THE HANDWRITING ON THE WALL
written for
KEEPERS OF THE FLAME

THE HANDWRITING ON THE WALL
—————— *written for* ——————
KEEPERS OF THE FLAME

B O O K I

Teachings from the Mystery School
The Healing Power of Angels

ELIZABETH CLARE PROPHET

PEARLS OF WISDOM
TEACHINGS OF THE ASCENDED MASTERS
Mark L. Prophet • Elizabeth Clare Prophet
VOLUME TWENTY-NINE • 1986

SUMMIT UNIVERSITY  PRESS®

The Handwriting on the Wall
written for Keepers of the Flame
Elizabeth Clare Prophet

Pearls of Wisdom 1986
Volume Twenty-Nine Book One

Published by
The Summit Lighthouse®
for Church Universal and Triumphant®

LIBRARY OF CONGRESS CATALOG CARD NUMBER: 87-62298

INTERNATIONAL STANDARD BOOK NUMBER: 0-916766-83-7

Printed in the United States of America

Summit University Press®
First Printing

Contents

Contents *ix*

Pearl
Number

Page
Number

VII

Teachings from the Mystery School

Contacting his amanuensis Mark L. Prophet in Washington, D.C., the Ascended Master El Morya, Chief of the Darjeeling Council of the Great White Brotherhood, founded The Summit Lighthouse in August 1958 for the purpose of publishing the teachings of the Ascended Masters. The anointed Messengers Mark and Elizabeth Prophet were trained by their Guru El Morya to receive the Word of the LORD in the form of both spoken and written dictations from the Ascended Masters. Since 1958, the personal instruction of the Masters to their chelas in every nation has been published in weekly letters called Pearls of Wisdom. Before his ascension on February 26, 1973, Mark L. Prophet transferred the mantle of the mission to Elizabeth Clare Prophet, who continues to set forth the mysteries of the Holy Grail in current Pearls of Wisdom, Keepers of the Flame Lessons, and at Summit University. These activities, headquartered at the new-age community at the Royal Teton Ranch in Montana, are sponsored by the Brotherhood as the foundation of the culture and religion of Aquarius. For information on other volumes of Pearls of Wisdom published since 1958 and numerous books and audio- and videocassettes distributed by The Summit Lighthouse, write for a free catalog.

The Ascended Master El Morya
Chief of the Darjeeling Council of the Great White Brotherhood

Belshazzar the king made a great feast to a thousand of his lords, and drank wine before the thousand.

Belshazzar, whiles he tasted the wine, commanded to bring the golden and silver vessels which his father Nebuchadnezzar had taken out of the temple which was in Jerusalem; that the king, and his princes, his wives, and his concubines, might drink therein.

Then they brought the golden vessels that were taken out of the temple of the house of God which was at Jerusalem; and the king, and his princes, his wives, and his concubines, drank in them.

They drank wine, and praised the gods of gold, and of silver, of brass, of iron, of wood, and of stone.

In the same hour came forth fingers of a man's hand, and wrote over against the candlestick upon the plaister of the wall of the king's palace: and the king saw the part of the hand that wrote.

Then the king's countenance was changed, and his thoughts troubled him, so that the joints of his loins were loosed, and his knees smote one against another.

The king cried aloud to bring in the astrologers, the Chaldeans, and the soothsayers. And the king spake, and said to the wise men of Babylon, Whosoever shall read this writing, and shew me the interpretation thereof, shall be clothed with scarlet, and have a chain of gold about his neck, and shall be the third ruler in the kingdom.

Daniel 5

The Karma of America
The Goddess of Liberty

I come from the Temple of the Sun with a message of
victory for the people of America and the people of the world.
I come as the spokesman for the Lords of Karma. I come in the
feminine ray of Truth to exalt that Truth of the feminine ray
within you. I come to speak of karma as the law of cause and
effect, and of karma as the destiny not only of America, but of
every nation upon earth.

You have heard of individual influence within the self and
within the family and within the community at large. I say that the
influence which the individual can exercise and which the individual nation can exert rests squarely on the proposition of karma.

Where you are in consciousness rests upon karma. Many
among you have very good karma. Karma then becomes your
opportunity to fulfill your divine plan. And none of you are
without those negative aspects of karma that have brought your
souls into incarnation on Terra [the name given to planet earth]
once again to try again to fulfill the law of an inner destiny which
God has willed and which you have affirmed.

I AM the Goddess of Liberty. I have stood before each and
every one of you as you have passed before the Lords of Karma
prior to taking incarnation in this life. Now I am activating the
memory in your soul of this experience of speaking with me.

Look into the face with your inner eye—my own face and
that face focused in the Statue of Liberty. Recall now this gaze
of the one who represented the Divine Mother to you. Recall the
admonishment of your soul and your vow made to me in person
to go forth, to carry that torch of Liberty and to give rebirth to
the Christ flame and the Christ consciousness.

You are here in America—some by birth and some by the
destiny of your karma. You find yourself in this place in time and

space because I made a commitment to you in the hour of your birth that you would come to know the teachings of the Ascended Masters, that you would meet those lifestreams who could impart to you the knowledge of the Law and the knowledge of your vow to serve the Great Law. I promised you that you would meet my representative of the Mother flame.

Why did I make this promise? Because each and every one of you who is seated here tonight expressed the concern to me, as the representative of the Mother flame, that you would forget the knowledge of the sacred fire, the law of your karma and your promise to keep the flame of Life; and you implored me to promise you that you would have the opportunity to know the Law.

Therefore, I have fulfilled this night my vow to many of you, and you are here. And so I also expect, as you expected of me, that you will fulfill your inner vow to the Lords of Karma and to Saint Germain to make a more than ordinary effort in this life to balance your karma and to make yourself available for the fulfillment of America's destiny, to take the flame of the Mother and the Christed ones and to expand that flame into the world dominion of the Christ consciousness.

Well, we have come into a time, into an age, when it is imperative that those who have made their vows to keep the flame do so. Therefore I proclaim again! Liberty proclaims within you the law of your inner being and the understanding that now is the time and the space for the Light of your own God Presence to shine within you. Now is the time to forsake the careless expense and waste of God's energies which are the natural resources of the Spirit—the energy that flows ceaselessly.

Now is the time to realize that your Christ Self is able to reverse the tide of darkness on Terra—that in that flame is the power, the wisdom of God to become the allness of God in manifestation. Now is the time to prove the law of the avatars. Now is the time to make yourself a part of the mainstream of the karmic destiny of America, for her destiny is to be the place where the Woman clothed with the Sun and with a crown of twelve stars rises to deliver the mandate of the Christ consciousness and to give birth to that Christ Child.[1] This is the Mother within you.

I have with me, then, the assurance from Portia of opportunity sealed and the dispensation of our board [The Karmic Board] to give opportunity to this group of devotees for a more than ordinary release of the fires of the Mother within you that your souls might be nourished by the Mother's love. For you yourselves have earned this dispensation; you have given service to that Mother flame.

Sometime, somewhere, your devotion and your service has been sealed. And so we capitalize on good karma this night to allow us to enter into the forcefield of your worlds, to unlock the fires of the Mother and to seal the raising of those fires for a manifestation of the God consciousness within you—a sealing of the Light of the heart, that you might understand and become the Christ.

It is America's destiny to reveal the culture of the Mother to the world. And the hierarchies of Aries and Libra, fulfilling the Light of the heart chakra, come to the aid of those who have heard the call and felt the flame throughout Terra, throughout the four planes of Mater. The hierarchies of the Sun come forth and their proclamation is this: that it is by the fires of the Holy Spirit and the all-consuming energy of your own I AM Presence that you will bring into manifestation the fulfillment of this fiery destiny.

Now, therefore, receive the assignment of the Lords of Karma, that assignment being to surrender a portion of mis-qualified energy into the flame that it might be transmuted, that you might have returned to you God's energy purified to work the works of God on earth.

The assignment from the Lords of Karma is to give the mantras and the invocations to the violet flame for the freeing of this nation, for the reestablishment of spirals of victory to move forward during this period of the Dark Cycle and to establish the initiation of another one-hundred-year cycle [from the date of the Bicentennial—July 4, 1976] wherein the initiations of Maitreya can be given, wherein the Teachings of the Mother can be pro-claimed and the Mother's children can come into the fountain of living flame and have their chakras nourished, their souls and hearts and minds nourished by the fires of living Love, of immor-tal Truth.

The flame of the Mother burns and expands. The heart of the Divine Mother calls the children of the One into the AUM, and that calling to the Home is the calling of consciousness back to the awareness of Reality.

It is the karmic destiny of America to experiment in God-government, to experiment with the divine documents of Liberty. It is the destiny of America to establish golden-age education. And in the education that is the unfoldment of the heart chakra, it is the destiny for the little children to rise up with that God-dominion and that mastery of the quadrants of Mater whereby they can teach to all nations the way of overcoming on the path of initiation under the Christ and the Buddha and the inner law written in the inward parts.[2]

So it is the destiny of America to fulfill the culture of the Divine Mother as Science—a science that, when applied, liberates souls from drudgery and the toiling that became the karma of those who were expelled from the God consciousness of Eden. And this is the technology of the Divine Mother. It must not be misused or abused. It must become, with Religion, the pillar in the temple of being, so that by the binding of the individual to God as Father in Spirit through Religion and the binding of the individual to Mother in Mater through Science, the aspects twofold of Spirit and Matter may be fulfilled within the individual.

The culture of the Mother is not to be despised. The championing of the individual God flame ought not to be misused through those who take advantage by greed of the system of capitalism and free enterprise. These are to be bound by the action of the sacred fire of the Lords of Karma; for those who misuse the Spirit of the individuality of the God flame are perverting the flow of abundance, the flow of the supply of God, into the hands of the children of God.

Let this nation, then, be restored to the divine economy and the divine principles of God-government. Let the essence of these principles be drawn from the Source, the one Source of the I AM THAT I AM, the true Lawgiver of each individual God flame. Let there be a restoration, a regeneration, a rejuvenation and a resurrection of Life in the four lower bodies of those who have chosen to be a free people! And let this choosing be transferred to every nation. Let the example be set and let it be transferred!

I speak to all who love freedom in every nation on earth: Fulfill the Light of your karmic destiny! Work to give forth the culture of the Mother in your nation! Whether it be Mother Russia or Mother India or Mother China or Mother America, let it be that the souls of the children of the one Flame respond to the call of the Mother in their own tongue, in their own culture.

And let their cultures be purified by the flow of the flaming ones—sons and daughters of God ascended, Cosmic Beings who gather on Terra at the portals of consciousness to accelerate God consciousness, to exalt those who would be exalted in the God flame, to bring to pass the saying that is written, "Death is swallowed up in victory."[3]

So let that culture of death (which is not a culture) be swallowed up in the victory of Life, and let Life flow from the heart of the Mother to her children. Let the Life that is God be the fulfillment of the fiery destiny of the individual unto the nation, unto the planet, unto souls and evolutions who must come forth to fulfill their divine plan on earth.

And this brings me to the question of population control. I am very concerned with the control of the incarnation of life-waves on Terra, for we who are the Lords of Karma plan the incarnation of souls who will contribute to the overall pattern of perfectionment on earth. We are the ones who pass on souls who apply for incarnation.

Out of every one who applies, there are two who remain, who must be denied entrée into the portals of birth. Out of everyone whose incarnation is granted, there are percentages who never reach incarnation because of the current trends toward birth control through the abortion of Life.

And then there is that planning by those who advocate zero population growth, and there is the indoctrination in the mass consciousness against giving birth to children in this age. And therefore, those very precious and important lifestreams whom we have assigned to Terra are denied entrance into Terra by the free will of mothers and fathers who have taken the vow at inner levels to give birth to souls but in their outer minds have accepted the brainwashing of the mass consciousness.

I am a mother conscious of the Mother flame in cosmic dimensions and I am very conscious of the gaps in the evolution-ary chain of hierarchy now occurring on Terra. I am concerned with coming decades and the absence of those lifestreams who have been denied opportunity to live, to move, to breathe, to overcome, to attain God-mastery on Terra.

What will you do in twenty-five years when the scientists and the great avatars and those who espouse mankind's freedom, those who are returning to liberate the masses, are not there because you have denied them Life?

What will you do when the ages turn, when there are wars and rumors of wars and pestilence and plague and cataclysm taking the life of many, when the dearth of population comes and there is not the replacement for those souls whose karma will take them from the screen of life?

What will you do, O mankind who have made yourselves prey—fodder—for the manipulators? You have believed the lie; and as it is written, "your condemnation is just,"[4] because you will have made your own karma. As you say, you make your bed and you lie in it.

This is the story of karma; karma is the exercise of free will. I ask you now, have you exercised free will or have you been manipulated?

You do not exercise free will until you know both sides of the story. Did you know this side of the story before I spoke to you? Did you know that there are thousands of Christed ones awaiting incarnation? You have been told of their courage. You have heard that they come, they are aborted, and they volunteer again, knowing that they may pass through that trauma of dying in their mother's wombs. Yet they volunteer again because they are determined to set life free!

They are far more determined to liberate the masses than many among embodied mankind. For they see above and beyond the manipulation of the death cult, and therefore they see your souls crying out, pleading with the Lords of Karma for help, for intercession. They behold the prayers of children, they behold the praying of babies in their mother's wombs praying for life, praying they will come to maturation to be born in Mater—souls waiting to incarnate who are mature, advanced lifestreams not only from Terra but from other planetary bodies and even volunteers from other systems of worlds.

They have knocked on the doors of the Lords of Karma in our chambers in the Royal Teton Retreat. They have pleaded for opportunity. We have shown them what they will be up against and yet they have said: "We will go, we will try! We will work with mothers and fathers, we will find our place. We will find room in the inn on Terra." And so they come and they continue to come.

Now see what the question of abortion brings as karma to the feet of a nation! See what war brings as karma to the feet of a nation! Understand that those who kill with the sword must be killed by the sword.[5] Whether the sword is on the battlefield or in the surgeon's hand, the taking of life bears the consequence. And these consequences place a heavy karma on the people of America, whose destiny it is to bring forth the Christ consciousness not only in the little children, but through the sacred fires of the heart.

As the Spirit of Christmas covers the land with the light of the I AM Presence, that Spirit of the Christ Mass also comes knocking at the door of your heart, asking that you might pray for the little ones that they might be born in this auspicious year of 1976, that they might come as the crown of rejoicing of the Goddess of Liberty in celebration of Freedom and of Life—and of living and of the giving of self.

I tell you, precious ones, there is no greater fulfillment in all of cosmos than the fulfillment of creation—a holy maternity, a holy paternity, father and mother standing as representatives of the Father/Mother God giving birth to the Christ Child. Unless the fulfillment of creation be manifest within you, whether by giving birth to a child or by giving birth to the Christ light in yourselves and other lifestreams, you will not know the fulfillment of cycles.

Do you understand that the manipulators of the souls of humanity would take from them the fulfillment of the cycles of creation—would abort those cycles? Is it any wonder that we have a sick society and sick people for the very reason that they are not allowed to create in the image and likeness of God, but are told to create the ugly and the sordid and the astral and the psychic and the discordant sounds and art forms? And thus deep within the psyche, deep within the souls of mankind, there is a longing to be free to create as God creates.

O the wonder of creation! The wonder of watching before your very eyes a friend, a member of your family being transformed in the image of the living God because you have allowed yourself to be the instrument of that Flame! O the wonder of wonders to see the newborn child and the rebirth in the Spirit! You can be instruments for the magnetization of the God flame. You can be instruments for the salvation of a planet and a people.

I speak it now and I will speak it again and again, for I AM delivering into your total consciousness, being and world the promise of Life and of Victory through the fulfillment of your vows. I stand before you fearless in the face of the carnal mind and the mass manipulations of the carnal mind! For I know that one word spoken now in your own heart as a prayer to God to transmute that influence—to commit it to the flame—will be answered instantaneously by the edict of the Lords of Karma.

I therefore give you an opportunity, a moment of silence, to make your prayer to Almighty God, for in this cosmic moment there is opportunity of legions of angels who come to intercede and to bring to your hearts that which you invoke in the light of freedom. [27-second pause]

The Lord Christ has said, "Ask and ye shall receive, knock and it shall be opened unto you."[6] Each and every prayer uttered in the heart is adjusted now by the wisdom of your Christ Self and by the action of the will of God. And therefore, any who ask amiss will find their calls adjusted in the Christ consciousness and the answer to the call will be forthcoming.

Some of you have asked for a world and some of you have asked for the individual. Know this, Children of the Sun: that God is not limited, that the infinite consciousness of God can fulfill your prayer, for the one or for the billions of souls, with equal flow and equanimity, with equal action of the fire of freedom. Therefore I say, whatever call you have made for an individual, according to the will of God and in keeping with that will, it shall be multiplied for every lifestream on Terra.

This is my promise and the fulfillment of that promise, that you might understand each and every day of your life that that which you call forth for all mankind will be fulfilled for all mankind. We refer to this as the maximizing of your calls.

Do not limit your calls then! But realize that if you pray for one who is sick, there are millions who are sick and millions more who know not that they are sick who require healing in the mind and in the emotions and in the subconscious.

Therefore, let the multiplication of the loaves and the fishes by your own Christ Self be for the feeding of the multitudes through your invocations and decrees. And do not fail to include in your decrees, "This which I call forth for myself and my family, I call forth for all sons and daughters of God and for all evolutions of Terra on every plane of consciousness."

So then, watch how the Divine Mother will answer your calls made in the name of the living Christ. Understand the truth that the call does compel the answer!

And let me, if you will by your free will, release now into your forcefield the flame of Faith, the flame of Hope, and the flame of Charity amplified by the angels of Liberty who come now to maximize in the field of your consciousness your faith in the law of God, your faith in the science of the spoken Word and the science of the aura,[7] your faith in the Teachings of the Ascended Masters, your hope in your own Christ Self for salvation, and the charity which is the flow of the flame giving and receiving and being the outpouring and the inflowing, the unfolding and the infolding, of the sacred fires of love descending from the Most High God.

O America, fulfill your destiny and free mankind to fulfill their destiny! Stop the slaughter of the holy innocents and give birth to the Christ children who come knocking at the doors of America—because this is the place where destiny must be forged and won. Must we send them, then, to other nations—to China, to Russia, to India, to those places where there is not the control of life—or will you give them room?

I place this question before America this night and I demand that you give answer! Either you make room for the avatars and the Christed ones or the torch will be passed and other nations who will prepare them room, who will make way for the coming of the Christ, will receive this dispensation of the avatars.

I AM knocking at the door of America this night! I demand answer and I ask for the prayers of the Keepers of the Flame for the American people, for their enlightenment, for their awakening in this age.

When you deny the Mother flame, you deny the Christ Child. When you deny the Christ Child, you deny your own salvation. For salvation is through each and every one of these little ones who come to be admitted to raise up a golden-age civilization which can yet be born in this nation and throughout the nations of the world.

Now let the Keepers of the Flame be solemn in their consideration. You play the role of mediator: You stand in the place of the Christ consciousness for and on behalf of every member of your nation and your community and your family. You have a supreme responsibility to amplify that Christ flame, and I know of no better way than in the exercise of the science of the spoken Word.

You have a responsibility to see to it that the knowledge of this karma and also of this teaching is spread abroad throughout the land. You have heard the admonishment not to hide your Light under a bushel[8]—that bushel of neglect! You cannot sit home on your haunches and there give your decrees and deprive mankind of the knowledge of the Law.

You must go out into the highways and byways and become teachers of mankind. You must rescue the little children who are born, who come into the schools and who are programmed away from their immortal destiny. You must take up the cause! You must enter the fray! You must fight the good fight for the Goddess of Liberty.

Remember, I have kept my promise to you this night: I have put you in contact with the Teachings. Now I say, will you say no to the Divine Mother? Will you say, "I have forgotten my vow"? Or will you stand up tall, take your responsibility seriously and your word that you gave?

Do you not remember that "By thy words thou shalt be justified and by thy words thou shalt be condemned"?[9] So it is written; so it is the law of the judgment.

I remind you that ere a century has passed, all of you will stand before me once again and you will have in your hands to present to the Lords of Karma the harvest of good work or a crop that has failed. And you will stand alone to give testimony to the Lords of Karma. You will make your report as to the use you have made of this life and this quotient of energy.

And then, if you have not succeeded in earning your ascension, you will be there knocking on the portals of birth. And then you will be faced with that dilemma of a programming of a civilization against the birth of the Christed ones and you will face the karma of your neglect, of your failure to inform the nations of this karma of denying life.

So then, the cycles turn quickly. Many are called but few are chosen,[10] and those who choose to be the elect of God are those who win.

I am counting on you, Keepers of the Flame, to be winners in this life! And I back you with the full momentum of my lifestream if you will choose to win for Light, for Freedom.

I thank you, ladies and gentlemen, and I bid you good evening.

This dictation by the **Goddess of Liberty** was **delivered** through the Messenger of the Great White Brotherhood Elizabeth Clare Prophet on **Saturday, November 22, 1975,** during the weekend seminar *The Greater Way of Freedom* held in **Washington, D.C.** (1) Rev. 12:1, 2, 5. (2) See Elizabeth Clare Prophet, "The Cosmic Clock: Psychology for the Aquarian Man and Woman," in *The Great White Brotherhood in the Culture, History and Religion of America,* Summit University Press, pp. 173–206, $10.95 (add $1.00 for postage); and *The ABC's of Your Psychology on the Cosmic Clock,* 8-audiocassette album, 12 hrs., A85056, 12 lectures, $50.00 (add $1.30 for postage). (3) Isa. 25:8; I Cor. 15:54. (4) Rom. 3:8. (5) Matt. 26:52; Rev. 13:10. (6) Matt. 7:7; Luke 11:9; John 16:24. (7) **Science of the spoken Word and the science of the aura.** See Mark L. Prophet and Elizabeth Clare Prophet, *The Science of the Spoken Word,* Summit University Press, $7.95 (add $1.00 for postage); *The Science of the Spoken Word: Why and How to Decree Effectively,* 4-audiocassette album, 6 hrs., A7736, $26.00 (add $1.15 for postage); and *The Control of the Human Aura through the Science of the Spoken Word,* 2-audiocassette album, 3 hrs., A8075, $12.95 (add $.90 for postage). (8) Matt. 5:14–16; Luke 11:33. (9) Matt. 12:37. (10) Matt. 20:16.

Pearls of Wisdom®
published by The Summit Lighthouse

| Vol. 29 No. 1 | The Beloved Great Divine Director | January 5, 1986 |

The Handwriting on the Wall:
Read It and Decide Your Destiny
I
The Sealing of the European Continent

Lightbearers of the ages, I am come in a visitation of the Spirit—your Great Divine Director. I come to magnetize an inner energy field of Light for the reparation of the shattered lines of force striated throughout this continent by the records of war, infamy, and the abuse of power by various ignominious ones who have played their parts on the stage of life. The continent has been vulnerable due to layer upon layer of records of the shedding of blood, division, and all of those conditions thou knowest well.

For the healing of the breach at inner levels I am come. I am come for my love for my disciple Saint Germain and his heart full of desire to assist you. A blanket of violet flame is needed over all. As you place yourselves in this sanctuary prepared by your love and increase the calls to the violet flame and build the momentum, these will be multiplied to an extraordinary power by all legions of the seventh ray of cosmos.

I urge you to continue this vigil of the violet flame this night and to call to the Lords of Karma, for it is the conditions at inner levels, records of akasha tied to the subconscious of the people, that allow in the next cycle the repetition of history. This history is dyed deep. And every soul slaughtered on the battlefield of life cries out for justice, even from succeeding incarnations. And many have fallen again and again.

Is it any wonder that there is cynicism here or even a sense of hopelessness? Some have not known hope in many lifetimes. Consider how blessed ye are to have, then, the perception of Light, the calling to Light, and the dedication to Light. Consider, then,

O Lightbearers of the ages, that many need that which is now in your grasp—the flame of freedom, aye, and much more—the illumination and the joy of the Mother.

I do anoint you in her name that you might go forth bearers of the Word, messengers of the Messenger and of the Ascended Masters, truly to give the Teaching, to clear the way, truly to know that this is the hour and the day when many shall receive the Holy Spirit, many must preach the Everlasting Gospel and clear the way for the Aquarian age.

Beloved hearts, our message must be spoken again and again. Therefore we have asked that you take this Teaching and understand that step by step you are being liberated by coils of Light released by the Messenger. This is a concentrated experience and once you have it, when you present this Teaching, I again will be present to help those who desire to serve with Saint Germain.

Remember the great calling and the hour. And remember that we cannot bare to your hearts the full knowledge of the possibility of consequences when action is not taken and when the dark clouds and dark tides are allowed to continue to roll across this continent unobstructed. Where you have not the power to challenge by military might, nor the desire, truly you may challenge by the Word and the spoken Word. Nothing is fruitless, no effort without result. The only failure is not to call to me to act in the face of day-by-day events unfolding.

The members of the Karmic Board each have a very important role to play in the outcome in the European theater. Therefore know our offices and know that Cyclopea with the All-Seeing Eye of God, when you give his decree, will increase your vision of the future and a sense of your own direction. I myself when called upon seal you in the blue sphere of Light that is indeed the replica of the great blue causal body.

In the intense fire of Love, the integration of yourself in the I AM Presence is protected by Nada, who comes in this year with Mighty Victory to sponsor you and your beloved twin flame to the fulfillment of holy purpose.

I am contacting now your chakras. I am releasing Light for a new day, for the sense of resurrection, that all things that have passed in your life may be turned as prologue and you may write the first page of the first chapter of a new book.

Opportunity's cycles through justice come through beloved Portia—mercy for the washing of the records in the violet flame of Kuan Yin. Pallas Athena sponsors unerring Truth and should be diligently called into the media, who do not reach the people with the facts.

Such a veil of lies and propaganda, such a calling of black "white" and white "black" is continuing that the great masses of the people have no comprehension of the forces at work. The enemy is confused for the friend; the friend is confused for the enemy. And people lash out in great fear and terror to destroy that which is the greatest opportunity of the ages.

Thus, it is important to center with the Goddess of Liberty, for balance is something that has long been absent in Europe. The balance of the threefold flame of Liberty would give dynamism, true illumination, and enlightened action. Still we find the serpents dividing the people in political parties, economic philosophies—the same stale arguments that went on tens of thousands of years ago, the same players so worn out that if anyone would take note they should observe that even their skin is grey.

Beloved ones, it is the presence of Saint Germain which can indeed make the difference. We, as the Lords of Karma who sponsor the dispensations given to us by the Cosmic Council, truly wait for your word and your action and your response. For by and by, as the new year turns, we must go before the Cosmic Council with the report of the fruit of this rescue mission of Sanat Kumara through our Messenger and through yourselves. We must determine what new impulse or dispensation of freedom may be given in the new year as the result of your unceasing efforts to gather Lightbearers, to teach them the importance of decrees and the entering in to the joy of the violet flame.

Saturated is this earth with the blood of righteous Abel. Thus, beloved, how does one build a golden age upon such a foundation? How does one indeed? Thus the purging will come, I assure you. And it can come fully through Freedom's fire, else nature will take her course.

I trust you understand how vital is the free will of every individual. And that free will is the right of choice based upon knowledge and vision. Thus, it is right that you are aware of the power of the illumination, the purity of the Divine Mother to assist you.

If a tidal wave were announced, men would leave their plows and their fields and take shelter. If war were declared or hordes were approaching or a plague of locusts, the announcement thereof would cause concerted action—at least to escape the onslaught. We cannot cry any of these into your midst lest we be guilty of the same crime of the false alarm of "fire!" shouted in the midst of a crowded hall.

You see, beloved, there is in reality no accurate prediction. For, as Saint Germain has well learned and often said, the human consciousness is unpredictable. It is accurate to say that the challenges are moving toward your doorstep every day. It is accurate to say that when they arrive you must have Light in your lamps and already a momentum of understanding. It is accurate to say, as has been said already, be prepared for sudden changes. Be prepared for anything and then you shall indeed be prepared.

We have prepared a place in the wilderness, foreordained, because it is necessary. Whether or not it is necessary for you specifically only you can say.

I have come from other planes and other worlds to be with you, for I am deeply concerned for the outcome and the safety of many Lightbearers in various places on earth. Because of humanity's response in past ages, and as has been explained to you regarding the rejection of Saint Germain, we in fact are limited as to that which we may tell you. For often in a period of mounting karma it is best to focus the attention upon the Light. But then, of course, those who come are those who love the Light with all their hearts and would come in sunshine and in rain.

Prophets of doom always manage to extract from society fearful followers and their purses. We have no such desires. We will not clutter our retreat with those who are running from their own shadows or have not the courage to face the challenge in their own states. But, yes, we provide a haven of safety for those who fight the good fight and win and dedicate that life that God has given them to the rescue of other souls.

The noble captain and shipmates rescue those who are their passengers in time of calamity. But we have seen the example of all jumping overboard and taking the lifeboats and leaving the passengers. We would not have such co-workers. We would have those who become the Light and become a living pillar and pass through the night untouched and carry many in their arms. This is the way of the Ascended Masters.

To quote the Lord is fruitful: "Work while ye have the Light." The Light is come in the person of the Great White Brotherhood. And those of you who have seen the miracle of souls who reach out for a blessing have understood that something more than a human being has wrought this miracle, something more than any of ourselves. Truly, it is the entire Spirit of the Great White Brotherhood. Thus learn the meaning of a dispensation and a sponsorship, and be grateful that we can so sponsor you while we have the Light of a single Messenger with you.

By the fruits of the aura and the quickening, know the Truth. Beware, then, of psychicism and pride declaring itself our representative when it is not so and signs do not follow that are signs of Light but rather only signs of psychic phenomena. There is danger, and those who are hooked by such ploys know it not. Thus, the false gurus will be there forever and a day until their cycles too are spent and their hollowness rent. We come with a sign of victory to those who will seize the victory. It is only the way and the only way.

Beloved ones, the Path is accurate. The progress can be swift. But once you receive the Light and the blessing and you squander it and then squander it again, do not expect us to come with pitchers of Light to continually pour the oil into your chakras because you have taken another round in the valleys of delusion.

These are serious times. For your very health, for your very mindfulness you ought to conserve the life-force. You ought to denounce the fallen angels who purvey their rock music to steal from you by the syncopated beat the power of the Kundalini. You have never seen a rock star with a raised Kundalini. It does not exist. It is lowered, creating the magnetism out of the very bowels of the earth.

Blessed ones, these have burned out their chakras long ago and must amass the Light from the Lightbearers who follow them. Thus their auras are magnetic and they seem filled with a certain power. But it is not the power of that which is Above but the power of that which is beneath that hath but a short time.

Those cycles are arrested precisely on the schedule of the Great Central Sun. We neither hasten nor lessen their configuration, for we are confident in the judgment of the seed of the wicked. This one thing is certain—they come to naught. What is not certain is what will the choice be—the freewill choice of every soul of Light to be or not to be in the highest octaves.

We can never force, nor have we any desire to do so. For anyone convinced against his will becomes rebellious and hateful. Thus, the power of conversion belongs to the Holy Spirit in all. And only by the Great Central Sun Magnet is a soul truly demagnetized of Darkness and remagnetized to the Light.

I give you the vision to see and know the fruits of the evil seed and to see and know the fruit of the Ascended Masters. I caution you above all to guard the Light and let no one take it from thee. Let no one displace thy path of victory and overcoming. Lean upon the arm of the LORD only.

I have come in my Presence and I am radiating through you and to all of you as long as I am speaking, giving you the inner vision. And I will continue to do so this night. We do maintain the etheric retreat called the House of Rakoczy not far away yet over those nations not fully free—not fully free to be as you are today.

Blessed ones, read with me the handwriting on the wall and decide your destiny. I urge you to decide your destiny, to no longer be manipulated by forces within or without, to realize that your

decision will become fact as you summon all forces of the Divine
Mother and the Ascended Masters, as you have been taught.

This Teaching is powerful. There is no failure but the
failure of the individual to apply it. Thus, beloved, I am also a
voice that cries out in the wilderness.

Do you know, beloved, that conditions on Atlantis prior to
her sinking in some areas were not as vile as they are right here
in this country today? The Lords of Karma and the Cosmic
Council have long forestalled the karma due for the misuse of
the sacred fire by the fallen ones. And to allow the practices of
Satanism in this or any nation is folly, for all people pay the
consequences for their failure to object.

Blessed ones, it may be true that the LORD gave freedom to
Satan to tempt Job. But he did not deny Job the power of the Word
to challenge that Darkness. Thus, you must engage the sword of
blue flame and let this be a battle that is won by Archangel Michael.

Thus, my legions and my friends, my children of long ago,
I embrace you. I have fulfilled my reason for being in the sealing
of this continent. By placing yourself in my presence you have
indeed served as electrodes. And you will be blessed for as long
as you keep that flame by your own love and determination.

I am immensely grateful for efforts made on behalf of this
mission to the heart of every individual who has so given. I bow
before the Light. And I breathe upon that heart flame the breath
of the Holy Spirit to increase and increase and increase.

To fan the fire of the heart and the flames of freedom
therein—what higher gift? The flame is the flame of immortality.
To increase it by one-thousandth of a percent is to add immea-
surably to the Christ consciousness of a soul.

Oh, let us commune together in this flame of Liberty. Let
us come now into the center of the room where this flame is
enshrined for the duration of this retreat. Let us enter the heart
of that threefold flame.

Now journey to our retreat and abide there while you take
sleep, or keep the flame of the violet flame here—for truly
heaven knows the gratitude of the beings of the seventh ray to
all who assist in that mighty cause.

In the name of the Lords of Karma and Saint Germain, I bid
you a most fond good evening.

"The Summit Lighthouse Sheds Its Radiance O'er All the World to Manifest as Pearls of Wisdom."
This dictation by the Great Divine Director was the opening address **delivered** through the
Messenger of the Great White Brotherhood Elizabeth Clare Prophet on **Saturday, November 2,
1985,** during the 3-day *Seminar for World Teachers* on the Teachings of the Ascended Masters
in Flevohof, Holland.

Pearls of Wisdom®
published by The Summit Lighthouse

| Vol. 29 No. 2 | Beloved Lady Master Nada | January 12, 1986 |

The Handwriting on the Wall:
Read It and Decide Your Destiny
II
The Empowerment of Love

Away! Away! interminable delays to the internalization of the rose of the heart. Too long have I, Nada, awaited the coming of souls to the fount of Love.

My angels come with those of the Great Divine Director, the Lords of Karma, Mighty Victory, the Holy Kumaras, and Venus. We come, blessed hearts of Light, in the empowerment of Love and the dispensations of Chamuel and Charity from the LORD God for the judgment of the forces of anti-Love in the earth by the power of the ruby ray. This call and decree [33.00] should be given daily by all who truly understand that the lost chord in earth is Love.

With love as compassion and forgiveness, there are few conditions that cannot be resolved among Lightbearers. The most notable condition that does not respond to love is that of the force of Antichrist and the seed of the Wicked One in the earth. When you send love to them, they spurn you and mock you and use you.

Thus, in all other circumstances Love shall prevail. But in the challenge of the fallen angels it is Love that intensifies to the pure power of the Holy Spirit—white fire and the ruby ray as the essence of the Body and Blood of Christ. This call, then, becomes Love's judgment by the Lightbearers in their challenge of the forces of the entire false hierarchy misrepresenting the Holy Spirit and the great legions of Light who minister unto mankind by Love.

Jesus, who held the chohanship of the sixth ray before that office was passed to me in this age, taught of that hatred which would be coming into the world, setting members of the same household against one another, causing children to betray their parents. This hatred, beloved ones, is engendered today by the sinister force. Every Lightbearer and Keeper of the Flame must be alert to this force, as it does come insidiously into the mind and heart, into the solar plexus, creating a cast of darkness, of criticism of fellow brothers and sisters of Light on the Path, of division amongst the new-age movements, and even the spurning of the very spirit of prophecy that comes through this our Messenger as though somehow it were from beneath instead of from Above in Light as that incredible communion of all saints Above with all saints below.

Beware, then, the force of Antichrist on the third ray of Love. Indeed, pursue the Light of the Maha Chohan, who is the representative of the Holy Spirit and a hierarch of tremendous intensity that will send needle rays of Love to your chakras to remove those very forces opposing the petals. The intensity of the ruby ray is a power of the incisiveness of Love.

Now, then, beloved hearts, I come to admonish Keepers of the Flame in Europe. I come to admonish you concerning the necessity for more intense decree work. Your path of dynamic decrees must be in imitation of the fervor and the fire which you see always in the decrees of the Messengers. You are no longer babes in my arms but true freedom fighters on the line keeping the watch where the light of Love meets the darkness of human hatred and deviltry and swallows it up.

The fervor of the sacred fire in your spoken Word will create fervor of fire in your chakras. Henceforth when you enter the cities, enter in the name of the Messengers of the Great White Brotherhood. Enter in the name of Sanat Kumara, Gautama, Maitreya, Padma Sambhava and his mantle upon that Messenger. Enter in the name of the Mother. And let your chakras be beacon lights because your daily fervor does increase.

It is also time to fast and pray with fruit juices and specific herbs for purification, strengthening, and a higher and more intense perception of those saints above you. For when you see those armies of Light, you will be empowered by a fervor of love such as you have not experienced in many lifetimes. When you realize how the dark ones fall, how they are bound, how they are astonished as they have been challenged and bound through the calls of our team, you will come to realize that truly it is the

LORD's day in this continent and you have but to claim the cities and the nations for Saint Germain and the light of Aquarius, and you will see what can be done.

Expect miracles, thousand-petaled miracles of the rose of the heart. Expect them, beloved. For the old order and the old rules no longer apply. This is a new day of acceleration. I announce it to you, as some others of our bands have, to assure you that there is no limitation, that many await your coming, and that these stumps have been given primarily, as you would say, by the marines and the shock troops who land and immediately descend into the pits of Death and Hell to clean out the dark forces in the cities.

This has been a first-ray endeavor by those who truly have wed themselves to Morya, Hercules, and Archangel Michael. Now you will see that it will be easier to go into these cities and others, and you may always go with this mantle and momentum [of the Messenger's Stump Team] yourselves. For much preparation is intended for the hour and the day when Saint Germain can do that which he desires to do for these nations.

Therefore this day I have looked again to Atlantis and the records. And I have shown the Messenger in meditation that darkness of debris of Atlantis which yet is upon the Eastern Seaboard of the United States—a deleterious momentum whereby dark forces yet gain power over the minds of the people. Then, too, on the borders of Europe, here on the side of the west where the seas touch the landed areas and moving across the entire span of the land we see the mists of Atlantis and dark momentums.

I descend this day with legions of Chamuel and Charity and of Mighty Victory. I descend in the full fury of the sacred fire of Love which has been called in biblical terms "the wrath of God." Indeed it is his fire and that of the Sun behind the sun that does leap and lick and burn up now additional records. And you will see at inner levels the ruby ray and the violet flame blazing! blazing! blazing! blazing! blazing! blazing! blazing! burning now and consuming that substance! burning and consuming those records! burning and consuming now all that has confounded the tongues of the people, depriving them of the communion of Love in the Holy Spirit.

Therefore, beloved hearts of Light, I am Nada in the full support of your effort. I am burning through all psychic encumbrances, dependencies, and false teachers. Let the Light of the Christ appear! Let the Mind of God as the I AM Presence be the solace and the solution and the source to every opinion opining and opportunity descending.

O beloved hearts, what need have you of all of these paraphernalia and all of these psychic props and hooks when you have God within you and God is your sufficiency of communion, healing, restoration infilling with Light?

Oh, let the true spirit of the prophets of the Great White Brotherhood come forth. Let the purifying power of the gift of prophecy be known for what it is. Let us leave off of all psychic predictions and pronouncements, for, beloved, *Light is the alchemical key!* You have need of no other.

Develop, then, your sacred sun centers. Fear not to cut the ties to the astral plane, for all saints await you in the highest mountain of being. I demand the purging and the answer this day! For that which is of the psychic borders upon witchcraft and does not come under the aegis of the Great White Brotherhood.

Now, then, I have come with one word. The word is *dig*—to dig deeply into the astral maya of this continent with your intense decrees to Archangel Michael, to call to cut free those who are enmeshed in lower orders of activities who think they are a part of Saint Germain's wave of the new age yet they reject his violet flame, his dynamic decree, for all sorts of other manifestations involving glamour and the human personality and pronouncements made and promises of healings or cures by this method or another.

Take care, then. Thy aura is sanctified and made holy by thy God. Let not any man tamper with thy aura or chakras or physical body, but rather go directly to the mountain of God. Call upon the LORD in the name of Sanat Kumara. Let the archangels be your teachers and follow a path that is known, verified, and that does submit to the mathematical formula of the Logos. The Word itself is the great tester of men's hearts and of their path homeward.

We, the Ascended Masters, sponsor you on the path of the ascension. No other mystery school is founded for this purpose in the outer octave. All other good works may be promoted elsewhere but those works leading to the acceleration of Light and your soul's assumption unto God in the name of Mother Mary. This is the mighty work of the ages for those who have come with the author of the faith and those who shall return to the octaves of Light with the finisher of that faith.

You may be surprised at the intensity of my presence here, thinking that a Lady Master ought to be soft-spoken. My beloved cohort, the Great Divine Director, has pleased you with the soft speaking of wisdom and the withholding of the fervor of

his mighty power. I come as the Mother flame, pressing into
your being, penetrating through.

By your free will you sit in these rooms. Therefore I come, for
you have called and anticipated. Therefore I press. And I place
pressure upon you to renounce that which is unreal and the
human personality itself and the personality cults that are spawn-
ing everywhere in interference with your oneness with the Light. It
is a disease of every nation, I can assure you. It is understandable.

There are very few chelas in embodiment who have the full
mastery of the Mother flame of Love and of the Lord Shiva.
I commend you to pursue it, for then you shall become the daily
exorcist in Kali and Mighty Astrea's name, who is indeed the
Maha Kali. No more powerful mantra exists to the Divine
Mother than the call to Astrea [10.14].

If you would succeed in Love, you will be assailed by all
psychic entities and fallen ones. Therefore you must have your
momentum to burn through by the power of the ruby-ray judgment and the calls to Astrea and the charging of the chakras.
For in love, as masters, ladies and gentlemen of the power and
wisdom and love of Love, you will go forth and take your stand
in the earth—a stand that is needed by El Morya and Kuthumi,
who would pass the torch to third-ray chelas but find therein
those surfeited in their own human selfishness, wallowing in
their own self-pity, when these are the very ones who can
become the masters of Love here and now!

And you need not delay! You can declare it today and say:
"Lo, where I AM is the Almighty Love! I AM the incarnation of
Almighty Love. I will follow the saints of Love. I will follow the
Sacred Heart. I will be the unfoldment of the rose of Light of
the heart. I will be Nada in embodiment. I will be that Love
unflinching, unwilling to in any way hesitate before any force of
anti-Love!"

Blessed hearts, all forms of necromancy and spiritism and
spiritualism come under the false hierarchy of Love because it is
a false hierarchy of the Holy Spirit. Do you understand? This
cavorting with the forces of Death and Hell is an immense
danger to your soul. Yet you are called upon to balance the
threefold flame and you have served earnestly with El Morya,
with Kuthumi, and with beloved Saint Germain. Now is the
hour for the mastery of Love, which demands God-control in
the four lower bodies. It does demand the ultimate sacrifice, for
Love is by nature self-sacrificing.

Blessed hearts, this entire movement is a third organization in a trinity of effort. The entire organization of The Summit Lighthouse is to bring forth the Lighthouse of Love. The power of that Love, then, is in the teaching and the preaching, the ministering, the healing, the shepherding, the caring for each and every little one who does touch the hem of the garment of Love in this Teaching of the Mother.

Realize, then, that those who are truly engaged in Love will save the world! And those who fail to submit to the fiery trial, to subject their words and works to the power of Love, will not be given the empowerment of Maitreya to go forth for this work!

The balancing of the threefold flame is incumbent upon you. And when you do pass the initiation of the fiery trial and the fullness of the baptism of the Holy Ghost, beloved ones, this Love flame will give new brilliance to your wisdom, new strength to the will of God in you. And you will see how Love is the instantaneous magnet of the Divine Mother in you. Then you will find the path of your ascension readily at hand. And you will know at any day and hour you may be called by God that you are ready for that ascension.

And I tell you, the majority in this room right now are not ready for that ascension! And you ought to be concerned because those things that are coming upon the earth may indeed catapult you out of the physical body. And then you will wish that while you had a physical body you had heeded my word and my coming and my call in the European theater.

Present yourselves a living sacrifice and Serapis Bey will truly come knocking upon your door. And you will see what it means to be initiated by the fourth-ray Master of purity and sacred fire. And you will know the confidence of giving your life to God, for no one can take that life from you when you have earned your ascension. Therefore you are free and you do not fear danger. You do not fear death any longer, for your life is truly hid with Christ in God and you are a pillar of fire now and forever, as Above and so below.

And this is the understanding, then, of the power of the Masters of Love. Those who think they kill them know it not, but instantaneously these Masters produce another electronic fire body and they go forth and they manifest through the chelas and the Lightbearers until they are born again in another womb.

There is no dearth of bodies available to those who have merited the ascension yet have not yet taken it, as well as those who are Ascended Masters of Love who do come and manifest through the unfolding rose of your heart. But if you do not go forth and secure that rose of the heart, beloved ones, how will the Masters of Love manifest through you? For the chalice must be here and now, here below.

And this has been the entire message of this stump. This is the essence and the summum bonum of Love. It is the power of Love, the power of the flame. And you must seek Love early in the morning. You must seek the angels of Love with the dawn and seek to be the helper, the comforter, and the one who enlightens.

O beloved ones, by the fire of the Mother I am melting thousands of years of human recalcitrance which you have allowed to remain in you! And you should understand what is the meaning of the fire of the Holy Spirit that does come forth through the one who is truly anointed of the Great White Brotherhood and does bear in her aura and in her chakras those specific forcefields of Light.

Do not compare, then, those who give psychic dictations to one who has the mantle who can deliver the initiation of fire, who can deliver to you the power of Sanat Kumara and bring you as close to heaven's court as is deemed advisable and safe for your lifestream. Recognize this dispensation and understand that while you have this Light with you, serve to become that Light. Emulate that example and move on, for you must become that incarnation. And as you know, the souls of Light who represent the Light cannot always carry that Light for you or balance that darkness. And therefore no one may know the hour of the comings and the goings of the Messenger.

Realize, then, that this is truly the option for the sons and daughters of God. And light rays pouring through this crown chakra now are contacting every Lightbearer on this landed surface. And none is excluded. And all have, from the crown of the Goddess of Liberty, those rays that truly contact the heart and initiate the heart in the power of the threefold flame to give those souls an opportunity to prepare themselves to be initiated by the Goddess of Liberty on the path that you have indicated in your call.

Therefore we send forth feelers, light rays—preparatory—that call, awaken, and give hope to souls. As they respond, so they will be prepared, then, for the initiation of the Goddess of Liberty. And I tell you this very day, it is the Goddess of Liberty who walks with troops of angels of Liberty across the entire continent, north to south. And therefore there is the searching for those who are born of Liberty, and added protection and light is given unto them.

I say to you all who reside here in these nations: Follow in the footsteps of the Goddess of Liberty. Follow in the footsteps of angels of Liberty. Go forth and find them. Tell them! Tell them of the mighty message of the Coming Revolution, their own personal revolution in Higher Consciousness.

For it is the day of the appearing! And the Light does go! And the Light does proclaim! And the ruby ray is come! And you will see changes! Therefore, keep the flame in my name.

I am Nada. And you have never seen me so determined to give every opportunity to you and the Lightbearers to make it. For I have come many times in past ages and been rejected as Saint Germain was rejected. I come, then, in his stead when he no longer has the dispensation. I come myself, therefore, willing to pay the price.

I will stand in the end of the age before the Cosmic Council and I will speak of Europe. And I will speak of the British Isles. I will speak of Scandinavia. I will speak of Spain and Portugal and Eastern Europe. And I will say, "I have gone forth. I have delivered the Word. I have stood by every Lightbearer. I, Nada, vow to you, I have given them the opportunity of the flame of Love. If they have not come, if they have not answered the call, nothing more can be done. I have used the Light you have given me, Alpha and Omega. I have opened the door to all."

May all enter and know the LORD as the manifestation of the Goddess of Liberty herself.

I withdraw into the rose of your heart.

To the Mother of Exiles

O Liberty, bless'd Mother dear
By thy great love, hold me clear
Nearer to thy mighty flame
To serve our blessed Saint Germain.
He is thy son in freedom's birth
Who lifts on high the souls of men
Invoking vict'ry for the earth
The golden age shall come again.

[The Messenger and audience sang "To the Mother of Exiles," song 725 in *The Summit Lighthouse Book of Songs*.]

"The Summit Lighthouse Sheds Its Radiance O'er All the World to Manifest as Pearls of Wisdom."
This dictation by the Lady Master Nada was **delivered** through the Messenger of the Great White Brotherhood Elizabeth Clare Prophet on **Sunday, November 3, 1985,** during the 3-day *Seminar for World Teachers* on the Teachings of the Ascended Masters in Flevohof, Holland. Beloved Nada gave this dictation in a fiery intensity that must be heard in order to be fully assimilated (cassette B85145, $6.50 postpaid).

Pearls of Wisdom®

published by The Summit Lighthouse

| *Vol. 29 No. 3* | *The Beloved Goddess of Liberty* | *January 19, 1986* |

The Handwriting on the Wall:
Read It and Decide Your Destiny
III
A Good Report

Sons and daughters of Liberty, I stand here! For in my wandering about the continent I could not fail to make a stopover here in the gathering of heart flames to whom I desire to give my torch of illumination, a portion thereof, measure for measure according to the wisdom flame in your own heart. For I perceive the great love of Nada and I know that the Path of Love must be enlightened by wisdom's fire.

Wise must you become—wise as the serpents, the fallen angels, yet harmless as the doves of the Holy Spirit. Yea, I say, your wisdom must exceed that of the fallen angels! And it is God's wisdom I impart from the heart of the Father.

Now, then, feel the focus of the Eastern Seaboard of the United States. Feel now as the flame of Liberty and the violet flame and the Light of God continues to consume these deleterious records.

I AM your Mother of Liberty forever, and I come to reinforce now that which is given by Nada. We are determined that not a single soul in this entire group of nations shall hold any being in heaven accountable for their ignorance of the Law, for their failure, for their darkness and old night.

I say to you, beloved, may you have enough enlightenment to realize that you also will desire to make the same report to the Cosmic Council in the hour of your ascension. You will desire to say:

My Father, my Mother, I did live in thy body given to me in that hour and day and age. I did hear the call of Nada, the Great Divine Director, and the Goddess of Liberty. I did heed the call. I did give my life to find those Lightbearers and transmit your message!

My God, my Elohim, I have said I have left no stone unturned in seeking out the Lightbearers. Therefore, here I stand, O God! Here is the harvest of souls. Here is the fruit of our joint effort. Here is the victory—hearts afire for the love of Liberty. See how they have ignited a world! See how earth has become Freedom's Star!

I thank you, my Father, my Mother, for the Opportunity of sharing in the noble work of the ages of saving the Lightbearers from the Darkness of the fallen ones. So it is done, O God! Now, may I receive my assignment for the next world which does require my call and calling.

Thus, beloved, let it be a good report, an honorable one, a report worthy of the Son of God in you.

We long ago won our victory and attained our ascension by this path. I became the Goddess of Liberty, having liberated personally millions of souls on a number of planetary homes prior to my ascension. And since then I have never ceased to bear that flame of Liberty to those just about to come into their own who needed a transfusion of Light of my heart.

O beloved, I have rejoiced to see their faces, their hearts, and their souls aglow. I give to you that infusion that you might be myself in form. Thus, beloved, I ask you now to sing the mighty song of the blessing, the blessing for those who are of the I AM Race and the nation which I guard heartily for your coming— "God Bless America."

[The Messenger and audience sing "God Bless America"* and salute the Ascended Master Saint Germain:]

God Bless America

While the storm clouds gather
  far across the sea
Let us swear allegiance to a land that's free
Let us all be grateful for a land so fair
As we raise our voices in a solemn prayer.

Chorus: God bless America
  Land that I love
  Stand beside her and guide her
  Through the night with a light from above.

From the mountains, to the prairies
To the oceans white with foam—
God bless America!
My home sweet home.
God bless America!
My home sweet home.

Hail, Saint Germain! Hail, Saint Germain! Hail, Saint Germain! Hail, Saint Germain! Hail, Saint Germain! [applause] Thank you. [applause]

I just wanted to tell you that in most of my recent embodiments I have been in Europe. My last embodiment was even in this century, terminating in 1918. So I recall lifetime after lifetime serving in these various nations in various capacities. And I have the great sense that in my desire to help Saint Germain and bring Light here the Lords of Karma, especially the Goddess of Liberty, answered my call to allow me to be born in America in the state of New Jersey on the coast—a very few miles, as the crow flies, from the Statue of Liberty. There I was born of European parents, as you know, who kept the traditions that were familiar to me.

Standing before you today makes me very certain that you are my very own brothers and sisters and that I was sent to America to be initiated there, to speak the language of her people, to know truly what it means spiritually to be an American and to carry this torch of Liberty and Saint Germain so that the day could come when, after my training to be the Messenger for Saint Germain and the Great White Brotherhood and my receiving the gift of the mantle of the Teaching, I could come back into your midst where I have served before, this time to give you the real and only true gift that could make the difference in your lives.

It is a great privilege to be here among you, to honor your nations, your flags, your path, and also to be the bearer of the standard of Saint Germain and the Goddess of Liberty and all the American heart friends of freedom who love you, many of whom gave their lives in the two world wars that scarred your nations. And you also gave your lives and then reembodied for today's challenges so that we might all meet on this battlefield and realize what the power of the Flame of Freedom can do to erase not only in the akashic records the terrible scourge of war but also its residue of cynicism in men's hearts.

It is such a great new day. All the more because we are here to share it with one another. Not one of us here has ever had such an opportunity on European soil as we have in this moment to stand in the presence of the Goddess of Liberty and Saint Germain.

I would be most grateful if you would do me the honor of having the flag of my country next to me here on the platform so that I may also sing to that Opportunity that has brought me back to you, and I ask you to join me in singing "America the Beautiful."

Edward, may I ask you to hold the flag for me up here.

I'd like to introduce all of you to my husband, Edward Francis. [applause] Because he keeps the flame at the Ranch and at Camelot as well, I could come to you and stump Europe for Saint Germain. So because of Edward, I am here. And he has joined us, arriving just yesterday, for the end of the Stump. [applause]

I am hoping that Edward will also speak to you a little bit later today and perhaps answer some of the questions you have.

[All sing song 685.]

America the Beautiful

O beautiful for spacious skies
For amber waves of grain
For purple mountain majesties
Above the fruited plain.
America! America!
God shed his grace on thee
And crown thy good with brotherhood
From sea to shining sea...

[Following the singing of "America the Beautiful," the Beloved Messenger, Edward L. Francis and audience gave the salute to America, right hands extended toward Old Glory:]

America, we love you! America, we love you! America, we love you! And our Love is great enough to hold you eternally victorious in the Light!

As we go to take our lunch, we are in anticipation of the coming of Saint Germain today for the sealing of this wonderful conference. So I'd like to play that song to the freedom flame with all of the flavor of America tucked in. You're welcome to sing it and to march to it. First I'm going to dedicate the flames.

Dedication of the Flames

Beloved Mighty I AM Presence, send forth these flames of Alpha and Omega from our hearts as the witness of the Spirit of Liberty embracing the Atlantic. From both sides we march with the Goddess of Liberty. From all of Europe and the Isles, from all of America, North and South, we send to you, Almighty God in the Great Central Sun, our gratitude for the Goddess of Liberty, for Saint Germain, Nada, the Great Divine Director, the Lords of Karma, and All Saints in heaven.

In Jesus Christ's name, Amen.

"Hail, Freedom Flame! (Americana)," song 708, sung

"The Summit Lighthouse Sheds Its Radiance O'er All the World to Manifest as Pearls of Wisdom." This dictation by the Goddess of Liberty was **delivered** through the Messenger of the Great White Brotherhood Elizabeth Clare Prophet on **Sunday, November 3, 1985,** during the 3-day *Seminar for World Teachers* on the Teachings of the Ascended Masters in Flevohof, Holland. Copyright © 1986 Church Universal and Triumphant, Inc., Box A, Malibu, CA 90265. All rights reserved. Printed in the United States of America. Pearls of Wisdom and The Summit Lighthouse are registered trademarks of Church Universal and Triumphant, Inc. All rights to their use are reserved. Published by The Summit Lighthouse. Pearls sent weekly (to USA, via third-class mail) for a minimum love offering of $40/year.

Pearls of Wisdom®

published by The Summit Lighthouse

Vol. 29 No. 4	Beloved Saint Germain	January 26, 1986

The Handwriting on the Wall:
Read It and Decide Your Destiny
IV
The Decision and the Vow

Now let me tell you, beloved hearts, that the expansion of the flame of my beloved Portia is indeed the calling. It is the light of Opportunity and Justice.

I would extol these virtues of the Almighty God embodied, then, by beloved Portia. For each and every one of you has been blessed by her hand and her caress as you have taken incarnation in this life. For without the flame of Opportunity and the Justice of God meted out and apportioned on behalf of your fondest hopes and best dreams, you, beloved, would not be seated here this evening. And without the dispensation of the Lords of Karma, you would not see the full fire and fervor of my being delivered to you through this instrument who has truly functioned on and on through these days.

Therefore we desire each and every one of you to know that the power of God is greater than any instrument, and the power of God is available to those who seize the opportunity to be the instrument and present themselves the living sacrifice for the many. So it is rare to find those souls of Light across the earth who will stand with the Lords of Karma, who will not go wandering after the curious, after those things which adorn the ego.

We have empowered this Messenger to read any of your past lives, to tell you all kinds of things about yourselves should she choose to do so. When she does enter your aura she rather does draw the veil and seeks only to know the perfection of your Christhood. And therefore this office has never been abused by that flattery and by that idolatry and by that pursuit of a following based on those things which, when it comes to the kingdom of heaven, simply do not count, beloved hearts. Understand this great truth and cut yourselves free by yourselves from the fat of human selfishness and indulgence.

Who has taken from you your sense of holiness? Where is the glimmer of the light that does shine from you as holiness unto the LORD? I will tell you! That sense of holiness has been denuded from you by those in church and state who have come with their false revolutions of every kind, therefore seeking the lowest common denominator where all activity is common and is never endowed with devotion or a flame or an appreciation or the looking on high. And thus it does show upon your faces to the utter chagrin of your Mother who stands before you.

Therefore, we say take the flame of Opportunity and know that you did not take embodiment to be upon the socialist treadmill or any other treadmill of any other economic system where you are controlled from above, controlled from beneath, and boxed in as though you were fleas or mice or some variety of the animal species.

Beloved ones, you are more than men and women. You are God-free, immortal beings! And I desire to strip you by the sacred fire this night because the flame of Opportunity is kept in this universe, because that flame does glow, and because God Justice demands for you another opportunity!

When receiving so high a gift and calling you ought to be humble, not before me or the Messenger but toward the littlest chela and the one who serves. When you can be humble before the one who you think is beneath you in rank, then you have begun the ladder of life. For all may have some sort of affection for the Messenger, and why not? For the hand that feeds ought to be blessed. But, beloved, when you revere the God flame in one another as we revere it in you, then you will understand the dignity of human worth—of the individual and the individualization of the God flame.

That individualization of the God flame, beloved hearts, is far more important than building human empires. If we could find but one individual who would not stop the pursuit of God-identity, who would truly put himself on the line of that tough chelaship of Morya and Archangel Michael, which this Mother is able to deliver to those who are able to bear it, we would find therefore the means to forge a world union.

But so many come to be pampered. So many come, then,

with their pet theories and ideas, seeking ratification for these rather than to truly listen with the inner ear and the soul and to actually say to me when I enter the room, "Saint Germain, strip me of my pseudoself!"

Let me hear those who dare make that cry.

["Saint Germain, strip me of my pseudoself!"]

That is not fiery enough and I will not accept it!

[*"Saint Germain, strip me of my pseudoself!"*]

That is indeed an improvement.

Beloved hearts, you can increase your fervor in every way and it is the need of the hour. I, too, have come to please many over the centuries, but the time is long past to wait for anyone's human consciousness to come to the place of consecration. The hour is so terribly late, beloved ones, that I urge you with all your heart and mind and soul to not postpone the Day of Opportunity. The only day you can guarantee is today. The future is in God's hands and it is in the hands of the Law and the Lawgiver, who has already given you free will. And therefore karma rules the earth and the multitudes and the schedules and the timing.

You ought to be in the position of an Ascended Master today. I would give you the eye view of what it is like to know that your hands are tied. In fact, you are freer than we are to act, for you are on stage and we have already played our parts and can only ratify the acts of those who determine to summon the greater cause.

Understand that we ourselves are at the mercy of human will and human karma, but you are in the position to change it, to make the fiat. And when you know that you have the power of cosmic beings and Ascended Masters, beloved hearts, when you know that by your call we can truly step through the veil through you, then we can increase opportunity.

I tell you, you ought to have a role reversal tonight and realize that the Spirit of the Great White Brotherhood that can be effective on earth *is you* and that we are the ones who are waiting in the wings—waiting for the opportunity that you may possibly give to us to turn this planet around in her spin and straighten that axis and bring in a golden age.

Beloved ones, the earth is heavy with the dark ones, as you have been told. Their infamy spans many centuries. These dark ones are truly tipping the balance in many areas of life where the scales of justice weigh in favor of Darkness because the people want the Darkness. "And men loved Darkness rather than Light, for their deeds were evil."

When the people vote for tyrants and systems of tyranny, when they vote for terrorism and terrorist acts, it is free will on the stage of life. And it is your free will not to commit the sin of omission but to seize the right hand of Portia as opportunity to open the doors of your chakras, to open the portal of unity, to stand forth and to say, "Thus far and no farther. You shall not pass!"

Becoming active, then, in stopping the fallen ones in all ways is key and essential. But it must begin early, catching the sun before even she has awakened, going to the Light before the light has crested the horizon and beginning those morning calls. You will not defeat the adversary no matter how many social programs you have for the next million years. You will have to go to the eye of the serpent and to the serpent's tooth and tail! You will have to go to the very core of Evil! And only Archangel Michael can prevail in that arena.

I say to you, strip yourselves of indulgences and fat and squandering your Light. Let us see you as fiery yogis, yogins the next time we meet. Let us see you in the mode of self-sacrifice of the victors of the age.

Beloved hearts, heaven can only wait. Do not expect me to make some vast prognostication concerning your future. You are writing your future right now. You can see what you are doing. You can see what you have accomplished thus far in your life. You can predict what will happen to you if you keep on as you have been five, ten, twenty-five years. You can predict your own end, depending on your decision today.

I will not indulge you in your desire to have me tell you all things, as though I should read a crystal ball and make pronouncements and all should go away and say, "Saint Germain has said thus, Zarathustra has spoken," and therefore conclude we are the wise ones. Nay, you are the wise ones! You are the ones who now can take the very nucleus of life and knowledge—the keys of the kingdom which I have given to you through your Messenger. You can take these and decide to become the Wonderman of Europe, the Wonderwoman of Europe!

How would you like to have that appellation? Well, I can tell you, I will be the first one to give you that title when you have succeeded the miracle worker of the age. For after all, beloved hearts, I have given you much knowledge of alchemy as well as a sword and I have given you my momentum. For I, too, say unto you: He that believeth on me, the freedom flame that I AM, the seventh-ray Master that I AM, the works that I do shall he do also; and greater works than these shall he do because I AM in the heart of the Father.

Therefore take the first steps. Take them and take them well. I am waiting in my alchemical laboratory at the Cave of Symbols in the United States. I await your coming, but each time you are about to advance as an adept on the alchemical path, you let some foolishness or nonsense become the very thing that trips you—some digression, diversion, entertainment this way and that way.

Beloved hearts, to be an initiate of the seventh ray demands decision. The decision must be taken and the vow made. Without decision and the vow, you do not have the support of the heavenly hosts. You can say, "Maybe I will do this today. Maybe I will be an adept tomorrow. Maybe I will study alchemy on the next day and maybe I won't, for, after all, I am free! Saint Germain has said I am free. Therefore I must be free!"

Well indeed you are free, beloved hearts, but you may not enjoy the constancy of angelic support for the inconstant causes of your self-concerns. Of course, you can do anything you want to in the whole universe. You can do something different every day of your life. You can try a new hairstyle, a new outfit, a new fad, a new type of drug any day and any hour, and heaven will champion your freedom!

But, beloved hearts, is there any future or any progress in being the dilettante? I think not. I have watched many not only go to ruination but embody as those individuals who have nothing to say about anything and about whom the heavenly hosts have nothing to say either!

Beloved ones, I tell you, the vow is a serious commitment. The vow and the decision means that you abide by it. For you have given your word to the Almighty, the Almighty has accepted your word, and the Almighty sends his angels to assist you in keeping that word.

Then you enter a path of discipline and you follow the Teachings I have given, and they are many through this activity alone. And each and every Pearl and dictation, I tell you, contains such alchemical keys that if you could perceive how far you could advance on the Path in becoming that alchemist, you would begin immediately. In fact, there would be a stampede to the door! And that is exactly what happens at inner levels when souls finally wake up and realize that their greatest desire is to study with me at the Cave of Symbols.

Beloved ones, I do not accept all. I send them first to the Royal Teton Retreat and then to the Chief of the Darjeeling

Council of the Great White Brotherhood, beloved El Morya. And when they become chelas of whom Morya can be proud, whom Morya can trust, the Chohan of the First Ray will say, "Saint Germain, may I present to you my chela who is my trusted friend." I tell you, it is a moment in Darjeeling when I am invited to that occasion each year, when a few chelas can be presented to me and I may say, "Come now. Come to the Cave of Symbols."

Beloved hearts, it must be so, for I am a serious professor. I am serious in my art, for I see the world slipping down the drain. I see the avalanche of the dark ones and the astral plane, and I see many souls being lost daily.

I do not expect you to have the vision of the hierarch of the seventh ray. Therefore I give you some of it. And I trust you will no longer block that vision by clogging your chakras and your bodies with heavy foods—one more round of ingesting that dense substance, retaining the weight you do not need. You see, the enlightenment and the true seeing and the true spiritualization must come because your cell centers are filled with light unobstructed.

First the decision and the vow, the determination, the commitment. Then angels will take thee in their charge and protect thee. Then comes the definition of the Path and the period of study—study and chelaship—that you might become, therefore, knowledgeable in those Teachings so carefully given, so meticulously pronounced. So much there for you to find.

It is inescapable and unquestionable that you must master the English language. I have chosen now a number of embodiments to use this language. It is fruitful and vast. Borrowing from all other languages, it does become an instrument of the universality of the Christ Mind.

Be it so, I, too, am subject to the Lords of Karma. And if they have decreed it, set aside your questioning and your resistance and get on with this mastery and take the Mother's gracious offer—opportunity in the name of Portia to study and master the [English] language in such a very short time and therefore to be able to delve into the mysteries that are revealed in the Word. Our translations are for you the opening of the door. You must push it wide open and step through and get on then with perfecting yourself as examples of myself throughout Europe.

Blessed hearts, I speak out of profound love. And you must understand how Love does teach his children. Love, as the Mother flame within me, must come after you to let you know that in many areas of learning on this continent there have been highly disciplined ones who have become masters of science, of art, music, and every branch of human endeavor. They have stood out in the centuries, and always they are characterized as the ones who have been self-disciplined for a virtue, for a cause, for a talent, for a vision, for a goal.

One-pointed. One-pointed are these. It is a fraternity of the one-pointed ones who keep the flame of their field. Alas, many have functioned with very little light or spiritualization of consciousness, and yet we have also used them to bring about invention and discoveries of cures for diseases and therefore lifted the karmic weight of the planet.

We could do much through disciplined hearts. We could do much through those who would come prepared for their lessons, having mastered that which has gone before. You must understand that I do not speak merely out of yesterday. I speak out of having known you for 70,000 years and appealed to you—some of you many times over! And I wonder why you still wait, peeping through the curtain to see perhaps if anyone is looking at you looking at me. And if your neighbor should find out, you might just slip away from the Path lest you be disgraced or embarrassed.

O beloved ones, the reasons are manifold. But when it comes to the point of action, we know who does present swords sharpened—not for an effort but for a victory, and there is indeed a difference. Many like to say they have tried. But the victors are silent, for they receive the laurels and the applause of heaven and earth. They need not protest or justify or explain. We do not need such words. We know them all. We have read the letters of cowards in our day. We know the excuse of nonbeing. Let them have their excuse. One day they become as ghosts, fading beyond the windows and into the night while the bright stars shine.

There seem to be a million stars in the sky. There seem to be many, but when you approach, the magnitude of the one is the All. I said the magnitude of the one is the All! For the one has become the All and all things to all people.

I have tried to be this. I have gone hither and yon, here and there, bearing my wares of Light, finding little appreciation. I do not lament it in the sense of dwelling upon it. I count it a part of the work of my LORD.

I could regret many things. How many areas of the planet have slipped from an area of freedom to totalitarian control? I could regret the brainwashing of the masses in these areas of darkness. I could indeed regret the acceptance of the people of the condemnation of America.

My heart is heavy and it is also joyous. For truly I do rejoice to see you and to have presented to me this platform of opportunity. It is indeed a grand night of Opportunity for many in heaven and many of you. And you have placed me betwixt yourselves and heaven, and I have been happy to fill the vacuum. And I will always be happy to fill the vacuum of your hearts with some point of joy.

Let us make that joy count, beloved. Let us make that which we know become the star, the evening star of His Presence appearing. For all of your great effort and magnanimous hearts I praise the Almighty and your blessed souls who have indeed seen a vision and caught it—even more than caught it today from the heart of the Goddess of Liberty, Nada, the Great Divine Director, who have comforted me in many centuries when my endeavors have not culminated in a fruit of action of permanent and lasting freedom.

I look at South America, vast land of the Great Divine Director. I see there the potential of the golden age, yet setback after setback. Is it any wonder, beloved hearts, that we would not know where to place our support when all sides have corruption and darkness? Yet in the hearts of the freedom fighters there, in the hearts of those who truly love liberty, who must face those regimes which would overtake them—in those hearts a flame burns and we give support.

But where is the support of the West and of the people of the United States? Where is the support that would return the Goddess of Justice and the Goddess of Liberty to their nations? You see, the little people who fight on the battlefield for my cause must be reinforced by the superstructures of governments and nations who are yet free.

Blessed ones, some carry the myth that somehow freedom will win out because it is the nature of man. They have never reckoned with forces of Evil that are absolute. They have not wrestled with the forces of hell. They somehow think "the sun also rises" and that by some automatic process, which they romantically categorize as movements of the people in these nations, the whole earth will be restored. But this has not been the pattern.

The destruction of Afghanistan is before your eyes. Who will run and save it? No one dares. They are cowards! Before what? Before a military establishment that has been defeated year in, year out by the bare hands of the mujahidin?

Do you understand, beloved hearts, the configuration of

forces in the earth? Where there is might and power the beast has become lugubrious. It moves, or does not move, as some ancient reptilian form—mindless, awkward, unable to save even a company of men who are left to die at the hands of terrorists for want of right decision and right command. They [the captives] are the angels of Light! You are the angels of Light! But where shall they sound the fire of heaven when those in positions of power have betrayed them in every nation?

So the betrayal of the light of Vietnam has been complete, and devastation is through. And those of culture, of light have all been murdered and destroyed. It is a wholesale destruction of the populations of Lightbearers in every nation we see. Yes, they have their lists. They know who they will go after the moment they are in power, nation by nation.

India is their goal. Your nations are on their target. Yet the people have not focused because there is no energy in the third eye or the crown, for all wallow in their own sensuality and thralldom. They party and drink and make decisions great and small affecting the centuries and billions to come. How long can a body of Lords of Karma sponsor an evolution that fails to challenge the greatest enemy that has assembled itself out of Assyria, out of Babylon, out of the fallen angels? And if you only knew how as nothing they are.

Let us rejoice in victories. Let us see that even an eye of victory can be expanded and increased and enlarged. A following of Lightbearers can suddenly appear, and a great world communion in the Great Central Sun can produce in action a solid wall, flanked by angels, of saints in embodiment robed in white and those in the etheric octave.

Have you seen Elysian fields? I have seen them! You call them the dead. I say they are alive forevermore, championing, defying the fallen ones, calling to your hearts while you sleep at night—calling to you, telling you of atrocities and darkness. And you wonder why you cannot sleep. It is not always the dark forces, beloved. It is your brothers and sisters in the etheric octave who are prodding you and telling you, "Something is wrong! You must act in a big way for those things that have already come upon us and will come upon you also if you trust the wrong ones."

Beloved hearts, behold the panorama of life evolving in all octaves on this earth, waiting the day of the coming of the Light, waiting the day and seeing the dawn. Earth—earth knows the coming of the Light that you have heard and seen. Some fear it. Some run from it. Some immediately assail it. Others take the wafer and the wine, internalize the Light and become ourselves. But some of these are ignorant. Their education has been manipulated and they are unable to stand for us in high-level places where decisions are being made daily to defeat the human race.

Beloved ones, I only ask you this. Take each twenty-four-hour day and do the most you can for Light, for Freedom where you are. Do the best you can by making the best decisions for the best possibilities. Understand, beloved, there are always choices. Some waste time or are centered on inconsequential endeavors that do not lead to major victories. And even minor ones, when tallied day by day, count mightily. Take your twenty-four hours and realize it is a gift of Opportunity. Do not take Life for granted, or Freedom or this Teaching. Apply it now and see what you can do.

Come together in your nations. Form a plan and a strategy. What is most essential is to bring the Teaching and to nurture it and to teach people the fiery decree—not mere chanting of words, as I sometimes hear you give, but a fervor of the heart that does truly bestir the highest angels of heaven who leave off tending the Central Sun to see what is that fire burning now on planet earth.

Beloved ones, we have not called our decrees chants, others have. We have called them decrees because they embody will and fire and determination. Do not always lower the sound or reduce the volume. Go somewhere where you can shout and know that you have reached the star of my causal body. I will be there as I am here, for I am always in the heart of Opportunity.

While I have life and breath and dispensation and the ability to work with this planet, you can be certain I AM here, I AM there, and I AM in the star of your own causal body. I am Saint Germain. And I am grateful to you for having received me and prepared this place for me and for my Messenger. I will not forget the fight that you have fought, the good fight that you have won in this session and round. I always bless. I always increase. And I shall continue to do so, for it is the way of the seventh ray.

In my eye is the reflection of your soul—what you will be ascended in the Light and free if you choose to be; what you will be in abject Darkness if you take the left-handed path. Remember, I have told you. There is no predestination except God. Thus all will choose. And all will know that they have chosen because they have heard and seen and decided. Better to choose in knowledge than to be caught up in ignorance and to go down to defeat, never having known why failure has turned to death and darkness. At least one should have the knowledge of why one has failed, that one may perchance live again if Opportunity keep her flame.

You see how much you depend upon us? There are flames not kept for earth, for there have not been Masters to keep them. For you yourselves made the choice not to be a Master long ago. But where there are Masters and you do have that momentum and flame that is accessible, I tell you, you depend upon it mightily. Reverse the roles and see then how we depend upon you and how you are dependent totally upon your daily choices.

I come not to weary you but to love you. I come not to fault-find but to praise the most precious hearts that have ever come forth out of this continent in this age.

Precious hearts, I love you. I send you to find more of my own. Then we shall see what can be done.

I salute you in the name of my beloved Portia, my comfort, my love. May you also know her and realize that her flame burns in you also.

We seal you for another day of striving and bless you mightily now from our causal bodies.

[standing ovation]

O Saint Germain, Send Violet Flame

Beloved mighty victorious Presence of God, I AM in me, thou immortal unfed flame of Christ-love within my heart, Holy Christ Selves of all mankind, beloved Ascended Master Saint Germain, beloved Mother Mary and beloved Jesus the Christ, the beloved Maha Chohan, Archangel Zadkiel, Prince Oromasis, all great beings, powers, and activities of Light serving the violet transmuting flame, beloved Lanello, the entire Spirit of the Great White Brotherhood and the World Mother, elemental life—fire, air, water, and earth!

In the name and by the power of the Presence of God which I AM and by the magnetic power of the sacred fire vested in me, I invoke the mighty presence and power of your full-gathered momentum of service to the Light of God that never fails, and I command that it be directed throughout my entire consciousness, being, and world, through my affairs, the activities of The Summit Lighthouse, and all Ascended Master activities, worlds without end.

In thy name, O God, I decree:

1. O Saint Germain, send Violet Flame,
   Sweep it through my very core;
   Bless'd Zadkiel, Oromasis,
   Expand and intensify more and more.

Refrain: Right now blaze through and saturate,
   Right now expand and penetrate;
   Right now set free, God's mind to be,
   Right now and for Eternity.

2. I AM in the Flame and there I stand,
   I AM in the center of God's hand;
   I AM filled and thrilled by violet hue,
   I AM wholly flooded through and through.

3. I AM God's Flame within my soul,
   I AM God's flashing beacon goal;
   I AM, I AM the sacred fire,
   I feel the flow of Joy inspire.

4. The Consciousness of God in me
   Does raise me to the Christ I see.
   Descending now in Violet Flame,
   I see Him come fore'er to reign.

5. O Jesus, send thy Violet Flame,
   Sanctify my very core;
   Blessed Mary, in God's name,
   Expand and intensify more and more.

6. O Mighty I AM, send Violet Flame,
   Purify my very core;
   Maha Chohan, Thou Holy One,
   Expand, expand God's lovely sun.

Coda:* He takes me by the hand to say,
   I love thy soul each blessed day;
   O rise with me into the air
   Where blossoms freedom from all care;
   As Violet Flame keeps blazing through,
   I know that I'll ascend with you.

And in full Faith I consciously accept this manifest, manifest, manifest! (3x) right here and now with full Power, eternally sustained, all-powerfully active, ever expanding, and world enfolding until all are wholly ascended in the Light and free!

Beloved I AM! Beloved I AM! Beloved I AM!

* To be given at the end of the decree.

"The Summit Lighthouse Sheds Its Radiance O'er All the World to Manifest as Pearls of Wisdom."
This dictation by Saint Germain was the concluding address **delivered** through the Messenger of the Great White Brotherhood Elizabeth Clare Prophet on **Sunday, November 3, 1985,** during the 3-day *Seminar for World Teachers* on the Teachings of the Ascended Masters in Flevohof, Holland.

Pearls of Wisdom®

published by The Summit Lighthouse

| Vol. 29 No. 5 | The Beloved Goddess of Liberty | February 2, 1986 |

The Handwriting on the Wall:
Read It and Decide Your Destiny
V
Allegiance to the Law of the One

I come bearing the torch of the Central Sun, a rekindling fire of Illumination. I am Liberty, mother of nations and planetary spheres and of your blessed hearts of fire.

I am come for the awakening of the ancient memory. I come for Illumination and the consuming of that which burdens the mind and soul. And what is that burden, beloved? It is the burden of ignorance of the Law and the ignoring of the path of Love. Thus, I call all of those who are of the Light from one end of the earth to the other into the very heart of allegiance to the Law of the One.

O one eternal, indivisible Light of Liberty, I am in the very center of the Temple of the Sun over this city, directing now seven flames of Light through these seven chakras of our Messenger, delivering, then, the frequencies of the Lords of Karma to each and every one so gathered and all who are seeking and crying out to the Lord Christ, to the Lord Buddha, to the Lord Krishna— whatever the name of that Light.

O beloved, we come to answer the call by Illumination's fires. And in the quickening of Illumination, so let it be that the violet flame does burst forth as transmutation, as love, as allegiance in the very heart to the deliverance of a planetary home.

Leave now your nets of karma, human confusion and occupation! For I, the Goddess of Liberty, will indeed make you fishers of men. I will draw you to the shore. I will show you the

Note: Revelation 11 was read by the Messenger prior to this dictation at the request of Saint Germain.

boundless sea and the expanse of Light. I will show you how to first harvest light as skeins from the far-off worlds and how to use that light to harvest souls, that they, too, might know the flame of Liberty and be converted thereby.

O Light of the Central Sun, now intensify! Now go forth. Now let the earth be filled, for indeed the kingdoms of this world are become the kingdoms of our Lord and of his Christ in each and every heart that so ordains by free will the coming of the LORD I AM THAT I AM.

Let the message be crystallized as law written in your inward parts. Let there be a penetration and the exposure of the manipulation of the minds of the people by the controlled dissemination of information through the media and the press that does not come as the absolute God Truth or as fact itself but as a contrivance to separate, divide, and amass people toward this side or the other. Let those who are indeed not fools understand that they must not allow themselves to be fooled but study in the very heart of Saint Germain what are the true conditions in the earth in this hour.

O America, do not trust here and there those who say they lead, those who sit in the seat of shepherd and authority. Trust, therefore, the inner Light. Trust the inner warning. Be independent and striving ones and therefore find the positioning of Truth, and be not wedded to personalities or parties or unions where there is the intent to use you, then, for other purposes than those so stated.

This is the line of the three o'clock. I stand at the line of the nine. I am directing the arcing of the rainbow rays of light over America from New York to Los Angeles. I am intensifying the piercing light of Truth. Let all who are a part of freedom lovers in the world demand first and foremost the sword of living Truth from on high, from Pallas Athena and the Lords of Karma, to cleave asunder now the real from the unreal so that you can determine your fate and know that you champion right causes and the whole earth full of Light.

O beloved, it is indeed the hour of the coming of Saint Germain. It is indeed the hour of the sounding of the seventh angel who will not cease to sound through you, each and every heart, as you allow him—through our Messengers and Keepers of the Flame worldwide, through all who love freedom and espouse its cause.

So he is sent forth in this hour on that mission. So, beloved hearts of Light, it is indeed a new day for beloved Saint Germain.

And those last vestiges yet untransmuted of burdens upon his own altar are now swiftly passing into the flame. And we know that in the days to come you will indeed keep the vigil of the violet flame that the conclusion of the seventy-two weeks might indeed be the clean white page.[1] In anticipation of this fulfillment of that cycle, as you intensify in the coming fortnight a fourteen-day period to immerse the planet in violet flame, we release to you now the flame unfurled and the Light of the God of Freedom to the earth.

The beloved Ascended Master Saint Germain, beloved hearts, stands now on this platform as physical as the Law will allow him to be in this city of New York. [standing ovation]

"The Summit Lighthouse Sheds Its Radiance O'er All the World to Manifest as Pearls of Wisdom." This dictation by the Goddess of Liberty was **delivered** on **Sunday, November 17, 1985,** during a weekend seminar held at the Penta Hotel in New York City, where Elizabeth Clare Prophet was stumping for Saint Germain's Coming Revolution in Higher Consciousness. **(1) Seventy-two-week vigil for Saint Germain.** On July 1, 1984, Arcturus and Victoria announced: "As you take advantage of these hours and weeks, weeks in the seventy-two, beloved, understand that that may create anew an original leaven, a momentum of freedom which will give to Saint Germain the balance for all of those endeavors for which he has secured grants from the Karmic Board in the last 400 years"—grants for which he has had to "pay the price for faithless, reprehensible mortals who stole his light. . . ." Arcturus and Victoria promised: "That culmination of your service in the seventy-two weeks for planet earth can lay before the Lords of Karma, through the violet flame, through your invocations, the paying of the last farthing of all that has become the debt of Saint Germain," who therefore will "once again be permitted to go before not only the Lords of Karma but the Great Central Sun for a brand-new dispensation of Light."

Cup of Freedom

Beloved mighty victorious Presence of God, I AM in me, O thou beloved immortal victorious threefold flame of eternal Truth within my heart, Holy Christ Selves of all mankind, beloved Great Divine Director, beloved Saint Germain, beloved El Morya, beloved Jesus, beloved Mother Mary, beloved Goddess of Liberty, beloved great God Obedience, beloved Archangel Michael, beloved Mighty Astrea, all ascended beings, powers, activities, and legions of Light, angels and activities of the sacred fire: In the name of the Presence of God which I AM and through the magnetic power of the sacred fire vested in me, I decree:

1. O Masters of Love in Symbol Cave,
   Come now, make me true and brave
   By the royal flag of Light,
   Radiance of gold, blue, and white!

Refrain: Emblem of America, heart of Freedom dear,
   Keep our land in integrity here,
   Always aware that in God we trust,
   Each child of the Light, now make just!

2. Protect, direct, and arm us with Light;
   Goddess of Liberty, flood us with might.
   Cup of Freedom to the earth,
   O America, thy love is heaven's worth!

And in full Faith I consciously accept this manifest, manifest, manifest! (3x) right here and now with full Power, eternally sustained, all-powerfully active, ever expanding, and world enfolding until all are wholly ascended in the Light and free! Beloved I AM! Beloved I AM! Beloved I AM!

Pearls of Wisdom, published weekly by The Summit Lighthouse for Church Universal and Triumphant, come to you under the auspices of the Darjeeling Council of the Great White Brotherhood. These are presently dictated by the Ascended Masters to their Messenger Elizabeth Clare Prophet. The international headquarters of this nonprofit, nondenominational activity is located in Los Angeles, California. All communications and freewill contributions should be addressed to The Summit Lighthouse, Box A, Malibu, CA 90265. Pearls of Wisdom are sent weekly throughout the USA via third-class mail to all who support the Church with a minimum yearly love offering of $40. First-class and international postage rates available upon request. Notice of change of address should be received three weeks prior to the effective date. Third-class mail is not forwarded by the post office.

Pearls of Wisdom®

published by The Summit Lighthouse

| Vol. 29 No. 6 | *Beloved Saint Germain* | *February 9, 1986* |

The Handwriting on the Wall:
Read It and Decide Your Destiny
VI
The Passing of the Old Order

Most Gracious Friends of Freedom,
  Sons and Daughters of Liberty,
    I greet you in the new freedom of the hour. And I AM
Saint Germain. And I AM the presence of the seventh angel and
I AM sounding and resounding the mysteries of the infinite
Light through your hearts in this hour.

O beloved, I say to you with beloved Portia, hail to the
Light above! Hail to the Light below! Hail to the Light in the
torch of the Goddess of Liberty. Hail to the Light in the hearts
of the faithful, Keepers of the Flame always, who have cleared
the way for my coming in this hour.

Beloved ones, ladies and gentlemen, please be seated in
my flame.

It is a splendid day to know that we may move forward
together. Fear not, for the release of darkness and karma of the
seed of the wicked in recent earthquake and turmoil in Mexico
and South America, here and on the West Coast and around the
world—these things are for the passing of the old order.

Now in this hour you can anticipate intense sacred fire and violet flame. And as you capture that Light and as you determine as
never before to keep the vigil with me, I promise you that we with
the Lords of Karma will do all in our power to mitigate that which
may be scheduled to descend as world karma but which I tell you
can be consumed in the very air by the Light you hurl, the Light you
send, the Light in which you rejoice by the sounding of the Word!

As I am sounding, so you are sounding. And so it is the eternal sound. So it is the full power of the AUM. And it is the I AM THAT I AM. And it is the flame of freedom bursting.

O beloved ones, know, then, the signs of the times and know the meaning of the ascent of the Two Witnesses. For the plane of heaven to which they ascend is indeed the plane of appearance in the etheric belts of the earth, then, in the upper chakras—the chakra of the heart, the throat, the third eye, and the crown. And there in that heaven plane—there is your own personal resurrection! And your soul must needs be resurrected this day from preoccupation with the lower chakras in thy temple.

Let these be healed and sealed! Let your four lower bodies be healed, for my gift in this hour is indeed a healing, a magnetization towards wholeness that you might live forever on earth in your heaven world, that you might understand the power of the Mother to raise up the sacred force within you as a life everlasting, that you might know indeed the Mother flame in your midst, that you might learn to love every precious angel of the violet flame that comes peeping through your keyhole and your windowpane, that comes in the morning to waken you with joy.

O beloved, do not be crestfallen. Do not be set back by that which you meet. Let it be doused in violet flame. Go forth with the joy of precipitation. Take my "little book,"[1] this precious book given to you by the devotees and staff and co-workers, by the Messengers therefore manifesting that concerted effort to see the physical manifestation of that which I have long desired to have in print.

I hold it in my hand in this dictation for a very purpose. For I am charging this copy and through it every copy of this book with the full, flaming presence of my new day, my revolution to all. May this book itself find its goal in every nation and in every language.

It is a handbook. It is the little book which may be devoured, and it will begin the alchemicalization. It will begin the process worldwide of the raising up of the coil of the violet flame. To this, then, be dedicated, and know that I have indeed come again, my mantle with me, our beloved Alpha and Omega and the Cosmic Council so decreeing that I may go forth in this hour and that I may truly have the opportunity of the quickening.

Beloved hearts, the mantle given to me for this Stump,[2] which I have placed upon the Messenger, has been the very dispensation to galvanize Lightbearers. May this Word continue through you. May you also understand the message that is the

stepping-stones of life whereby those lost in a dead doctrine may
be the quickened who come first to the understanding of eternal
Life and then to its Love and then to its manifestation by that
courage and honor of the heart.

Beloved ones of the sacred fire, take, then, my trilogy of the
threefold flame of the heart. Internalize it and make it your
own. By the true study of this fourfold work on alchemy you can
become the alchemist and the adept right where you are. We
bridge the gap. Indeed we bring the altar of Israel to your very
heart and home.

Oh, know the Lord as the *Sanctus.*³ So the holiness of seraphim rest with you and violet-flame angels clear the path for
their coming. Remember the teaching of Serapis Bey enfolded
then and sealed for your heart in the *Dossier on the Ascension.*
Remember the teaching that the seraphim of God come at any
hour that you call to them, place their angelic presence where
you are, burn through and consume and dredge from you all
that is past and cast it into the sacred fire.⁴

The angels of the LORD, the legions of Light attend your
acceleration! Oh, do not hold back. Do not any longer stay in
the recalcitrance of a waywardness and the stiff-necked generation of old. Let all these things pass.

I send my flame to the very hearts of those laggard evolutions
in the Middle East who have held back the full price of glory.
I send legions and the solar ring of seraphim in this hour to
encircle those nations, to intensify the sacred fire, to give all the
opportunity then to beat their swords into plowshares and their
spears into pruninghooks.⁵

Beloved ones, let there be war no more! And let this be the
conclusion of this Summit conference. Let it be the conclusion
of all hearts in the earth to bind these fallen angels by the power
of the dynamic decree to Archangel Michael and his rosary said
daily. For the declaration of peace on earth must be reinforced
by the sacred Word, which is the sword of the Word. It is the
living Word that cometh out of the mouth of the Messengers of
God. And you are indeed emissaries representing the Godhead,
and you must send forth that Word daily. For those who desire
war for their own evil designs, beloved hearts, will not say die, will
not recant, will not turn back except the Light move *en force!*

Beloved hearts, you can call to march with Archangel
Michael and his legions of Light while your physical bodies
sleep at night. You can be with the saints robed in white. You
can place your very bodies on the line of Darkness, and you can

absorb and swallow up that Darkness as you are engulfed in the living presence of the seraphim of God.

They come in numberless numbers. Angels of the Lord descend, then, to this very planetary home.

O children of the Sun, look up and behold, for the day of opportunity is nigh! And that opportunity comes to you in this hour in the living presence of my beloved twin flame, Portia, who stands with me now as ever to direct her love to you and to speak to you of the promise of old—the opportunity for initiation through the twelve gates of the City Foursquare.

So receive, then, my beloved Portia, whose hour of victory is also come, as is mine. [standing ovation]

"The Summit Lighthouse Sheds Its Radiance O'er All the World to Manifest as Pearls of Wisdom." This dictation by Saint Germain was **delivered** on **Sunday, November 17, 1985,** during a weekend seminar held at the Penta Hotel in New York City, where Elizabeth Clare Prophet was stumping for Saint Germain's Coming Revolution in Higher Consciousness. (1) *Saint Germain On Alchemy: For the Adept in the Aquarian Age,* Summit University Press, $4.95 postpaid. See Rev. 10:2, 8–10. (2) See Portia, October 13, 1985, "A New Mantle for Saint Germain's Mission from the Cosmic Council," 1985 *Pearls of Wisdom,* vol. 28, no. 50, pp. 601–2. (3) *Sanctus* [Latin]: Holy One. "Sanctus" from *Saint Cecilia Mass* by Gounod was played as the meditation music before this dictation. (4) See Serapis Bey, Seraphic Meditations I and II: "The Great Electronic Fire Rings," "The Sea of Glass," in *Dossier on the Ascension: The Story of the Soul's Acceleration into Higher Consciousness on the Path of Initiation,* Summit University Press, pp. 120–31, $4.95 postpaid; and *The Alchemy of the Word: Stones for the Wise Masterbuilders,* s.v. "Seraphim," in *Saint Germain On Alchemy: For the Adept in the Aquarian Age,* Summit University Press, pp. 447–49, $4.95 postpaid. (5) Isa. 2:4; Mic. 4:3.

Pearls of Wisdom®
published by The Summit Lighthouse

| Vol. 29 No. 7 | Beloved Portia | February 16, 1986 |

The Handwriting on the Wall:
Read It and Decide Your Destiny
VII
Cosmic Christ Initiators Knock at the Door

I speak to your souls, O Lightbearers of freedom. I speak in the name of the Lords of Karma and of Sanat Kumara and the desiring of the hosts of the LORD that some should come, then, to that path of the ruby ray, that some should demonstrate the twelve gates and the twelve hierarchies.

I speak truly—truly in this hour of your opportunity held by the Goddess of Liberty to convene at the Inner Retreat, to let yourselves pass through the sacred fires to become the immortal God-free being who you are here and now and to never, never again consider death as a passageway to anywhere. For the transition must needs be only the soul's acceleration. Yet how can the soul accelerate at that hour of the passing if the momentum has not been built while on earth?

It is true that Jesus called your Messengers to found that Inner Retreat. And the one who stands on this side of the bank of the river and the one who stands on the other[1]—these do fulfill our promise to you to draw together your twin flames, to draw together your souls of Light in those highest unions of the divine family for the sponsoring of the children of the new age.

We do not relent in our God-determination to see this planet fulfill her fiery destiny. So the cycle of the twenty-two months is at hand. It is the sign and the number in Hebrew of the alphabet. It is the sign of each and every letter outplaying itself as a nucleus and molecule of sacred fire intensifying the manifestation in the earth in these twenty-two months beginning this day.

This cycle is given to you to assimilate all of Saint Germain's teaching in the little book on alchemy. See that thy soul does profit, for know ye not that the Master does overshadow you and promote the full alchemy of Light in your being? As you study and internalize this teaching and place yourself directly in the heart of the science of the spoken Word daily, taking that book also and giving that violet-flame call to the ten,[2] you will see that the twenty-two months are for the gathering—the union of hearts in molecules of service all over the earth, focusing the amethyst jewel, coming together for the balancing of karma and then the service of a chalice forged of a mosaic of souls. Understand that here and there and everywhere this gathering of molecules of violet flame is the only answer to those conditions at hand [as the result of the Four Horsemen and the Seven Archangels pouring out the vials of the last plagues of mankind's karma].

Do not forget this meeting or that I have spoken, for I have been with you, each and every one of you, in the hour of your previous transition. I am indeed Portia, the Goddess of Opportunity, so called because I embody the flame of opportunity that is the open door to the union of your soul with your Mighty I AM Presence, and in that union the reintegration here on earth of the white fire bodies of your twin flames.

Now be seated as I give to you that sacred fire in this hour.

Understand, beloved, that through your acceleration, through your making your pilgrimage, as to Mecca, to the Heart of the Inner Retreat, you then will pass through veils of the untransmuted substance. You will change your garments and prepare for that initiation of the transfiguration in the mountain of God.

It is absolutely essential that at inner levels and in the plane of the I AM THAT I AM and the Holy Christ Self—your soul reaching that plane by dynamic decree and meditation and service to life—that you are one with your twin flame and that you complete your reason for being on earth in this hour.

Hear my statements, for they apply to each and every one of you! Where it is not possible for you to contact that twin flame physically, it matters not. The inner union and the reinforcement is the key. Where it is not possible, we assemble lifestreams who are soul mates or have a similar path and attainment, who have good karma together and who may serve as receptacles for the I AM Presence of the twin flames of themselves and each other, forming a cosmic cube in the earth.

Thus, beloved, endeavors in the earth must have the presence

of the wholeness of Alpha and Omega and the single call you make
each day:

Lo, I AM Alpha and Omega of the twin flame
white fire bodies of myself and my beloved
manifest here in action!
Lo, I AM Alpha and Omega,
the beginning and the ending
of our white fire sphere of wholeness!

To affirm here below, therefore, the oneness of yourself and
twin flame will place upon you the mantle of these twin spheres of
Light to accomplish the purposes to which you are set.

Fear not, then, to be divested of unreality. Fear not to take
swift strides and giant steps to the Sun, for the need of the hour
is great. We will do all that is possible to avert world cataclysm,
O beloved hearts. Only remember, the one individual, the Keeper of
the Flame, the finger in the dike—that one with God is a majority.

And sometimes when you recall the voice in your heart and
respond to that call and give the dynamic decree in any hour of
the day or night, you may be the sole one on earth whose prayer
reaches the hosts of the LORD that can stay the hand of great
darkness coming upon this or any city. Understand your value
and worth. Understand the path of individualism and know the
reality of the Great White Brotherhood.

I am Portia, your advocate before the Court of the Sacred
Fire, before the courts of the world, and before the court of
public opinion. And I speak to all devotees in all new-age movements, in all paths and teachings that go beyond the orthodoxy
of the major world religions.

Beloved hearts, the forces of darkness would splinter and
divide you. You must understand the union of Light of the avant-
garde of the age and be not so mindful or critical of separate ideas
with which you differ. It matters not, beloved ones, if you do not
agree on every point of the Path and Teaching and Way. What
matters, beloved hearts, is that you see the union of those who are
climbing the highest mountain and that you realize that when all
arrive at the Summit of Being all will understand and know the
Law of the One.

What is important in this hour is that there be a worldwide
awareness of the oneness of those seekers after Truth and that
their union be based on the principle of Truth and common
survival. For if there be separation, you will see then how here
and there the smaller groups are cast down, as those who fear
the coming of the new wave of Light do organize to put down

by every means anyone who goes forth with a message of the coming revolution of Light.

Understand, beloved ones, that it is time truly for the Great White Brotherhood and those who understand the meaning of the saints robed in white to stand together and to defend one another's right to pursue their own perception of the living Word and the universal Reality, to defend everyone's right to pursue a path to union with God. Defend that right in concerted effort!

Beloved hearts, if all can even receive this book of beloved Saint Germain and take some of it as real and active, then Saint Germain will forge a worldwide union of freedom fighters and you will no longer experience the darkness that has come upon those who have been the true revolutionaries, who have had the courage to go after whether the false gurus or the true, the very courage itself to seek an alternative to a dead and dying doctrine that indeed shall be quickened by the LORD's presence in and with you.

I am calling, then, for the unity of hearts on basic principles and [for you] to set aside [your] differences. For if the new-age movement cannot come together in a worldwide ecumenism, I tell you, then, it is no better than the old order of those who have been bickering for thousands of years while the world and its children have been left untended.

The solving of the problems of man's view of theology is not the urgent need of the hour, beloved hearts! The urgent need is the assuming of the Holy Spirit and the descent of that Light into every man's temple regardless of what that man may call that Light or how he may define it. The Light is the Light, and the Light is true! And the vibration is known. And all that is less than that vibration is *not* of the Light and should be therefore shunned.

Therefore let there be the dividing of the way. And let the Lightbearers of the world unite in the name of freedom! in the name of the flame of freedom of my beloved Saint Germain! who is truly the champion of every seeker everywhere regardless of any erroneous concepts or burdens that may separate that one from the fullness of the blazing reality of the noonday sun of his I AM Presence. For Saint Germain takes everyone's hand and leads that one nearer and nearer to the Light as he is willing and able.

Therefore, beloved hearts, please do not interfere with the trek and the momentum and the rhythm of new Lightbearers on the Path. Let them take his cup as they are able while you keep the flame in joy and love. Be free, then, of criticism and see how the ground swell of those who are the liberated souls in the world will make their voice count not only in religion but in the governments of the nations, will take their stand and see the way through to the holding of the balance for the economies—and in this nation especially. And the sacred fire infolding itself must collapse the old structures and build upon the foundation of the white cube and the stone of the masterbuilders.

I call you, beloved hearts, to a path of Love. I send you forth to acquaint yourselves with those who are following whatever path, that you might be emissaries of Love and Justice and the message I bring that the opportunity to pursue Truth by all of these groups *must* be preserved, *must* be protected by a union of hearts throughout the entire planetary network. O Keepers of the Flame of Saint Germain, will you help me sponsor this endeavor?

["Yes!" standing ovation]

The false gods who have positioned themselves in the earth truly have one fear, and it is indeed the fear of the people. When the people rally around the standard of Christ and the Christ-bearers, when they act in concerted voice and heart, then they must only recede.

The power of Victory is in your hands. Do not forget it. Receive, then, the torch of illumination of the Goddess of Liberty. Seize it in Saint Germain's name! Bring illumined action to the world—action based on awareness of the I AM Presence and the Christ Self.

I call for helpers to publish our battle cry, the magazine of the Coming Revolution in Higher Consciousness. I call to you to understand that exposés must be written, that the truth must be stated, and many are needed. Let talents developed by you for ages now be focused on the physical victory. For there is no other victory that we desire except that physical victory, for it is the foundation of all others.

If there be not the physical victory in America of the claiming of the land and the resurrection of hearts and of the restoration of fairness to all peoples regardless of their race or ethnic origin, their status in society or their religion—beloved hearts, if this is not won here, how can it be the gift of this people and this torch of Liberty to every other nation?

Fanaticism must be consumed in this hour!

And I, Portia, stand therefore with the banner of the hordes of hell. And I put it to the torch. It is the banner of fanaticism in every field and area. Let the cultists of fanaticism go down, for their banner is consumed! And in its place the banner of the living Christ, universal in all people, is raised on high this day! It is the rallying cry. It is the standard of all people of Reality.

Rejoice that our God is come into the earth and into your hearts in this hour, and purge the earth of that fear and hatred that breeds terrorism and would take from you any one of these little ones!

I AM in the flaming presence of Opportunity. And the opportunity and its day is done for the fallen ones and these possessing demons who mouth their words of fanaticism in every quarter of the earth. Their day of opportunity is done! They have had their opportunity to unite under the banner of Maitreya and Sanat Kumara and Lord Gautama. Now let them retreat and let the Lightbearers march then! Let them march on Fifth Avenue and in the highways of our God! Let them march through the towns and the cities of the earth! Let them come as those freedom fighters who sang the "Yankee Doodle Dandy" and knew whereof they spoke.

O beloved, it is an hour of freedom. Can the earth contain it? ["Yes!" standing ovation]

I promise you in sealing this hour that *none* can deter you, *none* can stop your victory! The way is clear. You have only to march and claim the planetary field of consciousness for the angels of the LORD.

No one can deter you except your own self or doubt or trepidation. These, too, in your name I cast into the sacred fire! May you do so daily as you advance on the cycles of the cosmic clock and know indeed personally the blessed representatives of the hierarchies of the Sun who knock upon your door in the name of Christ and say to you as the sun signs change and your birth cycles turn, "May I enter, O soul of Light? For I deliver to you now a message and the testing of your soul of the Cosmic Christ."

Will you open the door of your heart and receive the Cosmic Christ initiators, beloved ones? ["Yes!"]

So we thank you, we love you, we seal you, and we say, watch and pray. Keep the vigil and keep the flame, for the day of the seventh angel's sounding is truly upon you.

The past is prologue. Move forward in Light.
[standing ovation]

"The Summit Lighthouse Sheds Its Radiance O'er All the World to Manifest as Pearls of Wisdom." This dictation by Portia was **delivered** on **Sunday, November 17, 1985,** during a weekend seminar held at the Penta Hotel in New York City, where Elizabeth Clare Prophet was stumping for Saint Germain's Coming Revolution in Higher Consciousness. (1) Dan. 12:5. (2) See "Ten for Transmutation," in Mark L. Prophet and Elizabeth Clare Prophet, *The Science of the Spoken Word,* Summit University Press, pp. 113–25; $5.95 postpaid.

Pearls of Wisdom®

published by The Summit Lighthouse

| *Vol. 29 No. 8* | *Beloved Lady Master Venus* | *February 23, 1986* |

The Handwriting on the Wall:
Read It and Decide Your Destiny
VIII
The Lost Chord of Twin Flames

Lightbearers of Love unto the New Age,

I AM grateful to descend in the matrix of sacred fire, in the cone expanded for the descent of Light.

I am come by the forcefield abuilding. I am come by elementals and angels and by your leave, dear hearts who reach out for Love and the Beloved.

Know that all things must work together for good to those who are called and chosen of the Ancient of Days.[1] Know that we must also move planetary forces and that our mission in this hour through this company has been to establish and lay the foundation for the penetration into the earth of pillars of sacred fire held by Holy Kumaras and legions of Victory's Light, especially here in this area of the third-eye chakra of the nation anchored in the Temple of the Sun.

We come, then, for many reasons to release the Light through the spoken Word now passing through your chakras so prepared. Angels of Venus of Love bring forth the delicate vibrations for the restoration of soul sensitivity, refinement of creativity, and restoration of truly that which is the lost chord of your harmony with your beloved twin flame.

Souls, now I call to you out of the seat-of-the-soul chakra! Rise by the power of the resurrection flame and the mantra of the Lord Christ:

I AM the Resurrection and the Life of the sacred fire
burning in my heart and soul and mind and body.

I AM the Resurrection and the Life
of holy purpose in twin flames of our causal body.

So, beloved, the turning of cycles is come. Earth has experienced darkness and calamity and the Fourth Horseman in this year.[2] Thus, Death has been the pale rider. And you, beloved, have seen, day upon day, wondering what next might appear across the continents of the earth. But fear not. All this must come to pass. Let the cycles of the night burn themselves out. Let the morning doves ascend now up the spiral to the fount of love of twin flames.

Beloved, in the dark night of earth's history, be the candle as you are. Go forth in the full promise of Saint Germain, for we reinforce this commitment. And the legions of Light of the Holy Kumaras are working in the sea and under the sea, into the very heart of the continent to establish balance and the magnet of Divine Love.

Light of the Central Sun descending now, Holy Spirit, Maha Chohan, draw the ring of fire and the figure eight through the very nexus of twin flames. Accelerate then, accelerate then the Light! In the name of Brahma and Vishnu, in the name of Shiva, we release that sacred fire, consuming records here, going to the very heart of the people of this area and going to the heart of those who also must be taken, for their malintent and darkness has proven a grave vulnerability to the manifestation of equilibrium in this area.

Beloved ones, so it was said—one is taken and another is left.[3] And this is the hour of the sifting and the weighing and the measuring of the court. So let there be the measuring now.[4] And in the Central Sun, by the power of that magnet, let twin flames descend. Let the power of your I AM Presence descend. Let the power of the Light descend in the vortex of the secret rays.

In the Light of Mother Mary and on the path of the sacred heart, we open the door and kindle a flame. I have come for the fulfillment of a certain cycle, beginning in the hour of Sagittarius, of that begun by Vesta.[5] Thus, in the fulfillment of the All-Seeing Eye of Scorpio, I initiate the sacred fire whereby you become, by the momentum and the thrust of Sagittarius, that flame of Maitreya, that flame of the Love of the Buddha who is indeed the Cosmic Christ and the Teacher of the Mystery School come again.

So in the year's conclusion in the cycles ahead the entire Spirit of the Great White Brotherhood calls to you even now to remember the acceleration of the violet flame and the harvest and the judgment of the seed of the wicked and the clearing of the way for the little ones. So it is a year [1985], beloved, know this, that could have been much worse for this nation and the nations of the earth but for the Lightbearers everywhere, but for the prayers and the good intent so manifest in right action.

I then stand, anchoring the Light of the Holy Kumaras for a purpose. Darkness is taken from your auras. For you have come to the fount seeking the knowledge of twin flames, aye, and you have found more than a dissertation—you have found a meditation and a path of the mystics. And you wonder, "What is this?" I tell you, it is the true mystery of Love that is found in the intoning of the Word and the communion, as Above so below, with hierarchies of Light.

Twin flames approach. These are they who are counted among the Ascended Masters. Some of you seated here, then, have with you in this moment the Ascended Master who is your twin flame, overshadowing and quickening, opening the way and leading you in the direction of the highest mountain of opportunity. For you the path of twin flames is truly integration, as Above so below, as your four lower bodies serve as the anchor point for your soul's attainment and the final lowering into the octaves of the earth of the other half of your self who has gone before you to keep the flame in heaven as you keep the flame on earth.

So it is with your Messengers. You are not alone but must also rise in the understanding of such a responsibility as to not turn back and not relinquish the intensity of your pursuit for the ascension. You are the one, then, who remains balancing vestiges of karma of both—the instrument of the Light for the conclusion in the Omega cycle of your joint endeavors.

Cherish, then, the opportunity to be in alignment with the masterful presence of your own Beloved. Count it not a sacrifice, then, to continue to strive and to give, for all that you sow will be the fruit in twin causal bodies. And by your planting and your harvest, when you shall have ascended both will return to the scene of earth to anchor through the records left new Light and a clearing of the way for others.

Now there come out of the etheric octaves and the temples of Light twin flames of those here not yet ascended yet working diligently in the etheric retreats, some as initiates and adepts, others as disciples and neophytes under the Ascended Masters of the Great White Brotherhood. These are not in physical embodiment in this hour, but you are working closely with them as you make the call to be taken to the Royal Teton Retreat while your body sleeps at night. This association at inner levels is yet accomplishing your mission, and you must be mindful that some must of necessity have this condition of circumstance. Be not concerned, for truly you are one in the innermost Being.

Strive, then, to be the example and the embodiment of the higher attainment of yourself and your Beloved as you keep your role in your family and community, in your profession and service. Marriages on earth amongst those in embodiment may be [entered into] with those who also have twin flames in the etheric temples or ascended. These, then, anchor the Light of both twin flames, creating that cosmic cube which we have spoken of.

This is very important, beloved—that you have the sense of the presence of the gathering from all levels of being of those who serve together in what is called *the entire Spirit of the Great White Brotherhood.* For some have truly overpreoccupied themselves in the quest for the twin flame instead of accentuating the path of the internalization of the Word and the AUM and the I AM THAT I AM and the power of the Light descending of causal body.

I speak, then, to those of you who seem extraordinarily burdened sometimes. And you wonder why, when you are on the Path, you seem to be so weighted down. Alas, you also may have the condition of a twin flame not necessarily in embodiment but manifesting on the lower planes, in the astral plane itself or in physical embodiment in dense spheres of consciousness and out of the path of Light. You, then, become the better half of the whole in the sense of the acceleration of Light, and upon you depends the survival of a soul yet floundering, whether [one who is] in embodiment or one who is your partner or one you know not.

This, then, is the hour to recognize the tremendous power of the Elohim Astrea and this mantra to the Maha Kali that is the most powerful mantra to the Divine Mother—the call to Astrea [10.14]. Your vigil, then, becomes a great necessity to cut free hour by hour yourself and your counterpart from the overriding demons of death and suicide, alcoholism and drugs and the dark things that hang upon the human spirit. This walk, then, is also a challenge, of another kind. But you must recognize that the Reality of your beloved twin flame is always in the Universal Christ and in the representative of that Christ to whom you have sung, Lord Metteyya.[6]

Therefore, beloved, be not dismayed, for all Life is one. And when you are fighting for the freedom and the survival of the Beloved, you are truly taking your stand for all in such a plight. And you yourself, by the strengthening, by the courage of heart, are also gaining dominion over your four lower bodies.

The time may come when you will decide, as others have done on Atlantis and in ancient civilizations, to leave then the octaves of the habitation of your counterpart and enter into the ritual of the ascension, that you might have the maximum Light to magnetize that soul up in the evolutionary scale to also yearn and seek and know and find you in the higher planes of Being. This, my beloved, is exactly what the case has been for those whose twin flames are ascended today. You are the ones that were left behind, for whom they fought diligently in previous lifetimes. And because they elected to mount the fiery coil and take that ascension, you are seated here and now. You are striving. You are seeking. You feel the tug on your heartstrings of someone above who loves you.

Thus play your roles, beloved, and realize that there is hope indeed in all octaves for the return to the white fire core in balance. Some of these Ascended Masters in previous lives have had to make the decision to enter the orders of the Great White Brotherhood when their counterparts would only malign and misuse their good intent and the good Light they brought forth. These were very painful partings, beloved, but they were to that end of your victory. Thus, when you make your decisions of coming together and separating based on the prior and original Love of the white fire core of Being, based upon your first allegiance to the Almighty One, you may always know that the blessing counts for your Beloved even though in the moment it seems almost a cruel fate.

Blessed ones, remember, karma as justice is also mercy. And there is no injustice anywhere in the universe. I bring your hearts comfort in the struggle of life, in the burdens and temptations. Blessed hearts, when you win the victory of Light in your heart, that victory always counts for your Beloved. And when the Beloved is ready, so then will that entire momentum of your victory serve to catapult that one almost in the twinkling of an eye to new planes of awareness.

So you become the sponsor of not one but many parts of Life left behind, and [left behind], I might say, by their own recalcitrance. And sometimes being left alone is the only way the one addicted to the material senses may find renewal and the urgency of coming up higher. For the loss experienced is great, I am certain you realize.

I speak, then, to those of you whose twin flames are at your side, you who have the opportunity in this life to know physically, face-to-face the Beloved. And I say, when the karma of the past and the injustices inevitably practiced toward one another in the past arise between you, let them not destroy the beauty and the oneness of Love. For proximity, when twin flames retain ancient karma, may become even a contempt, a sense of injustice, a sense of "How could you have done these things to me?"

In the pain of parting and anger or argument, beloved, in the moment of separation which discord brings as well as the destruction of the filigree pattern of the renewal of this ancient tie, there must be seen the value and the preciousness of the oneness in the white fire core of Being regardless of all outer manifestations.

Thus, there is a holiness and a grace between one another that must be observed. Often the shortcomings of twin flames are similar, therefore mutually aggravating. Beloved hearts, angels of the sacred fire have worked centuries to bring you together. [Therefore, guard the union, guard the harmony.]

I speak, then, to those who are in the relationship of soul mates or karmic unions. In all cases and regarding every part of Life, it is well to deal with gentleness and respect and honor. For, you see, the love that one gives toward child or friend, teacher or employer, toward one's partner in life, whoever—that love always ascends ultimately to the heart of the twin flame.

Thus, you will seek and find the Beloved of the Light in each expression of love, each service rendered, each forgiveness given. The heart tie is never broken. And therefore also out of respect for the Beloved, remember, when you sink into sadness and denial, worthlessness, even condemnation, the one you love most is the one you hurt the most; for the twin flame even ascended bears all of this. It is consideration and care that allows one to be tender toward all Life, never aborting cycles in any plane or octave but giving unto God and all, knowing that one gives unto the Beloved.

The lessons of Love that come from Venus and the heart of Victory, whose sign is also Sagittarius, must indeed be learned on earth. For an age of freedom has as its foundation Love itself. Only Love can give true freedom to the Beloved and every part of Life.

Thus, let the doves of the morning freely fly to the sun. For when their time is come, they must be gone with the wind and the fire. They must be then no more a part of earth. Thus you know where the twin doves have flown, and you say to yourself, "May I and my Beloved also fly to the heart of the distant star whence we came, but not before we have gained some magnanimous victory for earth and her evolutions."

O Ascended Master Cuzco, governing now the earth changes from the retreat at Suva, so I say to you, receive the transfer of Love of Venus, holding the balance in the electronic fire-ring. Receive, then, the Love of Heros and Amora! Receive the Love of Chamuel and Charity!

By the Light of Surya and Cuzco, the Light descends, sealing the sheaths of the four lower bodies of earth, gaining time and a half a time and space in the Buddhic mind for you, beloved, to find the way and the Path and the loving-kindness toward all.

In the name of the living Christ Jesus, in the name of Saint Germain, I commend you—walk with God, mindful ever of thy Beloved. And be free in the tenderness of the rose of Light of the heart.

By the Seven Holy Kumaras, I wrap the earth in the swaddling garment of Love without end. May this truly be the purging of all hatred and the transmutation of fear. Take courage, for this is the age and the coming of age of the heart.

By our Love are we one. I AM Venus of the Flame.
[standing ovation]

"The Summit Lighthouse Sheds Its Radiance O'er All the World to Manifest as Pearls of Wisdom." This dictation by the Lady Master Venus was **delivered** on **Sunday, November 17, 1985,** during a weekend seminar held at the Penta Hotel in New York City, where Elizabeth Clare Prophet was stumping for Saint Germain's Coming Revolution in Higher Consciousness. (1) Rom. 8:28. (2) **Fourth Horseman.** In his New Year's Eve address, December 31, 1984, Gautama Buddha warned, "It is the year of the Four Horsemen and of the fourth. Life, then, in its intensity, must cancel out anti-Life." See Rev. 6:1–8 and 1985 *Pearls of Wisdom,* vol. 28, no. 6, p. 64. (3) Matt. 24:40, 41; Luke 17:34–36. (4) **The measuring.** Ezek. 40, 41, 42, 45:1–6; Zech. 2:1, 2; Rev. 11:1, 2; 21:15–17. (5) See Vesta, January 1, 1985, "New Love," 1985 *Pearls of Wisdom,* vol. 28, no. 7, pp. 67–69. (6) **Metteyya.** The name for Maitreya in Pali, the sacred language of the Theravada Buddhist canon. *Maitreya* is derived from the Sanskrit *maitri* ("friendliness").

The Covenant of the Magi
by El Morya

Father, into thy hands I commend my being.

Take me and use me—my efforts, my thoughts, my resources, all that I AM—in thy service to the world of men and to thy noble cosmic purposes, yet unknown to my mind.

Teach me to be kind in the way of the Law that awakens men and guides them to the shores of Reality, to the confluence of the River of Life, to the Edenic source, that I may understand that the leaves of the Tree of Life, given to me each day, are for the healing of the nations; that as I garner them into the treasury of being and offer the fruit of my loving adoration to thee and to thy purposes supreme, I shall indeed hold covenant with thee as my guide, my guardian, my friend.

For thou art the directing connector who shall establish my lifestream with those heavenly contacts, limited only by the flow of the hours, who will assist me to perform in the world of men the most meaningful aspect of my individual life plan as conceived by thee and executed in thy name by the Karmic Board of spiritual overseers who, under thy holy direction, do administer thy laws.

So be it, O eternal Father, and may the covenant of thy beloved Son, the living Christ, the Only Begotten of the Light, teach me to be aware that he liveth today within the tri-unity of my being as the Great Mediator between my individualized Divine Presence and my human self; that he raiseth me into Christ consciousness and thy divine realization in order that as the eternal Son becomes one with the Father, so I may ultimately become one with thee in that dynamic moment when out of union is born my perfect freedom to move, to think, to create, to design, to fulfill, to inhabit, to inherit, to dwell and to be wholly within the fullness of thy Light.

Father, into thy hands I commend my being.

Pearls of Wisdom, published weekly by The Summit Lighthouse for Church Universal and Triumphant, come to you under the auspices of the Darjeeling Council of the Great White Brotherhood. These are presently dictated by the Ascended Masters to their Messenger Elizabeth Clare Prophet. The international headquarters of this nonprofit, nondenominational activity is located in Los Angeles, California. All communications and freewill contributions should be addressed to The Summit Lighthouse, Box A, Malibu, CA 90265. Pearls of Wisdom are sent weekly throughout the USA via third-class mail to all who support the Church with a minimum yearly love offering of $40. First-class and international postage rates available upon request. Notice of change of address should be received three weeks prior to the effective date. Third-class mail is not forwarded by the post office.

Pearls of Wisdom®

published by The Summit Lighthouse

| Vol. 29 No. 9 | Beloved Archangel Michael | March 2, 1986 |

The Handwriting on the Wall: Read It and Decide Your Destiny

IX

Archangel Michael Dedicates an Altar and a Sanctuary

The following scriptural passage taken from Chapter 12 of the Book of Genesis has been selected for this dedicatory service by Archangel Michael.

Now the LORD had said unto Abram, Get thee out of thy country, and from thy kindred, and from thy father's house, unto a land that I will shew thee:

And I will make of thee a great nation, and I will bless thee, and make thy name great; and thou shalt be a blessing:

And I will bless them that bless thee, and curse him that curseth thee: and in thee shall all families of the earth be blessed.

So Abram departed, as the LORD had spoken unto him; and Lot went with him: and Abram was seventy and five years old when he departed out of Haran.

And Abram took Sarai his wife, and Lot his brother's son, and all their substance that they had gathered, and the souls that they had gotten in Haran; and they went forth to go into the land of Canaan; and into the land of Canaan they came.

And Abram passed through the land unto the place of Sichem, unto the plain of Moreh. And the Canaanite was then in the land.

And the LORD appeared unto Abram, and said, Unto thy seed will I give this land: and there builded he an altar unto the LORD, who appeared unto him.

Hail, Sons and Daughters of God!

I AM in the Presence of the LORD on the LORD's Day of Vengeance. For truly I have come into this land and nation for the redeeming of the Light and the Lightbearer and the LORD's vengeance unto those who have been the destroyers in the earth.[1]

Therefore, beloved hearts, as I said to Moses and to Joshua, Put off thy shoes from off thy feet, for the place whereon thou standest is holy ground.[2]

Blessed ones of God, so stand in honor of thy Presence and know that where I AM is the Presence of God. And where you are I AM, for I have taken you to my heart, O beloved—I have taken you to my heart. Thus understand the meaning of the three-in-one. I AM with the LORD God, thus the two-in-one, and thou with us art three.

O beloved, know truly that thy precious feet[3] are desired of the earth. Remember, then, thy God and remember that the LORD, He is God in the very center of the earth. The LORD does love thee, and the Buddha of the Ruby Ray in the center of the earth[4] sends forth the mighty currents of that ruby ray.

And therefore I AM in God, I AM in thee, and thou art God in manifestation. And if thou shouldst remember thy name in God—I AM THAT I AM—therefore thou shouldst remember all of the ways and the covenants and the honor and the word of thy God that must at all times proceed out of thy mouth, else keep the silence.

(Blessed ones, be seated in the heart of the threefold flame.)

Oh, to know the divinity of God! To know that divinity and to come into that heart. To understand thyself as the Light-emanation of the One, therefore never to stray from the holiness of God.

Indeed, I went before Abram before the LORD God gave him the new name of Abraham.[5] I called him out of the land of the Chaldees, the land of Sumer.[6] Beloved hearts, I called him from the idolaters and the idolatrous one.

Thus I went before him and he saw me face to face. Therefore he builded an altar unto God. So this altar has been built* and I AM grateful for another opportunity in this nation† to come through the hearts of devotees and to anchor a pillar of fire, yea, twin pillars of fire of the blue ray into the heart of the earth for the securing of this continent.

Blessed ones of God, so it was El Morya and Lanello who went forth.[7] And so they were willing to leave the land of their

* in the home of Keepers of the Flame in West Germany
† The Messenger returned to West Germany after the European Stump.

origin for a new land that I would show them. And yet this land that was ordained was already filled with the Canaanite. And the Canaanite were these fallen angels who had come to rule the earth and they were the giants among men in those days.[8]

Thus all of you are called from the land of your Father in the Great Central Sun. You have been called as pilgrims to journey, then, in this and that nation; and yet you are still passing through to the appointed goal of that land of the gathering of the seed of Sanat Kumara—the land America that is truly overrun today with the Canaanite.

Therefore, as Abram moved in stages and each place that he went he builded an altar unto the LORD God[9] whom I revealed to him, so do thou likewise. And let the altar of thy heart and the altar of thy house be then entrusted to my care. I have come not only to dedicate an altar and a sanctuary, I have come to rededicate hearts whose full fire of dedication and devotion must yet be tried by the ruby ray—whose full fire of purpose, as was Abram's, must yet be known and displayed to the soul.

Comfort ye my people! Comfort ye my people![10] My people of Light is scattered throughout this continent. Therefore let the heart be upon the three-in-one.

The Covenant of the Chela
(Prayer of the Humble Heart)

Where I am, there is Archangel Michael, the angel of the LORD. And where he is, there is God.

Therefore *I will* put off the shoes of my karma, my misunderstandings, my grumblings, my burdens, my cares, my opinions about others.

I will put off all of these and let my feet and my soul be naked unto God, unto the earth that is God's.

I will go once again as the child of his heart without the sophistication of the pride of ambition of the things of this world which I have acquired from the Canaanite and his civilization.

I would be divested of all these things this day, O God. I would return to the pristine glory I knew with thee in the Central Sun.

So I AM thy heart, O God. Purge me now. I desire to be delivered of all these things, that I, too, might know Archangel Michael, face to face.

So it is the prayer of the humble heart that understands that his sins are as rags and old clothing from which he may divest himself at any moment that he so choose. It is the humble heart that knows that sin cannot dye the soul unless the soul, of free will, refuse to surrender.

Thus, beloved hearts, I have called this Messenger in this week. I have called this Messenger to my altar in the upper octaves of Light and I have called for her to give invocations on behalf of certain among you who have come here. And these invocations directed by myself have been to cut you free, each one, from that [substance] of past karma and human momentums which had not theretofore passed into the flame.

And these old momentums, crusty and sometimes wicked, have indeed attracted to yourselves the opposition of black magicians, who thereby have gained entrée into your worlds through that old familiar "electronic belt." You understand that of which I speak. It would be useless to bind the false hierarchies that beset you when within the subconscious you would still retain the very magnet that draws them to you.

Thus we understand the value of the Messenger. Therefore the Messenger did come to you at inner levels and call for the binding of this substance, but not until she did secure from each of you the bending of the knee before the Lord Sanat Kumara and his Christ and Christ in the Great Spirit of the Brotherhood and Christ in the Great Spirit of the embodied chela. Therefore, if we bow to the Christ in the Almighty, we must bow to the Christ in the heart of the least of these the brethren.[11]

Therefore understand that when the human creation besets the soul, it can be such a vise grip of witchcraft self-imposed that the soul must then [perforce] resist the bending of the knee. And thus, the call is given again and again by the Messenger: "If you would *serve* the Light, if you would *see* the Light, if you would *be* the Light, then bend the knee and confess that Christ the Light is LORD." And in order for the soul to come to that point of absolute confession, the Messenger had to implore the binding of substances of karma and burdens that bound you to the old ways of the fallen ones and the Canaanites.

Such is the insidious nature of the pride of these fallen angels that has hung upon the souls [even of the Lightbearers]. But I am joyous to tell you that as my gift to you the binding of this substance and the binding of the fallen ones did result in your freedom—those for whom the calls were made—to truly bend that knee and therefore in sweetest remembrance of thy origin to confess that Christ is LORD of your house and not the human ego and the human creation.

Thus, unwittingly the Lightbearers of the earth yet worship in the religion of the Canaanites. Therefore I call to all Lightbearers of the earth in this hour to truly build an altar to the LORD and an altar to myself, Archangel Michael. And I call for this as Mother Mary has appeared and called for the building of churches in her name. For to me is given the dispensation—and that dispensation [is] to bind the hordes of Death and Hell and to work an extraordinary work for the Keepers of the Flame in this activity.

Thus, we do announce to you the beginning of that inner work that must proceed for many of the Lightbearers on earth for the clearing of records which do impede the full work of the Teaching Centers and Study Groups and individual chelas in the service of the Light.

Therefore, those who desire to receive this work and this call, do place your petition before the blessed Mother who is your Messenger that you might receive your cup filled and running over, that you might cooperate with this endeavor and that you might see how it is possible for much of the old Atlantean records to be stripped from you that you might fulfill your purpose in this land of Germany and in your respective nations.

I speak of this land, for this is where I have sent my Messenger for a very key and holy purpose. It is for that purpose of the clearing of the records of all wars that have been fought upon this soil and the black magicians who linger in the astral plane or in the pits of Death and Hell and for the clearing, therefore, of all that has come out of the astral plane and the records of death and some of the discarnates that still have not been taken.

Beloved ones, this nation has been so burdened in so many ages by fallen Venusians, by fallen lifestreams from various origins around the galaxies who have come here and who have singularly placed such a burden upon the Lightbearers as they have perverted the path of Divine Love. And they have therefore unbalanced the threefold flame.

And they have purveyed a doctrine of materialism and materialistic science and the building of the human ego and various cults that yet survive, including those that are psychic, of the false teachers and the false channels of Saint Germain who have come to this country again and again to lead the children of Light astray, always by the glamour of the personality, always by every manner of entrancement and entrapment that has to do with the psychic realm.

Beloved ones, had Abram tarried on the way from his home country to the promised land to which he was sent, I tell you, beloved, the course of history from then till now would have been entirely different. In every age there are key lifestreams who know in their hearts that they can make the difference, that they can be the instrument for the turning of the tide in the world. So in this age you must know in your own heart that each and every one of you here is such an individual if you choose to be, for God cannot choose you unless you choose to be—even if he has chosen you from the beginning!

If you choose, then, not to hallow the ground whereon you stand, to hallow the words of your mouth and the light of your body, if you choose not to walk in the dignity in which you are chosen and that you have chosen, beloved hearts, I fear there is not much beyond what has already been done for you that can be done.

I must tell you truly that there is nothing magical about being chosen by the LORD. Every man and woman in his time is chosen for the anointing. And those who are chosen by the very choice of God are those who also know and can do. And yet, no archangel or avatar or Lord Buddha himself may come into your house and change the order of things or tell you to stop your squabbling or tell you to correct this and that. By the very dignity of God where you are, you must stand and determine that what you say and what you do and how the course of your life unfolds will be according to that highest purpose.

And you must be astute after the Messenger has left on the morrow to understand that when you come to a point of resistance in yourself, when you refuse to overcome those conditions of the human personality that abort not only your own divine plan but also that of your family, your spouses and children, your community, and this worldwide movement—when you come to that place and you know you have hit another level and layer of human stubbornness, of self-deceit and of [unconscious] anger, you must call to this Messenger to intercede for you at inner levels, to make calls to me for the binding of those forces in your electronic belts which have become the sorcerer's apprentice.

We do not leave you comfortless. We have ordained a Messenger because you need us in physical embodiment. You need this presence here to intercede for you. With travail and great groanings within your spirit and within your soul, you need a comforter and you need the one who will fight the adversary with you—not for you, but with you! Understand this, beloved hearts. When you reach out and desire to be cut free from those things that beset you, know that this is precisely why there is a Messenger in embodiment whose physical voice may speak and quiver the physical atoms of your being and release the Light of Sanat Kumara that will bring about change.

Therefore, I have directed [the building of] this altar and set it as a prototype under the direction of the Messenger that you might see what I desire to have even in a simple room, a small room where only two or three may fit, even a closet if that is all that is available. But, beloved hearts, let me have the color and the quality and the fire; and therefore you will see I will place my pillar where you erect such an altar.

I will place it there and I will use the twin pillars of my being to anchor in this continent the maximum forces that you allow me to do by your call and by your life to avert war and those coming predictions that will surely come to pass upon this continent, I tell you, as prophesied, unless you can see the Light and know that in addition to the altar, which is the first step, there must be a reaching out as never before to find those Lightbearers—

To go after the ones contacted, to anoint them with Love and more Love and with the teaching of Wisdom and with a fervor to pursue the Will of God and to anoint them again with Love as the violet flame of mercy and to woo them as angels have wooed you to the Path by every form of means whatsoever at their disposal to coax you and to cajole you and to move you nearer the place where you can laugh, as the mighty Buddha does laugh, all of the human nonsense into the sacred fire each and every day!

O beloved, be ashamed to go to bed burdened by human nonsense! Be willing to stay until you can purge your souls, for you are in the grips of the toilers of the black magicians from the very depths of hell when you cling to these burdens that beset you. And the Messenger can report to you by her own experience in this land that indeed the darkness is heavy and does cause those very conditions of harshness and sharpness and the clinging to the memories of the past and the old momentums of gossip that she herself has found in endless relatives that yet remain on this continent from this and previous embodiments.

There are momentums here that come out of focuses of Death and Hell beneath this very soil. There are momentums in this land carried on by the Canaanite in the land as they move about their work. There are momentums of darkness here from all of these fallen races that have gathered on this continent and that still evolve here and have not determined to turn and pursue the Light in all of the thousands of years of the example of the saints and the miracles manifest by Mother Mary and myself and Saint Germain and Jesus and those in embodiment who have walked among them.

Realize, then, that we know this. And we do not suggest that you desire or attempt to convert the alien in your midst, the 'Canaanite', or these who still worship dumb idols and the dumb idols of themselves. We are determined that first and foremost you shall go daily before this altar protected by myself and dedicated to the God, the Mighty I AM Presence of you, in whose presence I stand—there to be divested of the black magic and the practices of Satanism that are upon your auras and therefore produce an action akin to black lightning and silver and red flashes of crimson. For in this state, beloved ones, it is very difficult for you to expand and balance the threefold flames of your hearts.

And thus the Messenger does indeed understand your burden, as I understand it. But we come to bring the enlightenment of Apollo and Lumina:* that these forces must be defeated because at the present moment they are defeating the full expansion of your heart flames that could come about if you were more wise and astute and did apply definitely with greater fervor those Teachings that you have already been given.

Thus realize, beloved hearts, that every nation and continent has its peculiar conditions, yet these conditions are not unknown in America or elsewhere. They may come in different packages. They may be more familiar and therefore somewhat neglected by the inhabitants of a nation who have grown accustomed to certain vibrations and, rather than cut through, as Maitreya would say, "they accommodate."

And accommodation to human error and the devil's consciousness is the most dangerous and insidious and pernicious disease of the mind that you can allow to stay in your soul and being. Believe me, beloved hearts, if you succumb to any force pressing against your aura, whether it be jealousy, whether it be the burden of the beast of socialism, whether it be the demons from under the earth—whatever the condition, if you grow accustomed to it and therefore the branches in your trees do not grow straight but crooked [in order] to grow around these [forces], then, you see, you are "accommodating." You are saying, "I will take the course of least resistance. I will not fight until finally this problem is consumed [of itself] where I am."

But, you see, beloved hearts, where you are, God is. Now then, you see, it is upon God himself that you allow the encroachment. You hear of Mother Mary defamed and you are ready to fight to defend her. But will you defend Mother Mary where you are? Will you defend her as yourself?

* Elohim of the Second Ray of Illumination, whose retreat is in the etheric plane over Lower Saxony, Germany.

You are already Mother Mary, except you do not know it, you do not realize it, and therefore you do not act the part. Because you think you are human and puny and insignificant, you do not mind to allow the encroachments of these burdens upon your bodies—whether it is physically in your diets, mentally in that aggressive mental suggestion, emotionally in the turmoil that comes upon you when you attempt to organize and to move forward with the outreach of the movement worldwide.

I tell you, all of the devils in hell laugh when you get into the pettiness of argument and accusing one another when you should be about the business of the LORD. They laugh, for their own prophet Satan has told them that this is exactly what you would do and that this is how you would be defeated. And he has given them all of their tricks and formulas to catch you and to trap you and to prevent you from realizing that unless the Lightbearers be raised up out of this continent there will not be a place preserved for life to prosper.

These are hard words in a time of prosperity, yet I tell you the Law as a great dragnet is closing in. And that Law is intensifying and that Law has within itself a mathematics. And therefore understand that the Law itself will not tolerate beyond a certain level mankind's blasphemy against the LORD God, who has placed his very own flame within their hearts.

Understand therefore, beloved, that we seek no continuing city here,[12] but we seek to build an altar unto the LORD that the LORD might be glorified, that his pillar of fire in the earth might utterly consume and wipe out from this continent that darkness of Death and Hell. When you shall have performed this service [as Abraham did], you will be called to move on.

Do not escape your responsibility of dharma where you are now in service in your homes and Teaching Centers or in your professions. Realize that you must have a victory so intense—a victory like unto the transfiguration—that you are so filled with Light that you literally consume all unlike God around you and then disappear from the midst, the very midst of that action, as Jesus did.[13] For you have created a vortex of fire and you may step therefrom and go on to the next challenge.

And truly, I tell you, the challenge is great in America, for the Canaanites indeed have infested the land. They have infested the land, and therefore the kin of Joshua must come—Joshua the great leader. The kin of this one must come and all of those lifestreams who proceed therefrom who are the Lightbearers of the Christ [Presence] of the Ancient of Days. For we have battles that must be

fought and won in every area in America. And I can tell you that
the Messenger and staff have hardly the strength to carry on day
upon day to meet the challenge and the crisis they must face in
order to deliver to you weekly and hourly, monthly, yearly, faith-
fully the Word and the message and the promise of our Teaching.

Blessed ones of God, you are called to be a part of those who
come. And you must realize that today there are forces working
not only in the immigration service but in the intelligence services
and the secret services of that nation [the United States]. And
there is a growing network worldwide—a determination on the
part of the Christian movements, every sect and mainline religion
joining one another, determining to wipe out the voice of Truth
that comes through you and this Messenger and the Teachings [of
the Ascended Masters] and the very dictations themselves.

Do not underestimate any of these forces. We work night
and day. We work through you and your call. And you must
understand that their determination is to see to it that the Lightbearers who are of the I AM Race, who are 'Americans'* from
their very origin in the Central Sun, are not allowed legally to
enter that country and to remain. I need not tell you what a
serious crisis this would bring to our mandala (that consists of
the twelve tribes and the 144,000 of the Lightbearers and the
sons of God who are to ascend in this age) if, in fact, this plot to
keep them out of the United States were to be successful.

Beloved ones, this does need your attention and it is the
concern of the Darjeeling Council this day. And it is the concern
of beloved El Morya that you realize that this is one of the plots
on the drawing boards of the seed of the wicked.

Now, therefore, beloved ones, understand that I have told
this Messenger that there is no nation on earth where the international capitalist/communist conspiracy [the ICCC] is more
advanced in the free world than in the United States. The
advancement of that conspiracy in some areas is not even as
advanced in the Soviet Union. And I speak of the cancer that has
taken ahold of human hearts and souls because of the constant
bombardment of the people in America—whether with rock music
or with the perversion of sex in all manner of media and motion
pictures, whether through the infestation of the bodies of the
people with drugs.

When you consider that in the neighborhood of a tenth of
those living in New York are on drugs such as cocaine,[14] you
begin to understand the enormity of the problem that we face in

*In a metaphysical sense, the word *America* is composed of the letters *I AM Race* and signifies a 'race of
Lightbearers' having descended from Above with the Presence of the I AM THAT I AM.

rescuing the Lightbearers and establishing the foundation of a new civilization. And in these areas of the conspiracy you do not see such advancement today even in the Soviet Union, where the people are literally smothered in the blanket and consciousness of the Lie of World Communism.

Understand, beloved hearts, that America is the Promised Land, and yet through the misinterpretation of scriptures many Christians have believed that Israel is the Promised Land. And therefore, more than a billion dollars a year goes to the defense of Israel to the neglect of the United States and the building of the true City Foursquare.

Thus, through the milking of her resources, through lack of knowledge and abject ignorance, want of illumination of the Christ flame and the Holy Spirit, Christianity today in America is a milquetoast and a sop and has not even the fervor to challenge Darkness and that Darkness that is pitted against the Blessed Mother of Christ and the Darkness that is pitted against the little children or the Darkness that is pitted across the land through this disease that is come upon the nation, and the nations, of AIDS itself, which you know very well.

And I tell you from the heart of this altar, [which] you have given to me most graciously, that that disease is truly a judgment of the perversion of the Mother chakra and the tampering with that life-force. And yet those individuals who are lethal in their [auric] presence and in their ability to transmit this disease are yet free to roam society, and not only to roam society but to travel the world around. And so they [the wicked among them] do it when they know they have AIDS.

And when they are in their last months and year of their life, they will seek out [sexual partners in] these other nations and they will go to them for their last fling. And they will in some cases convey the AIDS virus into the bodies of hundreds and hundreds of children whom they engage in this child sex ring that goes around the world. And this is how AIDS is being transmitted today, because the fervor of the righteous has not spoken up to curtail the activities of those who are known AIDS carriers or victims, therefore to restrain them and to restrict their passports [to interdict them] from free journeying around the globe to infest these nations and an entire lifewave.

Beloved hearts of Light, it [this propagation of AIDS] is the greatest threat to the survival of the true genes of the Lightbearers. Understand that we are dealing with the science of genetics and that the progeny of Almighty God must remain pure in order to

pass on to the new souls of Light who must embody those traits
and character manifestations that come from the Great Central
Sun in order that truly the highest souls may in turn come
through them, and the seventh root race may come into embodiment on this soil and the soil of the entire blessed earth.

Understand what we see, beloved ones. If those who are in
embodiment today who are so beset by these diseases that truly
affect the genes, who are beset by drugs that also affect the genes—
if all of this war on the seat-of-the-soul chakra then produces a new
generation of individuals who no longer have the genetic material
to bring in a golden age and a golden-age race, what do you sup-
pose the Cosmic Council and the Lords of Karma will do? Do you
think that they will allow the seventh root race to embody through
those individuals who are incomplete, who do not have the capacity to endow them [these new souls] from their causal bodies of
Light with those things that are necessary to their evolution?

I tell you, they will not. The Lords of Karma and the
Cosmic Council have spoken to me and they have said with
absolute determination, "We will not allow the seventh root race
to embody on this planet unless there is promise that they may
have the full flowering of that which they are." You do not even
realize in what a balance the earth hangs simply because of this
disease and other diseases and the use of drugs in treating diseases which in turn also affects the genes.

Beloved ones, it is a precarious hour. Those of you who know
that your bodies are pure, I say, be forewarned and do not allow
yourselves and your children to be contaminated. And begin to be
concerned about public places and your use of public places in all
manner of situations that affect the body, and begin to guard and
guard well. For I tell you, you are targeted for these very conditions
and burdens [by those on the astral plane who would] prevent you
from fulfilling your mission, and I know whereof I speak.

Thus, beloved hearts, I come. I come with many things on
my heart this day. I come because I AM grateful to send forth
my voice in this nation, in this dictation, as my cohorts of Light
have done. I AM grateful to now feel the power of God passing
into the earth for the rolling back of those conditions which
I have observed here for centuries.

Some of you remember well the story of Joan of Arc. You
remember the burden upon her, and you know that I was with her
and led her. And you must realize that if the Maid of Orléans
can come forth and lead armies, then you, precious hearts, surely

Note: If you desire to establish an altar and a sanctuary to Archangel Michael, write to Rev. E. Gene Vosseler at
Camelot for paint samples and a photo of the Chapel of the Holy Grail to see how the "three blues" are applied,

can do anything—surely, in your faith in God and the conviction of his promises, you can do anything.

And I can assure you that *I AM with you,* and when you call to me *I AM physically present* in the room. And I say physically because I charge the atoms and molecules of your being with my being to such an extent that it qualifies as saying that Archangel Michael has stepped through the veil!

Beloved hearts of Light, of all things, do not take lightly the gifts of God, nor should you consider that you yourself are therefore favored or selected because somehow you are better than others. You must understand that God in you is worthy. And as the apostle said, "Let God be true and every man a liar."[15]

Is any man's human creation worth defending in the presence of God? Is it worth defending in the presence of such life-threatening, civilization-threatening conditions? Is any man's human creation, starting with your own, worth defending in view of the fact that you must carve out your destiny from here, attaining the victory all the way to the United States and see to it that none there can assail you and remove you and send you back where you came from? This in itself is a challenge of a lifetime.

Is any man's human creation, any woman's human creation worth defending when so great a salvation[16] besets us? I, for one, say nay!

Beloved hearts, in the fervor of the Blessed Mother, my angels have gathered. And they form that amphitheater of Light above, that the pillars might be established and this altar dedicated. Please rise.

[Archangel Michael chants in angelic tongues 1½ minutes.]

Above this Messenger stands your own Ascended Master Lanello, who continues in this invocation in angelic tongues as Above and so below for the anchoring now of these twin pillars at the place where this altar stands. Therefore, the twin pillars of Archangel Michael and the Almighty One stand here.

And therefore, beloved hearts of Light, know that Alpha and Omega as the twin flames of God anchor now this wholeness and this action of the sacred fire. And wheresoever you shall so establish this altar in like manner and play this dictation and be pure of heart and keep the harmony, so I will come and so I will establish that forcefield.

And so it is done. And Alpha and Omega have decreed it. They have called it forth. And these pillars extend from the heart of the earth to the heart of the Great Central Sun. And

separated by moldings, etc. You can begin with a closet or basement or attic storage area—even if there is only room for one or a few seats. It's Archangel Michael's matrix and the fervor of your decree momentum that counts—and that connects you with all other altars and sanctuaries dedicated by him worldwide!

they are sustained so long as this altar is kept, and when this altar is no longer kept they are withdrawn.

And therefore keep the flame. Keep the flame of Life and of Freedom and of the Will of God. And tend to the flame, O *bhikkhus.*[17] Tend the flame, O devotees of Buddha! Tend the flame, O devotees of Sanat Kumara, Alpha and Omega! Keep the flame in the heart of the earth!

Archangel Michael I AM! And I cry to you, O people of God worldwide: Wake up and fulfill your role, for only then can God choose and in so choosing know that he, too, is chosen by you.

In the oneness of the Trinity, I AM where thou art. We three—God, Archangel Michael, and the Son of God in you!

It is done! May you act upon it and be free! I AM THAT I AM evermore in the heart of the devotee of freedom. In the heart of earth I stand until the Lightbearers are free and the dark ones bound.

In the name of Mother Mary, I bow to the Blessed Virgin at this altar. May you also kneel to her honor.

Consecration of the Altar Chalice to Mother Mary

Blessed Mother of God, I consecrate this chalice of the will of God, offered here in my name, to thy diamond heart and the diamond heart of El Morya and thy chelas forever.

Blessed Mother of God, Mary, in thy name we serve to rescue thy children. Let thy honor, thy beauty, thy love, and thy presence be vindicated. Even so, as thou hast placed with Raphael the healing thoughtform over this place, let it be done unto all who so qualify themselves on the path of Light as these blessed servants have done.

Therefore that which is done in secret the LORD God shall reward openly. Seek diligently, therefore, the service of the chela and let thy God reward thee, O children, for truly the reward of all lifetimes comes due. Beware and be at peace.

"The Summit Lighthouse Sheds Its Radiance O'er All the World to Manifest as Pearls of Wisdom." This dictation by Archangel Michael was **delivered December 6, 1985,** in West Germany. **(1)** Rev. 11:18. **(2)** Exod. 3:5; Josh. 5:15; Acts 7:30–33. Congregation takes off their shoes. **(3)** Isa. 52:7; Rom. 10:15. **(4) Buddha of the Ruby Ray.** See 1985 *Pearls of Wisdom,* vol. 28, pp. 484 and 571. **(5)** Gen. 17:1–5. **(6) Abraham and Sumer.** Gen. 11:31; 15:7; Neh. 9:7. See Z. Sitchin, *The Wars of Gods and Men* (New York: Avon Books, 1985), pp. 251–350. **(7)** El Morya was embodied as Abraham, and Lanello as Lot. **(8)** Gen. 6:4; Num. 13:32, 33; Enoch 7:11–14; 9:8. **(9)** Gen. 12:7, 8; 13:18. **(10)** Isa. 40:1. **(11)** Matt. 25:40, 45. **(12)** Heb. 13:14. **(13)** John 8:59. **(14)** See James Gross, "'Crack,' a New Form of Cocaine, Alarms U.S. Experts," *International Herald Tribune,* Nov. 30–Dec. 1, 1985, p. 3; and the *Statewide Comprehensive Five-Year Plan, Second Annual Update,* October 1, 1985, published by the New York State Division of Substance Abuse Services, Bureau of Evaluation and Research, p. 20. **(15)** Rom. 3:4. **(16)** Heb. 2:3. **(17) Bhikkhu** [Pali, fr. Sanskrit *bhikṣu*]: Buddhist monk, religious mendicant.

Pearls of Wisdom®
published by The Summit Lighthouse

| Vol. 29 No. 10 | Beloved Sanat Kumara | March 9, 1986 |

Teachings from the Mystery School
I
The Retreat of the Divine Mother
at the Royal Teton Ranch

In the heavenly hierarchy there are appointed mentors of the Spirit unto souls striving, surviving, intensifying Light here below. These mentors function under the offices of the four quadrants, whose hierarchs you have been told are myself, Lord Gautama, Lord Maitreya, and Jesus the Christ.[1]

Thus, under these Teachers, as we serve on all the rays, are individual tutors quickening communion through illumination and love, who accompany souls especially devoted to a greater Light. These tutors are almost omnipresent. They accompany such souls close to the Christ Self and with the voice of conscience proclaim the right—and reason with the soul for the highest office and decision. Especially do they reinforce the inner will and determination to fulfill the individual divine plan.

Sometimes it is necessary in the life of a soul to take a meandering route while friends look on in dismay at choices and decisions made. The soul will unerringly, because of the presence of the tutor, elect the path of progress best made through the balance of karma, through the fulfilling of old commitments and the rendering of assistance to Life.

Whatever develops the flame of the heart and increases the light of the chakras, this too is the amplification of God's will until one day that soul, filled with the light of Love, yet surfeited in the pleasures of the world, may return to a path that more likely represents the higher calling perhaps so obvious to friends and yet not yet, in the timing of cycles, the path that is to be chosen.

This knowledge, beloved ones, should not give to you any excuse for taking the detour on the path of Life. It is given to you that you might have compassion for others as well as for yourselves and your own past.

All things that have come upon you in this life have presented a certain necessity, else you yourself should have departed quickly. The necessity for the repetition of lessons is not always understood by schoolchildren. They cannot understand that when they think they know something they must rehearse it again. There is a certain satiation of the soul that must come about through the spiritual light and fire, the reinforcement of the fibers of inner being.

Beloved ones, in the simplicity of the God flame there is also a nobility. Thus, trust your heart to the keeping of the Christ Self and know that you also have a friend. And when you call to Archangel Jophiel and call for greater wisdom and the breaking of the barriers of the mental body and the pressing beyond to the Higher Mind, there is also a mentor who is sent—ofttimes an angel, sometimes a Master graduated from earth's schoolroom.

Therefore it is possible to increase in learning, to increase in knowledge by application. And through the Holy Spirit's gifts of wisdom and knowledge there may come to you a quickening far more quickly than would be realized in the ordinary course and patterns of human learning. For, you see, human learning is to a certain extent the programming of the computer of the mental body; but divine awareness comes with a flash of light and the steady stream of the crystal cord. It is an awareness that is a permeation rather than a repetition. It is an infusion rather than the rehearsal of sums and words and figures, all of which, of course, are necessary for the building blocks of the mind.

Beloved ones, by devotion and the love of heart and the diligence to the Law of the One, you may indeed unfold the flower of eternal Love in this hour. Following the path of the rose of the heart with Nada and Rose of Light and the saints such as Thérèse, you come quickly and approach the path of the ruby ray.

Four lines of ruby fire. When they are in the square, they present the maximum challenge. When they form the diamond, we see the transcending of the square to the Light of the heart. These four lines cannot be askew or tossed as pickup sticks on a table.

Visualize now in your mind these four lines as you would

place them with your hand.* Visualize your hand putting in place these four lines of ruby fire. Thin lines but intense, they mark the sign of the base of your pyramid of Life. They mark the sign of a path of overcoming by Love, pressing through the lower vehicles of the four lower bodies and centering in the heart by the raising of the Mother flame from that four-sided and four-petaled base chakra.

All things that are troublesome, all things that are wearisome, all things that defy explanation may be resolved in the divine flame of Love forevermore and forevermore.

I am come this day, and Lady Venus with me. We come to bless and heal. We come to anoint severally and specially the chelas who have approached our altar through this fall quarter [1985]. We come for blessings and healing to our staff and students and community worldwide. We come to extend the rays of love from Venus and from the Central Sun. We come for the qualification of Light and the unity of purpose. We come to assist at the Royal Teton Ranch, and we ask your assistance also in the laying of the foundations to fulfill Morya's plan and the cycles of the Cosmic Clock which tick loudly.

Therefore know that we are in readiness and we are in motion to fulfill all things. Thus the Light has gone forth and dispensation from brothers and sisters of Light of Venus. To consecrate this Inner Retreat, this entire Ranch to the flame of Love, is truly their desiring. And as they come to assist, it is for the fulfillment of all Love's promises to all Lightbearers who shall gather there—fulfilling the imperfect, the incomplete, the longings of yesteryear, but raising them to a higher point and goal.

Therefore, let there be surcease from trouble and being troubled in the soul. Let there be the infilling of the being in this hour with gentle love, with love so gentle as to accustom the soul to itself. And when the soul is at home in the gentleness of Love, the love increases, the love intensifies, the love becomes gentility, and from gentility a strength and from strength a wisdom and from wisdom the power of Almighty God present and alive within you.

Love, then, is the Great Central Sun Magnet. Love is never without white fire or the trinity of the threefold flame. When we speak of Love, we speak of an enveloping light that surrounds and becomes the dominant force of the other three comprising the square. Likewise with Wisdom. It becomes the enveloping cloud of golden yellow light, yet within is the Purity and Power and Love.

*on the Cosmic Clock, connecting the numbers 12, 3, 6, and 9, forming a square dissecting the circle on those points.

Blessed hearts of the seven rays and the root races, blessed hearts who are angels who have come once again to enter the path of shepherding, teaching, preaching the Word—you also are called to be tutors of the Lightbearers of earth with the World Teachers and the hierarchs of the ruby ray.

O Buddha of the Ruby Ray in the heart of earth, O Buddha from the Sun, expand now and reach forth. Touch these souls in the profound sense of becoming. Touch them for the quickening. Touch them with a ruby fire that there might be seized from them now, by the quality of the ruby ray, substance to be taken—and not to be taken lightly—for that darkness must be removed ere the precious flowers can grow in the garden of the soul.

We have heard the call for the clearing of Darkness. We have heard the call for the clearing of world condemnation.[2] Legions of Light move, for this force of action will surely deliver an open highway to Saint Germain. Let it increase. You need no invitation to gather in the Holy Grail and set yourself to the task of the alchemists of the age.

Earth is changing ever day by day. The Light does increase. The Darkness is thereby uncovered, and when uncovered it is just as quickly swallowed up—if you will not tarry in its burdens or the hooks that are indeed rusty. For they come from far beneath in the astral plane in the holes of Darkness and Death and Hell.

Therefore, beloved, as quickly as the gross Darkness, and the force of the anti-Mind that you feel, does come upon you, recognize it is [that this chemicalization (or backlash) is the result of] the marvelous work of your alchemy and therefore rush to send into it [into that Darkness, into that sinister force] billows and streams of cosmic Light descending. For these are already preparing the way for winter solstice and the opening of the womb of the Cosmic Virgin, the Divine Mother who does send forth, oh, such souls of Light to be caught up by you in arms of Love!

So the opening of the door of the temple of the Divine Mother and her Inner Retreat is also come. And this Inner Retreat, positioned now as a vast center of Light, is indeed above that "Place Prepared"—prepared, of course, by the Divine Mother— the entire area of the Royal Teton Ranch.

The Mother has waited long for the coming of the Buddha out of the heart of Shamballa. She has waited long for your coming. And she does hold the balance of ancient civilizations that have occurred, both on Lemuria and Atlantis and those long forgotten upon this continent as well as in other areas of the earth.

This great and vast temple of Light, beloved, has been prepared over aeons. It is the place of the gathering of the culture of all nations and peoples. It is the place of the drawing together of many lifewaves. Therefore minister to them, understand them, feed them the teachings of the path of their own resolution, their own calling, and their own tradition.

In the very heart of Lady Venus, who keeps the flame of Mother Earth with you, there the flame of the Divine Mother of Love does abide. Thus Venus, initiator with the Holy Kumaras of the path of the ruby ray, does position herself in this hour in the Retreat of the Divine Mother over this Ranch in the etheric octave, arcing her heart's love to the retreats of the earth, to the Goddess of Liberty, and to every soul who must journey there.

I pray you will call to beloved Venus in the name of the Trinity and the fourth—of Sarasvati, Lakshmi, Durga, Kali. I pray you will understand that in the heart of every manifestation of feminine being these four personages of God as Mother are in balanced manifestation. Every mother of Light above and below is Mother according to the degree of her entertaining of Her Being, internalizing these aspects of the Mother.

The Mother has much to teach her children and requires all of the tutors assigned by us, the restoration of the culture of heaven, and the best of earth. We seek not to re-create human patterns but to show the cultivation of Light behind every expression, however great or meager, of the peoples of earth.

May your songs to the Divine Mother echo far into the night and welcome then Lady Venus, who with me does also welcome the Mother and her team and all Keepers of the Flame of Europe and the earth who continue to make possible the stumping of the nations.

Your welcome home to the Inner Retreat the very next time you are there, beloved, will be in the arms and heart of Venus. Remember to call to Love, to call to Chamuel and Charity and Heros and Amora, to call to the Holy Spirit and millions of angels of love of Venus for the resolution of all problems assailing your mighty endeavor in this age.

Blessed ones of Summit University, the mantle and the cape of Saint Germain upon you are blessings to your heart.[3] With the scepter I hold, I touch you now and every heart of gold who has upheld our standard in these months. So it is done.

May angels now serve to you the Communion prepared, that there might be a passing to you, beloved ones, of the very substance and essence of our Light.

Receive, beloved, our Love. And visualize the strong arc of

golden light from the Royal Teton Ranch to the retreat of the God and Goddess Meru,[4] spanning then the hemisphere and providing the escape and the open door for souls to approach the throne of grace in the etheric temple of this Retreat of the Divine Mother.

Once Omega did place a focus of her retreat over La Tourelle. So, you may know that that entire retreat and forcefield, removed at the hour of the passing of this property to other hands, has been held in the etheric octave until the announcement of the opening of this vast retreat of the Mother over this wilderness land, over this park and ranch.

May the world rejoice that the temples of the Divine Mother of Lemuria may come again and that her bells may be heard and hearts may be won because they are taught by you with angels—by Love and Love forever.

I seal you in the living flame of Love.

"**The Summit Lighthouse Sheds Its Radiance O'er All the World to Manifest as Pearls of Wisdom.**" This dictation by Sanat Kumara was **delivered** through the Messenger of the Great White Brotherhood Elizabeth Clare Prophet on **Sunday, December 15, 1985,** in the Chapel of the Holy Grail at Camelot. It was the concluding address to the students of Summit University Fall Quarter 1985, sponsored by Sanat Kumara and Lady Master Venus. (1) **Offices and Hierarchs of the Four Quadrants.** On the path of the ruby ray, Sanat Kumara, Lord Gautama, Lord Maitreya, and Jesus Christ hold the offices of the hierarchs of the four quadrants. These offices (embodied by the Four Cosmic Forces) are noted in Ezekiel 1:10 and Revelation 4:7 as the Lion, the Calf (Ox), the Man, and the Flying Eagle. As diagrammed on the Cosmic Clock, Lord Maitreya represents the Father on the 12 o'clock line (etheric quadrant) in the office of the Lion; Lord Gautama, the Holy Spirit on the 9 o'clock line (physical quadrant) in the office of the Calf; Jesus Christ, the Son on the 3 o'clock line (mental quadrant) in the office of the Man; and Sanat Kumara, the Divine Mother on the 6 o'clock line (emotional quadrant) in the office of the Flying Eagle. See Sanat Kumara, *The Opening of the Seventh Seal,* in 1979 *Pearls of Wisdom,* vol. 22, pp. 121–28, 201–3; diagrams, pp. 136, 142, 186, 274–75. (2) **Clearance of world condemnation.** On December 8, 1985, the Messenger inaugurated a series of seven Sunday services of invocations and dynamic decrees to the sacred fire for the clearing of individual and world karma in the misuse of the seven rays and their corresponding chakras and lines on the Cosmic Clock. The week preceding this dictation was dedicated to the clearing of Keepers of the Flame and the entire earth body of the perversions of the 12 o'clock line and the crown chakra—especially the momentums of personal and planetary criticism, condemnation, and judgment—and to the restoration of God-Power to the Lightbearers through the causal body of the Great Divine Director. (3) Traditionally, at the conclusion of Summit University Level I, Saint Germain, Gautama Buddha, their angels, or one of the Ascended Masters places a mantle upon each student— sometimes gold and sometimes violet—with a five-pointed star on the right collar, which is made permanent the hour the student completes all of his assignments. When the grades are tallied, the mark of attainment is embroidered upon each robe by angelic hosts of the Buddha. (4) The retreat of the God and Goddess Meru is located in the etheric plane over Lake Titicaca.

On December 13, two days before Sanat Kumara's dictation, a Keeper of the Flame was driving her six-year-old daughter to school in Bozeman. About five miles outside of town, the child suddenly exclaimed, "Mama, look at that city up in the sky! You know, there are no cars in the streets." And then she laughed, "But there are fairies along the streets." Later she said, "And, Mom, the air—you should have seen the air [aura]—it was all gold!"

"...And Jesus saith unto them, Yea; have ye never read, Out of the mouth of babes and sucklings thou hast perfected praise?" (Matt. 21:16)

Pearls of Wisdom®
published by The Summit Lighthouse

| Vol. 29 No. 11 | Beloved Lanello | March 16, 1986 |

Teachings from the Mystery School
II
A Report from the Darjeeling Council

Beloved Hearts of Light,

The blessed Mother Mary and I come as emissaries this holy night of the Darjeeling Council where we have been meeting in expectation of our presentation of our message here with you.

Great is our love and most sincere the greetings of the brothers and sisters of the Diamond Heart who salute each and every one of you who keep the flame of the will of God and tend its sacred fires daily through the giving of this rosary to Archangel Michael.

And therefore, the Chief would send us with this report—a good report to you—that as the result of this rosary and its saying far and wide, good things have come to earth, dark things have been averted. One does not see what the Great Law has sent back to the astral plane, saying, "Thus far and no farther! For my own have sent forth the call and the Great Law must confer." Therefore this conferring of blessing by the stemming of the tide should be understood.

It is reported that this has been the worst year for air traffic disasters, deaths, earthquake. But, beloved hearts, do you know, or will mankind ever know, how much, how far greater disaster should have come upon the earth and to various individuals that has not come to pass? Will mankind know of the great darkness that has been taken from the earth by your persistent calls?

Let me tell you, then, for those who have performed the service deserve the reward of knowing just how far-reaching and resounding is this call to the angels in the octaves of Light, who respond with mantras and singing and affirmations such as Gregorian chants.

Thus, when you call upon these choirs of angels, know that their affirmation of the Word is the quivering of the ethers, the quivering of fire and air and water and earth. And, beloved ones, this quivering is a shaking. It is a leveling and a balancing simultaneously as it is an uprooting. Thus the power of sound by the power of nine as you send forth the call has indeed opened the bowers of the Great Causal Body of the Great Divine Director, who has been able by karmic decree to send this staying action as well as the binding of the most insidious of dark ones.

Thus, count your blessings, for cataclysms there were scheduled and many more. And terrorists desired to do far more damage than was done. And the hordes of Death and Hell and certain discarnates that feed upon the blood of the dead did lust after that Light, yet they were contained by the call. And Archangel Michael went forth to bind these demons that are vampires indeed.

And because they are vampires they must create situations that cause the untimely death and the shedding of blood. And they are most insidious. And I bring them to your attention this night, for had this knowledge been released to you many years earlier it should have been a fright to many of the new souls whom we also welcome to our hearts this evening. And yet we say [to you] with the warning of our forces of Light that this is truly a path of those who would be enlisted in the forces of Light of Archangel Michael—the armed forces, for they are armed with the sacred science of the Word and the sword of the Spirit itself.

Thus, the uniqueness of the Mystical Body of God can be known and seen, for it is mighty indeed as that mighty work of the ages. And so, you might say it is a Holy Order of orders, [comprised of] those who have chosen to be a part of The Faithful and True and his armies[1]—saints whitened by effort,[2] by lives lived in the honor of the flame of Love.

Therefore, beloved ones, concerning these discarnates and others, I would reiterate to the Messenger and to you openly that the Friday night Ascension Service that comes under the Order of the Golden Lily sponsored by the Goddess of Liberty is most necessary for the weekly housecleaning and the sweeping of the planet on the physical and astral and mental planes of these discarnates and the debris of current events of that week, many of which have punctured the auras of the people with great sorrow at the untimely passing of loved ones, as in the accident of the Arrow Air.[3]

Beloved ones, these things ought not to be. And it is the [fault of the] greed and neglect of those who enter the marts of private commerce, taking advantage of the capitalist system. Thus, loopholes in regulations and those who apply them leave the door wide open for accidents that ought not to be.

And do not put aside the understanding of world terrorism in all of these things. For even though on the outer, accidents may occur out of ignorance or ignorant animal magnetism (as you have called it) through the neglect of maintenance, on the astral plane that ignorance becomes a virulent malice. And it is an act of terrorism enacted by astral hordes, specifically the demons who are called vampires.

And therefore, they are determined that there shall be the shedding of blood of innocent children, as in Afghanistan and other nations where the forces who are the agents of Death and Hell working through the Soviets and others do not stop before women and children but desecrate their bodies and minds and souls before the final act of the shedding of blood.

And I call the vampire entities "individuals" because they are the darkest of fallen angels. And some of them are even in physical embodiment and some are on the astral plane. And this killing and desecration of life that you find in these nations, of women and children especially, where war is not fought by men against men but it is fought against the most precious and vulnerable part of a man—his wife and child—where these things come to pass you know that you are dealing with demoniac forces and that those who execute them [women and children] are a part of those forces.

Thus, beloved ones, the Friday night service is for the clearing of the planet on the astral plane, and the physical as much as possible, of these dark ones who prey upon humanity in so many ways, as well as for the clearing of those who have passed from the screen of life for whom calls must be made to take them to the retreats of the sacred fire.

When this weekly housecleaning is not given priority by the saints, when they are lured to other places of entertainment and pleasure, then I tell you, beloved, it causes a suffering in the entire week which follows. May I advocate, therefore, that those of you who generally have commitments on the evening of Friday which take you away from the sanctuary come and give this vigil at five in the afternoon or earlier or in the early hours of the morning so that the twenty-four-hour cycle of Friday—which is the Good Friday, always in memory of the crucifixion of the Lord Christ—

may be covered by you and may have the full action of the release of the sacred fire of the golden lily of the heart [your own threefold flame and that] of the Goddess of Liberty and therefore of all those who have attained to her level of Cosmic Christ attainment.

Understand, beloved, when you have a cosmic being such as the Goddess of Liberty sponsoring an order and a decree action, the Law requires that all beings of that level of attainment and below must also combine their forces as a part of the Spirit of the Great White Brotherhood in that sponsorship. Therefore, the higher in hierarchy the sponsoring Master of any endeavor, the greater the numbers of those who sponsor with him. And therefore the canopy of the Goddess of Liberty and those who serve with her, who are of other spheres and cosmic worlds, is bent on the clearing of this platform of earth of these unseen forces.

Understand, beloved, that where you see the shedding of blood in accidents, these very vampires contrive—through drug entities, alcohol entities, sleep entities, chemicals of all sorts, including prescription drugs—to cloud [the mind and to distort the reflexes] and thereby to set up the individual so that he is partially not focused through all his senses and therefore not capable of dealing with difficulties in traffic. And thus, accidents come about.

The shedding of blood in this wise or the [arranging of] death without the shedding of blood is still the means whereby these vampire forces collect the life-force of the people of Light. And tragedy of tragedies, which you come to realize now, is that inasmuch as the life essence of the individual—the Light [or Christ consciousness]—is contained within the blood itself, the vampires seek to arrange plots and situations where the highest of evolved souls are the very ones who come into the danger of these plots.

Therefore, beloved ones, come to understand that the higher the echelon, the higher the rung of the ladder that you seek to abide in and to serve from, the greater must be your determination—*your God-determination*—that there is nothing more important in your life than to establish and reestablish your protection.

And if perchance the force should whisper in your ear and tell you that you are not worthy, blessed hearts, tell that force that those for whom you care—those who are your dependents, those across the planet who need your dynamic decrees—they themselves are worthy if you are not! And therefore, tell the force as you tell yourself that God is worthy somewhere on earth of having your life preserved—even if in the moment of darkness and temptation sent by these fallen ones you come to believe that something you have said or done does not make you worthy of the graces that flow freely from the altar.

Beloved ones, there is a mighty band of violet fire twixt the congregation and the altar wherever the LORD God has established that altar. And so that band of violet flame is the mercy of the Law. And it is there that you seek sanctification, purging and purification, atonement and the law of forgiveness in order that you also might then be worthy of some light of the Holy of Holies that can be transferred to you by the cherubim of God.

See, then, that you understand that when you feel least worthy, that is when you ought to enter. And if there be no one in the sanctuary, then begin a mighty marathon to the violet flame. Drench yourself in it. Take a physical shower. Do a day of fasting. And with God-determination seek to find the causes and conditions in your life, in your chemistry, in your emotions, in your karmic record that made you vulnerable to that act which you now find uncomplimentary and not in keeping with the good order of your being.

Beloved ones, there is a cause for vulnerability. There is a cause for backsliding. And those who experience this must understand that it is incumbent upon you to discover the cause and to go to Kuthumi and to call to him and to see that you receive that understanding and that you do not leave that backsliding alone until you have Cyclopea on the very button [of the cause, effect, record and memory] of that condition!

I tell you, beloved ones, you do not even stop to think how repetitive are those points where you continue to fall as you skip on the Path lightly, seeking to catch up with the Lord Jesus. And just when you are about to catch up to him and walk with him you find that you are tripped by your own vulnerability and you fall.

But you do not realize that there is a point within yourself that makes you vulnerable. And sometimes it is simply not caring that you are sloppy in a certain area of speech or in your behavior patterns. Sometimes it is this carelessness. Sometimes it is ignorance. Sometimes the fire of desire has simply not been kindled within you to show you that there is a way of God-Mastery and it is up to *you* to figure it out.

Thus mastery begets mastery. And you must be master enough of your world to figure out why you are not the full master of your world! And you may think that this is impossible, but it is not impossible. For the mantra and the white fire core of the mantra, the flaming fire in the center of every decree, is able to illumine you. And thus, through your dynamic decrees you do rise. And you can look upon yourself and you can say:

I AM Determined!

This particular human habit is getting the best of me and depriving me of my victory under situations of great tension, great darkness and heaviness.

Therefore I *will* to win when all circumstances are the most difficult for me and *I AM determined* to discover that key in every way.

And I *will* eliminate anything and everything from my life that is costing me my victory. For I love Mighty Victory and his legions too much to ever again have this Light taken from me by any form of human nonsense whatsoever!

Therefore, this day and date of December 24th to the 25th, 1985, _____, I take my stand with Lanello:
_(Insert today's date here.)

_____.
(Here insert your specific declaration for your God-Mastery on any point of the Law.)

And *I AM determined* with Godfre to set aside all those things which so easily come upon me.[4] And *I AM determined* to go forward in the Law and to know myself as God more and more each day.

So shall I determine to embody the virtues, the powers, the principalities of angels and all of those good momentums of God-qualities which they have determined to devote themselves to over so many thousands and millions of years on my behalf.

Beloved ones, this is a message that is eternal. It ever has been. And in these hours where the road narrows because you are focusing on one point which is the goal—and therefore the narrowness of the road means that you have excluded many things of this world which simply no longer interest you—there is one thing that interests you most: it is the goal of God-government in yourself and in this planet. It is the goal of God-Mastery where you are by the power of God-Love. It is the goal of Truth itself. It is attainable.

And you see, beloved hearts, the very heart of my message from the heart of the Chief and those who have met in the Darjeeling Council in the past few days is the following—that there are many who desire to embody on earth. Even Ascended Masters would like another round to come forth and help humanity in this dark hour. It is up to you, therefore, to secure the place, the proper forcefield and environment. For the Lords of Karma have said unequivocally that certain things must be accomplished before these highest ones can descend.[5]

First and foremost, then, on the agenda is the securing of the Inner Retreat and the Royal Teton Ranch in all ways. The specifics of current and proposed and upcoming projects as well as those completed and the funds necessary, therefore, are on their way to you in a letter from the Messenger and Edward in this very moment. Take to heart this message, for it is these goals we desire to accomplish and, parallel to them, a mighty expansion of this Work and a calling of those who will come to the Path and realize how important is that Place Prepared.

Thus, we must see a certain stabilization, not necessarily on the surface of the world but a stabilization in the hearts of many Lightbearers who will hold the balance and not be moved to the right, to the left, and up and down each time adversity or some problem comes their way.

We cannot count on such chelas. In fact, we do not call them chelas, for they are like yo-yos. One day they are smiling and one day they are frowning. And one day they come with a black cloud and the next day they are inundated with light. Beloved ones, you must carry the light through the downward cycles and throughout the undulation of the sine wave.

Realize, then, that there is a portent of great comings and great events. But you will have to understand that all of you must become a magnet of the Great Central Sun, qualified by the action of the violet flame. You see, the Great Central Sun Magnet is as the white sphere in the center of the Great Causal Body. This Great Central Sun Magnet may then be charged by Elohim, in answer to your call, with a specific type of magnetism of the seven rays.

Thus, you may call for the Great Central Sun Magnet to be supercharged with the action of the violet ray and you may become together in this Mystical Body that Great Central Sun Magnet of the violet flame of freedom. And in this power and presence of that magnet of the violet flame you can consume and transmute on contact the great darkness that has rallied itself against this movement, Messenger, and Teaching. Fear not, for the Great Central Sun Magnet is the power of God to consume it. Yet the body bulbs must burn brightly and the molecules must be present. For this magnet must become physical in order for it to work through you in the physical octave.

Therefore, I suggest that those who truly understand the meaning of holding the balance for this Great Central Sun Magnet write to me at Darjeeling and propose their own confirmation in the Inner Order of the Great Central Sun Magnet. Beloved ones, our confirmation will come to you at inner levels. Your outer self may not be aware of it, but you ought to pursue the Path of those who have the calling. For when you pursue the Path you make your election sure[6] both in our minds and in your own.

This organization needs a commensurate action of violet flame to go after and chase the blue-lightning angels [in order] to consume with a tremendous power all that this blue flame does break loose from the very bowels of the earth. The violet flame is indeed the "cleaner-upper," as Omri-Tas has told you. It can be used for every household chore and the chore of digging out and consuming the darkness of the astral plane.

Like any other ray or power, beloved ones, you can develop a momentum on the violet flame. And therefore, when [you have a momentum on it and] you call it forth, it is released with far greater intensity, for your aura is already the intensity of the violet flame. And you have only to open your mouth and the violet flame rushes through, reinforced by all of the beings of the seventh ray.

Beloved ones, you have known individuals whose auras have been charged with anger. And the moment they open their mouth they are angry and they are releasing darts of wickedness and fear. These individuals have a momentum on anger.

Thus, as you have been told by me, you can have a momentum on anything.[7] When your forcefield is intensified by coils of violet flame and you open your mouth to send that fire forth, it does consume all hatred and condemnation, all darkness and plots of the seed of the wicked. *Nothing can withstand the Great Central Sun Magnet supercharged with the violet flame.* Thus know Alpha and Omega in the seventh ray and be at peace, beloved ones.

Beloved ones, there is an intensity of action taking place as we draw you into the circle of fire of the Darjeeling Council. We draw you into an awareness, into the etheric matrix of our discussions which shall be impressed upon your finer bodies this night while you sleep that you might be participants at inner levels in those things which concern us.

We see, then, that our thought has conveyed to you a certain stimulus of the mind, a certain oneness of the heart with El Morya. Those who have stood for the will of God with

Archangel Michael and who have [to their credit] mighty accomplishments at inner levels, having participated with his legions of Light, deserve to know, then, what beloved El Morya and the Darjeeling Council are thinking about, are talking about, and are determined to accomplish.

First of all, you must know that you can trust the mantle of the Messenger. When you hear her invocations and when a service is dedicated to a specific action as it has been this evening, know that it comes directly from our heart and our deliberations, for the Messenger's service is the first point of contact with Darjeeling and the release of that knowledge.

Thus, trust the direction that you hear both individually and organizationally and follow the lead. Give the calls to the will of God and to Cyclopea and much violet flame and you will soon uncover how these points of the Law transmitted through the very aura of the Messenger may be stepped down into action for greater productivity and service and acceleration of your beings in whatever path you are consecrated to.

Considering this consecration of the Path, beloved ones, there is no higher calling than to join forces with the delivery of this message of the Coming Revolution everywhere on the planet. If you choose a lesser road, we bless you and we will help you all that we can. But, beloved ones, whatever is the outcome of Saint Germain and his forthcoming and expected balance, by his chelas, of that karma of individuals' misuse of the violet flame,[8] it must be realized that *the time is short.*

Whether conditions lighten or worsen, the time is still short in which to deliver this message. For, as you have seen around the world, unless knowledge is in hand and the dynamic decree is a tool sharpened by use and exercise, the best of servants and the most sincere are not able to defend themselves in the day of darkness, in the day of the returning of their karma or in the day of the plots of the sinister force even to take them from the screen of life.

We therefore have much to convey. But much that we convey is given directly from the Master to the chela at inner levels. And when you are on the correct wavelength of your I AM Presence this direction does come through, and it comes through yourself as a determination to act.

Trust, then, your first impressions. Surround them with love and light and the sacred fire and it will be revealed to you not merely the rightness or the wrongness of the path, but its advisability—what is the preference, what is the priority, what is the fine line of the real and the pragmatic.

Beloved ones, you may think this is hardly a Christmas Eve message. I will leave that to the Blessed Mother. I speak to you my birthday message—my birthday from this embodiment past.[9]

I speak to you of the hierarchy of Capricorn and its initiations. (And I have spoken to you this evening already in the Teachings given.[10]) It is the pressing on and beyond previous limits. Do not for one moment expect or accept the limitations you have had in 1985.

The new year which begins at winter solstice is a very open door, beloved ones, a very open door. And if you would be careful, it is necessary to close the door which you have passed through before you open the next. For when you leave doors open behind you, you allow that which is past to follow you. And therefore seal the place where evil dwells[11] and let the violet flame penetrate it. Move forward in the open door of your Holy Christ Self.

Anything is possible with God and nothing is impossible. What remains is for you to get this profound truth through your own head and simply to act upon it—to defy the forces of rote and mechanism and the desire of the mental body to not think. The carnal mind is an idolater and a slave and a tyrant, and therefore by these traits it snuffs out creativity.

Realize, then, that in the fullness of the sacred fire you can go forward if you break the stupefication of that part of the four lower bodies which is as the computer that functions in accord with that which you have programmed into it.

Wise are the parents who build perfect patterns of light. Wiser still those who enfold this training with purest love. But wise is the individual who is not overcome by the errors of his parents or others but understands the plastic nature of the four lower bodies, which means that they may be molded, changed, reformed, refined, and overcome.

Even within an hour one can transmute with the violet flame a particular programmed momentum of an entire embodiment. You do not *do* it because you do not *know* it or *believe* it—and you do not take the time to focus on this aforementioned subject of dealing with the most vulnerable points which cause your backsliding.

If you will take up that violet flame and if you will be sponsors, one and all and any, of starting these violet flame sessions at any hour of the day or night, using them for your own blessing as well as for that of the activity and the planet, you can direct such a concentrated ray of the violet flame from your heart, from your soul and mind, from the momentum of your aura and from the Great Central Sun Magnet of the seventh ray, that you can dissolve these momentums with an action of Light like a violet-flame laser beam which you direct into your electronic belt; and the very same wavelength [of human discord found in your own subconscious momentums] can to a large extent be consumed in relatives as well as in those of similar genetic strains, national traits, geographical or economic influences.

There is no limit to what the sacred fire can do except your limited concept about what the sacred fire can do. The sacred fire is the omnipotence of God. Decide what you will and it shall be done. Only be certain that what you decide is in keeping with the divine plan and the will of God, with Honor, Integrity, and Truth always filled with compassion.

Thus, when you decide upon that which God has decreed or that which the Ascended Masters have told you and all of your forces are moved in motion on that point, you *will* have your victory! And you *will* walk this earth as masters of your destiny as you should, as living examples that the path of the Ascended Masters and their chelas is the highest, [and that it] is reflective of the universal order of the Guru/chela relationship.

If others following lesser paths do better, accomplish more and are more successful, why should any man follow this one or follow its adherents? Jesus was victorious and influential by his example. He stood out as against the fads of the day. He dared to be different and thus he is and was forever the peace-commanding Presence.

Go *be* all that thou art in Christ, all that thy Christ is, O beloved. Go *do* that perfect thing and mighty work for which your souls were sent long ago as in Bethlehem, descending on a cold night, you vowed with your Lord, "Lo, I AM come to do thy will, O God: [12] In love perfect my soul!"

Thus, beloved, decipher now my birthday message, for I will return one day, hopeful to find you closer to my heart, to my causal body, and to my mission.

For the moment I leave you with the Mother and the Divine Mother who is the true Mother of All Living. [13]

"**The Summit Lighthouse Sheds Its Radiance O'er All the World to Manifest as Pearls of Wisdom.**" This dictation by Lanello was **delivered** through the Messenger of the Great White Brotherhood Elizabeth Clare Prophet on Christmas Eve, **12:16 a.m., December 25, 1985,** at Camelot. **(1)** Rev. 19:11–16. **(2)** Dan. 12:10. **(3) Arrow Air accident.** On December 12, 1985, a chartered Arrow Air DC-8 jetliner carrying 248 soldiers and 8 crew members crashed about a half-mile after takeoff at Gander, Newfoundland. The impact and fire totally destroyed the aircraft and killed all on board, making it the worst military air disaster ever. The soldiers, members of the 101st Airborne Division, were returning to their headquarters at Ft. Campbell, Kentucky, after completing a 6-month tour of duty in the Sinai Peninsula with the Multinational Force and Observers—a peacekeeping force assigned to monitor compliance with the 1979 Egyptian-Israeli peace treaty. The flight had originated in Cairo, Egypt, stopped at Cologne, West Germany, and then Gander for refueling. The cause of the crash is still under investigation by the Canadian Aviation Safety Board and members of the U.S. Federal Aviation Administration (FAA). Arrow Air ranked second highest in consumer complaints received in 1984 by the U.S. Transportation Department, and in 1985 agreed to pay a $34,000 civil penalty to the FAA for operational violations dating back to 1983. An inquiry on Defense Department policies for moving military personnel on chartered aircraft will be conducted in February by the House Armed Services subcommittee on investigations to examine Arrow Air's safety and maintenance records as well as details on the specific plane involved in the accident. A recent safety investigation of U.S. airlines revealed safety violations in 33 percent of the inspections and a high level of serious violations. The FAA was found to be inadequate to conduct the number and the depth of airline inspections required in the airline deregulation environment, and airline managements were cited for not ensuring a high degree of public safety by failing to comply with FAA rules. **(4)** Heb. 12:1. **(5) Incarnation of Lightbearers.** In a dictation given on Palm Sunday, April 4, 1982, at the Inner Retreat, Lord Maitreya told us that "certain avatars will not embody here until those who comprise the Community have sufficient attainment to hold the balance for that Light—not because they are afraid, but because they would not jeopardize your own Path." (1982 *Pearls of Wisdom*, vol. 25, Book I, "The Living Book," p. 62)

On March 30, 1983, Archangel Gabriel warned: "I tell you that it is inevitable that Cosmic Councils will decree and put a ban on the incarnation of Lightbearers if there is not the binding of the world beast of drugs. . . . Though there is a great need and though there be a place prepared, the Four and Twenty Elders have reported to Alpha and Omega that they cannot allow souls of great Light to descend and then be taken over by drugs." He said that "unless this planetary home be raised to a new standard and a new level of cosmic consciousness, that edict will go forth. . . . In the hour when Cosmic Councils in past ages have decreed a stop to the incarnation of advanced souls on a given planetary system, it has meant the stopping of evolution and the beginning of a great darkness." (1983 *Pearls of Wisdom*, vol. 26, no. 24, pp. 196–97)

On July 3, 1983, Sanat Kumara, speaking of the "coming race," explained: "Whether or not these souls of Light will come into embodiment is dependent upon the offering and the dedication of mothers and fathers together. . . . The Lords of Karma cannot contemplate the entrusting of souls when their early years become years of neglect by parents, by sponsors, and by teachers. . . . Incoming souls of Light have often overcome the drawbacks of their parents, but, when it comes to a new age and laying the foundation thereof—and a new race which can be brought forth in this Community—I tell you, we must have more."

On December 6, 1985, Archangel Michael told us that the propagation of AIDS "is the greatest threat to the survival of the true genes of the Lightbearers" and that the Lords of Karma and Cosmic Council will not allow the seventh root race to embody if those on earth today "no longer have the genetic material to bring in a golden age and a golden-age race." They have said with absolute determination: "We will not allow the seventh root race to embody on this planet unless there is promise that they may have the full flowering of that which they are." (1986 *Pearls of Wisdom*, vol. 29, no. 9, pp. 63–64) **(6)** II Pet. 1:10. **(7)** See Mark L. Prophet, "Momentum," on 2-cassette album *Sermons for a Sabbath Evening I* (A8073), $9.95 postpaid; single cassette B8073, $6.50 postpaid. **(8)** See 1986 *Pearls of Wisdom*, vol. 29, no. 5, p. 33, n. 1. **(9)** In his final incarnation, Lanello was embodied as the Messenger Mark L. Prophet, who was born Christmas Eve 1918, in Chippewa Falls, Wisconsin. **(10)** The Messenger's Teaching is contained in "The War on Drugs: Fighting to Lose," *The Coming Revolution: The Magazine for Higher Consciousness* (Summer 1986), pp. 32–41, 80–89; $3.00 postpaid. **(11)** Job 14:17; Rev. 20:3. **(12)** Heb. 10:9. **(13) Mother of All Living.** Translation of the name Eve, from the Hebrew *Chavvah,* lit. "life-giver." See Gen. 3:20.

Pearls of Wisdom®
published by The Summit Lighthouse

| Vol. 29 No. 12 | Beloved Mother Mary | March 23, 1986 |

Teachings from the Mystery School
III
Love's Revolution

Beloved ones, the Christmas message of the holy night bears with it always the dharma. If you would have the message, then you must accept the obligation which the message brings—unless, of course, you come but for entertainment and to listen again to the old, old story. But, of course, there are many places of worship where you may satisfy this desire.

You see, when you desire to know something you have not known before, when you seek enlightenment, you must know the path of the wisdom ray, the second ray of Lord Lanto and Confucius and the Buddhas and Bodhisattvas and Archangel Jophiel and Christine, whose emissary I am in this hour. For my Son came to bring wisdom and illumination in the midst of utter darkness.

Thus, when you seek Christ it is truly wisdom you seek and the Mind of God. But you must ask yourselves why must you go here and there to receive it. If this kingdom of God as his Mind is within you always, then realize, beloved, that if it is not a working knowledge for you, if you have not accessed this plane of your causal body, it is by the law of your own karma. Bypassing that law, the Ascended Masters come to bring you wisdom, not to set aside the Law but that the advantage of wisdom might give you the opportunity to balance that karma which deprived you of getting that wisdom from your own Source.

Do you see, beloved, how important is this point of the Law? Therefore, know that every dictation of the Ascended Masters is indeed a dispensation that allows you to bypass the karma of ignorance and go to the source of our causal body and your own to gain the enlightenment whereby you may now descend the ladder of life and conquer those elements that opposed your getting of that understanding as you might have.

Inasmuch as the Masters of the Great White Brotherhood must pay the price for you to have a dispensation which you have not earned, the message brings with it the obligation to use the knowledge to set other parts of Life free. These other parts of Life may have a greater karma than your own and we may not be allowed to go directly to them. Thus, in giving to you we expect a return, as does the Law. And your return is to act in our stead on behalf of these lifewaves. Such is the order of hierarchy. Such is the coming of the Word.

This is the real reason why many betray the Word or have fled from our presence. They sense the burden of the LORD.[1] And that burden is the burden of obligation. And they say, "We will not pay. We have done enough today. We will go thus far and no farther. Do not ask us another sacrifice or another service. Enough is enough."

And when you say this to a Master, beloved, he bows gracefully from you and says, "The Law is the Law, and you yourself embody the law of your being which you have made."

By your placing the limitation on your ability to respond, so you have set the seal of limitation concerning that which you can receive. And even if you should hear it or read the Word intellectually, that Word itself as the Light-emanation of Logos and First Cause, beloved, will not act to come into your being and burn the old matrix and transform and convert by the Holy Spirit[—because in setting the seal of limitation upon your own head you have ratified the law of your own mortality].

And every word that is uttered through the Messenger is that same power of magnetizing the soul to the polestar of Being— back to its original course where the very axis of one's soul aligned with the Presence is pointed to the Great Central Sun.

Thus, beloved, seek to know in a dictation that you hear what action, what inner work is called for. For you see, when you complete it, then and only then will the Light and the Law of the Light allow you to absorb the full intensity of that dictation and its release in all of your four lower bodies.

Hear, then, the word of my heart this evening. Hear, then, how Chamuel and Charity have come in this year to defy the force of anti-Love that has kept apart twin flames and soul mates even within the walls of this heart center.

May you be grateful all the days of your life for what Chamuel and Charity and Morya himself have done to sponsor you in these marriages, consecrated before the altar of the Holy Grail.[2] May your gratitude, then, for this intercession itself remind you of Love's obligation to stand for Love in the same determination of Chamuel and Charity for the binding of the forces of anti-Love which are anti-Buddha, anti-Christ, anti-Yourself.

Blessed ones, when you push back these forces on behalf of others, as you can thread the eye of the needle and open the gates wide, you will see that the twin flames and soul mates that will be magnetized to this activity of the sacred fire will be complementary in nature to your own service and to your children. Therefore, to fail to challenge the forces of anti-Love daily by the ruby ray is to act against one's highest purposes.

One can realize the divine plan a little bit and one can realize the divine plan magnanimously in the full effulgence of the Light. One can meet basic requirements or one can go above and beyond that call of duty and thereby expand one's causal body and be the benefactor of right choice.

Blessed ones, this is a Lighthouse of Love. And I would anoint you now as stones of the Lighthouse. And therefore I would ask you to come forward in this hour and receive the promised blessing.

[Ten couples married at noon Christmas Eve proceed to the altar to receive the blessing of Mother Mary.]

Come to the steps and kneel.

Petition for the Ruby Ray Wall

Our heavenly Father, I am your daughter, Mary. And I come before you seeking dispensation for this Summit Lighthouse of our Love, the fond child of the heart of Morya.

Our Father, I would tell thee of the assailing of the bastions of this Lighthouse by evildoers who have come, some as wolves in sheep's clothing, some appearing as angels of Light yet emerging from the depths.

I present to you, our Father, these souls of Light dedicated to the heart of Love. Let them be as an ensign. Let them be as a remnant who do stand with all others in this activity worldwide who have embraced the path of the ruby ray of Sanat Kumara.

Our Father, in my heart's deliberation I truly believe that those who have borne the burden of world hatred and condemnation and the declaration of war against this activity and Messenger—those, then, who have kept the fires of Love burning in the face of all of this—deserve a surcease and a dispensation of a wall of ruby fire that twinkles with the violet flame when necessary and with the blue lightning when deemed expedient.

Our beloved Father, I ask, then, for this wall of the ruby ray around those who become the components of Love's Tower of Light. I ask, beloved Father, that this wall of ruby ray, whose center and orifice is the Buddha of the Ruby Ray, shall be the force for the dissolution of discord and all that is sent to destroy this outpost of the Messengers of the Great White Brotherhood.

With this ruby ray, then, I touch these souls who may with it choose to start their revolution of the ruby ray in proclaiming Love's Word, that all who see them might understand that in each and every case harmony was the key to Love's victory—harmony in one's members, harmony together, harmony in service and love—a harmony that extends from the individual to the workplace to all who are a part of this activity and beyond.

By this law of harmony, O Father, by this example, guard it with all due fervor. It is my heart's determination to receive the dispensation to give from my causal body the ruby ray, forged and won through my heart that is called the Immaculate Heart.

Beloved Father, we know not only potential but action, gone forth this year through the Messenger, supported by this team and all of this Community round the world. Our Father, you have before you from the recording angels the names of all supporters of this Stump and mission, the detailed report of their sacrifice and service and, where applicable, of their failures. You can see the high percentage of victories.

Beloved Father, some of these feats of Light, made possible by Saint Germain, have been unequaled up to this hour in the recent history of earth. Thus, I ask for the dispensation to descend now through this ruby ray for the propelling back to the point of origin of hatred in every form, maligning, gossip, condemnation, disinformation, and every plot and conspiracy to distort the Light and Truth and Teaching and to deprive the whole world of its blessing.

Receive, then, these stones as they have offered themselves, as their harmony has come through Love's sacrifice.

Our Father, I present my petition for this dispensation. And I ask you to release this blessing of the ruby ray through my Immaculate Heart that the spiral might begin and your decision might itself be the capstone upon noble effort.

Mindful of hearts who have won before, beloved Alpha, let the most immediate effect of the Darjeeling Council's meeting this night be that the one thousand souls nearest to the heart of this path be immediately sponsored and cut free to come to the Royal Teton Ranch, to Summit University. We ask it, O God, that this Great Central Sun Magnet of violet flame³ might have greater energies of consecrated hearts and that there might be enough co-workers to fulfill all requirements of the hour.

I come as the Mediatrix, Our Father. And this which I have asked I ask in the name of the infant Messiah, Jesus, as well as in the name of the full Ascended Master Jesus Christ of this moment. I ask it in the name of those who would be born and await thy answer.

We understand, O Father, that it is the response of this company that also must count—and their petition with my own ratifying the desire, then, for the ruby ray wall. And this desire and petition will be given in the full awareness by themselves of the obligation and commitment such a dispensation will bring.

Our Father, I thank thee. I seal my prayer. And I turn to instruct them once again.

You who kneel before the Lord God, understand the perfect power of purity of the ruby ray. Understand that the handling of such high-frequency energy involves the advanced initiations of the Holy Spirit. If you would ratify my petition for this dispensation, count well the cost. For there is no greater opposition on the planet than the opposition to Love and Love intensified in the heart of Shiva as the Destroyer of Darkness.

Because you have already raised up this flame, this activity has come under its recent onslaughts. To bring now the momentum of your call and your life-force to the crescendo where the victory is possible demands that you recognize the danger, foresee it, and be vigilant—I say, the danger of having this quantity of ruby ray light around you.

You have almost a year's running momentum in the giving of the rosary to Archangel Michael. Thus, you have already established the protection before the bestowal of the gift. You need only keep on keeping on what you have done and strive for acceleration, tapping new resources, [achieving] new breakthroughs into your own causal body.

And I say as your witness that you are capable of sustaining this now—not alone these twenty, but each and every one of you here and around the world who knows that I am speaking directly to your heart by the current of the ruby ray.

Therefore I come to touch you now. And you will receive only that which your innermost being gives consent to. As impetus to the goal of our receiving of this dispensation, let us keep the days ahead as a vigil to the ruby ray and its judgment. Let us see what the Lord of the World will report on my prayer to our Father this eve commemorating the birth of my Son.

Be it done unto thee according to thy true desire.

[Mother Mary blesses the ten couples joined in holy matrimony through the Messenger.]

I, Mother Mary, say to this company that the consecration of these vows this day is a part of the inner temple mysteries given to these souls because they have passed certain initiations of the test of the ten involving the solar plexus [chakra]—service, surrender, selflessness, sacrifice. Thus the hearts of men and women are known of God and the recording angels.

You may understand that these requirements are many and varied according to the long, long history of the evolution of the soul. Many are worthy among you, but these were called and chosen that you might know what lies ahead at the Inner Retreat. For the Mystery School of Maitreya, its sponsorship, is at the very core and root of this event, aided in many forms by the dictations that have occurred since that announcement,[4] not the least of which being the work of Chamuel and Charity.

May you strive and know that those who are the initiates of Love are always rewarded in Love. May you have renewed reason to pursue this path, not for the outer marriage but for the outer marriage which indeed signifies that the soul has taken the step—one step—toward becoming the bride of the Lamb.

I, Mother Mary, consecrate these marriages to that goal of union with the Lord Sanat Kumara. My sponsorship is upon you. And the Keeper of the Scrolls does report this night to Lord Maitreya who else among you already married may proceed and continue with the course which you have set to yourselves whereby you also have passed key initiations of the ruby ray. And for those following the Path outside of the vows of marriage, know that you are not forgotten and that your path has worked mightily indeed to advance you nearer to the pink sphere of your own causal body.

Thus, beloved, by the example of the few, others may gauge

their progress. Realize, then, you who kneel, the obligation to the cosmic honor flame to maintain the example you have set, that all who come to this Community might know the Path of Love that leads to the perfect union with the I AM Presence and the marriage that is made in heaven, on earth, or for whatever karmic reason that may lead the soul as stepping stones to the highest manifestation of twin flames and causal bodies.

It does not matter what the reason outwardly or karmically for the marriage such as these. It only matters what you make of it, what you do from this moment on, how you set your goals. Is it not wondrous, beloved, that the first page of the day of your life together, a new life, is yet a clean, white page which you shall write on on Christmas day.

I, Mother Mary, seal you in the fiery cloud of Love, safe from all prying of lower forces. Keep the harmony and know perfect peace. Go, then, the way of Love's joy and example, sharing and inundating the whole world. For we mean nothing less than the igniting of a fire of Love's revolution. Many torchbearers have captured it and passed it. To you is given the opportunity, then, to receive it and run.

In the name of Sanat Kumara, in the name of the Father, the Son, the Holy Spirit, and the Mother, Amen.

The Serving of Holy Communion

Mother Mary's direction concerning this blessing is that that which the couples have received may be conveyed to you by their serving of Communion now. And you may call for and accept the Body and Blood of the ruby ray of the Lord Jesus Christ in this hour. As the desire of thy heart is, so shall the gift be.

The bread and the wine saturated by the causal bodies of Lanello and Mother Mary await you, then, at the altars. You may take your positions and serve. May we sing to Sanat Kumara as this takes place. (Song 546.)

I thank you for your love and support and wonderful presence this day.

"The Summit Lighthouse Sheds Its Radiance O'er All the World to Manifest as Pearls of Wisdom." This dictation by Mother Mary was **delivered** through the Messenger of the Great White Brotherhood Elizabeth Clare Prophet on Christmas Eve, **12:53 a.m., December 25, 1985,** at Camelot. (1) Jer. 23:33–40. (2) See 1985 *Pearls of Wisdom,* vol. 28: Archangel Chamuel and Charity, July 7, 1985, "The Mystery of Love: The Judgment of the Ruby Ray," and October 10, 1985, "The Light Is Gone Forth and the Light Shall Prevail," nos. 39 and 46, pp. 475–86, 549–57; Chananda, July 5, 1985, "Twin Flames on the Path of Initiation," no. 32, pp. 407–16; El Morya, July 5, 1985, "The Mission of Twin Flames Today," and July 19, 1985, "The Inner Temple Work of Serapis Bey," nos. 33 and 43, pp. 419–25, 521–26. **(3) Great Central Sun Magnet of Violet Flame.** In his Christmas Eve address, Lanello told us that we must become, in the Mystical Body of God, the Great Central Sun Magnet of the violet flame of freedom to "consume and transmute on contact the great darkness that has rallied itself against this movement, Messenger, and Teaching." He asked that "those who truly understand the meaning of holding the balance for this Great Central Sun Magnet" write to him at Darjeeling and propose "their own confirmation in the Inner Order of the Great Central Sun Magnet." See "A Report from the Darjeeling Council," 1986 *Pearls of Wisdom,* vol. 29, no. 11, pp. 79–80, 82–83. **(4) Mystery School of Maitreya.** In his May 31, 1984, Ascension Day address delivered in the Heart of the Inner Retreat, beloved Jesus announced the dedication of the Inner Retreat as the Mystery School of Maitreya in this age. "You realize that the Mystery School of Maitreya was called the Garden of Eden. All of the Ascended Masters' endeavors and the schools of the Himalayas of the centuries have been to the end that this might occur from the etheric octave unto the physical—that the Mystery School might once again receive the souls of Light who have gone forth therefrom, now who are ready to return, to submit, to bend the knee before the Cosmic Christ. . . . Maitreya truly is more physical today than ever before since the Garden of Eden. For his withdrawal into higher octaves was due to the betrayal of the fallen angels and the acts of the fallen angels against Adam and Eve and others who were a part of that Mystery School. Thus, the long scenario of the fallen angels and their devilish practices against the pure and the innocent have ensued. And one by one, each must come to the divine conclusion of the Return. Each one is accountable for leaving the Mystery School, and each one is responsible for his own return and his making use of that which is available and accessible as the divine Word." See Jesus Christ, "The Mystery School of Lord Maitreya," 1984 *Pearls of Wisdom,* vol. 27, no. 36, pp. 316–17, 324.

Pearls of Wisdom, published weekly by The Summit Lighthouse for Church Universal and Triumphant, come to you under the auspices of the Darjeeling Council of the Great White Brotherhood. These are presently dictated by the Ascended Masters to their Messenger Elizabeth Clare Prophet. The international headquarters of this nonprofit, nondenominational activity is located in Los Angeles, California. All communications and freewill contributions should be addressed to The Summit Lighthouse, Box A, Malibu, CA 90265. Pearls of Wisdom are sent weekly throughout the USA via third-class mail to all who support the Church with a minimum yearly love offering of $40. First-class and international postage rates available upon request. Notice of change of address should be received three weeks prior to the effective date. Third-class mail is not forwarded by the post office.

Pearls of Wisdom®

published by The Summit Lighthouse

| Vol. 29 No. 13 | *The Beloved Messenger* | *March 30, 1986* |

Teachings from the Mystery School

IV

The Christmas Rose

Messenger's Invocation for the Lighting of the Altar Candles:

O Light of the incarnate Word, we salute thee in the eternal Spirit of Christos. Evangelical angels proclaiming the Word of Messiah, hear our call this Christmas morn! Inundate the earth with thy Light. Clear now the way by the power of the Holy Spirit.

Let the Lord Christ Jesus descend in his Second Coming into the hearts of those who have raised up the sacred fire by the power of resurrection's flame. Even so, come quickly, Lord Jesus Christ.

Come, Holy Christ Self of me! Occupy this humble abode. So receive us, Lord, in the manger of our hearts. Upon the altar thereof, we ignite these flames.

O love flames of the sacred fire, secret rays of spheres, causal body blazing bright, intensify now the action. O come into the hearts of those sons and daughters of God, children of the Great Central Sun who in this hour may understand with Nicodemus[1] that we must be born again out of Spirit, baptized by sacred fire, and therefore be received of Him as we receive Him now.

O Jesus Christ, come into my heart and live there forever. O beloved Son of God, be thou the Christmas Rose—the Rose of light and love and truth and peace and mercy and freedom.

Lord Sanat Kumara, thou Ancient of Days, draw now the geometry of the path of the ruby-ray rose and of the Buddha of the Ruby Ray and of Lord Gautama and Maitreya.

O fourfold City Foursquare whose base is the cosmic cross of white fire, be now the foundation of my heart's love of Christ. O path supernal of Love eternal, hear our call this day, that Love might consume every planetary force of anti-Love and the Lord Christ might reign forevermore because Love does triumph o'er all.

Blessed One of God, thou Manchild, living flame of Love, thou who hast descended in this very hour of Light's portent: O come, beloved heart, Manchild of the sacred fire, with the Blessed Virgin.

We behold thy face, thy presence, thy perfect design and divine image in the heart of hearts of all children of the Light. O let thy presence and the pressure of thy electronic light body now transform the mind and heart and soul and consciousness of all who live upon earth.

For this is the day and the hour of the appearing of the Daystar from on high[2] to all people. The sign of the risen Christ, born again, is the great joy, the eternal joy of this our Christ Mass.

We salute thee, O Ascended Master Jesus Christ, all thy saints and angelic hosts.

In the name of the Father, in the name of the Mother, in the name of the Son, in the name of the Holy Spirit, Amen.

A very, very joyous Christmas to each and every one of you.

"Merry Christmas, Mother!"

Thank you.

We would sing to our beloved Christmas Rose, the Rose of Jesus Christ's own heart. Number 214. Let us intone the mighty Word that is made flesh in this hour: *AUM AUM AUM*

The Crowning Rose

A rose so tall crowns us all
God's mercy 'round our feet
His light of love from above
Reveals man's life complete
Reveals man's life complete.

No flaw can mar his reality
No blight can harm the soul.
Before the heart the rose does start
To make all mankind whole
To make all mankind whole.

Domain of Light and beauty
Freedom rules the mind
The hand of Christ-Reality
Teaches now, be kind!
Teaches now, be kind!

I AM all one, enfolding all
My Light rays from above
Renew in heart the divine spark
For which the Christ does call
For which the Christ does call.

From the heart of Saint John:

The Incarnation of the Eternal Word

In the beginning was the Word, and the Word was with God, and the Word was God.

The same was in the beginning with God.

All things were made by him; and without him was not any thing made that was made.

In him was Life; and the Life was the Light of men.

And the Light shineth in darkness; and the darkness comprehended it not.

There was a man sent from God, whose name was John.

The same came for a witness, to bear witness of the Light, that all men through him might believe.

He was not that Light, but was sent to bear witness of that Light.

That was the true Light, which lighteth every man that cometh into the world.

He was in the world, and the world was made by him, and the world knew him not.

He came unto his own, and his own received him not.

But as many as received him, to them gave he power to become the sons of God, even to them that believe on his name:

Which were born, not of blood, nor of the will of the flesh, nor of the will of man, but of God.

And the Word was made flesh, and dwelt among us (and we beheld his glory, the glory as of the only begotten of the Father), full of grace and truth. John 1

Let us give the "Forever Thine" and the "Adoration to God."

This is the message of the Lord Jesus Christ, our Christmas Rose—that this Word came into the world. This Word is the I AM THAT I AM. This Word is the God Presence and the Holy Christ Self.

Today we celebrate the new birth of this Christ Jesus, one with the Holy Christ Self of our hearts. Let us truly imbibe and assimilate and experience this consummate Love, his reason for being. We fail not our Lord. We come together to worship by affirmation of his presence within us. We come always to the altar for the purging Light of the Holy Spirit, the sacred fire of Love's intensity by which we realize the great immensity of God, worlds without end.

Our reason for being is defined this day by the Lord and Saviour, the Child in the cradle and the Cosmic Being whom Jesus our Lord is become.

Oh, we would worship at the fount of this Reality, and by contact with our own Mighty I AM Presence we would send showers of Love to the whole world that Jesus might be resurrected from a dead Roman paganism into the universal Life and intimacy of Love which he truly bore this morning in Bethlehem.

This very morning he is intimate with the little people, with the elementals, with nature. And this is a sign to all people that Christ is come for the regeneration of all kingdoms—elemental, human, and angelic. And these three together as a trinity are the moving force to defeat every power of anti-Love and anti-Christ, which we declare in Jesus' name has no power by this our decree:

Forever Thine

In the name of the beloved mighty victorious Presence of God, I AM in me, my very own beloved Holy Christ Self, Holy Christ Selves of all mankind, beloved Lanello, the entire Spirit of the Great White Brotherhood and the World Mother, elemental life—fire, air, water, and earth! I decree:

My mighty great God Presence
On shining wings of Light,
Come blaze thy radiant Light rays,
Be a beacon through the night.
High in thy constant watchtower
Of the Summit now you blaze;
Deep within the hearts of men
You're anchored there to raise
All to Love,
All to Love,
All to Love.

My mighty great God Presence
On radiant sunbeams bright,
Come with thy Faith, Hope, Charity,
The threefold flame relight.
Release now through the Summit
That Ascended Master touch
That harmonizes heart with heart
With each responding, oh so much
To thy Love,
To thy Love,
To thy Love.

My mighty great God Presence,
With thy being I AM one;
I but invoke thy radiance
To know that thou art come.
The tower of power upon the Rock,
The Summit is enduring;
Deep in men's hearts, its healing rays
Abide, all evil curing,
By all thy Love,
By all thy Love,
By all thy Love.

My mighty great God Presence,
Our consciousness so raise
Till we know such joy of being
We lift our voice in praise.
From hearts of children everywhere
Is gratitude now pouring;
Releasing chords of harmony
Their own God Self adoring
With all their Love,
With all their Love,
With all their Love.

I AM, I AM, I AM adoring Thee
With depth and breadth and height
Of consciousness as it expands
With radiating Light,

Beloved I AM,
Beloved I AM,
Beloved I AM.

Adoration to God

Beloved mighty victorious Presence of God, I AM in me, my very own beloved Holy Christ Self, by and through the magnetic power of the immortal victorious threefold flame of Love, Wisdom, and Power burning within my heart, I decree:

Beloved Mighty I AM Presence,
Thou Life that beats my heart,
Come now and take dominion,
Make me of thy Life a part.
Rule supreme and live forever
In the Flame ablaze within;
Let me from Thee never sever,
Our reunion now begin.

All the days proceed in order
From the current of thy Power,
Flowing forward like a river,
Rising upward like a tower.
I AM faithful to thy Love ray
Blazing forth Light as a sun;
I AM grateful for thy right way
And thy precious word "Well done."

I AM, I AM, I AM adoring Thee! (3x)
O God, you are so magnificent! (9x)
I AM, I AM, I AM adoring Thee! (3x)

Moving onward to Perfection,
I AM raised by Love's great grace
To thy center of Direction—
Behold, at last I see thy face.
Image of immortal Power,
Wisdom, Love, and Honor, too,
Flood my being now with Glory,
Let my eyes see none but you!

O God, you are so magnificent! (3x)
I AM, I AM, I AM adoring Thee! (9x)
O God, you are so magnificent! (3x)

My very own Beloved I AM! Beloved I AM! Beloved I AM!

This understanding of the mission of the birth of Jesus Christ became a profound realization in the heart of beloved El Morya when he as Melchior, one of the three wise men, visited the place of Jesus' birth and beheld that Divine Manchild who had the Holy Spirit from his mother's womb. And so, this El Morya has held in his heart these two thousand years the understanding of the universal nature of that Child— that Child who could not be circumscribed by dogma or orthodoxy or any creed.

It was the Universal Light that he saw. It translated to El Morya, not as a flesh and blood God, but as the very imminence of the Word that was with God in the beginning, draped immaculately with garments of flesh. And so, in his heart, Melchior went forth determined to transmit the personhood of God, the nature of the universality of the Light to all people.

I have never heard a sermon preached concerning the three wise men as the very first ones to witness unto him and therefore to have the authority from his point of origin to proclaim his divine doctrine from the cradle and the very moment of his birth.

The apostles who circumscribed him and established their orthodoxy knew him only in the last three years of his ministry in Palestine and, though Peter proclaimed him Christ, the Son of the living God,[3] they knew him more as the flesh and blood Saviour and less as the ever-appearing I AM THAT I AM. For by their testimony, their unbelief, their hardness of heart for which he rebuked them in the last hours before he took his leave of them,[4] we perceive the absence of the full quickening of the Word that could translate to them the mystical union with the one we know as the Christmas Rose.

Thus, dear Morya went forth to translate his understanding in the mystery school of Camelot. He saw the power of the Divine Manchild to slay all of the "isms" that had come out of the Serpents' preaching of their false doctrine to those in the mystery school of Eden. He, as Arthur, King of the Britons, came forth to slay those twelve kings,[5] representative of the Canaanite consciousness with which Joshua before him had been sent to do battle accompanied by the valiant of the twelve tribes. He saw that the application of the Spirit of the Divine Manchild must be in society, in government, in holy orders, and in the internalization of the Word on a path, a very personal path of individual Christhood, forged and won.

Thus, the highest holiday of the year, the day of Pentecost, celebrating the descent of that Holy Spirit upon the apostles after Jesus' ascension, became the cyclic going forth and return of the knights that they might render their reports to the king and queen on their initiations slaying dragons, championing the poor, defending maidens in distress and challenging the illusions of witches and foul queens and the forces of the underworld, their magic and entrancement, as they went bearing that Christ flame in quest of the Holy Grail.[6]

So he came as Becket and More and Akbar. So he came as this mystical figure—Abraham reappearing in many guises, all of which were to frame and portray how this Manchild whom he had beheld so transcended the boundaries of any and all religious tradition of which he might be a part in his succeeding embodiments. We cannot say that Thomas Becket (1118–1170) or Thomas More (1478–1535) were typical Christians. In each case it was the Christians of the time who murdered him, who told him, "You need not make such a sacrifice, only give in and concede to Henry's wishes."

So we find the quintessence of the Christmas star in the heart of El Morya, and this El Morya is truly the wise man of our Christ Mass. For it is he who has called us to the same birth, teaching us that we must be willing to bear in the same lowly estate that magnificent Light.

By contrast, what is there special about the manger and the animals and the hay and the cold night and the plains? The only thing that is special is the diamond heart of the Christ—no props or pyramids or palaces or royal robes and jewels bedecking the princes and powers of this world. Only one star shone that night and it was not the star of materialism, it was not the star of Communism: it was the star of the Spirit, the Lord's and yours and mine—of the I AM THAT I AM. The Mighty I AM Presence of the Universal Christ shone over Bethlehem, and out of the Great Causal Body of the I AM Presence, the Saviour Jesus Christ descended the shaft of the crystal cord and entered into that form prepared.

We see and we understand, then, that all of the baubles and trinkets and riches and power and success of the world is a competitive ploy to make us forget that the only star we can ever keep, the only diamond that can provide the chalice for the infinite Light, is the heart of Christ in us—our own Christmas Rose unfolding. All other events, all other moments of history pale into insignificance. For the birth of the Avatar is the turning of the ages.

We are here that his birth and his message be not lost. Only we can prove that he lived and that he lived for a mighty purpose as we are willing to be that babe, born not in a palace, but in a manger.

And so God and man conspired. And in the great vision of the Mighty I AM Presence and the tube of light we see the facsimile of the Lighthouse. It is a Lighthouse of Love.

And so, El Morya thought and thought upon the mission of the Divine Manchild in this century. And as the result of his deliberation upon the Will of God, he called his Messenger Mark Prophet, sent him to Washington, D.C., that alabaster city where the facsimile of the Lighthouse of our Mighty I AM Presence is to be seen in the Washington Monument—the 555-foot obelisk that is "a pillar of fire" and "a tower of power upon the rock."

And he said to Mark, "This is the conspiring of Ascended Masters and unascended disciples of the living Christ. Let us, then, take this our Tree of Life, this our Mighty I AM Presence. Let us come together. Let us make of all of the presence of God that we have individually externalized one tower, one Lighthouse of Love.

"Let all of the Light of the chelas of the Will of God become one blazing Light in that tower. Let it be the Summit Lighthouse whose beacon calls every man and woman and child to the summit of Being. Let it be built of the stones of the wise master builders of all ages who would build the pyramid of Life. Let each stone signify a chela wed to the Will of God by the Christmas Rose, who declared in his descent, 'Lo, I AM come to do thy will, O God!'"

This mystery, then, of a Community of the Holy Spirit, an organization, if you will, that is called The Summit Lighthouse, is taken directly from the mysticism of the Path of Love borne in the heart of one Melchior, a wise man out of the East, as he came to Bethlehem with Caspar and Balthazar—now the Ascended Masters Djwal Kul and Kuthumi. They came, then, not only offering gifts—gifts as focuses of protection, initiation and of the threefold flame, signs of gold, frankincense and myrrh—signs of the Order of Melchizedek—but also sealing that Divine Manchild as they, the Three Kings of the Orient, represented the entire Spirit of the Great White Brotherhood. After taking their leave of the Holy Family, they secured for them safe passage into Egypt and escape from Herod's henchmen.

And so, the beloved wise men of old are still our guides today, and so they have lent themselves as pillars of fire to go before us as emissaries of that ancient Brotherhood whose calling is also ours in the name of the Ancient of Days. And we see that all who follow the Three Kings to the path of the Mighty I AM Presence come to the path of the building of this Lighthouse of Love.

We give praise unto the LORD for this dream of Love come true through the heart of Mother Mary, through the heart of Lanello, our own beloved Mark, who was the one chosen by the Darjeeling Council to head it. We can see that through the receptivity of his heart to Morya's call to found The Summit Lighthouse and the Order of the Child that he also mounted the spiral staircase of the Lighthouse to become one with its beacon.

This we may also do. This many disciples of El Morya who have passed through the halls of Summit University have also done. That we might become fully a part of the beacon Light—this is our Christmas prayer.

And so, Mark left for us a poem, giving to us his understanding of this Lighthouse of Love so that we might not forget the fundamentals of humility upon which it is built nor the formula by which it is maintained.

I invite you to sing this song now by way of becoming that pillar of fire this Christmas Day. Number 513. Please stand.

The Lighthouse of Love

From the Sun Center of Love all divine
Through Thy great star-studded universe mine
Flowed emanations of perfect good cheer—
Lo, it is I! Lo, I AM right here!

The Summit Lighthouse is a victory flame
Light overcoming all darkness and blame
The Lighthouse of Love will guide all below
Who bask in the glory of purity's glow.

No favorite son, ye all are divine
Made in His Image—restore us, let's climb!
We come for thy blessing, Father of all
Thy Light is pure love, we answer thy call.

Away in a manger, beautiful Christ
So meek and so lowly, filled with delight
Spurned by the world and rejected of men
Was honored by some—He cometh again.

The world shall be changed and painted so bright
By charity's beams and pencils of light
The Summit presents the Masters divine
O let us then hear them while there is time!

Purpose in living descends as a flame
Enveloping garments, gifts in Thy name
'Round us forever and heals every woe
Thy Spirit directs, reveals how we go.

O Mary and Jesus, Saint Germain dear
Remove all our density, cast out fear
Thy flames enfold us to resurrect light
Cast out all death and fill us with Life.

The Summit Lighthouse of creative power
Releasing bright radiance every hour
Charges the world with harmonious rays
That change all your darkness into great praise!

Thank you. Won't you be seated.

Let us be the Christmas Rose. We will give decree 30.04. Please visualize the pink rose unfolding in your heart, and as you give this decree the pink rose becomes the mighty blue rose and then it becomes the yellow rose and the violet rose and the white rose.

You can see the power of the Great Causal Body of the Lord Jesus Christ unfolding in your heart, and therefore the heart is the all-purpose beacon of Light. It sheds its radiance, and whatever is the need of the hour becomes the qualification of your heart. This is God-Mastery on the Path of the Sacred Heart, the ruby ray of Jesus Christ. Together:

Love Me

Beloved mighty victorious Presence of God, I AM in me, my very own beloved Holy Christ Self, Holy Christ Selves of all mankind, beloved Lord the Maha Chohan, beloved Mother Mary, beloved Paul the Venetian, beloved Archangel Chamuel and Charity, beloved Heros and Amora, Elohim of Love, beloved Lady Masters Nada and Venus, beloved Goddess of Liberty, beloved Jesus the Christ, beloved Lanello, the entire Spirit of the Great White Brotherhood and the World Mother, elemental life—fire, air, water, and earth!

By and through the magnetic power of the immortal, victorious threefold flame of Liberty and the adoration flame ablaze within my heart, I decree:

1. I AM so willing to be filled
     With the Love of God;
   I AM calling to be thrilled
     With the Love of God;
   I AM longing so for Grace
     From the heart of God;
   Yearning just to see his face
     By the Love of God.

Refrain: As a rose unfolding fair
            Wafts her fragrance on the air,
            I pour forth to God devotion,
            One now with the Cosmic Ocean.

2. I AM hoping so to be,
   Made by Love Divine.
I AM longing Christ to be,
   Wholly only thine.
I AM so peaceful in thy Love,
   Feel at home with God above.
I AM at one with all mankind—
   The cords of Love God's children bind.
I AM fore'er one living Soul
   With angels, man, and God as goal.

3. I AM locked in God's great Love,
   His mighty arms of Power;
Cradled now by heaven above,
   Protected every hour.
I AM alight with Happiness,
   Wholly filled with God Success,
For I AM love of Righteousness.
   I love Thee, love Thee, love Thee,
My own God Presence bright;
   Love me, love me, love me,
Protect me by thy might.
   Remain within and round me
Till I become thy Light!

Jesus placed upon my heart this morning a very special sermon. He desires me to read to you from the Book of the Acts of the Apostles and the Gospels, that he might expound on the Teaching contained herein. It is a very powerful presence of the Lord Jesus Christ who comes to transfer not mere knowledge but the power of the Holy Spirit this Christmas Day.

And so I shall read to you from the tenth and eleventh chapters. It concerns Peter. Peter, as you know, was given the keys of the kingdom of heaven,[7] which means the power of the Christ to open the causal body of the individual that the descent of the Holy Ghost might take place therefrom and out of the living presence of the Lord Jesus Christ.

Peter exercised this gift of the keys of the kingdom first on Pentecost, when the Holy Ghost came upon the apostles and the Gospel and baptism was given unto the Jews.[8] And every man heard the message of Christ spoken in his own tongue. Thus, we understand that this ancient people of the Light of Sanat Kumara must receive the opportunity to walk in the path of the Eternal Christ.

Now we come to Peter's second use of the keys of the kingdom. And this is the story of that event—most precious, most personal, most human, and most divine:

The Gospel Given to the 'Gentiles'

There was a certain man in Caesarea called Cornelius, a centurion of the band called the Italian band,

A devout man, and one that feared God with all his house, which gave much alms to the people, and prayed to God alway.

He saw in a vision evidently about the ninth hour of the day an angel of God coming in to him, and saying unto him, Cornelius.

And when he looked on him, he was afraid, and said, What is it, Lord? And he said unto him, Thy prayers and thine alms are come up for a memorial before God.

And now send men to Joppa, and call for one Simon, whose surname is Peter:

He lodgeth with one Simon a tanner, whose house is by the sea side: he shall tell thee what thou oughtest to do.

And when the angel which spake unto Cornelius was departed, he called two of his household servants, and a devout soldier of them that waited on him continually;

And when he had declared all these things unto them, he sent them to Joppa.

On the morrow, as they went on their journey, and drew nigh unto the city, Peter went up upon the housetop to pray about the sixth hour:

And he became very hungry, and would have eaten: but while they made ready, he fell into a trance,

And saw heaven opened, and a certain vessel descending unto him, as it had been a great sheet knit at the four corners, and let down to the earth:

Wherein were all manner of fourfooted beasts of the earth, and wild beasts, and creeping things, and fowls of the air.

And there came a voice to him, Rise, Peter; kill, and eat.

But Peter said, Not so, Lord; for I have never eaten any thing that is common or unclean.

And the voice spake unto him again the second time, What God hath cleansed, that call not thou common.

This was done thrice: and the vessel was received up again into heaven.

Now while Peter doubted in himself what this vision which he had seen should mean, behold, the men which were sent from Cornelius had made enquiry for Simon's house, and stood before the gate,

And called, and asked whether Simon, which was surnamed Peter, were lodged there.

While Peter thought on the vision, the Spirit said unto him, Behold, three men seek thee.

Arise therefore, and get thee down, and go with them, doubting nothing: for I have sent them.

Then Peter went down to the men which were sent unto him from Cornelius; and said, Behold, I am he whom ye seek: what is the cause wherefore ye are come?

And they said, Cornelius the centurion, a just man, and one that feareth God, and of good report among all the nation of the Jews, was warned from God by an holy angel to send for thee into his house, and to hear words of thee.

Then called he them in, and lodged them. And on the morrow Peter went away with them, and certain brethren from Joppa accompanied him.

And the morrow after they entered into Caesarea. And Cornelius waited for them, and had called together his kinsmen and near friends.

And as Peter was coming in, Cornelius met him, and fell down at his feet, and worshipped him.

But Peter took him up, saying, Stand up; I myself also am a man.

And as he talked with him, he went in, and found many that were come together.

And he said unto them, Ye know how that it is an unlawful thing for a man that is a Jew to keep company, or come unto one of another nation; but God hath shewed me that I should not call any man common or unclean.

Therefore came I unto you without gainsaying, as soon as I was sent for: I ask therefore for what intent ye have sent for me?

And Cornelius said, Four days ago I was fasting until this hour; and at the ninth hour I prayed in my house, and, behold, a man stood before me in bright clothing,

And said, Cornelius, thy prayer is heard, and thine alms are had in remembrance in the sight of God.

Send therefore to Joppa, and call hither Simon, whose surname is Peter; he is lodged in the house of one Simon a tanner by the sea side: who, when he cometh, shall speak unto thee.

Immediately therefore I sent to thee; and thou hast well done that thou art come. Now therefore are we all here present before God, to hear all things that are commanded thee of God.

Then Peter opened his mouth, and said, Of a truth I perceive that God is no respecter of persons:

But in every nation he that feareth him, and worketh righteousness, is accepted with him.

The word which God sent unto the children of Israel, preaching peace by Jesus Christ: (he is Lord of all:)

That word, I say, ye know, which was published throughout all Judaea, and began from Galilee, after the baptism which John preached;

How God anointed Jesus of Nazareth with the Holy Ghost and with power: who went about doing good, and healing all that were oppressed of the devil; for God was with him.

And we are witnesses of all things which he did both in the land of the Jews, and in Jerusalem; whom they slew and hanged on a tree:

Him God raised up the third day, and shewed him openly;

Not to all the people, but unto witnesses chosen before of God, even to us, who did eat and drink with him after he rose from the dead.

And he commanded us to preach unto the people, and to testify that it is he which was ordained of God to be the Judge of quick and dead.

To him give all the prophets witness, that through his name whosoever believeth in him shall receive remission of sins.

While Peter yet spake these words, the Holy Ghost fell on all them which heard the word.

And they of the circumcision which believed were astonished, as many as came with Peter, because that on the Gentiles also was poured out the gift of the Holy Ghost.

For they heard them speak with tongues, and magnify God. Then answered Peter,

Can any man forbid water, that these should not be baptized, which have received the Holy Ghost as well as we?

And he commanded them to be baptized in the name of the Lord. Then prayed they him to tarry certain days.

And the apostles and brethren that were in Judaea heard that the Gentiles had also received the word of God.

And when Peter was come up to Jerusalem, they that were of the circumcision contended with him,

Saying, Thou wentest in to men uncircumcised, and didst eat with them.

But Peter rehearsed the matter from the beginning, and expounded it by order unto them, saying,

I was in the city of Joppa praying: and in a trance I saw a vision, A certain vessel descend, as it had been a great sheet, let down from heaven by four corners; and it came even to me:

Upon the which when I had fastened mine eyes, I considered, and saw fourfooted beasts of the earth, and wild beasts, and creeping things, and fowls of the air.

And I heard a voice saying unto me, Arise, Peter; slay and eat.

But I said, Not so, Lord: for nothing common or unclean hath at any time entered into my mouth.

But the voice answered me again from heaven, What God hath cleansed, that call not thou common.

And this was done three times: and all were drawn up again into heaven.

And, behold, immediately there were three men already come unto the house where I was, sent from Caesarea unto me.

And the Spirit bade me go with them, nothing doubting. Moreover these six brethren accompanied me, and we entered into the man's house:

And he shewed us how he had seen an angel in his house, which stood and said unto him, Send men to Joppa, and call for Simon, whose surname is Peter;

Who shall tell thee words, whereby thou and all thy house shall be saved.

And as I began to speak, the Holy Ghost fell on them, as on us at the beginning.

Then remembered I the word of the Lord, how that he said, John indeed baptized with water; but ye shall be baptized with the Holy Ghost.

Forasmuch then as God gave them the like gift as he did unto us, who believed on the Lord Jesus Christ; what was I, that I could withstand God?

When they heard these things, they held their peace, and glorified God, saying, Then hath God also to the Gentiles granted repentance unto life.　　　　　　　　　　Acts 10, 11

God Sent His Son to Save the World

And as Moses lifted up the serpent in the wilderness, even so must the Son of man be lifted up:

That whosoever believeth in him should not perish, but have eternal life.

For God so loved the world, that he gave his only begotten Son, that whosoever believeth in him should not perish, but have everlasting life.

For God sent not his Son into the world to condemn the world; but that the world through him might be saved.

He that believeth on him is not condemned: but he that believeth not is condemned already, because he hath not believed in the name of the only begotten Son of God.

And this is the condemnation, that Light is come into the world, and men loved Darkness rather than Light, because their deeds were evil.

For every one that doeth evil hateth the Light, neither cometh to the Light, lest his deeds should be reproved.

But he that doeth Truth cometh to the Light, that his deeds may be made manifest, that they are wrought in God.   John 3

Empowered to Become Sons of God

But as many as received him, to them gave he power to become the Sons of God, even to them that believe on his name:

Which were born, not of blood, nor of the will of the flesh, nor of the will of man, but of God.   John 1

Let us meditate for the dictation of Jesus Christ as we listen to the Vienna Choir Boys singing "Greensleeves."

Pearls of Wisdom®

published by The Summit Lighthouse

| Vol. 29 No. 14 | *Beloved Jesus Christ* | April 6, 1986 |

Teachings from the Mystery School

V

"Rise, Peter: Kill and Eat!"
The Engrafting of the Threefold Flame

Unto the sons and daughters of God I send my call of the Spirit of Christmas.

I AM come into the world a Light, and the Light of noncondemnation I AM. I AM the power of Love devouring as a flame, and a flame sharper than the two-edged sword,[1] as cloven tongues of fire[2]—an all-devouring flame[3] that consumes the fear and doubt of nations.

And I send Peace. And this Peace is sent through the seven sacred centers of thy bodies of Light. I send peace on earth through the etheric chalice of each and every one who has offered himself in this hour to be the receptacle of my Light by tarrying this day unto the hour of my coming. Therefore, Keepers of the Flame of Life worldwide, I address you in the Spirit of the Liberty[4] of the newborn Child of Christ.

Lo, I AM come. Lo, I come with abundant Life! Lo, I come with peace and a sword![5] Lo, I AM come in the flaming presence of the Ancient of Days. And I AM your Jesus of old and of new, for the new birth and the progressive becoming of God is a mystery of Life given to you to understand this day. So be seated in the spiral of your own becoming Light.

How, then, can Light become Light and become more Light? It is a question of the increase to the critical mass, the increase of the white fire core of Being. And thus, as the central flame expands to become the sun, the increase of the rings upon rings upon rings of the causal body does become an infinitude of the rays of God, twelve times twelve increasing.

Thus you find, when the causal body of the Sons of God does reach the point of the Maxim Light, the rainbow rays and the secret rays begin again. And thus there is the repetition unto redundancy of this abundant Life whereby beyond the blue of the sealing presence there begins anew the five secret rays and the seven again.

Thus, beloved, the causal body of Life does repeat itself again and again until you understand the meaning of cosmic consciousness in a sevenfold body of Light. This you may observe in great cosmic beings. And this we show not upon the Chart of the Divine Presence, that you might realize that this humanity must first rise to the single manifestation of these bands in divine harmony.

And that harmony consists of a mathematical formula whereby the increase of Light, band upon band, sphere upon sphere, is able to contain and hold that Light, increasing from the sun center and multiplying by the factor of the very geometry of God. And thus, you see, there is a golden ratio to the relationship of these bands of the Great Causal Body.

And now you are preparing, then, for the coming of Serapis Bey and the changing of the fourteen-month cycle whereby earth and yourselves will have new access to the great blue sphere of the causal body of cosmos and all cosmic beings and Ascended Masters and to the blue sphere of your own I AM Presence and body of Light.

Realize, beloved ones, that you are now in transition from the green sphere of that causal body unto the blue. You are sealing, then, the path of truth and science and healing and the All-Seeing Eye of God. It is well, then, while the gates are yet open of the path of the emerald ray, that you concentrate on healing and the decrees to Cyclopea and the healing thoughtform and the vigil of Mother Mary, that you realize the meaning of Wednesday as the day of the emerald ray and that you make this the final manifestation of that Light that does appear. For this sealing of that ring of Light shall be the very magnet, with those which have preceded, whereby the blue sphere may rise and increase and intensify in the next fourteen months.

Be here with me, then, this Saturday eve as I come with Serapis Bey to inaugurate fourteen months of the stations of the cosmic cross of white fire dedicated to the will of God fully manifest in sons and daughters of Light. And thus you have a running momentum on the blue flame by your acceptance and sheer devotion to Archangel Michael, this Prince of the

Archangels—this prince of the mighty blue sphere.

Blessed ones of God, the path of attainment is cumulative. You cannot increase Light, then squander it, then come again and be where you were in the last round. Thus you build upon foundation upon foundation upon foundation. And this is the realization of what it means to be the Buddha in manifestation for the ensouling of worlds and what it means to be the Mother.

And this is the goal of all twin flames, as by the figure-eight flow there is indeed the cosmic interchange, and the Alpha and the Omega in alternating cycles realize and define this path of Motherhood and Buddhahood, giving birth always to the universality of Christ in the plus and in the minus manifestations of the sons and daughters of God.

Thus we see the coming cycle of the blue sphere as a blueprint of Life, as the opening of the causal body of the Great Divine Director releasing the action of the power of the blue ray in elemental life and in the earth itself. And we see the blue ray necessitating the action of the violet flame on the part of those who understand the balance that is held by Alpha in the first ray and Omega in the seventh.

Thus the violet flame, as presented to you last evening in the Great Central Sun Magnet conception, supercharged with the violet ray and the seventh light actually coming from the seventh sphere of the Central Sun, is therefore, beloved ones, the key to progress in the blue ray.

Let us understand that God-protection to the earth can be given and God-government and the blue-flame will of God unto the economies of the nations. And this most magnificent opportunity that comes under the sponsorship of Helios and Vesta and the Great White Brotherhood through the hand of Serapis Bey is indeed the opportunity to call forth the Elohim and the beings of nature who are a part of that trinity—the blue flame of the trinity of angels, elementals, and men.

And therefore the path of elemental life is in focusing the power of God and the will of God throughout the physical matter cosmos. And so you understand it shall be an era where you as sons and daughters of God in the wisdom ray and you as embodied angels in the love plume shall go forth, beloved ones, and access the power of these beings of Light and mold and draw them into the divine design. And we will see what the momentum of Lightbearers in the earth can bring about, then, as the staying action of that cataclysm that is projected by mankind's karma in the Dark Cycle's turning.

Beloved ones of God: this is the magnificent opportunity and it comes from the initiation of cycles of the causal body of Lanello in the very hour of his ascension—beloved. And therefore the charting of the course is always the beginning when one Son of God passes through the ascension coil and the white fire [in order] that all those following after him might thereby gain opportunity, through the descent of his mantle of the Holy Ghost, and may go forward, then, [having been] given opportunity as time and times and a half a time,[6] as years and cycles to spread that Light—to spread it around the earth.

Truly, as the hand of the Mother does spread the butter on the newly baked bread, so there is the spreading of the oil of gladness, there is the spreading of the divine doctrine, there is the spreading of the nectar of the lily of the valley and of the gardenia. And the scent of the risen Christ in that Son of God does become the opening of the way for dispensations and opportunity, which indeed have come to you by the blessings and presence and indeed the sacrifice on the path of the ruby ray of your own beloved Mark.

And therefore I give you in this hour that magnificent vibration of the causal body of Mark that may bring to you his mystical presence in my heart and in the Lord Christ through the playing of "Greensleeves." And as this song is played, beloved ones, meditate upon the causal body of Mark. Meditate upon his heart and mind and you will find that my oneness in his causal body and in his heart therefore does bring to you the attunement with the profound love and wisdom, the inner knowledge of the Law and the Doctrine of my heart.[7] And you may assimilate that Word, beloved. And that Word's assimilation is for your power, your wisdom, and your love.

[Recording of Lanello's keynote, "Greensleeves," performed by the Philadelphia Orchestra.]

And so, my beloved, in this keynote which does key the causal body of one Son of God, may you come to understand the mystery of the Christmas Rose and the spinal altar and the ladder of Life marked by the intervals of the thorns. For the thorns themselves must tell you that the human consciousness and ego must be pricked, punctured, delivered unto the sacred-fire chalice of the rose ere the soul can mount the stairway of the degrees.

Beloved ones, I, Jesus Christ, do always radiate the fullness of my causal body through the causal body of your own soul, those [causal bodies] of the sons and daughters of God and the children of the Light. Understand, then, the meaning of the individualization of the God flame and the uniqueness of each one's own causal body. [By cosmic law] I may radiate that Light only as the sun of my soul does multiply the sun of your soul, as you yourself give consent.

And the most effective means of this radiating power of the Word—our Word together—is by way of your own internalization of your own causal body of Light as you meditate upon the rings of the causal body [visualizing them] surrounding your heart, beloved, and increasing until fully in deed and in the Word that was with God in the beginning[8] you are here below that I AM THAT I AM, as you are with me above that I AM THAT I AM.

Beloved hearts of Light enfired by the Christmas Rose brought by Mother Mary, O beloved ones of the Sun, as the Messenger awakened this morning, entering then her body, I showed to her how the angels were already building the ruby wall of light, the mighty wall of light called for by Mother Mary.

Thus, the Father has answered and the angels this day, beginning then at dawn, have begun this inner-level wall of the ruby ray, building the crystal. Crystal upon crystal, beloved ones! Oh, it is a wondrous sight! And as the Light of the dawn of the Central Sun of Being does shine through it, as the Light of your I AM Presence does shine through it, one can see all of the spectrum of the third ray of the Holy Spirit and even more as there does appear, then, the secret rays and the white fire core thereof.

Thus, rejoice this day in this peace on earth that is known by a path of Love and a wall of Light that becomes truly a Lighthouse of Love in the most literal meaning of the term. For it is literally a wall of Light, and angels of Light and sons and daughters of God may pass freely in and out. But the cherubim of the ruby ray, beloved ones, do not allow to enter anything that defileth, [neither whatsoever] worketh [abomination, or maketh] a lie or is in opposition to the mighty Light of the living Christ. [But they which are written in the Lamb's Book of Life, . . . they may freely enter in.][9]

See, then, that thou dost enter with the beloved Peter. Impetuous as he was, incomplete as he was in his mission, this heart I sought to work through; and therefore I gave to him the commission of the release of Light to those who were not of the original seed of Sanat Kumara but who were the [self-appointed] Lightbearers ready to receive my coming.

Beloved ones, the power is given unto the embodied Son of God, truly the Lord's Christ, who is always the one in embodiment that is the one who goeth before the Cosmic Christ. I was the Messenger of Him that sent me, beloved. I was the one who was the channel for that Light, and my words were the words of Him that sent me.[10]

Even so, I send my Messenger, clothed with the very promises that are spoken of this Word. For the Word does come into the world and no matter through whom It does appear, even through myself, the world does not receive that Word. The world does not understand it or comprehend it, for the world signifies the consciousness unwashed, unquickened, yet dead.

And so the Word comes to deliver a message to those whom the Word must first quicken that they might receive the message. And therefore, there is a necessary link to be established with the world that is, as one would say, the unformed, the not yet enfired. And this world must have belief—not yet faith but belief, beloved ones—belief in the name I AM THAT I AM, belief in the One Sent as the vessel of that Word. And therefore, this belief becomes fired even with faith by the Holy Spirit through the one who speaks my Word directly to you.

Understand, therefore, to those who believe on the name of the Son of God Jesus Christ and the Sun behind that Son and the Messenger of that Son there is given "power to make them sons of God."[11] There is given power to ignite in them the threefold flame. And this is what was given to Peter. The keys of the kingdom[12] are the key to the causal body and the threefold flame. And therefore, Peter must come to understand that that which is common and unclean, referred to as the godless, those having not the God flame within them—these ones, beloved, may be anointed. For that [creation] God alone can sanctify in the name I AM THAT I AM.

God therefore can raise up of these stones vessels for the threefold flame.[13] This, understand, is always the mission of the Great White Brotherhood and of every order that we have sponsored since the very earliest coming of the avatars to planetary systems of worlds. It is the igniting of a spark in the human form and figure that the soul might receive the breath of the Holy Spirit and become a living, vibrant soul—a spirit, a divine spark of Being.

This is the mission of my Life. And it is declared to you this day: "Rise, Peter: kill and eat!"[14] Understand the meaning of the word "kill and eat" or "slay and eat."[15] Realize that one must have material—alchemical material. And so Cornelius the centurion was chosen. And he sent men to Joppa.[16] And one of those men is a devout chela of this Messenger in this very hour.

Beloved ones, I tell you truly, you are called and you are the elect. And we have drawn you together from all ages. And by and by I shall reveal more and more of those situations of service where you have given your utmost devotion and where you have seen the glory of the Lord's Spirit and received that Holy Ghost.

Therefore, Cornelius was a just man, praying unto God, yet he was not a Jew. Yet he had heard the message of my coming. He was one who did fast and pray, and therefore the material was there—the something that could be quickened, beloved hearts. And this is a very necessary understanding, for that which is unwilling can never receive the engrafting of the threefold flame.[17]

Thus you also understand the rejection [by the human body] of the mechanical heart. When there is the rejection of the true heart of Christ, there is nothing that can be done whether by myself or the Messenger or the Elohim. For so to do would be the abrogation of the covenant of free will which God has ordained, and the Father does not supersede the free will.

Therefore, from among the Gentiles, from among those alien to the Word of God, some come forth desiring, some come forth and respond to the angel of the LORD and follow his instruction implicitly. What would you consider, beloved, had Cornelius rejected the angel, thought that it was a figment of his own mind, and, reasoning within himself, canceled out the opportunity [to receive the Holy Ghost] to his own house and relatives and family and friends and all generations who should come after them?

Recognize well, beloved ones, that to fast and pray [in order] that one might hear angels is important, but to be unwise and to fast improperly and to care not for the body in all ways of balance, one may find the result to be not the intercession of angels but the infestation of demons and demon possession. And this has occurred to many who have fasted without the overshadowing of the Holy Spirit through their devotion unto God.

Fasting, therefore, is for the increase of Light. And let your emphasis be on the spiritual path of fasting and not always fastened to the lower level of explanations of toxicity, et cetera. Beloved hearts of Light, let all these things be added unto you,[18] but may the focus of your fast be the sacred fire and communion with God.

Therefore, beloved, in my apostle was also one who obeyed against his own habit and custom, tradition and better judgment; for the vision I gave was to show that Homo sapiens—the human in and of itself, unquickened and without a threefold flame—is as the beasts of the field and the animal kingdom. There is no difference, beloved ones, only a higher order of the human animal evolution.

Thus, beloved, the command is given again, "Rise, Peter—

Rise, O sons and daughters of God founded upon the Rock of your own Holy Christ Self—kill and eat!" These two commands I would give to you as a mystical understanding. For, you see, in order to receive or assimilate that soul that is to be quickened, which must be accomplished by the apostle, by the Messenger whom I send, there must first be the *slaying* of the anti-self, the *slaying* of the demon, the *slaying* of the anti-Christ that is borne, many times, by those who have not the God flame.

I have not commanded our Messenger to eat, therefore, that which is common and unclean without first the slaying of the Darkness that is within it. Therefore, many who have desired me who have come to this activity, regardless of the condition of the threefold flame or the absence of it, have been received into the path of my discipleship, have been received by El Morya as chelas, have been taken at face value.

And we have said, "If you will follow the Path and reach that point of fiery initiation and trial whereby you stand before the Messenger, and the Messenger does receive me and receive the transmission of the Holy Ghost through me to slay that human creation, and if you receive that slaying by the power of the Word and allow the not-self to go down, then you can receive from me through the Messenger the transfer of that mighty power of the flame of the will of God which indeed the threefold flame is."

Understand this, beloved ones. You must bring material that is fit and meet for repentance, as John the Baptist gave the same opportunity to all who were in Israel [Judaea] in that day.[19] And he called them forth to that baptism by water that they might surrender that very substance of the godless and anti-God force within themselves.

Bring forth fruits meet for repentance. For repentance and remission of these sins must precede the enfiring of that three-fold flame [through the One Sent], which office is also upon your own Messenger as the Vicar of Christ, which means the representative thereof. And this is the meaning of her going forth in the stumping of the nations—to contact those hearts who will believe on the one whom we have sent and follow that ray, that thread of Light all the way back to our heart as we use our instrument who must be physical [in physical embodiment] for this transference of Light.

Beloved ones, emanating from my heart through the heart of the vessel, then, is a filigree Light through your own hearts. And when you are in alignment as chelas and do not shirk responsibility and do not turn aside from the wrath [sacred fire] of God and the strong winds of the Holy Spirit, when you receive it and allow the tatters of your garment to be blown from you and you are free to stand naked in the wind of the Holy Spirit, and when all the not-self then is put into the flame of the Holy Ghost—*you,* beloved ones, stand to receive that transfer of Light!

And I tell you, by the very power of my heart [transmitted] through the Messenger Mark, there did come to his very first secretary in The Summit Lighthouse at the conclusion of her life of service the gift of the threefold flame. And this was possible because we had a physical instrument whereby it might be conferred. And therefore, after a lifetime and several lifetimes of service to the Great White Brotherhood, she then did receive the opportunity to expand the flame of the Son of God.

Rise, Peter: kill and eat! Understand therefore that I speak also to the soul of Peter in this hour who is unascended. And I speak to that one and I say to you:

Christ's Admonishment to the Soul of Simon Peter

Rise! Kill, therefore, the human ego that has waxed strong for determined centuries since my coming! Kill it and slay it now if thou wouldst have opportunity—the same opportunity that did descend through thee that day in the house of Cornelius.[20]

As you did say, "Can I withstand the command of the Lord God? Can I go against his coming and his Holy Spirit?" Therefore I tell you, Peter, be humble this day that I have raised another in thy stead for thy failure and that thou must bend the knee also before the instrument as well as before the One who has sent that one to be the instrument.

Therefore, Peter, recognize that thou must indeed follow the Path from that point to which thou hast descended. For thou hast not continued in the wise use of the keys of the kingdom, and therefore they have been transferred to this one representative who did serve thee well in many incarnations.

Therefore, spurn not the purified and the humble sons and daughters of God who have advanced beyond thy calling because thou hast been neglectful in thy service, but seek once again to enter in. For in this hour of the cycles turning you, then, have your final opportunity to repent and be saved in the very living presence of thy beloved Archangel Michael.

Beloved ones, this which I say to Peter must be recorded in the physical octave. But heed well my word, for the same mandate applies to you and to your soul, whoever and wherever you may be on the Path of Life. I say, "Rise, Peter: kill and eat!" Slay that human creation! Slay that not-self! And fear not the coming of the Messenger of the Lord who comes with the refiner's fire.[21] And see that thou doest not enter into fear and doubt and trepidation and criticism and condemnation and judgment.

For truly I AM the one who does try the hearts of men. And I am trying your hearts, and I am trying this heart. And truly it is the world who is on trial and not the Messenger in this hour! For I have seen and I have known the purity of heart and thank Almighty God that you, too, shall also be known by the purity of heart and not by men's opinion, not by that which the media does report but by the very endearment of your heart to the Almighty God.

So is your path of discipleship secured, and not by the events of the past and not by the mistakes of the past but by the fervor of your soul's desiring to be all of that will of God. For every day is a new cosmos, every day is a new day in the will of God. Therefore understand that it is truly the hour when those [of my anointing] may take up the fallen mantle of this apostle and move forward, beloved, to cast out of the very Holy of Holies those priests and false pastors, those rabbis (who are not rabbis of the Holy of Holies), and all who misrepresent the Godhead.

Beloved ones, the fallen mantle of Peter has been reflected in the Church of Rome since the very beginning. Understand that one does not follow a disciple who has relinquished his hold upon my garment. One follows the vessel so long as the Light is in that vessel. One follows the vessel only because one sees and knows that Light.

Beloved hearts of living fire, it is time, as Saint Germain has said, for that Babylon the Great[22] [its tentacles in Church and State] to come tumbling down and for those who are the tyrants in the earth to find that they are no longer sitting in the seats of power.[23] It is time that the true religion that is never defiled,[24] that can never be turned back, that can never be diluted because it springs from the wellspring of Life—the mighty threefold flame—come to pass on earth and be preached in every nation and in every field.

You can preach this Teaching in every avenue of service and profession. It is not confined to religion. It has its application and its applicability, beloved ones, even as the Word itself has its adaptability, to every field of knowledge. So let space technology and electronics and the world of computer science, beloved ones, have the endowment of the threefold flame by the sons and daughters of God.

Rise, Peter: kill and eat! And therefore, let the scientists who are the materialists excluding God be not the forerunners of this age of the union of science and religion; for there must be the God flame in all areas. And there is, therefore, in the absence of that flame, a copying by humanity of a certain image of mechanization man. And the computer image of the perfect human machine has become a standard for many to emulate. And therefore they are perfecting the human self and the human mind, not realizing that they must have the endowment of the Holy Ghost and the threefold flame that did descend as on Pentecost in the house of Cornelius.

O beloved hearts, see how children are being given the standard of mechanization man and the godless who say, "We do not need the Lord's Messenger. We do not need the apostle. We do not need the Word of Christ. For we are sufficient unto ourselves. And we are rich and supplied and increased with goods."[25] Beloved hearts, go not after them, for their lure and their pride in the avenue of the senses is a defilement and a defying of this very step that must be taken if they are to endure unto eternal Life.

Therefore, I came not to condemn the world but that all might have eternal Life through this transfer of the Holy Christ Flame.[26] Understand the meaning of the Son of God, and that [it] is to raise up of these stones instruments of the original Logos from the beginning, whose birth in my form and heart and spirit and being in Bethlehem, the very place of God, you celebrate this day.

This, then, is the celebration, beloved ones, that the path of Christ is not an exclusivity unto those who fancy themselves a chosen people. If you were chosen by Sanat Kumara from the beginning, you ought to be humble before so great a calling. You ought to remember the motto *Ich dien* and noblesse oblige*— I serve, and I serve in the understanding that because I have God's flame of nobility within my heart as the mighty threefold flame, my obliging of his will [in service to the lesser endowed] is my great obligation. For those who know better must do better. Those who have the highest Light must increase that Light and let that Light shine as a magnet, truly as that Lighthouse of Love that those who have it not might therefore perceive their darkness and come seeking my heart through you, beloved ones.

Is there any desire for the Light if those in embodiment are not joyous in that Light and in its expansion? All things in the marketplace of life are sold by individuals who will tell you how wonderful such-and-such a product is and how much it has changed their lives, how much it has done for them. And I marvel

* *Ich dien* [German]: I serve—motto of the Prince of Wales. *Noblesse oblige* [French, lit., nobility obligates]: the obligation of honorable, generous, and responsible behavior associated with high rank or birth.

how Keepers of the Flame will sell this and that remedy or this and that doctor and path to the exclusion of the realization that all these things are, in themselves, merely a single line of the instrumentation of the Word. And that which they ought to be selling, therefore, is the "mighty threefold flame of Life, that gift of God so pure," as Zarathustra has spoken it.[27]

The mighty threefold flame of Life does heal all thy diseases, does bring alignment and the blueprint of Life. And that threefold flame, as the flame of the *Will* of God, as the flame of the *Wisdom* of God, as the flame of the *Love* of God, beloved ones, does bring you nearer to your divine plan and to the divine one within you.

And some of you are not with the one whom you should be with this day and this hour, though he or she be next to you in service—because of your ambition, because of your envy, because of your jealousy, because you desire to have another situation or another relationship, because somehow that other situation or relationship complements your ego and your lower self. And therefore you have missed the one who is right next to you. Beloved hearts, realize, then, that the threefold flame of Life is the key to the kingdom of perfect Love with your twin flame or the one sent to hold that focus of Love in your life.

Therefore, do not criticize and condemn anyone but recognize the complementary nature of all servant-sons and -daughters of God. And call earnestly to Chamuel and Charity in the fullness of the ruby ray, and give that ruby-ray call in conjunction with the ruby-ray exorcism written by Sanat Kumara naming all those conditions, and let these be named on your own electronic belt.

Rise, Peter. Kill pride and ambition! Kill envy and darkness! Kill self-centeredness that does blind thee from true Love! Beloved ones, cease your self-conception of yourselves in whatever image of the human you have carved out. Enter now into the perfect design as I take you by the hand—you, then, as children, you as the newborn child.

I come as your Ascended Master Jesus Christ. Place your hands in mine. Trust me as the child trusts the dearly beloved parent. I will show thee this day who thou art. I will show thee thy soul, created by God in the beginning, free of all these things, free of all these encumbrances. I will show thee the Path of perfect Love.

I have shown this Path of perfect Love to the Messenger regarding various chelas in the way. And she has remained silent for the unpreparedness of those individuals. Their own human pride makes them unwilling to see who, then, is the soul most complementary to the inner blueprint, for they have not yet humbly come as did Cornelius, trusting that Peter would be the instrument of the perfect message of the Lord Christ. They trusted as children and knew they would receive what was given by God through him for them. Their hearts were so opened by Love that the Holy Spirit did descend in its fullness.

Blessed ones, it is truly the hour to slay the force and forces of anti-Love. See, then, a mighty pink sphere, a cosmic clock. Read every line of that clock of human creation, common and unclean, as being the force of anti-Love, anti-productivity, anti-health, anti-creativity in your life. This is an hour that is a cosmic interval when this great sphere of Love comes down from heaven, as God did give the vision and I did give it to Peter of this sheet drawn at four corners.[28]

Thus, in the killing and the eating of the lesser self, in the assimilation of the Word, in the willingness that the Christ of thee and of the Messenger shall "slay and eat," you shall find yourself, beloved, in this alchemy of the Word whereby you are become your Real Self and there is no difference between the soul and the inner Bridegroom. And the soul does wear the mantle of her Holy Christ Self and does therefore bow to her Lord in [His instrumentation through] life's partner, life's friend, husband or wife, co-worker, leader, employer, or the little child in the way. When you can bow to the Lord in anyone and in yourself, then you will know who I AM in the one that is sent to you to be your spouse in this life.

I bring this message as [a help in] your ongoing understanding of the message of the Darjeeling Council that advanced souls and even Ascended Masters are applying to embody. If you do not rise and "kill and eat"—eating by way of transmutation in the violet flame, killing by way of putting out the forces of Absolute Evil that have invaded your being—you will not be prepared for the Archangel Gabriel who will come to you with the annunciation of "that holy thing that shall be born of thee which shall be called the Son of God."[29]

I, Jesus, give to you your Christmas assignment. Go forth with a renewed understanding of this science of Being and give birth to the Son of God within yourself. Then we will see what we shall do for this humanity. As I have done before you, so may you now do in my name and [in the name of] all who believe on me in this hour [and] in my name and [in] my instrumentation through the One Sent.

I begin to release that power that can make you sons of God. And that power will come with the fierceness of the Almighty, and its demand upon you will be "Rise, Peter: kill and eat!" Its demand upon you will be to be initiates of the sacred fire of Serapis Bey unto Sanat Kumara, threading through my heart— I who am your brother and friend.

For, lo, as I have promised from the beginning—Lo, I AM with you alway, even unto the end of the world[30] of your human creation, even unto the end of the age of your karma, even unto my Second Coming into your temple which is become the temple of God.

Even so, little ones, resist not the Holy Spirit who loveth thee always.

Messenger's Blessing of the Love Offering

In the name of Jesus Christ, I AM THAT I AM Sanat Kumara, Gautama Buddha, Lord Maitreya, I call forth the blessing of the entire Spirit of the Great White Brotherhood. I call unto Alpha and Omega to receive these hearts' love offerings for the breaking of the Bread of Life, for the multiplication of the Word in order that we might go forth sent by the Lord, the I AM THAT I AM through Jesus Christ our Saviour, through Saint Germain, our holy brother and deliverer, to preach to the nations the Everlasting Gospel, to rekindle hearts, O God, to ignite the Flame.

Goddess of Liberty, O ensign of this people, O Woman clothed with the Sun, hear our call as we accept in this hour even the mighty wall round about the people of Zion, the wall of the light of the ruby ray.

Ruby-ray angels and Buddha, Chamuel and Charity, Heros and Amora, Maha Chohan, in the name of the Christmas Rose, our Jesus Christ, we salute thee: O servants of the Lamb of God, we are one in his name. Amen.

"The Summit Lighthouse Sheds Its Radiance O'er All the World to Manifest as Pearls of Wisdom." This dictation was **delivered Christmas Day, December 25, 1985,** at Camelot. In her sermon before the dictation, the Messenger read John 1:1-14; Acts 10; 11:1-18; and John 3:14-21; 1:12, 13, which are included in "The Christmas Rose," 1986 *Pearls of Wisdom*, vol. 29, no. 13. Jesus' dictation, which followed, is an integral part of the ritual and should be played following "The Christmas Rose" service each time it is given at the solstices and equinoxes. **(1)** Heb. 4:12; Rev. 1:16; 2:12. **(2)** Acts 2:3. **(3)** Deut. 4:24; 9:3; Heb. 12:29. **(4)** II Cor. 3:17. **(5)** Matt. 10:34. **(6)** Dan. 12:7; Rev. 12:14. **(7)** Mark Prophet, born on Christmas Eve 1918, was embodied as Mark, the Evangelist, author of the Gospel of Mark, and as Saint Bonaventure (1221–1274), the "Seraphic Doctor," who wrote *Breviloquium, The Journey of the Mind to God, The Tree of Life,* and *The Life of Saint Francis.* Bonaventure's doctrine greatly influenced the Western Church. He was canonized by Pope Sixtus IV in 1482 and made Doctor of the Church in 1588 by Sixtus V, who testified that Bonaventure "whilst enlightening his readers . . . also moved their hearts, penetrating to the inmost recesses of their souls." Hence, the momentum of his service to Jesus Christ and his knowledge of the Lord's Divine Doctrine may be accessed from his causal body through this keying action (through his keynote, which is "Greensleeves") of the Ascended Master Jesus Christ. **(8)** John 1:1, 2. **(9)** Rev. 21:27. **(10)** John 6:29; 7:16-18, 28, 29, 33; 8:26-29, 42; 12:44-50; 14:20-24. **(11)** John 1:12. **(12)** Matt. 16:18, 19. **(13)** Matt. 3:9; Luke 3:8; 19:40. **(14)** Acts 10:13. **(15)** Acts 11:7. **(16)** Acts 10:1-8. **(17)** James 1:21. **(18)** Luke 12:31. **(19)** Matt. 3:1-12; Mark 1:2-8; Luke 3:1-17; John 1:6-34. **(20)** Acts 10:34-48; 11:12-17. **(21)** Mal. 3:1-3. **(22)** Rev. 14:8; 16:19; 17:5; 18. **(23)** See Saint Germain, Oct. 13, 1985, "The Sword of Sanat Kumara: The Judgment of the Rulers in the Earth Who Have Utterly Betrayed Their God and Their People," 1985 *Pearls of Wisdom*, vol. 28, no. 50, pp. 589–91; and Dec. 7, 1980, "The Judgment of the Great Whore," 1980 *Pearls of Wisdom*, vol. 23, no. 52, pp. 371–93. **(24)** James 1:27. **(25)** Rev. 3:17. **(26)** John 3:17; 12:47. **(27)** See Zarathustra, Dec. 12, 1965, "A Fiery Action of the Expanded Christ Consciousness," 1965 *Pearls of Wisdom*, vol. 8, no. 50, pp. 219–21. **(28)** Acts 10:9-16; 11:5-10. **(29)** Luke 1:35. **(30)** Matt. 28:20.

Pearls of Wisdom®

published by The Summit Lighthouse

| Vol. 29 No. 15 | Beloved Serapis Bey | April 13, 1986 |

Teachings from the Mystery School
VI
The Descent of the Mighty Blue Sphere
A Fourteen-Month Cycle in the First Ray of the Will of God

O Holy Ones of God, Seraphim Mighty,
  I, Serapis, call thee now from the heart!
    Seraphim, descend this shaft of light built by elementals at the command of sons and daughters of God.
    Hear the decree of the Word of Keepers of the Flame on earth.
    Seraphim of God, as thou dost keep the flame of Life in the Central Sun, tending the mighty altars of sacred fire, I bid you now: Come into the auras of these who have been sent from the Sun in the beginning—Light shoots of Alpha and Omega who have been green shoots these past fourteen months [of initiation in the fourteen stations of the cross in the emerald sphere of the causal body].[1] Come, seraphim of God, with Raphael and Mother Mary.
    Justinius, come now for the sealing of the auric light and the third eye in the mighty sphere of the emerald light. For Truth has gone forth in the science of Wholeness, the power of the Word, and all manner of Teaching that emanates from Vesta and Pallas Athena, Hilarion, and many Healing Masters.
    Beloved, all that has gone forth from the emerald sphere does now touch and qualify the succeeding sphere. Each gain of mastery from the white fire core of Being, from the beginning pulsating outward, does lend new enlightenment and enchantment, if you will, of the Word, of the Life, of the Love inherent in each and every flame and sphere.
    All attainment is cumulative if you will it so—if you do not let go, if you persevere. And the stairway of the degrees becomes

an exalted experience. And you can feel the increase of the rings of light around your four lower bodies. And you can feel the dissolution of darkness and former auric emanations that were left over from other lifetimes.

It is an hour of cycles turning and it is important to assess the net gain. Every soul periodically must of necessity engage in a certain introspection. Not so often—perhaps once or twice a year profoundly—for overattention upon the green shoot and the sense of self allows the individual to fall prey to the very diseases of the psyche that are passing through the flame to be consumed.

Thus, beloved, he who maintains the most concentrated attention on the I AM Presence and the one-pointedness of a goal, being swift as an arrow, he then is one whom we declare safe for the acceleration of the cleansing of the astral body, which must come about fast or slow as you decree it. Therefore, concentration and the strength of mind and will and heart on the assignments we give you builds [of] itself a shaft of light that is protective, and thus we are able literally to drain the astral body of toxins and diseases, darkness and shadows and entities of past lives. These pass into the violet flame with scarcely a notice from yourself because you are so one-pointed on the feat of service to Light.

Service to Light—this we extol in every heart. When you stop and start, spin and then break the thrust of the pinwheel of life and of the chakras, beloved, you become vulnerable to the very things that come out of the subconscious to be bound.

If you would, then, but strengthen this shaft of light emanating from the wonders of your attention upon Almighty God for the sealing of each of the four lower bodies, for the sealing of the place where evil dwells in the subconscious, you would find that the health and the right-mindfulness, the piercing light of the heart would allow us to then trust your own dedication and momentum that must be sustained in a continuous beat of harmony and a held strain of music without break that we might complete the surgery through the Lord Jesus Christ, who comes as the good physician to take from you the burdens and cares which, though they seem surface, are not surface at all but emanate from dark pools and cesspools long ago forgotten. For there is a world of darkness in the subconscious, where the quicksands of life yet are.

Therefore, beloved, when you are a start-and-stop chela, when you decree now and then but have no schedule, just at the moment when the cycle comes in the full power of the healing ray to truly engage your being in this work of the ages of the removal of these layers of substance, we cannot do it.

For just at that moment, all of a sudden you have taken a vacation from the Path, and the world rolls in and another round of its enjoyments. And, of course, we could not possibly begin this surgery, for the patient is not ready: the patient will not sustain the accelerated beat of the life-force in the heart and in the chakras so that that which must become a radical removal of subterranean substance can be taken according to the laws of cosmos.

Thus, I would speak to you of the mysteries of Lord Maitreya. I would speak to you of the Path as a spiral, step upon step succeeding the last. I would speak to you of the vast differences, from seat to seat among you, of chelas, of backgrounds, of cosmic history, of time that has been spent in our retreats over the centuries. Thus, I would tell you there are scarcely two alike among you, scarcely two of equality on the path of self-mastery, some concentrating here and there, some newly come to the realization of the earnestness of the path of the fourth ray.

Therefore, I would steal with you awhile and take a moment to reinforce in you my commendation, by way of my love, to tell you that many have made great strides and increased at inner levels in the building of the Deathless Solar Body. This you yourself may not necessarily observe concerning yourself, and it does require the Teacher to tell you that some have so increased and been diligent in areas pointed out that they indeed have taken giant steps toward the initiations of Luxor. And others, while thinking themselves fastidious, have merely ridden on the joy of those who are profoundly one with God.

Thus, beloved, no matter how many surround you, the Path is a lonely path. For the Path is one of your soul and your heart in communion with God—you and God alone in the universe of spiritual joy and bliss. On one plane of your striving this is as it is, and the soul does conquer here at night while the body sleeps, whereas in the day the karma of communities and families and nations and old ties does surround individuals with all manner of circumstances and duties, employment, burdens and joys.

There are many planes of existence. And some of you look forward to placing yourself at rest at night, not so much because you are tired but because you are anxious to get on with the inner work and the inner service that can continue uninterrupted [by the cares of the day] and [is therefore capable of] accelerating. And you know that by this inner work you are improving your lot in the outer planes as you journey to the [etheric] retreats [of the Great White Brotherhood], as you commune in Love, and indeed as you are initiated by the archangels.

Never fear, for the unseen victory of Love is always registered at Luxor. The 'computers' of the Mind of God, vouchsafed to us through the science of Sanat Kumara, are readily available by cosmic consent and your own. Therefore, we are able to monitor the progress on the Path of the Mother and the Path of the Ascension of every soul of Light on earth. Daily there are dispatched from Luxor seraphim of God who go to the side of Lightbearers to assist them, to show them the way to the next door and the opening of the Path to those very areas that require attention.

Beloved ones, it is by certain fiats that your Messenger has made concerning her life and the life of this Community and its future that we have been able to open doors of knowledge and understanding to her. Without these fiats, these probings, these challenges of limitation and ignorance and darkness—and the inner realization of the need to claim more of the cosmic unity—this information and expansion would not have come forth.

Thus, beloved, it is a wonderful joy to walk in the woods and by the streams and in the mountains and to shout unto the LORD God—to reach for the farthest star or the very nearest sparkle of the stream, to touch and contact God, whether with a still, strong voice of determination or with a mighty shout unto the heavens: **"O God, send me help for this requirement of the hour!"**

Beloved ones, I hurl to you now from my heart the choice—creativity that must come to you and blossom in you by a balanced threefold flame. I speak of creativity in meditation, of the genius of your own Christhood, and of the planes of heaven of your causal body. Remember, you dwell in a plane of effect and so-called limitation.

To break the barriers of mortality you must ascend this spinal altar and continue up the crystal cord. You must desire to mount and develop a momentum on climbing mountains of one's inner being to once again retrieve the lost chord of identity and to access from your own cosmic computer of the Mind of God all that you have been abuilding for millions of years of evolution.

Is it just that you should be cut off from this Universal Mind which once was your own? The law of karma says that it is just, for each and every one has entered into lows of ignorance and ignominy. But, beloved ones, the other side of justice is mercy. And you have abundant mercy in the violet flame. And you ought to pray to God and say:

O God, yet I be in this condition of limitation, bowed down in my body and being, yet I call to you for Mercy:

Heal me of all inharmony and diseases. I will to be harmonious Love forever.

O God, by thy Mercy Flame, transmute and consume in me the records of dark deeds that have cut me off from the full waking awareness of the totality of my mind in God.

Thus, beloved, do not cease to yearn for and to pursue the higher and higher Self. Do not categorize yourself at a certain age or level, or an attainment, even in the human sense, beyond which you foresee you will not go in this life. [Do not so limit yourself.] There is no limit to what you can become on earth through this form that you wear if you will determine to become the master of your life. To be an embodied Master is a worthy goal. And to do so in love without rigidity or superstition is commendable.

Thus master any art and apply it to the internalization of the Word. Be not satisfied with any area of indulgence of the self. But do thou indulge the greater Self and thyself within it.

Beloved, learn to think creatively and ingeniously as to how you can become more of myself in manifestation. For there is a way of Life and Eternity we would proclaim—the Path of the Ascension. And Lightbearers must be known for this path of Light and raised sacred fire.

O blessed ones of God, hear the elemental life who rejoice in all that has been manifest in the emerald sphere. We seal now the body elemental of every Lightbearer on earth. We seal the children of the Sun in the rays of the Healing Masters, in the heart of Mother Mary.

And so with cycle's door ajar unto the blue sphere, we come now accompanied by Archangel Michael and legions of Surya and Cuzco, who does hold the balance this night in the heart of the God Star Sirius for the descent to earth of the mighty blue sphere amplified by the white fire core of the Great Central Sun and of your causal body. Now you can see from the center to the periphery rings of expansion and joy as bells are ringing and the new chime of the new year and the new age does receive the very special quality of the blue flame of the Will of God.

Clear as crystal, direct as Morya, powerful as Hercules, faithful as Archangel Michael—so the blue sphere does descend around you. Oh, rise to greet it as a leaping hart, beloved ones! Rise into the very center of this sphere as it comes all around you and as your auras scintillate with fire.

As on a rainy night you may see rings around the moon, so visualize this ring around yourself. See the shimmering cobalt blue sparkling with turquoise and even shades of deep purple; see the aquamarine and the stellar blue of Mother Mary; see the blue of fountains, of sky and water; see the blue of the eyes of angels—all of this representing the depth and the power of the sea of God.

Beloved hearts of Light, this sphere around you is mighty indeed. And you are well able to magnetize it, for your devotion unto the rosary of Archangel Michael has truly saved so many lives since its inception, as we have told you.

Beloved ones, you have been running and gaining a running momentum to receive this blue sphere. Your devotion as chelas of Morya, your love of Archangel Michael, your desire to do well—all these things are qualities of the first ray and of the Will of God. And therefore, be sealed and know that the sphere that descends from your causal body in this hour is commensurate with that externalized blue flame that you have called forth in this and all embodiments.

Whether it is less or greater, be not concerned with thyself or with thy neighbor by comparison. But, beloved ones, know this—when you see Himalaya and Vaivasvata Manu and you see their mighty blue spheres and you see that of the God and Goddess Meru and the Great Divine Director, you may contemplate what it is to intensify and increase the power of the blue-flame sun and the blue-flame Central Sun Magnet.

Beloved ones, if another have a greater sphere than you, praise God and say, "Because my brother has won, I shall win too!" And this is exactly why we give you fourteen months—fourteen stations of the cross of Jesus and of the Mother and her children. In fourteen months you can multiply this sphere geometrically. This is the meaning of this dispensation from the heart of Alpha and Omega.

By the grace of the continuity of our dictations to you unbroken, you may know that such an opportunity is at hand. And you may proclaim it to all Lightbearers throughout this fourteen-month cycle. You may tell them how wondrous is the rosary to Archangel Michael, how wondrous are the blue-flame decrees and the blue-flame Masters. And you may tell them of the power of the Divine Mother in the white fire core of Being here and in the Great Central Sun to multiply that action.

And you may tell them, of course, beloved, how necessary protection will be in the coming year as you contemplate the change of the Dark Cycle, which will find itself on the 5/11 axis of the Cosmic Clock, signifying that this is the year, beginning April 23, 1986, when the backlash of the dark ones—for all of the

Light that has gone forth in the last twelve cycles of the clock—
may be unleashed upon an unsuspecting humanity.

Beginning on that day you ought to expect the revenge of the
fallen angels against the Light and the Lightbearer. And you must
understand that the wall of blue flame and the sphere of blue
flame is given unto you [in order] that when the Darkness comes it
may instantaneously be deflected and go back to its source. And
may the source of Darkness be destroyed by its own evil intent.

This is my decree, and this is my message to you that you
do not underestimate the meaning of the Dark Cycle of the
returning of mankind's karma and of the karma of the fallen
angels, who have in this hour great envy and jealousy of the
Lightbearers and the sweet children of Light. And their momentum of revenge has been smoldering as resentment for aeons.

Thus, beloved, to continue to build and to accelerate, to increase and intensify the blue flame is the surest defense and sign
of victory. God has already disposed and answered prayers ye
have not thought of. Angels have already begun to weave a
filigree net of blue flame, a most intense fiery blue. It is a tight
crocheting of an armour of mail made of light substance imper-
vious. It is draped now between the physical manifestation and
the astral plane for the protection of the earth from further
eruption of astral hordes and darkness that began when the
hour struck midnight December 31, 1959. It was then that the
spilling over into America and the world of the subcultures of
rock music and drugs paved the way for all astral horror and
Death and Hell to come into the physical plane.

There was therefore established [on July 26, 1964] a golden
chain mail connected at the great monuments of the world. But,
beloved ones, this golden chain mail was not [sufficiently] reinforced with dynamic decrees by those in embodiment, inasmuch
as the numbers of Keepers of the Flame and individuals decreeing
at that time were not nearly so great as they are today. Therefore,
I trust you will review this dictation concerning the golden chain
mail and realize that we enforce this now and reenforce it with this
blue chain mail of fiery blue energy and powerful protection.

Thus, we direct your attention to the principle of heading
off the dark ones at the pass. And if you will be seated, I will tell
you about this pass. [For] I myself have had great experiences of
holding back the forces of evil at the pass in the mountains.[2]
And I have seen it as an exercise and as an initiation that must
be forged and won by Lightbearers.

Beloved ones, there comes a moment when a group of

individuals on earth realize that they alone stand between oncoming hordes of darkness and their nation and their planetary
home. This realization has dawned upon you—and upon some
of you increasingly—until at this hour you have come to recognize that the superiority of the Path of the Great White Brotherhood, and especially of the path of the fourth ray, has lent to
you a Light, a Power, a Teaching and a Science whereby you
can stand on behalf of millions and invoke the Light and see the
results and see the response of angels and beings of cosmos who
have stood between mankind and descending calamity.

Thus, the principle of "heading them off at the pass" is the
principle of stopping the eruption out of the astral plane into
the physical plane of great darkness—darkness that is planned in
secret as conspiracy and plot against humanity, darkness that
does not want to be unveiled or exposed, darkness that comes
from extraterrestrials hovering and who have also taken embodiment, darkness such as sudden war or economic difficulties,
diseases that come seemingly out of nowhere, of which Halley's
comet has become the harbinger.

Beloved ones, there are messengers from the Sun. Some of
them are typified in comets. But there are angels who come
whether or no there is a comet to be seen in the sky. Such an
angel is Gabriel of the fourth ray, the angel of the annunciation.
To him I bid you call that you might have the realization from
his heart aforetime of those things that are planned to erupt out
of the astral plane as they come with sudden destruction[3] as the
return of planetary karma.

As you know, so much of this planet's karma is in fact the
karma of fallen angels which does not rightly belong to humanity
but which has been manipulated to their destruction. And we
have spoken to you of the fallen angels and their karma-dodging.
Therefore, you see, the creative call must be that their karma fall
upon their own heads and that this fiery mail of blue surround the
Lightbearers and the innocent and the youth and the children
that they might be protected yet another day and another hour
and another decade to find the Path and come into the Light.

Beloved hearts of freedom, when you think how in this year—
as Truth has gone forth, as healing seminars have been conducted
and the lost arts of healing proclaimed—souls have come for the
first time to the knowledge, whether of the Great White Brotherhood or of the Ascended Masters or of this Messenger and this
Path—when you think of the newness of these souls as babes reborn
in Christ, you say in your hearts, "What a shame, what a cosmic

shame it would be if these souls were deprived of the opportunity to realize the fullness of that Truth which is brought."

The wise, the heroes and the heroines of past ages have always seen this equation. And when they themselves have seen that they contained in their own hearts such Truth and the magnanimity of the Godhead, they could easily give their lives that others might have the same opportunity to bring to fruition this sphere of blue which is upon you.

And so you see, beloved ones, those to whom God has given so very much, of them much is expected.[4] And they expect much of themselves. For they have Light, and they know they have enough Light to also give—to give of their life in any way possible that others might have in this embodiment the continuity of the thread of contact long enough so that when and if they come to that point of transition [the change called death] they are able to continue without even a break in consciousness, higher and higher in the etheric octave to the very throne room of Gautama Buddha or Sanat Kumara.

[Of a truth,] many who have heard this Teaching and passed shortly thereafter from the screen of life are those who have come and seen the newborn Christ Child at the presentation in the temple and have said, "Now I have seen the Lord. Now I may go to other octaves."[5]

Thus, beloved ones, ye have been bought with a price.[6] And you are entering a year when you must buy with a price ten thousand times ten thousand Lightbearers on earth whose hour has come for this opportunity, this infusion of the mighty blue ray.

I say, press on and hold the pass. I say, prevent the darkness from penetrating through, and challenge with a sternness and a determination of the eye of Serapis that evil which has become commonplace as people have allowed themselves to be lulled into a stupor in the face of this culture of drugs that plagues the earth as the creeping and crawling things out of the pit have come unto the bodies of the very Lightbearers we have sent.

Beloved ones, I commend you and commend you again for securing this Inner Retreat and advise you to continue as directed. For one day you will see and know how important it was to "work while ye have the Light"[7] or, as they say, to "make hay while the sun shines."

Be grateful for the sun that shines and the fields that ripen and for the harvest. Be grateful for your mastery with elemental life and the alchemist Saint Germain, truly the Adept of adepts of this age. Be grateful that while you have youth and life and mind and will and the means to multiply substance, you can fully build and complete this retreat.

Beloved hearts, one day you will see so great a multitude approaching that you will have to turn many away and send them to qualify themselves for that rarefied Light just as we do at Luxor. The standard must be high. And this time Maitreya's Mystery School must endure.

O mighty cosmic forces four, seal now the earth. Seal now this blue chain mail. Seal now these spheres of blue.

O Morya, beloved, you have prepared them well to this time. O Archangel Michael, you have prepared them. O Mother, you have prepared them. And Lanello, your brooding spirit has not let the true ones stray.

O Elohim of the first ray, so [much a] part of the physical octave, you have set herewith pillars of blue flame. And therefore I, Serapis, dedicate this sanctuary of the Holy Grail as a shrine to the First Ray of the Will of God. Let it so be known. And let it so be the matrix until all is fulfilled here below.[8]

In the name of the starry blue Mother and her aura that fills the earth, in the name of the World Mother, Mary, in the name of her counterpart and all sisters of the Will of God, so let the devotees come into the heart of the blue flame and the cosmic blue egg.

It is sealed and thou art one. Preserve at all costs thy wholeness and thy circle of oneness that is Community—the cradle of the new age.

With the sign of Luxor, I seal you.

Power of the Will of God, go forth through these my own forever!

"The Summit Lighthouse Sheds Its Radiance O'er All the World to Manifest as Pearls of Wisdom." This dictation by Serapis Bey was **delivered** through the Messenger of the Great White Brotherhood Elizabeth Clare Prophet on **Saturday, December 28, 1985,** during the 5-day New Year's conference, *Teachings from the Mystery School,* held at Camelot. (1) See Serapis Bey, October 28, 1984, "Initiation from the Emerald Sphere," and Elizabeth Clare Prophet, "Fourteen-Month Cycles of the Initiation of the Christed Ones through the Spheres of the Great Causal Body," 1984 *Pearls of Wisdom,* vol. 27, no. 56, pp. 483-510. (2) **Leonidas.** In the fifth century B.C., Serapis Bey was embodied as Leonidas, the Spartan king honored throughout history for his courageous spirit in the face of insurmountable odds. In 480 B.C. Leonidas commanded the Greeks in their heroic stand against the immense Persian invasion at the pass of Thermopylae—gateway to central Greece. Before the attack, it was reported that when the Persians shot their bows, the arrows darkened the sky. In response, one of the Spartans cried: "Then we'll fight in the shade!" Leonidas, with 300 Spartans and about 6,000 Greek allies, resisted the advance of the Persian army under King Xerxes for two days. On the third day, when the Persians approached from the rear and no reinforcements were in sight, Leonidas dismissed most of his troops, and he and his 300-member Spartan royal guard fought to the last man. (3) I Thess. 5:3. (4) Luke 7:36-48; 12:48. (5) Luke 2:25-35. (6) I Cor. 6:20; 7:23. (7) John 9:4, 5; 12:35, 36. (8) In obedience to this decree of Serapis Bey, on January 2, 1986, Keepers of the Flame gathered in the Sanctuary of the Holy Grail to paint it a beautiful heavenly blue! And so it stands today, the chalice of the mighty blue sphere, the home of Archangel Michael and Masters and chelas of the First Ray of the Will of God, a tribute to the Ascended Master El Morya, founder of The Summit Lighthouse and initiator of our Beloved Messengers.

THE RADIANT WORD

THE COAT OF GOLDEN CHAIN MAIL

Given in Los Angeles, July 26, 1964
by Beloved God Meru through the Messenger Mark L. Prophet

And so there flows now the wondrous outpouring of our love from the Andes unto the world. And as this love flows forth, we urge that the golden armour of holy illumination's flame be placed in the consciousness of all as though it were wrapping and enfolding them round, so that the arrows and pestilences that infest the world to this present hour may be stayed and by the gift of divine illumination men may walk in robes of righteousness.

The right use of divine power will make this planet reflect the golden-age radiance which it is our will to expand now. And so, as I come to you this morn, it is my wish that you will feel the sweet gift of our grace imparted to you through the angelic messengers who issue forth from this retreat, carrying to your heart strands of golden substance that you may feel also the illumination of this precious substance as it is placed by angelic hands as a circlet of light around your brow.

The anointing of this holy gift is to intensify the flame of illumination and to decrease the density of the brain consciousness of man so that the Holy Spirit of illumination may flow forth unimpeded and expand our light to the youth of the world in this hour of cosmic need when balance is the call of the hour. . . .

As I am come to you this holy morn, I then come with cosmic purpose in view, bearing tidings of kindness and grace from the lovely Lady Meru, who is my consort. Today we shall not experiment, but we shall perform—we shall weave a network of light over the planetary body. And because this is the day called Sunday, we shall utilize the energies and devotion of many hearts to weave this great garment of light over the planet.

And it is our intent this day that this garment of light shall resemble a coat of golden chain mail so that we may plug the gaps in mankind's consciousness where the penetration of psychic substance passes and causes them to reinfect various areas of the world after the decrees and calls of the students of Light have effectively rendered them antiseptic. . . .

The Christ of the Andes, this magnificent statue of light, is now being charged while I am speaking to you by angel devas from many parts of the world and is also being touched by a rod of power held in the hands of the Angel Deva of the Jade Temple. This action of purity is talismanic in action and designed to cause a spiritual white radiance of cosmic light to be released from this statue in commemoration of the Cosmic Christ. And as this takes place, it is beamed out in an omnidirectional manner so as to contact the entire periphery of the earth's surface.

These currents, then, follow the curvature of the earth and will incite a cosmic action of Love and Light wherever they contact the spires of worship of mankind this morning, weaving together the energies of both Christian, Moslem, Jew and Buddhist, and the many religions of the world into a consecrated chalice and forcefield that the angelic hosts will take up and offer to the Karmic Board. This offering is intended to be carried directly to the Great Central Sun and laid before your precious Alpha and Omega. . . .

We hope to insulate mankind from the psychic realm as much as possible and establish a curtain of great power so that this realm will become somewhat isolated from mankind and exceedingly difficult to pierce. It is our hope that this will bring about a great wall of light between the octave of psychic substance and the human consciousness of mankind, making it extremely difficult for those individuals engaged in psychic practices to actually contact the psychic octave. . . .

It is the intention of the great Goddess Meru this morning to intensify the feminine ray in your midst while I amplify the masculine ray so that you will understand that the action of building this coat of golden chain mail is not an action of one second but is being accomplished in part while I am speaking and will be intensified in the days to come as you call for the amplification of the action which took place this morning. . . .

Now, precious ones, with the great release of substance of Light that is pouring forth across the planetary body this morning, I would like to tell you also that we are using some of the political focuses of the world, such as the Washington Monument, and we are tying in to the mighty ray that is anchored there as a silent sentinel for and on behalf of America. The action of Light this morning is actually weaving strands of great cables and extending these cables to tie all of the monuments that are constructive across the face of the earth into one vast network of Light.

Then the angelic hosts are contacting persons and places and conditions and things which are vibrating with an action of Light, and all are being interwoven into this marvelous pattern.

This is going to mean a tremendous boon to the earth in this day and age, but it will require the attention of the students in order to reinforce and establish it so that it may be a permanent action for the earth.

Do you see what I mean, blessed ones? This is an etheric gift which we are conferring upon the earth this morning. And this gift requires a specific action of mankind's attention being fed into it in order that the power of Light may retain this power of the golden chain mail armour anchoring mankind into the purity of his divine radiance.

I thank you and I am counting on you, as is the lovely Goddess Meru, to sustain this action of mighty assistance poured out in this day to the earth and all mankind upon it. . . .

Pearls of Wisdom, published weekly by The Summit Lighthouse for Church Universal and Triumphant, come to you under the auspices of the Darjeeling Council of the Great White Brotherhood. These are presently dictated by the Ascended Masters to their Messenger Elizabeth Clare Prophet. The international headquarters of this nonprofit, nondenominational activity is located in Los Angeles, California. All communications and freewill contributions should be addressed to The Summit Lighthouse, Box A, Malibu, CA 90265. Pearls of Wisdom are sent weekly throughout the USA via third-class mail to all who support the Church with a minimum yearly love offering of $40. First-class and international postage rates available upon request. Notice of change of address should be received three weeks prior to the effective date. Third-class mail is not forwarded by the post office.

Pearls of Wisdom®
published by The Summit Lighthouse

| Vol. 29 No. 16 | Beloved Archangel Uriel | April 20, 1986 |

Teachings from the Mystery School
VII
"Thus Far and No Farther!" Saith the LORD
The Judgment of Laggard Terrorists and Retaliators

Ho, Sons and Daughters of God!

Ho, Angelic Hosts of Light from the Sun!

I, Archangel Uriel, salute you in the dawn of the eternal Christos. O hearts aflame with resurrection's fires, know that the I AM with me is the I AM with you. And by the link of Light we are one, and heaven and earth are not separate. But the intensity of the Logos passing through the Light, I AM THAT I AM, is truly the perception of the All-Is-One of the Mystical Body of God.

Truly in this Light of our Lord, beloved, be seated now, mindful that you sit in the seat of Christ-authority that comes only from the divine spark, the threefold flame of your heart whereby truly you are ignited unto eternal Life.

Ones sent for holy purpose, I come with my mission of the LORD's Judgment as always.* I am now walking in the (physical) streets of Jerusalem. I am on the path of the sorrowful way.[1] I place my feet, and angels with me, throughout this city. And we come, therefore, for a purpose, beloved hearts. By the Holy Spirit sent by the Lord Christ, we come for the rebuke of those laggard elements throughout the Middle East who have perpetuated an ancient rivalry in their terrorism, in their retaliations, in their stealing one from the other.

O beloved hearts of Light, the LORD God has decreed this day, "Thus far and no farther! They may no longer call themselves a chosen people who choose to destroy life and to incite

---

* Archangel Uriel of the Sixth Ray, servant of the Lord Jesus Christ, comes to deliver the judgments of the Son of God. In *The Sibylline Oracles*, a collection of Messianic prophecies (200 B.C.–A.D. 200), he is the angel who brings the seed of the Wicked One to the judgment seal.

life." They may no longer call themselves Abram's seed, beloved hearts of Light, whether through Sarah or whether through the bondswoman.[2] Beloved ones, know the LORD and understand that the inheritance of Light is not by flesh and blood but by the descent of that Light and the fervor of the heart and the striving of the soul.

Therefore we say, angels of Light do gather for the binding of this international conspiracy against the Light. And those who care not and with wanton destruction incite this murder or commit it—both are equally guilty. And the world dares not point the finger of judgment upon those who are the real culprits in this hour.

Therefore I, Uriel, shall now point the finger, and it is the finger of the living God. And it has descended before. And this finger does write, and it writes again, "MENE, MENE, TEKEL, UPHARSIN." Thou art weighed in the balance and found wanting, and therefore the Judgment be upon thee this night![3]

And in this night of the Dark Cycle of returning karma they shall not escape.[4] They shall not create barriers, whether of dollars or of oil[5] or of conspiracy or glad smiles or justification by any means. Let the hordes of Death and Hell be so forewarned. For ye are bound this day! And the LORD has sent me, that by the power of the Word his Judgment might rest in the physical octave and be borne in your hearts and you might see and know that the earth is the LORD's![6]

And whereas there is no international solution for world terrorism, the LORD God Almighty does contain that solution. And angelic hosts are ready to deliver it day upon day and night unto night[7] as you offer the confirming Word. For here below in the footstool kingdom,[8] beloved hearts, *you* must ratify God's will and his ordinances and his holy Word and realize that free will is being outplayed in every area of the world and every arena of political and economic action.

Thus, the Lord Christ came to the darkest area of the world. He came there to rebuke the Darkness, and he rebukes it this day. And he has sent me to determine that the conspiracies of laggard evolutions shall not be allowed to encroach upon the entire planetary body and carry out their crazed designs of total destruction for the revenge of their blood, which is not the blood of Christ but the blood of devils who have incarnated.

Beloved hearts of the living Son, know that this earth has many mysteries. And lifewaves there are of Light, and tares among the wheat[9] have determined to snuff out the Christ in these little ones. And therefore we see this form of abortion aborting the divine intent for the city of God—that Jerusalem and the New Jerusalem that is the City Foursquare of the map of the entire North American continent.[10]

And you know whereof I speak. And you know the lie that has gone forth to destroy and disrupt the balance of forces in the Middle East. Beloved ones, ever and anon it has been that these dark forces have sought international control and sought to make the world carry the burden of their karma and their Darkness. "Thus far and no farther!" saith the LORD.

I AM Uriel, Archangel of the Sun. I AM in the flaming presence of the Son of God. I go before him in this city and throughout North America that the Light and the Power of the resurrection flame might be raised up in all people of Light [in order] that they might be quickened into the awareness of those coming events upon the earth so prophesied by the Lord Jesus Christ himself—

Not because prophecy itself is a predestination but because men and women of goodwill who are the Lightbearers in the earth and the very salt of the earth[11] may read this handwriting on the wall and see to it that by their free will espoused to God's own holy will, espoused to the living Christ, they may intercede— they may play the role of intercessor to secure, then, innocent life and to bring forth a bastion of protection, which, as you can see, beloved ones, can never occur through material means. For only the LORD can give protection to the innocent against the inroads of Death and Hell.

And so I marked well in the mind of the Messenger this place in Rome, the very exact place where this massacre took place.[12] There they stood, Messenger and company, on that very place. And so in the mind and memory is etched that spot and the realization in the heart of the Messenger—"There but for the grace of God go I."

And you see what protection the mighty archangels will afford the servants of God when they make the call. For by free will the call must be made. For we are archangels serving the will of God in the Great Central Sun and we come to serve the sons and daughters of God! But we may not, by the law of God, intercede in your life or interfere unless you surrender that human will and say, "Not my will, but thine be done. O LORD, come into my life and help me!"

Beloved ones, where Lightbearers have given the calls to Archangel Michael and the call for the tube of light, there has been protection. Thus, may all the world take up Archangel Michael's Rosary as the defense in the Day of Vengeance of our God.[13] And this vengeance is come upon mankind as the returning planetary karma of these fallen angels [embodied] in the midst thereof.

And I say, no Lightbearer—not *one* of these little ones— deserves to be taken from the screen of life. And yet, for the false pastors and the false gurus of East and West they have not known how to call upon the name of the LORD. And it is written, "In that day they shall call upon the name of the LORD, and they that call shall be saved."[14]

So it is written, beloved hearts, and so it is the Law. In the name of the Christ Self of all people, you may invoke God-protection for the righteous and the acceleration of the Judgment of the seed of the wicked and those devils in embodiment who prey upon Life.

And what is their course? And what is their goal? It is anarchy. It is chaos. And mercy does not abound, for these peoples have not accepted the descent of Jesus Christ as the Messiah. And they yet dwell in the "eye-for-an-eye" and "tooth-for-a-tooth" sense of God-Justice.[15] And they have set in motion causes of Darkness that will never end unless there be some giving, some coming to the table of God, which is truly the Round Table. For the square table always ends in confrontation, but the Round Table of the Mystery School of Camelot is where the divine resolution of the Holy Spirit does take place.

And those who are without mercy do not have the grace of God. And the grace of God is brought to men's hearts by holy angels. What shall we say, then, when we offer our way and our recourse to Him to these ones? What shall we say when they will have none else but revenge and retaliation one to the other, whether it is in the Middle East or Southeast Asia or on the playgrounds of life everywhere on earth? What shall we say when the mercy of Christ, delivered by our heart and hand, is rejected? We must withdraw, for we must respect free will.

Therefore, the rejection of the mercy and grace of the LORD and Saviour results in each individual having to come to grips with the forces he has set in motion. And there does not stand between him and his returning karma the great Mediator of the Word who is Christ the LORD. With the advent of the divine Mediator there is mercy, there is hope, there is renewed Life and opportunity. There is the opportunity to be washed clean from sin and past lives as well as the sullied garments of this embodiment.

What would you do if you could not implore the grace of
God in your life? And yet, beloved, know and understand that
there are relentless races of dark ones upon earth who desire
much more to have revenge and will take the consequences of
their spiritual suicide pact. They have been told that they will
be received by Allah or by Abraham, or whomever, in commit-
ting these deeds of the perpetuation of murder.

I tell you, they listen to false hierarchs and fallen ones who
are the impostors of the true and only living God of Israel whom
the archangels universally represent. We are the angels of the
LORD's Presence, and therefore where we stand is the I AM
THAT I AM. And therefore, we have said in the person of
Archangel Michael, "Put off thy shoes from off thy feet, for the
place whereon thou standest is holy ground."[16]

Do you understand that an archangel may hallow space
and time? Do you understand when you stand with the archangels, there is holy ground? For the LORD is with us and we are
his emissaries and we have been so ten thousand times ten thousand years and longer.

Beloved ones, those who do not perceive the sacredness of
[human] life, because Life is God, shall not pass, shall not deprive
the glorious resurrection of the evolutions and lifewaves of
earth! The LORD God Almighty has decreed it!

We, the archangels, descend, attending the year 1986. And
we summon you, soldiers of Christ, members of the army of The
Faithful and True, the Word of God.[17] We summon you and we
say, the sharper-than-the-two-edged-sword[18]—the power of the
spoken Word—will summon us.

I say to every one of you: Try me! For I AM Archangel
Uriel of the sixth ray of the Lord Jesus Christ. I go before him in
the fullness of the Judgment and in the fullness of the resurrection. Call to me and you will see that the LORD has truly decreed,
"Thus far and no farther! Either the Lightbearers of earth must
rise up and be the chalice of this living flame and determine to
deny the power of Evil, else the free will of the laggard evolutions will have their day."

Now the LORD has decreed it. *Now* we have spoken it. *You,*
then, must confirm it and see to it that all of the earth and her
evolutions do have your prayer and that there is the dividing of
the way and that there is a stripping action of the fallen ones of
all that light they have stolen from the altar of God and misused
against God's holy people.

Beloved ones, there are Lightbearers in the Middle East.

There are Lightbearers in Israel, in Jerusalem, and in every Arab nation. And these Lightbearers are the oppressed, burdened by the customs and the Darkness of their false leaders who have led them into a frenzy of a war of revenge, retaliation and Darkness.

O children of the Sun, shall we all lose our souls fighting over the patch of earth when the earth is "the LORD's and the fullness thereof"? Can any man claim the land, the sea, the stars, the sun as his own? Is it not enough to claim the Light within his heart as the Light that God has bequeathed to him?

After all, their lives are short enough. Is not somehow the eternal kingdom worth everything and the sacrifice and the laying down of arms? May not Jew and Arab and Christian embrace one another? Or else are they the false ones who are of the synagogue of Satan?[19] Are they not the real? Shall they not, then, be unmasked? And shall they not be known by their deeds and by their words and by their insults or their praise unto the Almighty One?

Blessed hearts of Light, I appeal to you, for you have been assembled from all areas of the world. You come from all nations. You sit together in Love—Jew and Christian, Buddhist, Hindu, those who have been atheist, those who have been Moslem. You are all *here* in this very congregation! And through your hearts I direct Light now back to the congregations and the nations out of which you have come forth in the true understanding of the I AM Race and of America, where all differences and shades ought to disappear in the mighty torch of the Goddess of Liberty and her initiation of your heart by the threefold flame.

Therefore I say, let bigotry and fanaticism and religious persecution and bondage cease in America this day! For these are the very seeds that beget hatred that begets terrorist activities and violence. You, then, who decry the actions of those beyond this nation must clean your own households and now embrace the mighty flame of tolerance and compassion.

Let love abide. Let love abide for the Eternal One who has sent his prophets and saints, who has sent the LORD into your midst. And agree to agree together on the Truth itself. All men can and should agree on the foundation of Truth that life is sacred. When life ceases to be sacred, then all sins proceed therefrom—abortion and maligning, desecration, molestation.

O beloved, archangels have vowed before the Great Central Sun in this twenty-four-hour cycle to go forth, to work through whoever shall work with us and call upon us. We are here and we are determined. And we know that the Dark Cycles can be turned by those who exercise their free will in the science of the spoken Word and enlist the company of angels.

O children of the Sun, remember, in every world religion the angels have been eclipsed and therefore you have been stripped of your intercessors. These are your companions, your brothers, your sisters, your servants.

We are in your midst. We are sent to perform this work. We can do the job! We are trained! We are professionals! We know how to bind the demons! Only call in the name of God I AM THAT I AM, in the name of his Son Jesus Christ, and stand fast and behold the salvation of your God![20] Stand fast and see the healing of the nations and the fall of tyrants!

It shall come to pass! It shall be! I have spoken it in the name of God and Jesus Christ, in the name of your heart flames, in the name of these little ones. It is spoken and the Word goes forth. It is the Word of Christ. And this Word shall not return unto him void.[21]

In the flame of Peace, know I AM THAT I AM.

"**The Summit Lighthouse Sheds Its Radiance O'er All the World to Manifest as Pearls of Wisdom.**" This dictation by Archangel Uriel was **delivered** through the Messenger of the Great White Brotherhood Elizabeth Clare Prophet on **Sunday, December 29, 1985,** during the 5-day New Year's conference, *Teachings from the Mystery School,* held at Camelot. (1) **Via dolorosa, the sorrowful way.** The path in Jerusalem which Jesus is believed to have followed as he bore his cross to Golgotha. The fourteen stations of the cross are marked along the way (approximately one mile in length), where pilgrims stop and pray in commemoration of the Passion of our Lord. It is said that this devotional ritual grew from the tradition that Mother Mary similarly visited the scenes of Christ's Passion following his ascension. (2) Gen. 16; 17:15–22; 21:1–18; Gal. 4:22–31. (3) Dan. 5:25–28. (4) I Thess. 5:3. (5) **OPEC and the oil market.** Within two months after Archangel Uriel's dictation, oil prices plummeted 51% from $27.06 to $13.26 a barrel. This is a sharp contrast to the drastic increase of over 1,800% in oil prices from 1971 to 1981 in a market largely controlled by the powerful Organization of Petroleum Exporting Countries (OPEC) cartel. "Over the past decade," reported *Newsweek* on March 7, 1983, "OPEC engineered the largest transfer of wealth in history. It threw the economies of the industrialized countries into chaos, and brought some Third World nations to the brink of ruin. It contributed to the unmaking of two U.S. presidents, and left deep scars on an American psyche that took pride in self-reliance." OPEC was formed in 1960 by 5 nations—accounting for almost two-thirds of the world's proven oil reserves and 85% of its petroleum trade—whose stated goal was to stabilize prices through controlling oil production. Today OPEC consists of 13 nations (Saudi Arabia, Venezuela, Iraq, Iran, Kuwait, Qatar, Algeria, Indonesia, Libya, Ecuador, Nigeria, United Arab Emirates and Gabon). The first major price increase came in 1971 when 23 oil companies signed an agreement with OPEC raising the price from $1.80 to $2.18 a barrel. Shortly after the start of the 1973 Arab-Israeli War, OPEC raised oil prices to $5.12 and Arab producers imposed an embargo against the U.S. for supporting Israel. In January 1974, OPEC capitalized on the crisis and more than doubled prices to $11.65 a barrel. A gas shortage ensued—although some observers, such as Christopher Rand, have claimed that there never was a shortage and that the oil industry, despite public displays to the contrary, actually welcomed the embargo and profited from it (see Rand, *Making Democracy Safe for Oil* [Boston: Little, Brown and Co., 1975]). Following the 1979 Iranian revolution and resulting gas shortages, OPEC raised prices to an average of $14.59 a barrel. By May 1981 the average price was up to nearly $35. Steadily increasing oil prices had a number of negative economic consequences, including higher consumer prices and unemployment, and were a factor in the economic recession of the early '80s. In addition, banks, professing to be confident of high, stable oil prices, loaned billions to developing nations so they could meet higher oil prices, helping to create the so-called "debt bomb." Cartel prices are notoriously unstable, and by 1981 several factors—principally conservation, energy efficiency, use of alternative energy sources, and a global recession—combined to decrease demand, creating a surplus and gradually lowering prices. In 1983, Nigeria, burdened by heavy debt and other domestic problems, became the first nation to break ranks with OPEC and dropped its price $5.50 to $30 a barrel. OPEC then agreed to set prices at $29 per barrel, its first official price cut. Thereafter, oil producers competed for shares of a declining oil market and by 1986 all efforts to control the falling oil price deteriorated into an all-out price war. Some analysts think a sustained drop in oil prices will benefit the U.S., Japan, and other oil importers by stimulating their economies, creating new jobs, increasing productivity, and perhaps decreasing the U.S. trade deficit. But there are also potentially grave repercussions. International banks, which loaned billions while oil prices were high, face potential bankruptcy because of the inability of oil-exporting countries—such as Mexico, Venezuela, and Nigeria—to repay their massive debts, and bank failures could trigger a cataclysmic economic crisis. Knowledgeable Washington officials believe that the Federal Reserve would never let major banks fail. Rather, they would artificially create enough credit to cover the losses. This, however, would set in motion a cycle of inflation that would be a problem of the same magnitude as the debt. It has also been suggested that a war might be engineered in the Middle East by the U.S. in order to curb oil production and raise prices, and thereby maintain economic stability. **(6)** Ps. 24:1; I Cor. 10:26, 28. **(7)** Ps. 19:2. **(8)** Isa. 66:1; Matt. 5:34, 35; Acts 7:49. **(9)** Matt. 13:24–30, 36–43. **(10) Map of the City Foursquare.** The Ascended Masters have called North America the map of the 'City Four- square', the Place Prepared and the Promised Land for the reincarnation of the seed of Light of Abraham. The tribes of Judah and Benjamin and some Levites have reincarnated among the 'Jews'. The other ten tribes of Israel have reincarnated among the Gentile nations of Europe. The half-tribes of Ephraim and Manasseh, sons of Joseph, are peculiarly tied to the United States of America, Great Britain and the Commonwealth nations—i.e., the English-speaking peoples. However, neither term, *Jew* or *Gentile,* can be correctly applied to the seed of Light of Abraham, who descended from the Ancient of Days, Sanat Kumara. For those who are of the I AM Race, being endowed from on High by the Mighty I AM Presence with them, are correctly called **"Hebrew,"** or *Ibri* in Hebrew, meaning "one who passes over" (from the crossing of the Euphrates by Abraham, c.1950 B.C.). *Ibri* is possibly derived from the Hebrew *Eber,* which means "the other side" or "across," and may have also been used in reference to the descendents of the patriarch Eber. Abraham, who descended from Eber, is the first in the Old Testament to be called "Hebrew" (Gen. 14:13). Some scholars believe that the biblical word for Hebrew, *Ibri,* is equivalent to the Akkadian *Habiru,* or *Hapiru,* which is found in ancient texts (c.2050–c.1000 B.C.) throughout the Near East. The term *Habiru* denoted a social class of people who were "wanderers" or "outsiders" living a rootless existence. According to theory, the biblical Hebrews may have belonged to this larger class of rootless people and thus would have been referred to as *Habiru* by the more established groups of society. Some who are called 'Jews' and 'Gentiles' today are in fact the reincarnated seed of Light of the twelve tribes, and some are not. Thus, by their fruits we may know the true heirs of the promises, whose Light has now been scattered amongst every tribe and nation and race and religion on earth. And the Light-essence of their consciousness in the Law of the One is the sign of their spiritual inheritance as sons and daughters of the Most High God. **(11)** Matt. 5:13. **(12) Massacre in Rome and Vienna.** On December 27, 1985, a team of 4 terrorists burst into the Israeli El Al Airlines check-in area at Leonardo da Vinci Airport in Rome, hurling hand grenades and firing submachine guns at travelers and passersby. Minutes later, 3 terrorists attacked the El Al Airlines departure counter at Schwechat Airport in Vienna. A total of 19 people, including 5 Americans (one, an 11-year-old girl) were killed and more than 110 others wounded in the brutal assaults. According to eyewitness accounts, the terrorists fired "wildly and haphaz- ardly," spraying bullets into a nearby snack bar in Rome and into a hair salon in Vienna. Both attacks occurred in areas open to the general public where no security searches are conducted. On November 7, the Messenger, traveling from Rome to Paris on her European Stump, was at the very spot in Leonardo da Vinci Airport where the incident occurred. Evidence indicates that the terrorist teams were part of a radical Palestinian faction, the Revolutionary Council of Fatah, headed by Abu Nidal—reputed as possibly "the deadliest terrorist alive." Nidal and his group currently operate out of Libya and were reportedly retaliating against the October 1 Israeli bombing of the P.L.O. headquarters in Tunis, Tunisia, which killed over 70 people and wounded at least 100 others. While Israeli leaders vowed to avenge the airport massacres, the U.S. urged restraint, calling for international sanctions against Libya, and ordered Americans living there to leave. **(13)** Isa. 34; 61:2; 63:4–6; Jer. 46:10. **(14)** Joel 2:28–32; Acts 2:16–21. **(15)** Exod. 21:23–25; Lev. 24:17–21; Deut. 19:21; Matt. 5:38–42. **(16)** Exod. 3:5; Josh. 5:15; Acts 7:30–33. **(17)** Rev. 19:11–16. **(18)** Heb. 4:12; Rev. 1:16. **(19)** Rev. 2:9; 3:9. **(20)** Exod. 14:13. **(21)** Isa. 55:11.

Pearls of Wisdom®

published by The Summit Lighthouse

| Vol. 29 No. 17 | Beloved El Morya | April 27, 1986 |

Teachings from the Mystery School
VIII
Seeking and Finding the Mystery of Life
"I AM Ascending"

How good it is, beloved, to be with friends this night to contemplate the meaning of winter solstice, once the hour of my birth.*

Once I became the Light descending in the earth's darkest hour. Thus, it is good on the 29th of December to contemplate beyond the merriment of Christmas to the portent of Christ's birth for every soul. In each life, beloved, there is then a new hope—a new star of hope, a new reason for being, a new mystery to be discovered in the Christmas Rose.

For each one does descend a single shaft of Light from the Mighty I AM Presence to embody that portion of the Word without which the world should suffer indeed. The world suffers greatly today for want of the expression by sons of God of that single Light of the Word incarnate which they have come to represent, to master, to embody, and then to transcend.

When little children are not shown a path of seeking and finding[1] the reason for Being, when they are not even shown how to contemplate the mystery of the apple, is it not a pity? Looking at the apple, one cannot know the mystery it holds inside; one must cut open the apple to find the heart and the seed of life. And then, of course, the apple is no more. Then ask the child as you show him this mystery, "Can you find out the seed of Light in your heart without cutting it open?"

Thus, Life is a mystery that must be probed without destroying its heart and essence—not knife but spoken Word and

* El Morya was embodied as Thomas Becket, born winter solstice, December 21, 1118, in London, England.
Copyright © 1986 Church Universal and Triumphant, Inc.

prayer, mystical union, discovering the heart of Life without dissecting it. Let games be played, even guessing games—games of blindfolding, finding treasure, searching for Easter eggs and precious toys handmade. Children must have a sense of the quest, developing a mental dexterity, an understanding of the need to rely on intuition and inspiration and compass and the stars and so many signs that nature gives to the mariner.

Beloved ones, do not so easily give to the child the answer, for the answer is not important. It is the ritual of seeking and finding in all things—having to muster the will, having to have enough desire in the attainment of the prize to pursue. Thus, competition in life, in sports and games is useful to a point. For the desire to excel is truly the excellence of the first ray. And that excelling, beloved, is fired by love for the prize. And the prize becomes more precious and more precious as sights are elevated. And soon the prizes of this world no longer satisfy.

It is good to win the medals and the cups. It is good to show the point of winning and victory only to realize that having thus conquered, one need not conquer again but one is ready for spiritual heights. And one knows that with effort and commeasurement and the inner sensing of the nearness of the stars one can achieve the goal of immortality.

Thus, it is well to understand in training oneself or one's child not to make the hurdle too great or too little but to instill enough challenge that demands enough effort that in striving the soul will exceed its former position and discover a new unboundedness, a new penetration of the larger Self.

Thus explore. Thus discover. Thus be creative. Do not rest on yesterday's victories; they are not equal to the next challenge.

Thus, I begin to you my counsel of the new year with a single lesson from Maitreya's school on goal-fittedness. Fit yourselves well for the good use and exercise of the four lower bodies, the skills, potentials and talents that you have, always knowing that you are building parallel lines of force with an inner summoning and an inner adventure of the spirit that takes place beyond the body.

Beloved hearts, we rejoice to have this mighty swaddling garment of the blue sphere around the earth and you and our Messenger and activity.* We rejoice that the armour of the will of God is well known to you as warriors of the Prince of Peace. Therefore, we take this opportunity to announce a new course of study at Darjeeling—a preparatory course for entering the initiations of Lord Maitreya, a course conceived by us here in Darjeeling

* See Serapis Bey, Dec. 28, 1985, "The Descent of the Mighty Blue Sphere," *Pearls of Wisdom*, vol. 29, no. 15.

whereby you yourself can pace yourself and ready yourself not for a fearful encounter but for a joyous one, knowing truly, "Lord, I am ready. Receive me now into thy heart and inner sanctum."

Beloved, the age of fear and doubt is past. Let it go by, passing down the hill as a stream that moves on. It is the age of joy and light, the age of alchemy and freedom and a new expression of the effulgence of the Christ flame. This is a path of Love expanded in your hearts in song and winged prayer with the Mother, whose heart's call has reached us in Darjeeling with many plans for this year of expansion and cutting free those ten thousand times ten thousand of Maitreya's bands.

Seize and grasp and sense the wind itself of freedom that is upon you. Sense the will of God, the desperation of humanity, the determination of the Almighty, the willpower of the chelas and the Truth blazing, reflected from the armour of our knights. A blinding light comes back in the eye of the enemy as the Light itself deflects the arrows. Let the will of God probe deeply, expose then the dark deeds.

Four murderers came—one for each of my four lower bodies.[2] They were determined to put out the Light of myself. But I could only mock the evil in their eye and behold the risen Christ who gave to me and my heart such grace as to continue to minister to the people of Canterbury and the world.

Thus, I did not die in vain, as you have never died in vain. For life moves on, outwits and outsmarts the evildoer. And they themselves return to the scene of life so blank and charred and hollowed out, with scarce an identity to continue their folly. They are to be pitied, beloved ones, but never to be despised. Evil itself may be despised for a moment as the ruby ray utterly consumes and dissolves it. For the ruby ray is always a laser beam that goes forth by the intense Love of the one who is, therefore, perfectly able to meet the adversary in the way.

Our God is a consuming fire.[3] And this consuming fire is indeed Love. Love fulfills her purpose in many, many ways. Love, of course, is the most creative and ingenious element, for Love seeks many ways to comfort, to uplift, to instruct, and to rebuke.

Therefore, we call upon those who see in the will of God a means of mastery in the detail of the Law of the Cosmic Christ. Detail, then, is the will of God—a thousand-petaled blue lotus, the sunflower herself and the many seeds thereof. The will of God is fastidious and detailed. It is [you have] fourteen months to master a skill, a trade, a profession, to bring to the point of excellence that which you would love most to lay upon the altar of God—that achievement, that ability which you know will enable us through you to build the house of God, to bring light to many a house now in darkness, to deliver souls of lifelong addictions. And these addictions go on lifetime after lifetime.

I tell you, beloved, the miracles that God can work through you are a million times a million, sparkling, gemlike. Sending back to you from the sapphire of my heart fragments of rainbow rays, I have seen the miracles of God again and again. To live in the life of miracles as the capstone on the pyramid, as the emerald crystal of the All-Seeing Eye of God, one must build the sure foundation of God's will.

In going through the fourteen months of each cycle of the causal body multiplied by the white fire core, beloved, you then have come to the practical and physical light. It is a light of Capricorn, the highest of the sacred fire, most profoundly embedded in the earth. Thus, the white-fire/blue-fire sun of the God Star ever shines more brightly now, expanded and reflected through your auras.

It is a wondrous opportunity to decree for God-government in this nation, to implement Saint Germain's call for the judging of tyrants everywhere,* to call for the amplification of the will of God from the Sun and the turning back of any and all harm which this comet may portend.

Many things can be accomplished with the blue flame. You will discover these as you give the calls to the will of God, as you saturate your beings by going through the entire blue section of decrees until you can hardly bear the blue flame any longer and must swiftly turn to the violet for the transmutation of all resistance to that inner alignment with the sapphire crystal.

Oh, the joy of Hercules this night! And Amazonia is with us as they approach this altar, beloved, sealing then the dispensation [of the blue sphere] of the Logoi, of Serapis, and Alpha and Omega. Thus Archangel Michael sends intensified Light, and Surya and Cuzco.

We come for the strengthening of the pilasters and the insertion in the earth of electrodes of blue fire. Almost as you would place toothpicks to hold together a cake or a sandwich, so we insert in the earth, through layers of subterranean disturbances and pressures, giant electrodes of the will of God thousands of feet in length, having a diameter the width of this altar [25½ ft.].

These the Elohim and the four cosmic forces are placing throughout the planetary body for the holding steady of the earth in a time when her molecules and substances are being bombarded

---

* See Saint Germain, Oct. 13, 1985, "The Sword of Sanat Kumara: The Judgment of the Rulers in the Earth Who Have Utterly Betrayed Their God and Their People," *Pearls of Wisdom*, vol. 28, no. 50, pp. 589–91.

with discordant sound, with chemicals and pollutions, with anger and war, experimentation, abuse of every kind and the shedding of blood. These electrodes will assist, beloved, in the absorption by earth and her evolutions of the new etheric body earth received almost a year ago.*

Now come to the heart of Uriel Archangel, whose radiance as perfume yet wafts upon this altar. Come to the heart of Uriel and position yourself there through the trials and tribulations which must be faced and then swiftly passed through.

We will stand indeed as one body, never alone. To this end was the Great White Brotherhood founded. With this inner knowledge of the science of the Law of the One have you assembled, truly in the knowledge that the circle of One is the protection of your life and in the understanding that it is living bodies and lively stones[4] that make up this circle of Community that is called "church."†

And well it is that church might remain as an alabaster inner city of Light, unsullied by mankind's poor attempts to imitate the City Foursquare. So long as the Church Universal and Triumphant shall stand as the white cube in the earth, so long [shall] the open door for angelic hosts to step through the veil and souls to ascend [remain].

Let the borders of this Church Universal and Triumphant expand. But let not the standard be lowered. Let Lightbearers come and be educated here and in Darjeeling and at the Inner Retreat, at Maitreya's Mystery School, and be shown how they may meet a standard of excellence and the self-mastery of the sacred centers of Life.

O teachers who would serve with the World Teachers, come, then! Come to Darjeeling. Come with Kuthumi and Jesus and Djwal Kul and me. Come, as with Mother Mary we take you to a comprehensive sevenfold way of reaching souls of Light.

For there are hours in the day when one speaks through this chakra and other hours when one speaks through another. There is a time for intensity and a time for gentleness, a time for communication of science and another for quiet meditation. Life is a great rhythm and opportunity. And the receptivity is according to the hours and the light rays and the Central Sun itself. [And these things must be learned.]

There are so many secrets to the mystery of Life for you to discover, beloved ones, as you unfold before all the world the Lost Teachings of Jesus Christ. They have waited so long that they have forgotten that they are waiting. They know not what they are waiting for, for they have long been told that they know it all,

---

* See Sanat Kumara, Dec. 31, 1984, "A Dispensation of the Solar Logoi," *Pearls of Wisdom,* vol. 28, no. 6, p. 60.
† church, or *ekklesia* [fr. Greek *ek* 'out of'; *kaleo* 'to call']: community of called-out ones.

they have it all, and salvation, of course, is guaranteed. A most unfortunate set of circumstances.

We would not dash the cup of hope from the lips of the hopeful. But we would say, sometime, somewhere the children of the Light must put on the garments of maturity, become wise, concerned, serious and responsible in seeking the kingdom of God, being willing to pay the price and coming to the realization that the price indeed can be paid. It is payable. It is earnable. And this we teach by the measured cadences of striving, to which I have directed your attention.

The more hurdles a lifestream learns to jump over, the more he can meet the hurdle of infinity, which, after all, can be contained "on the head of a pin"—and therefore not quite so far to leap as you had once thought. If in the twinkling of an eye the last trump of the human consciousness may sound and its karma go down,[5] if in that same twinkling of the eye of God you can know yourself in the totality of a universal Mind, beloved ones, then is anything too hard for you, held in the bosom of the Lord Sanat Kumara?

Precious hearts, you are indeed reaching for an infinite goal. But it is not a receding one; it is ever drawing nearer. Death is not its door. But in this life you can behold and see what grandeur of cosmos you can contain while still wearing bodies of which those you now wear in this octave are the facsimile. I say "facsimile," beloved ones, because as your bodies become purified and charged with light, they appear to be physical even to yourself, but they are [becoming] more a part of the etheric octave every day. This is why your diet changes and why you call for [require] other substances as you learn to adjust the body, the light body, to the environment of the cities of the earth.

You *are* ascending, beloved. This is my message to you this day, because this was my realization at the altar of Canterbury Cathedral. I said to myself in the face of these whose darkness was so great as to be so unreal—I said to myself, beholding His glory as truly Saint Stephen did, "I am ascending. I am ascending to the heart of God. This is the meaning of it all. This is the meaning of it all."

Beloved, at least it was action. After all, I wasted away in France for any number of years. They had had good opportunity to rally to the cause of Christ. Thus the karmic law descended. God called me home and allowed the drama to be outplayed with a particular contrast of Light and Darkness so typical of winter solstice.

You see, they were left to face the tyrant king. And Henry

must live with himself and his image and the world. Karma decrees therefore, and karmic law, that when individuals reject the representative of the Christ—which for that moment I was before pope and king and France and England, and soon all the world—when that messenger is rejected, then the Light is withdrawn and they must then overcome the Darkness by their own devices, else be swallowed up by it.

When they reject the messenger of Light, then, they must go their way until they become surfeited in Darkness and finally [perchance] come to the point of that same love of the honor of God whereby the honor is preferred beyond a paltry existence in cowardice, dumbness, ignorance and silent infamy. Some have come around since that hour in the twelfth century. Today the hour is late. And I can tell you that some of them have not changed a whit.

Take it from my heart, beloved ones—take it from me. Let God save whom he will through you. Be nonattached concerning the conversion of those who will not be converted and whom the LORD himself desires not to convert. Do not be stubborn in determining who shall be saved by you. Save no man. Give God that grace, for he will do it better than all of your contrivances.

But be a crystal gem, a heart humble in Light. Be an example of joy and joy in the LORD's achievement through you. Go forth, then, and establish good order and God-government in this Community. Commit yourselves to harmony, good-neighborliness, helpfulness and brotherhood. For we do indeed help one another. Beware, then, of evildoers who creep in to take advantage of your charity.[6] For charity must be given to the heart of Light, not Darkness.

I, El Morya, with Hercules and Amazonia, place now three mighty dots upon this altar for the sealing of the triangle of God's will with Morya and Mother and Mark—and you yourselves, three by three by three: for each one of you two Masters above forming the triangle of being. Realize, then, that we gird the planet round in this configuration and a grid of Light whereby the electrodes connect the blue chain mail, anchoring the etheric body of planet earth, fastened then by three dots again and again.

Thus, raise your hands thus [in this manner] now. Take the hand of two Ascended Masters and feel the flow of the will of God—each one a mighty bodhisattva standing staunch above you to the left, to the right. You, then, become the cradle of the *V*, the lowest point that has descended. And the hands you clasp complete the sign of the *V* of victory in this fourteen-month cycle. They pull you up and they let you down again as you serve in the lowest octaves, and draw you up again to the etheric retreats and the inner glory of the City Foursquare.

Have I spoken in poetry? Have I sung to you in song? Know this, beloved, that you have heard by my voice mysteries of Maitreya preparing you for his initiation. Study the text of my message and call for its inner blueprint to be anchored in your etheric body until the particular forget-me-not message for your lifestream, hidden in the very blueprint of my dictation, is fulfilled and does come to pass as fruition of the first ray in your life.

Above all, seek the qualities of the first-ray Masters. Become them. Do not flinch. Be uncompromising when it comes to the will of God. And as for compassion, in that be tolerant, forgiving, and bending. The will of God is the structure of steely white light that is your life and house and tabernacle. If the foundation and super-structure, if the skeletal frame be not perfect, naught else can be according to the plumb line of Truth.

Thus, in all matters of discipline under the will of God, be precise in defining your freedom of speech, your freedom of the press, your freedom to assemble, your freedom of religion, your freedom and right to own property and to preserve the value of your sacred labor—your right to have the abundant Life. Be precise, beloved, for the first ray of God's will will surely draw you into God-Mastery if you will only allow our devas and Masters of the diamond heart to tutor you now in the will of God.

Receive now the blessing and transfer of Hercules and Amazonia, who will speak to you on the morrow. I have prepared your inner bodies to receive the greater Light of Elohim. Thus build and build again, and be ready. For surely they come with a power unequaled.

In the name of the adorable one, Jesus the Christ, I seal you in my heart's love forever. Forget me not.

"The Summit Lighthouse Sheds Its Radiance O'er All the World to Manifest as Pearls of Wisdom." This dictation by El Morya was **delivered** through the Messenger of the Great White Brotherhood Elizabeth Clare Prophet on **the feast day of Saint Thomas Becket, December 29, 1985,** during the 5-day New Year's conference, *Teachings from the Mystery School,* held at Camelot. During the service before the dictation, the Messenger taught on the life of Thomas Becket. Her teaching and El Morya's dictation are published on cassette B86010, $6.50 ppd. (1) Matt. 7:7, 8; Luke 11:9, 10. (2) On December 29, 1170, after years of conflict with King Henry II of England over the rights of Church versus State, Thomas Becket, Archbishop of Canterbury, was brutally murdered in his own cathedral by four knights who acted on the king's desire to be rid of "this turbulent priest." Becket, who had been noncompromising in his defense of the Church, had just returned from France where he had exiled himself for six years in protest of Henry's abuse of power. (3) Deut. 4:24; 9:3; Heb. 12:29. (4) I Pet. 2:5. (5) I Cor. 15:51–53. (6) Jude 4, 12. Copyright © 1986 Church Universal and Triumphant, Inc., Box A, Malibu, CA 90265. All rights reserved. Printed in the United States of America. Pearls of Wisdom and The Summit Lighthouse are registered trademarks of Church Universal and Triumphant, Inc. All rights to their use are reserved. Published by The Summit Lighthouse. Pearls sent weekly (to USA, via third-class mail) for a minimum love offering of $40/year.

Pearls of Wisdom®
published by The Summit Lighthouse

| *Vol. 29 No. 18* | *Beloved Hercules and Amazonia* | *May 4, 1986* |

Teachings from the Mystery School
IX
The Power of the Will of God

Most Gracious Ones of Light,

We, Elohim of the First Ray, have positioned ourselves in the Great Central Sun for some time recently, there to contemplate our mission concerning this fourteen-month cycle of the blue sphere.

We have meditated upon the heart of Almighty God, communing with the powers of Elohim, Alpha to Omega. We have deliberated the cycles of cosmos, of planetary systems, and of this peculiar planet as a crossroads for many lifewaves who have come from far distant stars. They have journeyed here in spacecraft long, long ago, bringing with them laggard evolutions, all sorts of their own scientific creations that have evolved and become the animal forms you see on earth. Others have become as the robotic creation—godless, appearing as men yet not as men of God.

We see, then, key individuals everywhere on earth. You might wonder why earth could be so important. It has become the point of assembly of individuals who were either the key to Light and the acceleration of their home planets or the key to Darkness and their degeneracy.

Thus, they have arrived, for earth affords many amenities not found so easily, having the physical plane in its adaptability to many types of evolutions. Therefore, the sons of Belial—that ancient one that came from another galaxy—the seed of Satan, another rebel who took pride in his relationship to Lucifer, and many others yet have representatives here, though they themselves have passed before the Court of the Sacred Fire and gone through the Final Judgment and the second death.[1]

Genetically their seed is sown among the tares. By willfulness, favoritism, desiring to be liked by these gods, mankind and even the sons of Light have taken unto themselves certain genetic combinations that have given to them a propensity for pride and ambition, which, beloved hearts, is indeed not their original portion but which must then be overcome by a conscious determination. It is as though the shoes were worn by a certain step or a certain leaning of the foot and now you would attempt to right it. But the shoes have been worn in the wrong way and so now it is difficult to correct the step.

I tell you, all things may come into alignment with the will of God by your desiring, by your determination, by your conscious willing. For Elohim are with you, no matter what your point of origin or descent or ascent. We are here, following the dispensation of Alpha and Omega that those who believe on the Christ of the One Sent may also receive by that power accorded unto that mantle the gift of sonship through the threefold flame.*

Line upon line is the way of self-correction on the path of the first ray. El Morya and the Darjeeling Council surely represent well the first initiations and the fruits thereof that bring you first to the heart of Archangel Michael and then to the retreat of Hercules and Amazonia.

We, therefore, stand in this sanctuary for a purpose. And we ask you now to stand with us in honor of the will of God and God's purposes in the thirty-three-year spirals being outplayed.†

Beloved ones, we come for the steadying of the earth. For Solar Logoi have said, beloved, that they will not hold back the fury and the wrath of the blue-flame will of God. For want of allegiance to this flame, the very outer coating and seal of the cells of the physical bodies have worn thin, are no longer of that cobalt blue energy and fire to reject the viruses of every kind that penetrate the cell for the decomposition of the body.

These Atlantean scientists come from other planets have indeed created viruses. But they have continued because of mankind's consciousness, flattering themselves to think that they get away with the ignoring of the will of God. Beloved ones, where there is a breakdown in this mighty will of God, systems in the body and in society begin to break down—buildings crumble, bodies decay, the death spiral sets in.

We are come now for the increase and release of Light of Elohim. O beloved, hear our call! We will not hold back. Thus the shaft of blue flame is upon you. Thus receive it now and see

*See Jesus Christ, Dec. 25, 1985, "Rise, Peter: Kill and Eat!" *Pearls of Wisdom*, vol. 29, no. 14, pp. 112–15.
† See 1985 *Pearls of Wisdom*, vol. 28, no. 45, p. 548, n. 10.

how this cosmic cross of blue flame is formed about you by angelic hosts of Light. Stretch forth your hands and feel yourselves free as a starry body, an ovoid of light and this cosmic cross.

Know, then, that the arms of the cross, as you stretch your arms in this manner, do reach into infinity. And ultimately the lines that go forth from your heart meet on the other side of cosmos. And you are a part of a mighty ring of light that as far as you are concerned is indeed infinite. In the same manner, that pillar of fire that goes vertically through you now does continue worlds without end. Following the magnificent curve, it also does meet on the other side of cosmos. Thus you may wrap this cosmos in the arms of Alpha and Omega and know that you contain, all inside of this sphere of identity of Elohim, universes and the kingdom of God, which is also in your heart.

Now be seated in rings of fire as we would speak to you of the urgency and the dangers of the blue ray. Beloved ones, it is an immense power we bear—a power which when we vest it in individuals makes them of all people most unwelcome. This Power of the will of God is an agitation. In fact, when you have seen it in the Messenger you have noted well that many people may not linger in the aura of the Messenger for too long. Sometimes an hour is enough. And when strangers come into her presence they often find an acceleration of karma, though they may not connect it with the encounter.

Beloved ones, I tell you a mystery. Were we to increase the power of Elohim which this office [of the Messenger] can contain and which this lifestream has attained to, it would result in dire circumstances for ninety percent of the chelas in this activity. For you are not ready for the full initiations of the blue ray. Therefore, you see, we must temper this blue ray to the shorn lambs.* But we advise you, beloved, that we desire to form a real and living molecule of a sun presence of the first ray and to do so at the Inner Retreat where the land is vast enough to contain the energy that we would anchor into the earth.

Beloved ones, we come to ask you to consider a more fervent chelaship on the first ray, to truly come to the understanding of being El Morya in manifestation, of being Lanello and Mother Mary—to truly increase that will of God with decrees and to be prepared for the backlash and for the challenge to meet it with violet flame and joy and not to allow the power of God to draw you into cycles of irritation or anxiety or anger or argumentation or misuse of the sacred fire.

For power is the most difficult equation of life.[2] It determines

---

*"God tempers the wind to the shorn lamb." Henri Estienne, *Les Prémices*, 1594.

who, then, is sinner or saint, who is of the Light and who is not. For those who receive a little bit often become potentates in their own fiefdoms and immediately encircle themselves as prince of the realm, sending this one here and this one there and being in control.

But this desire to be in control, beloved ones, is seated in fear. Even the chelas themselves desire in some way to control the Messenger for their own sense of security. This can become a stifling experience to the Darjeeling Council, who then cannot use the Messenger as they would use her but must bear also the burden of those who somehow by association determine that they will steal the Light rather than earn it. It all boils down to this, beloved ones: Some determine to become the Light; some find one from whom they can curry it with favors.

Blessed ones, the will of God is free. The will of God is Light. The will of God is *the* Power of cosmos. You can have it, for the source of your causal body is there. Let yourself, then, pursue it with a joy of excellence, as you have been told.

For this is what the Cosmic Council in the Great Central Sun has said to us: The dangers on earth of not having in full force the Power of the will of God outweigh the dangers of having it. Therefore, you see, civilization is bowed down because of the rejection of the pillars in the temple. "Pillars of Hercules"[3] refers to the shafts of the will of God and those who will embody that will.

Beloved ones, let the Messenger be our tree planted—planted by the waters of Life, bearing much fruit. And when you are able, you may pluck that fruit. When you do not desire it, you may leave it upon the tree. And sometimes you may find it ripe upon the ground. But let the tree increase. Let it expand. Let it bear fruit for you.

Precious hearts, it is most important that you realize that the power of the blue ray does incite condemnation and gossip, revenge, the desire to get even when the blessing is not forthcoming because the offering is not acceptable. Thus, you remember how Cain was wroth because his offering was not received by Lord Maitreya, though he worked very hard.[4] So this very lifestream and others of the same seed have arrayed themselves against this church in this hour.

And those lifestreams did come from other systems, along with Serpents, i.e., fallen angels. And therefore the evolution of Light and Darkness unfolded as a karmic necessity on earth. For once the Lightbearers had toyed with the delicacies and the delicious ways of the fallen angels, [the Law decreed that] they must thereafter walk in those ways [of their karma] until they should be surfeited and return to the point of the One.

In the justice of the ongoing cycles, then, we must tell you that the more among you who espouse the cause of the will of God and this path of chelaship, the less Darkness will come upon the earth and upon this activity, because by your chelaship we will increase this blue-flame electrode round about the Messenger and correspondingly in you. If your chelaship does not accelerate, you may suffer loss. You may be driven and sawn asunder by the Power of God's will. This will is the immensity of the fire of the nucleus of the atom, of all powers and Matter forces in the earth and the sea and the land.

Beloved ones, you are dealing not alone with spiritual power but physical power. And therefore we, the Elohim of the First Ray, are referred to as the most physical of all Elohim. For by our very ray we are attached to the physical earth and your physical bodies. And so it is true with Archangel Michael and El Morya and those who serve this ray of the will of God. Likewise, the false-hierarchy impostors of these divine offices are also very physical. Thus, Armageddon is physical, beloved, but the victory is spiritual.

Realize, then, that a certain increase of Light [as the Christ consciousness] will come day by day. The key, then, is to espouse the flame of the God Harmony. For through the nexus of this great Master you find, beloved, that you truly will balance the molecules of the blue flame, the electrodes, the light itself. And when you balance this Alpha light with the violet flame, as the Great Central Sun Magnet of violet flame and seventh ray, then you will know truly one step of blue, another of violet, one of blue and another of violet. And you will be surefooted on the upward-spiraling staircase toward that point of the eye of the lighthouse where your Light with ours may be a beacon to the world.

We must speak to you of Mighty Cosmos' secret rays, for these rays concern the initiations forged and won in the brain, through the hands, the feet, the glandular system and the nerves themselves. The secret rays surround the threefold flame of the heart. The violation of these rays is like the violation of the nucleus of the atom for destructive purposes.

Some men in this world, false pastors in Church and State, have made it their business to move against the Great White Brotherhood and this activity. They have employed everything from psychotronics, mind manipulation by psychic and mechanized means to voodoo, blood rites, black magic and Satanism to prayers of malintent, which they offer in their churches, and calls to Jesus to destroy this entire activity and especially its Messenger.

Beloved ones, when these energies come upon you and loved

ones, they always manifest as chaos, confusion, accidents—especially accidents to the head, the feet, the hands, and in the area of the spleen. For it is a misuse of those secret rays by the power of the spoken Word, which is our ray—the first ray and the throat chakra.

When you find yourselves out of sorts, when you find divisions entering the circle of Love, quickly remember that you have entered this sanctuary—some for the first time. By your free will you have put yourself in the presence of Elohim. You now carry a portion of the mantle of the Great White Brotherhood; and therefore, the prophecy is also upon you to be "despised and rejected of men" as every Christed one was and is.[5] For it is the men who love Darkness because their deeds are Evil who despise the Light and the Lightbearers.[6]

Blessed sons and daughters of God, when you come to the source and the fount of the Great White Brotherhood, know that you have come to the highest dispensation on the planetary body that has come to the physical octave. There are Masters and unascended Masters in the etheric plane. But the release of Light by the mantle we have placed here is not duplicated. We say this by way of transferring to you the understanding that when you go out from this altar drenched with the Light of the will of God, you must be prepared to meet that which is the antithesis of that Light and those individuals who have sworn enmity against that Light from the beginning. They have entrenched themselves around the world.

Therefore I speak in the name of Archangel Michael. And I say to all students of every language, your priority this year with this fourteen-month cycle of the blue sphere is indeed to quickly translate Archangel Michael's Rosary. And when you lecture and when you teach, no matter what the subject, you may not give a lecture again without telling the people that whatever else they do, the giving of Archangel Michael's Rosary is the sole and unique prayer that will protect their communities and nations from the Darkness that is projected by evil minds.

I am certain that you can see what would take place out of certain lifestreams in the Middle East were they to have absolute power in the physical domain. Blessed ones, with the sale of technology freely from this nation to Communist bloc nations, Red China, and with the stealing of those secrets that go even to the Middle East, it is only a question of time until the forces of the abuse of power on earth may consider that they do indeed have the power to take on the nations of the West.

Beloved ones, remember that many lifestreams not of the Light who are the laggard evolutions have made a suicide pact to please their overlords, who promise them eternal Life when they give their life up in acts of terrorism. Is there any difference between terrorism—the throwing of bombs and grenades and the murder of innocent life—and the delivery of a nuclear weapon of any sort? It is only a question of degree and a sense of power.

Thus, when the power of God descends, be mindful that all the way from the anti-chela and the anti-Guru to the powers that be in the world to the disenfranchised ones who have not a threefold flame, there is a lusting after the Light and ultimately the willingness to commit suicide that those who have the Light may not continue their evolution.

They are as a web of Darkness. They are almost as microbes forming a net. It does not matter to them if some of the cells, some of the components of their conspiracy are no more. What they desire is the perpetuation of the false hierarchy itself and the consciousness of anti-God across the galaxies.

Let me tell you, beloved ones, that those key individuals who have come—and come to earth and been here millions of years and now approach the hour of their Judgment—they, then, must be bound and taken by the mighty archangels because, beloved, with them goes [there can be taken] the very core of the [false hierarchy of the] initiation of Evil on their planetary home or system.

This is why earth is a crossroads. This is why you have been given the various types of Judgment calls. For you have been a part of the Judgment of lifestreams.[7] And the reaction to that Judgment has been literally the liberation of worlds whose evolutions have known the source of that call [to be from the Lightbearers sojourning on planet earth] and who have sent praise and joyous shouts and gratitude to your hearts.

When you consider these dimensions, beloved ones, do you not understand that you also are a primary target? And therefore, you cannot afford to let down your guard *ever*. Let this entire movement swell with prayers and dynamic decrees during the upcoming playing out of the court cases and lawsuits that have beset the Church and the Messenger for a number of years.

Immediately following this conference these actions must be taken and decided. And therefore, let your prayers be to Alpha and Omega and to us, the Elohim, to the archangels and the Darjeeling Council to overshadow the trials, the courtroom and all those involved with the intensity of the will of God. For the will of God only is the solution to every problem of human entanglement and burden. Count it all as the lessons of life, the experience that is gained and thereby the mastery attained.

Beloved ones, your point of prayer and intensity is indeed necessary, for these individuals, appearing average, are not average at all. But they do represent key forces and other planes whence they have come. And therefore, much depends on the acceleration of the Judgment of the powers of Darkness that would use them and retain them as tools for as long as possible. We seek, then, a divine resolution in all things, that you might be liberated to be pillars of fire in the temple of our God.

We are accompanied now by great teams of conquerors and blue-lightning angels who will perform a service on earth while you stand and sing to the God Harmony. [number 467 sung]

The Light of the will of God must come! It shall descend! Let earth prepare, for the Light will right the four lower bodies of the planet. And those who will transcend the age are those who will be found in the heart of God Harmony, in the eye of the will of God.

O vortex supreme of the Central Sun, fiery whirl, descend! Now come upon earth. And we as Elohim say, then, with Morya, "Let the chips fall where they may!" For earth has a destiny. And a cosmic spin now is inaugurated by our presence here. And that new spin will be felt over the next century, subtly, for the righting now of the turning of a weary world.

Blessed ones, the impelling of the Light is up. Take no chance and delay, for the delay may cost you everything.

We convey our desire, our support and our best wishes for your victory in the Light of God's will in the new year. May you understand that we have played our part and shall continue to do so. But now, beloved, your victory is entirely up to you. The responsibility is upon your shoulders. Wise is the man, woman or child who identifies with the inner Christ and lets the government of his life, nation, and planet be upon those shoulders, capable, of the Lord Christ.[8]

In the name of the cosmic cross of white fire of Alpha and Omega, I seal you in your cosmic destiny! May you reach for it, seize it, and run!

"The Summit Lighthouse Sheds Its Radiance O'er All the World to Manifest as Pearls of Wisdom." This dictation by Hercules and Amazonia was **delivered** through the Messenger of the Great White Brotherhood Elizabeth Clare Prophet on **Monday, December 30, 1985,** during the 5-day New Year's conference, *Teachings from the Mystery School,* held at Camelot. (1) Rev. 20:6, 14; 21:8. (2) See *A Trilogy On the Threefold Flame of Life: The Alchemy of Power, Wisdom and Love,* in *Saint Germain On Alchemy: For the Adept in the Aquarian Age,* Summit University Press, pp. 267–85; $4.95 postpaid. (3) **Pillars of Hercules.** Two opposite promontories at the eastern entrance to the Strait of Gibraltar, said to have been erected by Hercules during his journey to capture the oxen of the monster Geryon (his 10th labor). (4) Gen. 4:1–7. (5) Isa. 53:3; Mark 8:31; Luke 17:24, 25; John 15:18–21; I Cor. 4:9–13. (6) John 3:19–21. (7) Matt. 19:28; Luke 22:28–30; I Cor. 6:2, 3. (8) Isa. 9:6.

Pearls of Wisdom®

published by The Summit Lighthouse

Vol. 29 No. 19	Beloved Lord Maitreya and Arcturus and Victoria	May 11, 1986

Teachings from the Mystery School
X
"I Draw the Line!"

Let Light dissolve this core of rebellion in every chela![1]

I, Maitreya, stand before you. And I challenge you to enter the true heart of hearts of your being. I demand that you see and know this dweller on the threshold standing in the door—because *you* allow it.

The doorway to higher consciousness has been opened by me and by your Holy Christ Self. But the tempter remains with arms folded, daring you to slay that dragon of the human will that continually overrides that which you *know* to be the Truth of your homeward path. And you allow it by continual rationalization.

Therefore, we cannot go forward with the Teachings that will empower you truly in the tradition of the Buddha unless you begin to take seriously what we say in dictation and message and lecture and understand that we are building before your very eyes the pyramid—the mighty pyramid of *your* Life. It is a great pyramid, having many stones. In fact, the pyramid of Egypt, beloved, is the size you should visualize as the structure of your own mastery in Matter.*

Ask yourself this question: How many stones may I leave out or remove and still retain the structure? As in any building, some may be taken. People may come and take souvenirs from your house of light. But if you omit the precepts and the instructions, you will find that we may not build the next level with you.

This building has come as a spiral from the beginning. In the 1950s, through the first messages through Mark Prophet, we determined in council in Darjeeling to bring through the dictations, the

---

* The Great Pyramid at Giza, Egypt, built 2600s B.C., 755 ft. per side at the base (13 acres), originally 481 ft. high.

Pearls of Wisdom, and all of our communications, beloved ones, *every stone required* for a graduate of earth's mystery school.

There are two mystery schools in earth—one on the outside, one on the inside. Those who are on the outside must figure out life's mystery by toil and many incarnations and, hopefully, insight gleaned from some experience. Those who enter the inside mystery school come to the very heart of the sun in the center of the earth, come to the very heart of that spiritual light and a universe all inside themselves.

Thus, beloved, I teach in the inner mystery school. I give on the outer ample keys to you who assemble and will build the Inner Retreat as your performance of the building of the pyramid of Life, even as we build this pyramid with you in the etheric octave.

The keys that I give cannot be interpreted until obedience is given. Therefore, beloved, listen well. We have accelerated the release of dictations that you might pass through those spirals. They are not too many to listen to. The *Only Mark* albums[2] are [contain] the very keys and steps essential to the Messenger's ascent as he bore world karma and therefore must bear the Light of the Brotherhood to transmute, to nullify, to put down the tempter at every hand.

One day another will come, and through all of these dictations [that one will] also find a code that tells quite another story of the soul's ascent. For you see what has already happened as with the release of this much Truth the persecution has descended upon your Messengers. But the new day shall appear, beloved, when Lightbearers, free of the grips of the toilers and their own subservience to their own rebellion, will find that those keys will unfold and that there will be greater and greater gifts of Teaching when those who are the lively stones[3] of this edifice of the entire Community can better hold the Light and the will of God.

I, Maitreya, come to you, therefore, to take full opportunity of these fourteen months for the protection and the perfection of the will of God within and without—Omega, the outward sign of our coming, and Alpha within. You find yourselves on the surface of the earth even as you find yourselves on the surface of your minds and bodies. But the journey to the heart of hearts is one to which I call you. Therefore know that the foundations laid may be traced by you. And it does not take many years to go through these publications but a diligent attention and a systematic self-assignment of daily reading.

I speak to you who have failed to listen to this call through the Messenger to become who you indeed are as both a spiritual

leader and one who sees himself moving toward the building of
the Inner Retreat:

I, Maitreya, *demand* that you ascend to your mantle and *cease*
your argumentation and resisting of the Call! Therefore, if those
who are chosen do not receive me, shall we go after the not-chosen
ones and anoint them when you reject the anointing?

Do not think that this is another dictation intended for someone else. It *is* intended for you! And no one can carry the physical
burden of this activity in any capacity whatsoever, small or great,
who is not willing also to wear our mantle. One is not a substitute
for the other.

Therefore I say to *you*, let the dweller at the door of the house
be bound! Let the resistance to the inner walk with Saint Francis
be bound! And let this movement move forward because there is a
purging, self-instituted, and a new willing for the new year!

You cannot forever postpone the Day of Reckoning. If you
do not accept the spiritual mantle, your karma will fall! I not only
predict it, I decree it! And no cause is so great as to make anyone
the exception to the path of our initiation. If you would stand at
the gate of the Inner Retreat and welcome the Lightbearers, then
stand also at the altar with the Mother and play your role, city
after city and nation after nation.

Beloved hearts, let no one who hears my word consider that
I am not speaking to *you*. For of all mistakes you could make, it is
the one of pointing the finger at another and saying, "I know of
whom Maitreya is speaking."

If the world has waited so long for the return of my path and
if an entire continent went down through the rebellion of the
fallen angels against the Buddha and the Mother on Lemuria, do
you not think that one of the reasons that we have indeed withheld this manifestation is not only because of the fallen ones but
because of the absence of seriousness on the part of the chelas and
their commeasurement to realize just what is at stake?

You are tired of the oppositions, the financial lack, the legal
problems, and all things that beset this organization. I say, take your
mantle and go as Elisha did[4] and part the waters of the Yellowstone
and see how Saint Germain will appear to you! And you will have
those experiences, because you are so determined—the experiences
which Godfre and Lanello and your own Mother have had.

Blessed ones, it is indeed an event. And thousands upon
thousands of Buddhists and other Lightbearers have waited for
this opportunity of my opening of the Mystery School. Yet so few
have understood the darkness of the false-hierarchy impostors

who say, "Lo, Maitreya is come here. He is come there. He is in embodiment. He is giving messages through me."

Beloved ones, I tell you, I have inspired upon the Messenger this lecture on the sugar entity because it is one of the greatest, if not *the* greatest threat. Coming through ignorance, this tempter causes the mind to rationalize and to say, "I need this for my disposition or my happiness or my reward."

Beloved ones, now you know, and you will know much more. But I tell you this—let my chelas who will come with me to the heart of the mountain now forsake this substance of the world. And consider now, as you remove yourself from the arena of all substances of sugar of any form—think of all these things of this outer world of which you will now not be a part, and you will have some sense of the withdrawal to the inner sanctum of the Holy of Holies.

You cannot have the world and the Mystery School as well. The world has come for the killing of the Buddha and then made it into a faddish philosophy.

O beloved, Serpents come again—their wares are the same. Go forth in my name and slay the beast of socialism! Its stench covers the vast landed areas of the earth. Its pollution is everywhere. It threatens the very fiber of this nation. How is it aided? It is aided by the sugar entity that makes people helpless as vegetables. And the sugar entity says through them, "Take care of me. Take care of us. We demand it."

O beloved, I tell you, the sickness and disease that mounts in America would be reduced 50 percent if processed sugar were withdrawn. I say only 50 percent because there are other karmic causes. But, beloved ones, with a 50-percent reduction and the fine-tuning and awareness of the people and their ability to grasp then, with minds full of light, the Path and the Teaching, the other 50 percent would go down by violet-flame transmutation and by planetary exorcisms such as you have engaged in this night.

All right, beloved. Look at that dweller on the threshold now. He is *shriveling* because I, Maitreya, stand before you and because you are awake! And you are seeing that dweller of rebellion and resistance to the Truth of your holy office for the liar that he is! And therefore, I come now to withdraw the energy vested in that dweller. And you by enlightenment finish the task. For it is your free will—*your* life, *your* door, *your* ascension.

And I, Maitreya, will not leave off from probing to the very core of your being! And my angels are fiery spirits and they come with a yellow fire that you cannot even imagine. It penetrates and uncovers and exposes. And if this is what you want from the Mystery School, this is what it portends.

And let all those who want some flattery for their egos and psychic talk of nonsense—let them go out, let them find the false gurus! For I, Maitreya, will stand with those who are determined to conquer self and conquer the dark ones in the earth and who are still determined with Saint Germain to make earth Freedom's star!

Beloved of the Light, my twin flame is present. I ask you to stand in honor of the glorious being of Light who is my divine complement. Thus the aura of my feminine counterpart does expand and expand and expand.

And this Shakti of Light therefore does continue to propel the incisiveness of the yellow fire into the brain, into the chakras, into the crown thereof, so that the enlightenment of all of the seven rays may come to you and so that those who are on the blue ray may understand that in the heart of that ray is the multiplication of the threefold flame. And therefore, we would not have you remain solely activators of good. But we would draw you who are the first-ray ones now into that Mind of the Buddha, who indeed has the God-Mastery of the entire Trinity and all complements of rays, secret and outer.

Beloved ones, illumination is a power to be contended with. Civilization is moved by ideas when conveyed correctly, and these ideas are for the conversion of souls. Thus, the Holy Spirit uses the power of the divine reason—and not the human—the logic of the Word, the understanding.

And you must pray to the Holy Spirit for the gift of understanding, the gift of wisdom and of knowledge—wisdom of the Spirit, knowledge of Matter. And you must pray for the means of conversion by enlightenment. And you will see that Americans, Germans, British, Australians, Russians—all desire the conversion of enlightenment!

The world is waiting for Maitreya and Maitreya's co-workers and servants. And they are also waiting for my twin flame, whom they know not. Thus, out of the octaves of nirvana she has descended in a golden orb of Light. And you will see how this presence of my beloved will multiply my action in your behalf.

Now see the great teams of conquerors. You have called to them. They are here! And if you see them not, watch how you will develop your spiritual senses by divorcing yourself from the world of drugs and sugar and marijuana and alcohol and nicotine.

Beloved, I long to see you free, and *we are determined!* And the Presence, then, in this golden sphere of causal body of Light of my beloved does arc the very presence of the Lady Master Venus in that

Retreat of the Divine Mother unveiled over the Inner Retreat,[5] so that Camelot, in this City of the Angels of the Christ and the Buddha, shall have that ray and that Light of my divine counterpart.

And you will know the Truth of Maitreya. And you will receive the initiations individually from my heart daily if you but inscribe, then, a separate letter to me this New Year's Eve addressed to your Mighty I AM Presence and Holy Christ Self, to me and to my beloved twin flame.

Then, beloved, you may apply to become my chela, my initiate. And watch well, for I AM determined to accept almost as many who call upon me, rather to give you the initiations and let you eliminate yourselves rather than I eliminating you without giving you a clean white page in 1986 to begin anew where you left off on Lemuria.

And I tell you, you did leave me in Lemuria and I come to claim you again! And you may determine to move forward, for I will bring you to that point of the union, whether inner or outer, of twin flames as only my office can accomplish. For it is my office that was violated by twin flames, and therefore through me you must receive that reuniting.

Thus, beloved, understand that wherever there is the beloved presence of Sanat Kumara and Lady Master Venus, there I AM. There I AM as heart filled to deliver their Light, as they have taught me forever and taught also Lord Gautama and Jesus and Kuthumi and all who have come to the union of the I AM THAT I AM.

Blessed ones of the Light, you must realize that the entire Spirit of the Great White Brotherhood is ready to cover the earth with this Teaching through you. We therefore are determined to make good your word and commitment by giving you the initiations. I pray that you will pray for the vision to see exactly what they are and to proceed with all due care and carefulness, which is indeed the virtue of the Goddess of Liberty. In carefulness, therefore, watch and pray.

I have come for the stripping action. And you ought to see your own fierceness of soul and your Holy Christ Self expressing through you the shriveling of that dweller as I speak, for I hold the balance. And when you are in an Ascended Master dictation, that being is holding for you a tremendous balance!

There is no greater time for surrender and inner determination than when we are present with you in the very room itself. And you then can go full force to tackle these substances and know you are protected in our auric spheres. And if you would continue to seal it by decrees thereafter, you may remain for the maximum blessing and victory which every dictation can afford you.

Now multiply this by all the dictations that have come forth and see how step by step, daily, hourly, monthly, weekly, yearly, you can go over those steps and receive the blessing, challenge the darkness and move on. And it does not take all day, for you will build a momentum, beloved ones. You will develop new capacities to absorb the Word and the spoken Word and the written Word. And you will even come to the place that before you read or listen to the Word the ideas will already be manifesting in consciousness, and as you read them you [will] find that you have already been assimilating them, whether out of the body or during sleep or just preceding the picking up of that volume.

Beloved ones, we do not set before you an arduous task but the straightest and shortest walk to God-Mastery and God-Victory which, when it comes upon you, you will see in this activity of Light an increase of members by Love, by a wall of the ruby ray such as has already been given you,[6] and by the action of the Light to repel all adversaries before they even begin to conceive of the plot of the sinister force against you!

This is the way this citadel of freedom must be guarded. *This* is the way an activity of the Ascended Masters must come to pass. *This* is the way the Great White Brotherhood desires to see their chelas function on earth, beloved ones.

We do not see you as toilers, burdened, then, by the tempters and the fallen ones. We see you as God-victorious! Now let us solve the old problems, and let us see you free and joyous, dancing on the hills, rejoicing and singing together all over Camelot, all over the Royal Teton Ranch. Let joy become the very miracle to repel all darkness.

And let there come upon the earth a fear and a silence before the hosts of the Lord assembling as Ascended Masters and cosmic beings. And know, beloved, that the earth has never been more ready for this message. And therefore, do not allow your own inability to move as quickly as the Lightbearers [who are] beyond these walls make you procrastinate in delivering that full message.

And I say to those who say that the world is not ready for Saint Germain and the violet flame, you have no power! And you will indeed reap the karma of your false prophecies and your psychic predictions, when you could have been the mouthpiece of Saint Germain himself in the liberation of people. You have rejected the decisions of the Great White Brotherhood and their timetable, and therefore they have rejected you!

Hear my word, beloved. The world *is* ready for Saint Germain and the violet flame! And I, Maitreya, am his chief promoter and exponent. And I demand that my chelas join me, that the world might know this great God of Freedom and be swept up in his very robes of Light.

So I have made my demand. It is not a request. It is not a suggestion. I draw the line. Let all enter who *will* and who will *love* and who will *be* all that they have been taught to be.

I love you with the intensity of the first ray of the will of God. Therefore let our Messenger *be!*

Beloved Arcturus and Victoria

Ho! Did you think we were finished?

Well, we of the seventh ray shall have the last word.

We, Arcturus and Victoria, place our seal upon you and our commitment of the violet flame that you may tackle these very entities so named and do so in the name of Saint Germain, that we may look forward to a victorious January 1, 1986, for beloved Saint Germain as our hero and the Master of the Aquarian age.

So there is yet time to give that action of the violet flame to complete all that the Lords of Karma require. This, then—may it be our last word on the subject of this responsibility that we have mutually taken on in the name of the God of Freedom.

So, we, Arcturus and Victoria, would sing to Saint Germain the "I Love You Waltz," that cosmos might be bathed in the twin causal bodies of the hierarchs of Aquarius.

["I Love You Waltz," number 237, sung to Saint Germain and Portia.]

"The Summit Lighthouse Sheds Its Radiance O'er All the World to Manifest as Pearls of Wisdom." These dictations by Lord Maitreya and Arcturus and Victoria were **delivered** through the Messenger of the Great White Brotherhood Elizabeth Clare Prophet on **Tuesday, December 31, 1985,** during the 5-day New Year's conference, *Teachings from the Mystery School,* held at Camelot. **(1)** Before the dictation, the Messenger delivered teachings from Maitreya on **sugar and hypoglycemia**—a disorder caused largely by the high percentage of sugar and refined starches in the diet, affecting an estimated 20 million Americans. Her lecture included a videotape exposé on sugar, *Sweet Nothing,* hosted by Diane Allen (Westinghouse Broadcasting and Cable, Inc.; producer J. C. Anderson), and instruction on: the symptoms of hypoglycemia; the various forms of sugar, including honey, fructose, maple syrup, molasses, and corn syrup; the identical assimilation by the body of "natural" and refined sugars; the advertising industry's programming of consumers to desire sugar; hidden sugar content; the relationship between sugar and nutrient deficiencies, hyperactivity, and criminal behavior; and how to treat hypoglycemia by avoiding sugar in all forms and regulating protein/carbohydrate intake. **(2)** The *Only Mark* series begins with the final dictation given through the Messenger Mark L. Prophet, February 18, 1973, and continues in descending order to 1958 to include every Ascended Master dictation released through him. Twelve albums (four 90-minute cassettes each) published to date, $26.00 ea. postpaid. **(3)** I Pet. 2:5. **(4)** II Kings 2:13, 14. **(5)** See Sanat Kumara, December 15, 1985, "The Retreat of the Divine Mother at the Royal Teton Ranch," 1986 *Pearls of Wisdom,* vol. 29, no. 10, pp. 70–72. **(6)** See Mother Mary, December 25, 1985, "Love's Revolution," 1986 *Pearls of Wisdom,* vol. 29, no. 12, pp. 87–89.

Pearls of Wisdom®

published by The Summit Lighthouse

| Vol. 29 No. 20 | The Beloved Great Divine Director | May 18, 1986 |

Teachings from the Mystery School
XI
The Call of the Central Sun

There is a star shining, beloved—the single star of your Christ-Reality.

I am in the blue sphere of my causal body of Light. As I am known [as] the Great Divine Director, an office accorded me by the Almighty One, I am a part of the radiant light rays descending as the will of God, as divine direction for the implementation of that will descending from each one's own star of cosmic Christhood.

The star of your causal body burns brightly tonight in the darkness of cosmos, in the void, throughout all Matter spheres. It is the causal body of the Sons of God that illumines the worlds. Think of the blackest night and know that when your causal body does appear, a whole town or state or planet may be illumined. Is this not a joy to know that you—in and as God—can therefore bestow upon every part of Life coming to the dawning and yawning realization of Selfhood some morsel of identification with the Infinite?

Thus, the physical stars are positioned (as you understand) as the outer manifestation of great causal bodies of Light of cosmic beings, a reminder to evolving souls that a point of relationship with the Divine One does truly exist and that because there is a commeasurement, an awareness within the soul of the point of Life, there is an inner recognition of a goal, a path—even a universal Brotherhood. For the manifold stars sing of a unity of purpose and design.

Therefore, beloved, without organized religion, but solely upon the principle of the love fire of the divine spark within, the evolving soul may begin to equate with Elohim. And the sense of distance does portray to the soul that there is a path and an over-coming, and a quest for the mastery of time and space and forces [that must be pursued] in order for the soul to reach that star.

Now, some have developed science to the place where the journey to the stars physically has become possible. But, beloved, they are yet going from point A to point B of the physical uni-verse. Thus, after long evolution in the science of Matter, one desires to part the veil, to scratch through the canopy of the heaven to see what is on the other side of the roof of the sky and the star itself. Indeed, many are curious to see the other side of the moon.

Therefore, beloved, there is inherent in the soul who has come from a Spirit cosmos far beyond all of this magnitude the desire to return to a spiritual Sun and a Being. Tasting the ulti-mate of love in this world and life, one only knows that one has not even begun to taste of the Love that is beyond, that is the source of the cup which one drinks in joy, in the fragile moment of Love's embrace that one would keep for eternity but that one can only keep for eternity if one will mount the spiral of Love and pass through the barriers into a space undefined, infinite and yet without time.

Beloved ones, the known is a comfort, but the unknown becomes a source of fear from which men may cringe and say, "I will take my way and life. Let me postpone to another day this probing, this voyage of discovery into the infinite Mind of God." And thus, in the long history of this planet a certain superstition, a social custom, that which is accepted as norms of activity, et cetera, has almost been a means of insulating souls and humanity and civilization against going beyond the wall—the wall that is built around the town to protect it from invad-ing marauders or enemies.

Somehow, had God not defined the bounds of man's habi-tation,[1] man himself should have drawn a limited circle about himself to contain his fears, to keep them under control so as not to have to think about his responsibility and his own beingness in the vast beyond that seems cold on a winter's night. Thus, he returns to the fire of the hearth and may be at peace and abide there for many centuries until he is confronted, as you are today, with conditions upon earth which truly trouble the hearts of little children.

There is, in fact, nowhere to hide, no cave so removed that it cannot be touched by pollution or nuclear war or astral hordes or false hierarchies who prey upon the Lightbearers. "Where shall we go, Lord? Thou hast the words of eternal Life."[2]

Ah, and then the soul begins to say to herself,

Nowhere may I go on earth or in this vast physical cosmos, nowhere may I go and be any closer in physicality to the infinite heart of Love. Where I am is the All. And when I am the All, I am neither in heaven nor in earth, nor in China or New York, for I am in the Holy of Holies of God where I am.

And thus, the soul may think to herself,

This planet earth with all of her problems—I might just as well perch here as anywhere, for the testings of soul would be the same and my absence of mastery would be no better, no less if I were suddenly removed with lightning speed to another planet across space.

And so it begins to dawn—the inner cosmos, the inner nucleus that has to do with the secret chamber of the heart and the cosmic interval that seems so tiny as physical dimension but is as vast as the Macrocosm.

Meditate upon your heart. See there the image of Buddha in meditation alway upon thy soul. Thus, in all of her musings and contemplated voyages and all decisions as to what to do here and there, the soul returns to the sense,

The whole vast Matter cosmos is a cage—confining, defining Life, yet in limitation. I am now ready, as the bluebird of happiness, to fly from this cage.

I have no fear. I AM the Knower and the known. That which is beyond that is cause of all that I have become here below must truly be ready to receive me. For if indeed this physical cosmos is a reflection, a negative manifestation of the divine polarity, then I should only find a more real, a more solid, a more permanent peace.

How can I fly beyond the roof of the sky? I must learn, then, complete adjustment of molecules of light of my own mind. I must understand that to pass through this nexus I must, of course, first find the pinprick. In all of cosmos, somewhere there must be a pinprick that I can pass through! So I will find it, and I will travel now the circle of the figure eight. I will pass over that in mind and heart and meditate upon the acceleration of sacred fire.

I will not only raise the light of the Mother within me, I will dance in the fountain of her light. I will become that light! I will swirl within it until I can absorb fully the intensity of the Light. For I know that somewhere this rising fountain passes from the negative polarity of Matter to the Spirit plus-polarity that gave that manifestation.

Thus, each day I will be the Mother's athlete. I will be the runner. I will learn to absorb more light. I will breathe deeply and take in the oxygen that is the carrier of light.

I will meditate upon the Word. I will know the science of sound and of mantra. I will let my gaze rest upon the yantra of the Buddha. *OM MANI PADME HUM. OM MANI PADME HUM.* Oh, I AM that jewel in the heart of the lotus! How magnificent! It is indeed the elusive crystal of Spirit.

I AM THAT I AM. I will follow the sound and the call of the Central Sun. I will listen now in the inner ear. I will cut off the senses from all of this turbulence of outer noisome pestilence. I will begin to attune with the movement of my heart and beyond its beating find the heart of the bird and the heart of angel, the heart of Elohim.

I will gaze upon the sun of Helios and Vesta with my inner eye, and I will then create a spiral, an undulation. And I will not go up and down the sine wave but I shall cut straight through as an arrow. In my meditation I will pass through the Central Sun of this system of worlds and back again in elliptical orbit. I can do this, for I AM the One.

I may know all the joys of this life placed here for my commeasurement with Love, but I may simultaneously and without fear build ring upon ring of my causal body here below as is above. I can enter the secret rays by the call to Mighty Cosmos. I am only conditioned to mortality. It has never been my reality.

I am standing now in the center of the Sun even as I stand upon the altar before the altar of the Holy Grail. Lo, I AM here and I AM there. I AM Mother and I AM Child, I AM Father and I AM Son, held forever in the embrace of Holy Spirit's cloven tongues of fire.

Now I climb the sunbeam back to the heart of the blue sphere. I hear in that ray of light the sound of the Great Divine Director. I am commensurate with the vibration of the will of God, and now I see how that will translates through Mother as surefooted divine direction. I may leap in the high mountains with those sheep and goats who know the way. I am so sure that my step is the step of

God, for I AM in the heart of the Great Divine Director.

Thus, I know no confinement. I gladly accept this opportunity, O God, to myself. Roll up as a scroll the record of every life that has ever been lived in mortality—subhuman, sinful, unaware, asleep. All these records can no longer be a part of myself, for I AM WHO I AM. I AM the living presence of Love where I AM. I have tapped the eternal fount. I have sailed to Venus.

But, O beloved, O beloved, when the worlds are known above and below, the worlds are become one where you are. Matter is not bereft of Spirit; Spirit is not bereft of Matter. Entering the eye at the point of the pinprick, then, you are in the center of the T'ai Chi.

In the sound of the Word accelerating, the great sun disc begins to spin. And the spinning of the T'ai Chi is the sign that I and my Father, I and my Mother are One. The oneness is the envelope in which I dwell—a pressed flower, an immortelle. I can be anywhere in God, for I have come to the nucleus of his will that is the blue-fire sun of divine direction.

O beloved Great Divine Director, now I know thee as thou art. For I have also passed by the way of thy soul's mounting to that blue starry body that I see in the heavens.

O Great Divine Director, come, now. Be the All of me as I AM the All of thee.

Thus, beloved, you have traced with me as I have traced the path of a chela moving from the will of God to its divine direction. Truly the Mother releases, as she is the Shakti, that which is the blue sphere of my attainment. Thus, the feminine part of myself, which you may also see portrayed somewhat in this facsimile,[3] is that which ties you in and keys you to your footsteps on earth in a very concrete step-by-step manner.

When you pray for the will of God and you feel saturated by it, you may still say, "But I do not know which way to go. I am in love with the will of God. I feel the fiery blueprint and the ruby crystal. I am a part of that eternal Light. Lo, I AM THAT I AM! But now, which way may I turn? Are my choices being made based on limitation? centuries, millennia of tribal superstition? fear, then, of outer things or perhaps even phobias?"

Beloved ones, as you have heard from Maitreya the beloved, a sound mind is based on a sound body.[4] And having all the rules of health with a capstone of knowledge concerning each functioning of the body is most important before setting the direction of one's life. Be certain you are not clouded by the problems that manifest from a body that is not well-tended, whose caretaker, yourself, has not understood the way of love and resurrection and accountability and, truly, the practical necessities of meeting the demands and stresses of life in a polluted, degenerate and burdensome physical planet.

Blessed ones, divine direction must begin from within. Neither the Messenger nor the Lords of Karma may respond to you this night or to your letters when you ask for the will of God but you yourself have not truly positioned yourself directly under that Tree of Life of Lord Maitreya. For when the fruit falls and the initiation is to be taken with bliss, you must be beneath the Tree of Life rather than here or there.

Thus, our advice to you when you have desires and plans, and these are uppermost, is to go and fill them. Fill your desires! Fill your cups! Play out your spirals. Learn, then, what you truly desire and what you do not desire. For the only portion of the will of God that you will ever successfully fulfill is that which you have made your dear and deepest desire.

You cannot tattoo the will of God on a wayward soul. You cannot wear the garment and yet not play the part. There is no adaptability to the inner blueprint of Life until all other choices have been eliminated by you—not us.

Therefore, I give you this hour to contemplate the will of God as your own desire—desires that you may think have no parallel whatsoever with the spiritual path; but they may indeed be a very important part of that path, simply because you contain them.

I have instructed the Messenger, who has mentioned this to you before, that she must be extremely careful as to any desire that may cross her mind, for any desire contained by the Messenger is immediately fulfilled. And this she has observed, for there is no substance to prevent the precipitation. Thus, considering that the cosmic law and the abundant Life should bring the fruit of desire, I have taught her to become most careful and economical with the power of desire, desiring always those things that are God's desiring, which are her desires truly.

And thus I have taught her to withdraw instantaneously all forces and energy and thoughts and feelings from any matrix unworthy, unprofitable, unfruitful, unnecessary and not achieving the desired goal of the glory of God's kingdom, of the golden age, of the spreading abroad of the Teachings, of the receiving of the little ones, of preparing the Montessori school and the

Ranch and all facilities, that everyone who might come who
hungers and thirsts after righteousness might be fed.

And with all of this grand design from the causal body of
myself, then there come the lines, the details of the filling in,
department by department of life, of that which must be done
so that no one upon earth of any evolution or persuasion may
not find some path, some morsel, some teaching, some truth—so
that no one ultimately may go away from this Community disappointed or unfed or feeling somehow empty and not filled.

Thus, how to do this as quickly as possible with the resources
and the volunteers at hand—this becomes a very exacting equation. And in this Mother Mary is the greatest asset as the admin-
istrator, as the all-seeing eye of the Community, having many
angels and scribes and secretaries who do undertake to give to
our Messenger and our leadership those reminders, those plans,
those ideas that best fulfill and fill in the missing pieces to a
Community that is designed to be a mosaic of the central sun of
Love with radiating light going forth.

And these rays of gold from the heart of the sun of Love are
pathways providing openings and entrances, all leading to the
heart of the Inner Retreat. This very land itself must be protected and prepared, for it has a very ancient, ancient spiritual
focus, beloved. It is indeed a cradle. But I would tell you that
the feet of archangels were placed upon that land long, long ago
in its formation, making etheric tracks in akasha and sealing
that place as a magnet for the drawing of pilgrims. It is truly the
shrine of this international movement. It is truly the point of
convergence of suns.

Let it become a more permanent place. Let the facilities be
there, for you will see that we will bring members of the nations
and the root races. Understand its link to the Grand Teton and to
the very heart of the earth. It is indeed a place prepared for twin
flames and the cosmic cross of white fire and solar lights and the
aurora borealis and the descent of mighty souls from above, in
those twinkling causal bodies, to waiting parents below.

I say then, beloved, determine in the next hour what are your
unfulfilled desires. No matter how mundane they may be, write
them down in a list and look at them. Confront them and say,
"Which of these must I most assuredly fulfill in order to be at
peace with myself and to move on surefooted to the rays leading
to the great blue causal body of the Great Divine Director?"

Put down, then, the spiritual goals of the Great White Brotherhood such as you understand them [to be], as they have been

defined by the Darjeeling Council of the Great White Brotherhood. Do this on separate sheets of paper and decide whether there be any human desires left over from many lifetimes of somehow nonfulfillment and aloneness, whether any of these desires may be sublimated in the fulfillment of higher goals, whether truly transmutation and resolution of the lesser or former desires may take place, and whether the joy you would receive from the fulfillment of spiritual goals for the saving of a planet would be adequate—adequate to compensate for the letting go of one of these.

Look, then, to what is needed most by you personally, what is worth most to you personally. And if there is something you have always wanted to do and you always come back to it and it will always be there nagging at you, it is best, then—if you are certain that you want that perhaps 'detour' in life—to go out and find it and realize it.

Then you must take these two lists as parallel lines and say, "Which of my own desires in the human sense are really God's desires for me? Which of these desires can link up and be an instrument for the fulfillment of the goals of the Great White Brotherhood? How, then, in satisfying my own soul's needs can I also satisfy the needs of a larger circle so that neither I nor the circle of Community will be deprived?

"After all, I have two arms, two legs—I have two parts to myself in every way. I am a dual being. As the Gemini Mind of God, I can handle the white-fire/blue-fire sun. I can understand the blue-fire sun of Sirius as that which must be done in the physical universe so that when my feet are lifted by angels above the earth and I find myself being carried aloft to other spheres, I will have no regrets, no sense that it is too soon to take that ascent.

"But I will truly have the sense, as I do this night in the heart of the Great Divine Director, that all past records of my former self may be rolled up as a scroll, put to the torch, for I AM WHO I AM. I AM in the heart of the great blue causal body. I AM the implementation of God's will through the extension of the light rays of the Great Divine Director."

Thus, beloved, I will tell you this cosmic secret—every desire of yourself which is legitimate as the blue-fire sun of your being, your lawful right to integrity and individuality, every such desire that is really a part of you and the Real You will *always* relate to the divine plan and the vast matrix of the goal of the Great White Brotherhood.

The circle of Community is drawn and it is the mighty blue sphere. Now know this—somewhere in the service of the Great White Brotherhood *you* can balance 100 percent of your karma. *You* can fulfill your fiery destiny and have all the real desires that you thought you had to put aside in a sense of martyrdom and false denial of self. This is not the true path.

When you come to those desires inconsistent in every way to the goal and the divine design of the Great White Brotherhood as you know it, then comes the hour, beloved, when you indeed must decide to pray fervently before the heart of the Blessed Virgin and ask that this desire be removed from you by cosmic surgery, as the incision of the surgeon removes a tumor that suddenly appears and has no reason for being.

Beloved ones, tumors benign and malignant are the sign of wrong desire unmanifest, festering, fed and nourished by human creation suppressed. Bear well my Teaching. For the cosmic flow between you and the great blue causal body of cosmos always flushes out those nuclei suns of wrong desire that ultimately become growths in the astral body, robbing you of etheric power and sacred fire, taking from your crystal cord and therefore depriving you of the energy that could make of your heart a cosmic heart and of your heartbeat a cosmic heartbeat.

Thus, if there be not flow because you are possessive of old wants and desires to possess people and things and power and money and so forth, this is the key, then, to an unclear temple— crosscurrents, miscurrents and misdirections to life where you may contain splinters of ten thousand former desires and your life is nothing but a sea of chaos, directionless, going a few steps here and a few steps there but never concentrating. For it is impossible to concentrate one's forces if one contains these grains and granules of desires that have been somehow dissipated and scattered through the aura.

If you would write to the Karmic Board, write for this—the prayer that all this debris of desiring this and that be consumed by the sacred fire and that you may have goal-fitting for goals you have set to which you can tether all of your forces with total commitment without dissolution.

Beloved ones, the individual on the Path who has a one-pointedness of purpose is truly approaching the Divine Wholeness. And those with psychological problems are always they who have wells of untransmuted desires that divide them and also build momentums and walls of hatred and despite and fear, all directed against the central moving force of the universe, whom they perceive to be antagonistic and not fulfilling their every wish. Tyrants are these, with a split personality split by split desires, always desiring to control the absolute center of the causal body of the Great Divine Director.

This is why those who walk in the power and aura and mantle of the first ray of the will of God are so despised by the powers that be of this world. For they cannot control them, they cannot defeat them! They can do nothing with the first-ray chela of El Morya and myself and Archangel Michael and Hercules and Amazonia. There is nothing to be done with a chela of the will of God who is become this shaft of blue flame, this extension of the Great Divine Director's blue causal body, this shaft of the will of God, this pillar of fire, an electrode in the earth such as Hercules has placed and Serapis Bey has brought.[5]

Understand, beloved, that the God-goals of the Great White Brotherhood are the white-fire sun. In Alpha and Omega these are one. May you resolve, then, in these hours and year to come all of your desirings here below as above.

My prayer for you, beloved, is may your blue-fire/white-fire suns be one where you are. Then there will be no journeying, for Spirit/Matter cosmos will be where I AM THAT I AM in you. And you will know God-free being anywhere and everywhere always and always and always because you have become the Alpha to Omega sun of flaming God-desire!

Oh, I commend you to the heart of the Buddha, Gautama.

"The Summit Lighthouse Sheds Its Radiance O'er All the World to Manifest as Pearls of Wisdom." This dictation by the Great Divine Director was **delivered** through the Messenger of the Great White Brotherhood Elizabeth Clare Prophet on **New Year's Eve, December 31, 1985,** during the 5-day New Year's conference, *Teachings from the Mystery School,* held at Camelot. (1) Acts 17:26. (2) John 6:68. (3) Before the dictation the congregation meditated on two slides of the Great Divine Director. The first depicts him with long golden hair and blue eyes, a flame upon his forehead and a ray of white light emanating from his third eye. At his throat is a luminous white sunlike disc; at his heart is a six-pointed white star from which is projected a golden beam of light. He is wearing a golden robe girded by his bejeweled blue belt and radiates an aura of white lightning against a Mother-of-the-World blue background. The second slide portrays the Great Divine Director surrounded by the concentric spheres of the causal body of the Cosmic Christ—a thoughtform which may be used to visualize the abiding Presence of the Holy Christ Self overshadowing and one with the lower self. (4) See Lord Maitreya, December 31, 1985, "I Draw the Line!" 1986 *Pearls of Wisdom,* vol. 29, no. 19, pp. 160–61, 164, n. 1. (5) See 1986 *Pearls of Wisdom,* vol. 29: Serapis Bey, December 28, 1985, "The Descent of the Mighty Blue Sphere," no. 15, pp. 125–27; El Morya, December 29, 1985, "Seeking and Finding the Mystery of Life," no. 17, pp. 144–45, 147; and Hercules and Amazonia, December 30, 1985, "The Power of the Will of God," no. 18, pp. 150–53.

Pearls of Wisdom®

published by The Summit Lighthouse

| *Vol. 29 No. 21* | *Beloved Gautama Buddha and Saint Germain* | *May 25, 1986* |

Teachings from the Mystery School
XII
"The Teaching Is for the Many"
New Year's Eve Conclave at the Grand Teton
Saint Germain's Burden Is Lifted

. . . It is, then, with great joy that I turn my attention to our center of Light, our Camelot. Let all who have gathered here at the Royal Teton Retreat now meditate profoundly upon the circle of Light as I reveal to you, O Lightbearers of earth who have assembled at the Grand Teton, how you are holding the candle of which I have spoken already earlier in my address—the single flame of Life whereby these whom you behold are called "Keepers of the Flame," and their Mother and Messenger is with them in physical embodiment, even as you are graced this evening by the Messenger who has addressed you—your own Teacher, Lanello.

Now we unveil Camelot to many thousands of Lightbearers who have gathered, selected and by invitation, escorted by seraphim to this New Year's conclave of Light. For we have introduced you to the Path of the Ascension and the World Teachers and the Ascended Masters. Now you may see gathered in California and throughout the earth at their stations those Lightbearers who deem it the highest privilege—O bhikkhus, O beloved daughters and sons of the Buddhic Light, the path of the East and all world religions—to savor the cross and the circle of fire, to take it, then, from the heart and extend it to earth. And these who have come from every nation to our Camelot out of the East and West therefore savor above all things to enter into this decree momentum of the Word which I have already given to you to witness.

Thus, beloved Keepers of the Flame, there have been watch-men and -women of the night who have observed the power of the spoken Word and the dissolution of entire pockets of the astral plane. And I have showed them what has been accomplished since Christmas Eve through the efforts of those assembled and the Masters' dictations. And they have fully realized, by this dispensation from the heart of Sanat Kumara, exactly what is the science of sound,[1] the science of the spoken Word.

Their enlightenment has been that which could have taken thousands of years of pursuit in the physical octave. For Sanat Kumara sent his angels some weeks ago to prepare the souls and four lower bodies and chakras of those selected from the earth to attend tonight's conclave here at the Grand Teton.

Thus, their preparation has been to raise their ability to see and perceive through my own Electronic Presence—which this night they have received for a period in time and space, that they might see through my eyes and heart and being and know all that has been taught by the Messengers in this century.

They have seen the violet flame. They have seen the blue-lightning angels exorcise the most intense, the most insidious forms of entities and demons. They have watched how Astrea and how the Seven Archangels have gone after the darkest of conditions and especially those affecting the youth.

They are eager, beloved ones, to be sure that when they return to their denser bodies they will have a memory of all that they have been taught at the Grand Teton, that they might also have some sign and contact. Their mentors have assured them again and again that they could find the books of the Teachings in the most prominent bookstores of this nation.

Some have lamented that they will not find translations in their own countries. And thus, there is born in their hearts, for the first time in this embodiment, a keen desire to study English and to come to America, hopeful that they will make the connection on the outer to that which they have been given within.

We have presented the vast panorama of the Great White Brotherhood. They have seen Mighty Victory and some of his legions of Light. They have stood present before the Lords of Karma, who have given to them angel secretaries to go over their private Book of Life with them.

Beloved ones, these are truly the best of earth's evolutions. Though not without karma, they are lovers of the Light, yet not in situations of having any advancement or prior outer knowledge of that which takes place at inner planes.

This experiment which I have sponsored has been my answer to Saint Germain's Stump to Europe and to the Messenger's call. For the effort of this team and the delivery of the Word night after night has made a deeper and deeper etch in the crystal of Matter and in the souls of Light.

It is truly an example of what we have taught you—that when the Word is spoken it reaches all upon earth of a similar wavelength and vibration. It is never limited to the immediate audience. And though without the amplification of satellite or modern systems of communication, yet the earth body itself records the Word, which is why the Word must be incarnate in you.

In the physical sense the Messenger cannot be everywhere. But in the divine sense Lanello *is* everywhere. And you must be his instrument. Thus, at anytime, wherever you may be in life, you may come upon a soul who has attended this conclave and therefore who has the inner awareness of all of the Teaching and the Law and the specific vision of the work of the angels as they implement the calls of your very divine decrees.

This dispensation has been made possible by many beings of Light. We have done all we could do for our part. Now we say, the particular call you may make is that these one hundred forty and four thousand and more be allowed to have the memory quickened in them of the inner planes' experience and especially that you might encounter them and give to them even a wallet-size Chart or some portion of the Teaching or a poster or anything that you might prepare that would be appropriate, that they might be drawn to that which is now a part of the immediate inner awareness—not something covered over that they knew twelve thousand years ago on Atlantis, but something they have had immediate association with.

Just as your calls have been answered with a fiery action throughout this conference, so, beloved, your calls may be answered to give help to these souls of Light.

Now, then, you understand the audience who hears my message, and you are part of the world of inner beings who recognize the office of the Lord of the World which was bestowed upon me by Lord Sanat Kumara. I am indeed grateful to have such disciples as yourselves, to have so many positioned around the world who in the very outer knowledge of being place their attention upon me in this hour and therefore receive, whether waking or sleeping, a current from my heart for the healing, the stabilizing, the regulating of the heart and the four lower bodies and the functions thereof.

And if you will be attentive to that which the Messenger has taught you concerning your health in this class and all that is to come in our seminar, you will retain a great portion of this light—a light for the regulation, the regularity of all functions of the body system. This regulation is established by the intensity of the resurrection flame, the full power of the threefold flame.

Almighty ones of Light I AM THAT I AM, now you understand that the Western Shamballa, sealed over the Heart of the Inner Retreat and extending for many miles radiating out therefrom, is a consecration of a shrine made holy by the footsteps of archangels long ago. Now you understand that the white-fire/blue-fire sun that has come in the establishment of the Retreat of the Divine Mother, with Lady Master Venus presiding over the Ranch, is also the polarity of that Western Shamballa. As you have heard, then, and understood, you can see that for aeons heaven has been banking upon this area as a place preserved, reserved, then, for evolutions who will come apart because they have been taken to the inner retreats of the Great White Brotherhood.

Now in this hour the Seven Chohans of the Rays bow before the Light and the altar of the Royal Teton Retreat where I am. They stand before me and they present their petitions to me before the Lords of Karma.

It is their request, made formal but deliberated by us earlier, to open, then, universities of the Spirit in each of their etheric retreats where they might welcome not dozens or hundreds but thousands and tens of thousands of students who will diligently pursue the path of self-mastery on the seven rays systematically, mastering most especially the first and the seventh rays whereby they might establish the Alpha and the Omega of their identity, whereby they might establish the will of God, the divine blueprint, the inner plan for twin flames and immediately begin an action of personal and world transmutation.

The plan, therefore, is for students to spend fourteen days in Darjeeling and fourteen days with Saint Germain at the Royal Teton Retreat and to alternate these fourteen days as they weave a balance and restore themselves to the commitment of the beginning and the ending of the cycles of life.

Having successfully passed certain levels, albeit beginning levels, nevertheless strong levels of accomplishment in the use of these rays, they will have a turn also with Lord Lanto and Confucius here at the Royal Teton and Paul the Venetian, who prefers to use in this hour the Temple of the Sun of the Goddess of Liberty, who is the Divine Mother of beloved Paul, and to anchor that action in the Washington Monument, as it has already had anchored there a focus of the threefold flame from the Château de Liberté.[2]

Beloved ones, this training, then, will be for the rounding out of the threefold flame in the wisdom of the Path and especially in the development of the path of the sacred heart, the expansion of love that they might rid themselves of fear and hardness of heart and records of death surrounding that heart.

Then, you see, comes the path of ministration and service, which is the logical manifestation of love and a balanced threefold flame. Through ministration and service in the retreat of Nada in Arabia, they will find, then, a place where they can give the same dynamic decrees you give here for all those untoward conditions in the area of the Middle East. And this shall be their assignment at inner levels even as they study the true path of Jesus Christ on that sixth ray as it has never been taught to them before.

Having come through these retreats, they are now ready to be washed in the purity of the sacred fires of the ascension temple for a beginner's course and for the first baptism by water of the Divine Mother. Then they proceed to Crete with Paul the Apostle and there Hilarion shows them the Truth of all ages, and the science of Being is unfolded layer upon layer.

Thus, having completed a round in all of these retreats—cycling fourteen-day cycles, some repeated in the same retreat, some interchanging—they will come again to second and third levels of training on those seven rays. It is desired that as quickly as possible through this training these may make outer contact with Summit University and attend its halls of learning at the Inner Retreat, as is our desire. For the expansion of Light and the increase of Light is far more possible there than in the dense areas and the low level at sea level here.

Beloved ones, we therefore desire that the knowledge of Summit University as the Ascended Masters' university shall be made known far and wide through every means possible and that the course contents will carefully be described according to the pattern set forth by the Seven Chohans.

We desire the knowledge of the persons of the Seven Chohans to go forth and the many series they have dictated in several forms to be there in the bookstalls of the world, that those individuals who are taking these courses might have something whereby they can make contact in the outer with our bands and truly begin that action of the sevenfold flame of the sevenfold Elohim in physical embodiment—finally, therefore, at that level to begin in earnest to balance their karma and prepare themselves for that world service which is their divine calling and make their ascensions in this life from that very Heart of the Inner Retreat.

This is our divine plan. This is our vision, the vision of Elohim and Great Silent Watchers of the City Foursquare to be builded there. We say, then, make haste to the mountain of God. For the summit beacon shining from those heights can be seen in the etheric octave as souls come and go to the Inner Retreat.

And as they come and go to that Royal Teton Retreat in the Grand Teton each night and pass over, the angels will show them the beacon and give them pictures in their mind and memory of that physical location so that by and by, by the repetitive action of seeing the beacon of the Inner Retreat, they may come to an outer awareness at least of the desire to take a vacation at Jackson Hole or Yellowstone Park!

And beloved ones, you must realize that you make things extremely difficult for our angels when you leave no outer signs of yourself in these areas. It is highly important that you understand that storefronts and signs and leaflets and individuals present to invite people to come to study the Teachings of the Masters—or whatever you may devise as films or situations that they may encounter along their journeys—are extremely important.

We have already sent Lightbearers to the area and they have come home without an awareness of your presence. And, in some cases, they have come home well-fed by you at The Ranch Kitchen with no idea whatsoever that there was the Great White Brotherhood and the path of the Ascended Masters, because you are so meek in the sense of fearing what neighbors and others may think of you if you are direct in your approach.

Beloved ones, you have to understand they have already formulated their opinions. And there is little that you can do about the obstinacy of human opinion but to let your Light so shine before men that they will see the Father's good work in you.[3] And those of the Light will glorify God and those not of the Light will condemn it, and it has ever been so. And therefore, be not concerned, for the mission moves on.

Beloved ones, it is indeed a warfare of the dark ones against the entire cause of the Great White Brotherhood. And you must outsmart them and you must use every means available to reach people in the physical octave. Somehow the lie has been spread abroad that this Teaching is for the few. I tell you, the hour is come and now is when the Teaching is for the many who are called.

The many indeed are called and for many reasons. If the few be chosen,[4] the few may still number in the millions. And you ought to be ready for the influx, for the harvest could not be more white[5] and the Light could not be greater.

And therefore the Goddess of Light, the Queen of Light, and the Goddess of Purity have come closer to earth than ever before. And they have determined that this light of the fiery ovoid described to you by the Messenger[6]—which was described to you simultaneously as they were addressing this company at the Royal Teton Retreat—shall become available to the pure in heart. This white fire, then, they bring to bear upon the auras of all candidates who have made known at inner levels and before the Seven Chohans that they are determined to regain the lost chord of their identity and to bring to bear on world events the full momentum of their causal bodies of Light.

And as for Europe, we have only scratched the surface. Now the Keepers of the Flame there will bring the Stump message on video to every town and city and prepare the way for dispensations before the Lords of Karma by our request—dispensations in which we ask for the opportunity to hold conferences in city after city and finally to see such a ground swell of support that these conferences may be broadcast by satellite throughout the world, that none on earth who have access to the modern systems of communication may be without the opportunity to choose this day whom they will serve,[7] to see manifesting clearly through the Messenger and yourselves the light of the angels, the angelic hosts, the legions of the Central Sun and know not only by the power of the Word but by their own inner sight that cosmic beings are addressing earth in this hour of her great peril and her greatest opportunity.

Beloved ones, 1986 can and shall be an open door as we together determine that it shall be and as you in embodiment do ratify our calls for these dispensations. Thus, the Lords of Karma, and I with them, have already approved this petition of the Seven Chohans. And in this hour it is formally granted to them to establish these universities whereby they will assist and increase in a very intense manner all that is being done by yourselves on earth.

Beloved ones, those who are in the great amphitheater surrounding the Grand Teton have stood to applaud this opportunity that is given to them in this hour. I bid you join them.

[standing ovation]

Beloved ones, I cannot even tell you the great joy of these hearts when they discovered the truth of this Cause and the presence of this activity. Less than one percent of those here had ever heard anything good or bad concerning this organization.

Therefore, those of you who think that the output of information in either direction has in fact had any impact on the greater population of the planet, I tell you it has not. And you can far exceed the positive statements you have made and the publications you have sent forth. And as for the darkness and the dark ones and their media campaigns, they are surely dissolved this hour by the Goddess of Light, the Queen of Light, and the Goddess of Purity.

Beloved ones, while you are standing, I present to you in this hour our beloved Saint Germain, the seventh chohan, as he does come forward and stand singly before me while the other six stand behind, and Portia now standing with the Lords of Karma.

Beloved ones, the hour has come, and it must come, whereby from our office we declare to you and all Lightbearers in all octaves that by the united effort of the entire Spirit of the Great White Brotherhood the burden complete of Saint Germain's incurred karma is lifted, transmuted, and sent back to the Great Central Sun purified.[8] [standing ovation]

Beloved ones, the Messenger has known at inner levels, in consultation with us and in conclave here, that if she and you together could endure to this night of December 31, 1985—already become where you are January 1, 1986—that truly this dark burden would come to an end and Saint Germain would be free once again to champion his cause through her and through the chelas as never before has occurred in these recent centuries.

Beloved ones, it is an immense relief to you, to the Messengers, in all levels of your four lower bodies. For truly you have borne sometimes ten times over the weight of karma of other lifestreams, whether from these decades of this dispensation or past dispensations through the centuries of those who have abandoned, betrayed, or misused the light of beloved Saint Germain.

Thus, beloved ones, you can see a new day! For you are the chelas of Saint Germain and you have borne his burden. You have been with him in his trial. You have been with him through all things. And he, then, is free to stand before us, before Alpha and Omega and lay before the Lords of Karma his plan and the plan of Portia for the inauguration of this age in the thirty-three-year cycle now under way as well as in the century entire to come.

Beloved ones, Saint Germain is brimming with hope and many plans that he has worked on for very long. He is beaming with a smile of joy and light. And I therefore give to him my place that he might address you in this hour. [applause]

[The Messenger: Portia does step forth now before Saint Germain. She does kneel before him as before the Lord of the World. And she does place in the hand of Saint Germain that mighty jewel of light—his focus of sacred fire that he placed upon the altar on behalf of all students of the violet flame and all whom he has sponsored in these centuries. Saint Germain does receive it now. He places it within a pouch, places it within his pocket, and does prepare to address all.]

Beloved Saint Germain

Most beloved friends of freedom of all planes of cosmos, I send the love of my heart to each and every one of you who has stood with me these long centuries of our joint efforts to reach the souls of the Lightbearers of earth that they might carry a torch of the violet flame to those lesser endowed who must be kindled by some in embodiment with the flame of freedom in government, in science, and in the mystical orders of religion.

I say to you one and all, our efforts have not been in vain. They have been costly indeed, and all have learned the meaning of paying the price—you keenly and I myself sometimes most painfully when I could not extend a hand until this tribulation, if you will call it that, was through. But, beloved ones, through it all, some have received the violet flame—not a few have ascended and are standing with me here tonight!

The knowledge of the seventh ray is abroad in the earth. And now, with a new fervor and a new hope and wisdom, I trust gained from any past indiscretions, we may once again lay firmly the foundation of our divine plan to sow and sow again the jewels of light and yet to so safeguard our sowings that neither you nor I, neither cosmic beings nor unascended chelas nor elementals who love me dearly should ever again become so encumbered by the situation of the misuse of the sacred fire by earth's evolutions once they have received the knowledge thereof.

Therefore, I bid you with all my heart's love a great and grand expression of gratitude. And I hurl to you now from my own being and aura, with beloved Portia, violets and lilacs and purple irises and all manner of wild and exotic flower that contains the violet and the purple spectrum. And to each and all who have ever favored me with a single kindness or a comforting word, I send this floral offering. And the fragrance descends. And you may know, beloved, that I am grateful.

In the name of the Goddess of Liberty and the Lords of Karma, my own beloved Portia, I am grateful to you, Lord Gautama—to you, Lord Maitreya, my brother Jesus and Kuthumi, El Morya and Lanello, and so many, many whose names I now say with all of my being. And a million times a million names are pronounced in the ethers that the whole of cosmos may know all who have ever helped Saint Germain and the violet-flame angels and the cause of freedom!

In this hour of rejoicing, I would address you, then. Most blessed hearts of Light, be seated in comfort and in our love.

Beloved ones, to me the most obvious solution for the protection of the Light and the protection of the Teaching is to use in the physical earth the matrix already provided by Archangel Michael and the Darjeeling Council with Mother Mary and the Messengers. The matrix of the rosary of Archangel Michael may be used now for a very specific purpose. And that purpose is for the protection of the Teaching, that it might come to Lightbearers, and for the binding of all Serpents and their seed—the binding of the dark ones immediately when they take it to use on the left-handed path.

I submit that the call to the archangels—directly to the heart of Archangel Michael through the decrees already written and this rosary for the protection of the path of the Great White Brotherhood, for the protection of the true souls of Light and the worthy and the instantaneous judgment of the usurpers of the Light—will go a long, long way in curtailing the advancement of abuses and therefore the incurring of karma for you and me and the increasing numbers of Ascended Masters who have come to join our cause of freedom from great heights of cosmos and the inner silence.

I must say that we applaud and bow in great reverence before the beloved twin flame of Lord Maitreya, who is here this evening, and welcome her and her decision to descend to these levels for the assistance of the feminine ray of this blessed and mighty Buddha warrior of the spirit fire.

And so, beloved ones, your knowledge and use of the tool of exorcism taught to you in the initial ruby-ray decrees given by Sanat Kumara is most valuable. Beloved ones, the Teaching and its practitioners and students must continually be protected. And immediately students must learn of these various forms of entities that beset them. And this army of Light must form, by the linking of arms, such a strength of union in the circle of fire that anyone who is burdened, who has been overcome by the dark powers, who is truly a son of Light, can be not only vindicated but swiftly cut free and protected.

Thus, we see in the building and the strengthening of brotherhood in the earth, of a true oneness and a determination to help one another, that there will also come an awareness of the penetration, if any, of our circles of charity[9] by alien forces that have no good intent but to spy upon our liberty[10] and misuse our Teaching and turn our words again that they might rend us.

Beloved ones, our students throughout the world have become very astute over the centuries. They have seen what the forces of Fascism and World Communism and the powers that be in every nation have done to undo the Lightbearers and the true freedom fighters and those who understand the path truly of peace with honor.

Beloved ones, therefore we see that with the intense protection and the fourteen-month cycle of the blue-flame will of God, we, as it were, may pull out almost all of the stops and let the Teaching go forth and let it truly be the sower of Aquarius who does sow the Word.

And where it is not on fallow ground, where it falls upon the rock and may be rejected,[11] let other angels come and pick it up and let others take it. Beloved ones, let us not leave the seeds sown anywhere to be misused, but let us make the call that the Lightbearers will come and pick up the crumbs that have fallen from the Master's table, that they will pick up the stone that was rejected,[12] the book cast away.

Therefore, the perpetual call to the seraphim is truly the key of Light taught to you by the Messenger. The seraphim come with swords and fiery auras recharged once in every seven days by the Central Sun itself. Thus they saturate those individuals who are of the Light with a mighty flame and perfume of roses. They lead them by the hand, they bind the demons—and where there is a will and a heart in those souls, they do indeed bring them to the fount of knowledge. But you, beloved, must establish those founts of knowledge, those places of availability and likelihood where many may pass in the marts of life.

You must become, indeed, the greatest salesmen in the world.[13] You must realize that you do have already the most salable item. It is the Teaching itself. The Messenger long ago realized this when torn and pulled and almost sawn asunder by those forces that determined to draw her into outer activities involving commerce and money.

Beloved ones, all of this is the lie that we have not provided you and this organization with sufficient material to create such an abundance, such a release of Light to the co-workers as for the building of the entire Inner Retreat.

The gold mine is here. It does not have to be sought and found. There is no need for merchandising in the marts of the world. There is a need for intense practicality in the presentation and packaging of the most interesting information and subjects and lectures and sermons that are going forth on the planetary body at this time.

And, beloved ones, had there not been so much opposition and such a weight of karma to be borne, you would have seen many, many more people taking the message for the message's sake itself. And wherever the voice of the Messenger is heard, people stop and listen. Yet they are told by many babbling voices, from their families to their ministers to their civic leaders, not to go after anything that is out of the norm of their established tradition. Tradition, you know, is a god in society, but no longer. For *we* are in the vanguard and we are at last free.

Therefore, beloved, I say to you—not by way of announcing a specific action at this time but by way of saying to you— may you propose what you will do and may we then bring your proposals before the Lords of Karma. And may we then state what is our request, based on the realism of the hour and your positioning of yourselves, as to what we will take as our responsibility.

We proceed with joy and the caution of experience that we must ask for those things of the Solar Logoi and the Elohim of which we may be certain there will be a fulfillment and a victory and therefore not result in a situation of the costliness of karma that does therefore affect the next and the next opportunity for our service.

We would rather that you yourselves be the daring ones, that *you* go forth and see what *you* will do and let us be the ones who respond. This is as it should be, for the Wise One, Lord Sanat Kumara, has said to me this very week,

"Saint Germain, you have been the champion. And when you have been in physical embodiment, those who are now a part of our activity on earth were benefited by your service and were advanced in their learning. Saint Germain, let them now come to center stage with the same courage that you had. Let them take on the responsibilities which you were so willing to take on when you were in physical incarnation and when you were the Wonderman of Europe, as you indeed are today the Wonderman of this world."

Beloved hearts, he said to me that I must let you play your part and that I must add to it and multiply it and must have, as they say, from you "money in the bank" by way of the assuring of the loan that I would then secure from the cosmic bank. Beloved ones, this is to say that there is a tremendous quantity of light that is available to me now in the great treasury of the Central Sun—a quantity of light that has been abuilding by cosmic beings proportionately as you have called the violet flame for the balancing of this accumulated karma.

Therefore, the substance of light is there. It is there on demand. And I am instructed to demand it as you present and show the most effective, workable, and successful programs for delivering this message to the world and for the building of the Inner Retreat.

In anticipation of the Light going forth, we have designated the Inner Retreat as a place that must be secure, must be the highest focus in the earth. For, you see, when the light goes forth it cannot be fully predicted what the response will be from the world and humanity. If these responses are an aggravation and a reaction creating a planetary chemistry that results in some world changes, it is necessary that the equivalent of the Great Central Sun Magnet be somewhere on earth.

And you know where that somewhere is. The eye of the Inner Retreat is the Grand Teton, and you are the body thereof. And that Great Central Sun Magnet can only be composed of your light bodies in physical manifestation.

As you already have understood, it will take great ingenuity to maintain the supply and the income in this area of the world. But, beloved ones, no one ever said that you could not go out and come in again, that you could not establish your base there and spend a major part of your year in those enterprising activities that promote both the Teaching and your own personal welfare, supplying you the needs of the hour for the blessings you desire to bestow upon your family and loved ones as well as upon this organization.

Thus, beloved ones, it is a question of the base. It is a question of having a retreat to retreat to and to go out from. This has always been the way of the Great White Brotherhood. Thus, you can expand your horizons and seek that place where you may also plant and reap a harvest essential to your God mastery in all planes.

I say to you, then, that in this hour of rejoicing and in this hour of the conclave, I am grateful to have been able to have shared with you the thoughts of my heart, the communications of the mighty ones, and certain parameters of our looking to the New Day.

My first actions will be to see to it that this activity is secure in every way and that the plans move forward according to the resolve of the Darjeeling Council and the Lords of Karma. I trust, then, you will seek a tidy conclusion to all those things that must be completed at the Ranch, made known to you and to be discussed later today.[14]

Beloved ones, having this activity secure is like the sealing of Noah's ark. We must know that our Lightbearers who have supported us in all ages will indeed survive to make their ascension in this life. And I tell you, beloved ones, I cannot guarantee that ascension but I can tell you that the Path itself and your following of it does guarantee it.

Keep on keeping on and do not avoid the eye of, or the encounter with, the Messenger. For you will find the surest incisive action of the violet flame keeping you moving toward the center of Being and your perfect Love.

Beloved ones, I have much to attend to, for there are many areas of the world that need my help. I will go forth confident that as you know exactly what these areas are, you will be mindful that I also need the action of Archangel Michael's Rosary that that which can be done for the government of this nation and all nations might be secured and that the fallen ones and the spies and the enemies of Truth and Life be bound, that they might not move in and take the dispensations that I am able to give of light and action toward a more perfect world, a world of union and understanding and the universality of Being and the entering in to the very nature of God.

Thus, beloved, in great love and deference to the Lord of the World, I return you to his heart of hearts that he may deliver now the conclusion of his message.

My beloved Gautama Buddha, it is my great joy to receive this honor and new freedom in your presence this New Year's Day. And I bow before you. For by your keeping of the flame for me and these Lightbearers, our Keepers of the Flame Fraternity has indeed been established and its members wax strong as the stars of your heart.

[standing ovation]

Beloved Gautama Buddha

Most gracious and beloved knights and ladies of the flame, Lightbearers of the world, I bid you once again be seated in our rings of light.

There comes to me an angel of the Keeper of the Scrolls. There comes an angel descending from the heart of Sanat Kumara, from the heart of the Central Sun. And the Solar Logoi have sent, therefore sealed, the thoughtform for this year, 1986.

I unroll the scroll of light, and oh, what a fiery scroll it is, beloved! Upon this scroll is inscribed the full outpicturing of the Mighty Blue Eagle—the angel formation of the legions of the God Star Sirius. This blue eagle takes the form, for this action for this planetary body, of the bald eagle of the United States of America. Yet it is blue, and when you study its components you will see that every feather and part is a blue-flame angel. And it is a vast formation that fills the starry heavens.

Beloved, the true and royal form of the flag of the I AM Race is the background of this eagle. It is the banner of Light. It is the Old Glory that has become America's flag. And yet it contains the secret within it of new developments within this nation which are to unfold.

The starry field represents initiates, and therefore its numbers may not be counted according to the outer. And the thirteen tribes are represented in this flag in the ruby and white, for it is [the red stripes are] not yet represented as the gold.[15] The ruby, therefore, has the filigree line of gold on either side of the stripe separating it from the white, thus signifying the path of the ruby ray and of the Body and Blood of Christ for the attainment of the ascension through those stars which I cannot number, for it is not lawful for me to reveal it.

These stars represent not only states but tribes of the nations. They represent compartments of root races. They represent the seed of Christ, the archetypal blueprint of all those who may ascend under the canopy of the Central Sun, its focus in the God Star, assisted by the protection of the Mighty Blue Eagle formation of angels.

Beloved, behind this there is a unique map of the earth. Laid out in spherical design, this map is translucent. And by means of adjustment electronically, one can look at the earth in this and past ages, going back as long as evolutions of Light have been on it and showing in those periods the various land masses, how the seas and landed areas were formed and how they are in this present era.

That which is center, beneath the heart of the Mighty Blue Eagle, is that portion of the earth that is indeed represented as the Western Hemisphere. Above that, the banner of the I AM Race.

Beloved ones, the sign of the thoughtform of the year is this: to restore in this hemisphere, specifically in the United States and in Canada (if her people and Keepers of the Flame do will it so), the return to the founding principles of freedom, the return by revolution of the Spirit—by education and enlightenment, by the path of the ruby and the gold and the white and the stars in the field of the blue-flame will of God—to the original divine design which Saint Germain held in his heart for this nation to be the instrument of the return of Lightbearers to the establishment of God's kingdom on earth and to their own ascension in the Light, that they may walk the earth once again as ascended beings to be the teachers of those not yet ascended and to bring this earth back to that point of that golden-age civilization seventy thousand years ago and in some cases millions of years ago.

Thus, beloved, this great thoughtform, which is large in dimension, does also retain at the very top the paintings of Saint Germain and Jesus, originally done by Charles Sindelar, and the Chart of the I AM Presence. When all of this is seen together in the grandeur of dimension, you can see that it fits very well on this giant tapestry.

This tapestry of the thoughtform of the year woven by angels will hang in the Grand Teton Retreat for all to see. It shows that America shall return, deserving to be, then, the nation sponsored by Saint Germain, her people going forth to transfer his science, his economy, his religion, his way of life, which represents that of the entire Great White Brotherhood, to every nation.

It shows that there is a key, and the key is that America must come to her original purpose and fulfill it. She has ever been established and sponsored by Saint Germain as the guru nation. Thus, though the chelas of Saint Germain and of America throughout the world may have in some areas perfected and gone beyond the disciplines of the people in this nation, yet the mantle has not yet been taken from them to restore the earth to the place of peace and freedom.

Thus, in the lower portion of the tapestry one can see the multitudes, and they come from every nation and they represent every tribe and race and people and color and evolution. And as these multitudes approach from the south this map of North America, there is in the center the dove of the Holy Spirit, the dove of peace. In anticipation of the presentation of this thoughtform at this hour, Lightbearers have been coming for decades and centuries from around the world that they or their progeny could be here in the hour of the renewal of the flame of the Spirit of Liberty.

Beloved ones, in the tapestry that proceeds out from around the maps there is a portrayal of major shrines of liberty of the earth, most notable that of the Goddess of Liberty on the right and the Grand Teton on the left.

Thus, beloved, it is an endless story that is woven into this tapestry, and it shows that the people of earth must bend the knee and confess the eternal Christ in the heart of Jesus, in the heart of Saint Germain, and in the heart of their own I AM Presence. And these brothers of the favorite son, Joseph, and of his sons, Ephraim and Manasseh*—these other tribes must come to that point of recognizing that the Father has a right to have a favorite son and to bless him. For that favor is not unjust or unequal but it is the favor accorded as the blessing of attainment. (Gen. 37:3–36; 41:50–52; 48; 49:1–29)

Thus, Joseph, as you know, was the beloved Jesus. And this is what you find—that the hatred of Joseph has become the hatred of America. America is the source of the Teachings, of the I AM THAT I AM sponsored by Saint Germain. And therefore he has sponsored this language of this people as the language of the Great White Brotherhood in this age. Therefore, there must be an acceptance of this and a bending of the knee also and not the constant quarreling by the other tribes—"Why are we not equal?"

You can be equal, but you must proceed under Joseph with his coat of many colors and under the prophet Samuel. You must go to their Promised Land. You must accept the Teaching and the Path and strive with these holy ones of God to perfect a Union long endowed. For sometime, somewhere the evolutions of other continents of Saint Germain have truly rejected him. And that karma is not removed from those nations, though it is removed from Saint Germain and the Lightbearers who have borne that world karma so long—especially the Messengers themselves.

Beloved hearts, the people of this nation have an endowment and a protection from the Master. Therefore, we make it known that for the integration of the Word and the entering into the universal age and an international unity of nations and peoples, it is truly a requirement that English be taught in the

---

* Jacob accepted Ephraim and Manasseh as his own sons, making each one the head of a tribe equal to the other eleven.

very lower schools to the littlest children of every nation upon earth. For this you must decree. For, beloved, how can they choose a path and a Master whose language and writings and entire dispensations and initiations are in a language that is foreign to them? Whether for commerce or education or the arts or brotherhood, there are manifold reasons why this, the language so rich in its incorporation of many other languages, should be the common knowledge of every schoolchild throughout the planet.

Thus, the thoughtform for the year may appear complex, but then the organization, the Path, and even the awareness of the average chela has also become complex in a nuclear and space age—an age of computers and technology accelerating the capacity of the mind to know Truth in every area of learning.

Thus, I say to you, beloved, that the complexity of your understanding of the Path can always be reduced to the simple simplicity of the Law of the One. When you study and know what we have taught through our many representatives, the Ascended Masters, you are the more able to feed my sheep.

Therefore, some of you will identify yourselves as a part of the body of the Mighty Blue Eagle, some of you as a part of those who minister at the altar of the I AM Presence and Saint Germain and Jesus. Others will see yourselves feeding and caring for the multitudes; others, the building of the Inner Retreat; others, the dealing with the nations and bringing them to the proper chord of response to our message. This tapestry, then, establishes an outline—whether within or without, whether in the maps of the earth in the ancient ages—of the Path for everyone who is to ascend through this dispensation and thoughtform.

Now the hour has come, beloved, for me to send you to rest. For we desire you to come now, straight as an arrow, to the Grand Teton mountain where you will be received, and the door in the mountain will be opened and you may enter for further instruction and initiation from Lord Maitreya which will be sealed in the concluding day of your conference when you return tomorrow, being this very day at Camelot.

In the blessed peace of the Buddha whom I represent, in the peace of Sanat Kumara, who has brought me to this office, I, Gautama, say to you, I am above all most grateful in this hour for the chelas of the will of God and Morya's diligence in bringing you to this point of keen receptivity to our heart.

May God bless you forever, my beloved. I am never apart from you, for our hearts are one in the heartbeat of the Ancient of Days.

"The Summit Lighthouse Sheds Its Radiance O'er All the World to Manifest as Pearls of Wisdom."
This dictation was **delivered** New Year's Eve, **12:05 a.m., January 1, 1986. (1)** See Elizabeth
Clare Prophet, *The Liberating Power of the Word:* Album I (6 cassettes), "Seven Steps to
Precipitation by the Command of the Word," $37.50 ppd.; Album II (4 cassettes, 111 color
slides), "The Science of Sound," $138 ppd. Also, "Sound: Life's Integrating Phenomenon," in
The Coming Revolution: A Magazine for Higher Consciousness (Spring 1981), pp. 24–33, 54.
(2) See 1982 *Pearls of Wisdom,* vol. 25, p. 494, n. 1. **(3)** Matt. 5:16. **(4)** Matt. 20:16; 22:14.
(5) John 4:35. **(6)** Before the dictation, the Messenger led the congregation in invocations and
songs to the **Goddess of Light, the Queen of Light and the Goddess of Purity.** She explained
that these three cosmic beings have "majored on the one-pointed goal of focusing the intense
Light [Christ consciousness] of God" and should be invoked daily. Their Light is especially
amplified at winter solstice. As you meditate upon the three giant ovoids of Light of the
Goddess of Light, the Queen of Light and the Goddess of Purity, "your attention becomes like a
straw . . . and you sip the nectar of this Light—as much as they will allow you to draw down into
your aura." The retreats of the Goddess of Light (in the Andes), the Queen of Light (above
Sicily), and the Goddess of Purity (on Madagascar) focus an action of the Trinity to the earth;
together these hierarchs draw the action of the cosmic threefold flame on behalf of her
evolutions. The Goddess of Light (Amerissis) made her ascension after an embodiment in
South America, where she had achieved great spiritual attainment but in an off-guarded
moment of overconfidence was trapped by black magicians who imprisoned the lower part of
her body in the form of a fish. For more than 300 years she served her fellowmen from behind a
counter, raising her thoughts ever upward and calling unto God to manifest Light, Light, Light!
As an Ascended Master, she once explained, "I am called by God's grace the Goddess of Light
simply because I have paid allegiance to Light for so long." The Queen of Light focuses the
action of the crystal fire mist and the crystal sword and may be invoked with her legions to cut
through the densest human creation. The Goddess of Purity focuses the flame of Cosmic
Christ purity. From her retreat, where the flame of purity has been sustained for thousands of
years, angels of purity carry light rays to the four corners of the earth. **(7)** Josh. 24:15. **(8) The
sponsorship of Saint Germain.** After his ascension in 1684, Saint Germain was given the dispensation by the Lords of Karma to return to earth and manifest in a physical body. The Comte de
Saint Germain appeared throughout the 18th-century courts as the "Wonderman of Europe."
His goal: to prevent the French Revolution and establish a United States of Europe. Though the
royalty admired his miraculous accomplishments and were always willing to be entertained by
him, they were not easily prodded to relinquish their power and move with the winds of
republican change. They and their jealous ministers ignored his counsel, and the French
Revolution ensued. In a final attempt to unite Europe, Saint Germain backed Napoleon, who
misused the Master's power to his own demise. The opportunity to set aside the retribution due
an age had thus passed and Saint Germain was forced to withdraw. Of his experiment on the
continent, Saint Germain once said: "Having failed in securing the attention of the Court of
France and others of the crowned heads of Europe, I turned myself to the perfectionment of
mankind at large, and I recognized that there were many who, hungering and thirsting after
righteousness, would indeed be filled with the concept of a perfect union which would inspire
them to take dominion over the New World and create a Union among the sovereign states.
Thus the United States was born as a child of my heart and the American Revolution was the
means of bringing freedom in all of its glory into manifestation from the East unto the West."
Saint Germain stood by George Washington throughout the Revolution and during the long
winter at Valley Forge. He inspired and directed the writing of the Constitution and anointed
Washington first president of the United States. In the latter 19th century, he assisted the
Masters M. (El Morya), K.H. (Koot Hoomi), and Serapis Bey in the founding of the Theosophical
Society. In this century, Saint Germain went before the Lords of Karma to plead the cause of
freedom for and on behalf of earth's evolutions. He offered the momentum of the violet flame
garnered within his heart chakra and causal body as a momentum of light energy to be given
mankind that they might experiment with the alchemy of self-transformation through the
sacred fire. Though the knowledge of the violet flame had never been given outside the retreats
of the Great White Brotherhood, the Lords of Karma agreed to release it to a certain nucleus of
devotees, and the experiment proved successful that they would illumine the masses as to its use.
In the early 1930s, Saint Germain contacted his "general in the field," the reembodied George
Washington, Guy W. Ballard, whom he trained as his Messenger. Through Guy and Edna
Ballard, he founded the I AM movement and released the dispensation of the violet flame.
When mankind en masse failed to respond, the Lords of Karma told Saint Germain they would
not give him "another allotment of energy for mankind to take and to dissipate and to waste." In
Saint Germain's own words, "after seventy thousand years of sponsoring various endeavors
for the enlightenment and the freedom of mankind . . . my wings were clipped. And I had but to
stand and hope that some other hierarch would come forth to implore a dispensation of Light

for humanity, for souls of Light." In 1958, El Morya, on Saint Germain's behalf, founded The Summit Lighthouse for the release and publication of the Teachings of the Ascended Masters and the establishment of the Community of the Holy Spirit in the Aquarian age. Saint Germain anointed Mark and Elizabeth Prophet as his Messengers and sponsored the Keepers of the Flame Fraternity. Mark L. Prophet ascended Feb. 26, 1973, and Elizabeth Clare Prophet remained as the embodied Messenger. On Sept. 3, 1973, Saint Germain announced: "As a result of the swelling of the Lightbearers and the swelling of the ranks of students of Light united in this activity, as a result of the expansion of the Mother flame through the Ascended Master University [Summit University] and the Community of the Holy Spirit and these endeavors in which you are jointly engaged for the victory of the Light, I have been given again a dispensation from the Lords of Karma! Thus I may once again step forth and pledge to you the energies of my causal body for the freedom and the victory of the Light in this age!" On Jan. 1, 1981, mindful of Saint Germain's long-standing desire for a stronghold of Light in Europe, Archangel Jophiel and Christine announced a dispensation for the reversing of cataclysm and war there. July 29 to Aug. 1, 1981, the Messenger conducted a conference in Ellecom, Holland, once again anchoring physically in Europe the causal body and flame of the Master, who extended to devotees of freedom in Europe a final opportunity "to form a ring of light, a union indivisible, indispensable to our Cause." (See also: dictations given in Flevohof, Holland, 1986 *Pearls of Wisdom*, nos. 1–4.) On July 1, 1984, Arcturus and Victoria announced the beginning of a 72-week vigil to "create anew an original leaven, a momentum of freedom which will give to Saint Germain the balance for all of those endeavors for which he has secured grants from the Karmic Board in the last 400 years . . . . That culmination of your service in the 72 weeks for planet earth can lay before the Lords of Karma, through the violet flame, through your invocations, the paying of the last farthing of all that has become the debt of Saint Germain," who therefore will "once again be permitted to go before not only the Lords of Karma but the Grand Central Sun for a brand-new dispensation of Light." In February-March 1985, the Messenger and her Stump Team carried Saint Germain's message for the Coming Revolution in Higher Consciousness to Australia, the Philippines and Hawaii. On Oct. 13, 1985, two days before the Messenger's departure for her Stump to Europe, Canada, and New York, Saint Germain blessed the Team and said: "If you so multiply my Presence as I would and as I have taught you, so you shall earn for me the return of that jewel which I long ago laid upon the altar of God in behalf of Europe. Thus having that jewel returned, I may act once again with greater dominion in the physical octave because it is your will that I might intercede. . . ." Beloved Portia then announced: "The Lords of Karma and the Goddess of Liberty this day do give to Saint Germain from the Cosmic Council that which is unexpected unto him. That mantle he has sought to earn by this mission, we give in advance that he might have the wherewithal to do greater works through you. And so we respond to the dedication of the European Keepers of the Flame and those of the Isles. Blessed ones, Archangel Zadkiel and Holy Amethyst place this purple robe upon Saint Germain in the gratitude of all of cosmos for his service untiring and for your response to that service and for his movement through the earth." The Stump concluded in New York on Nov. 17, 1985, the final day of the 72-week vigil. The Messenger delivered a dictation by the Goddess of Liberty, who announced that the last vestiges of the untransmuted burdens of Saint Germain were "swiftly passing into the flame" but asked that we continue the vigil, intensifying it in the coming fortnight "to immerse the planet in violet flame." In a dictation given at 1:00 a.m. on Dec. 31, 1985, Arcturus and Victoria told us, regarding our mutual responsibility "taken on in the name of the God of Freedom," that there was "yet time to give that action of the violet flame to complete all that the Lords of Karma require." The Messenger invited all to join in a violet-flame vigil, which began immediately following the dictation and continued for 23 hours until the beginning of Gautama Buddha's New Year's Eve address at 12:05 a.m., January 1. Gautama's joyous announcement of the complete balancing of Saint Germain's debt is the capstone of a long series of initiations given to Saint Germain and his chelas during the last 400 years. **(9)** Jude 4, 12. **(10)** Gal. 2:4. **(11)** Matt. 13:3–9, 18–23; Mark 4:3–9, 13–20; Luke 8:5–8, 11–15. **(12)** Ps. 118:22, 23; Matt. 21:42, 44; Luke 20:17, 18; I Pet. 2:6–8. **(13)** See Og Mandino, *The Greatest Salesman in the World* (New York: Bantam Books, 1968), available through Summit University Press, $2.95 ppd. **(14)** Refers to the New Year's Report on the Inner Retreat given by Edward L. Francis, Jan. 1, 1986, which included a brief history and slide presentation of the Inner Retreat and Glastonbury, a review of projects completed in 1985 and goals to be met before January 1987. **(15) Golden-age flag.** The inner design of the flag of America as it will appear in the golden age has gold stripes in place of the red, representing enlightenment and the gold of the Blood of Christ—the Life-essence of Spirit (Alpha). The white stripes represent the path of initiation and the ascension, the purity of the Mother (Omega). The thirteen bands symbolize the return of the twelve tribes and the thirteenth, the Melchizedekian priesthood—the order of Christed Ones in the service of the Lightbearers.

Pearls of Wisdom®
published by The Summit Lighthouse

| Vol. 29 No. 22 | Beloved Lord Maitreya | June 1, 1986 |

Teachings from the Mystery School
XIII
The Lord of the World's Path of the Six-Pointed Star
Taking the Hand of Maitreya's Messenger

Beloved Devotees of Lord Gautama,

We bow before his flame. Together with yourselves we have been in counsel with the Lord of the World.

And now we together—this our initial assignment since the beloved twin flame has come forth to join me in a mighty work for this age[1]—with our devotees and disciples, whom you call indeed bodhisattvas, some little while ago we began the procession from the Grand Teton to this chamber in a V-formation, ourselves together at the point of the initiation of the angle of victory, with two lines forming the V of the male and female bodhisattvas who have truly earned their position in the hierarchy of Maitreya and the World Teachers, all of whom serve under the Lord of the World.

All of these devotees, beloved ones, are wearing a gold costume of formal dress honoring the Buddha. It is a metallic gold and crystal. And therefore, as we have come, traveling high above the earth, the sun of Helios and Vesta and the heart flames of the God and Goddess Meru, together with those of Lord Lanto, Confucius, Jesus and Kuthumi, and Mighty Victory and his legions, have all reflected and shone in glistening white light and gold upon our garments and our chakras.

This may seem like pageantry, but it is a divine ritual—one to be impressed in the etheric octave and in the physical earth. For this indeed is what is seen in the golden ages of the Buddhas and bodhisattvas and Christed ones, as the anointed, the disciples of those who have been sent, may be seen in various parts of the earth outside of the retreats, moving together on their missions, crisscrossing the planetary home with illumination and love, song and comfort and teachings for hearth and home as well as universities and great gatherings.

Beloved ones, in the golden ages presided over by the Ancient of Days, the path of initiation of the Great White Brotherhood and of the Lord of the World is seen, of course, as the highest way. And those striving ones are to be esteemed and respected for the austerities or sacrifices or attainments which they have made and gained.

Thus, beloved, it is understood that those in training under the Lord of the World are preparing themselves one and all to be public servants in one path or profession or another. Their retreat is only for the preparation. In the latter years, so far removed from Shamballa, our disciples have spent one and several lifetimes in retreat in the recitation of the mantra and the inner disciplines whereby they might return to the point of the One and that point of integration where their office should bring them to the fore once again as the community servant.

Even though outer schools of Christianity or Buddhism or Hinduism may have lost the thread of this reason for being of the path of the bodhisattva, believe me, beloved ones, the epitome of attainment of the six-pointed star of the bodhisattva must include the victory as the warrior whereby the individual may fearlessly defend himself and his clan—that is to say, the cluster of devotees in his band—against every enemy within or without, subtle or gross. A very key point of the six is the attainment of that level of compassion whereby one is able to deal with all parts of life with poise, diplomacy, mercy, understanding and, above all, justice untainted by sympathy of the human sort but surely adorned with mercy's delicate flame of the Bodhisattva Kuan Yin.

Beloved ones, the light of purity crowned by the attainment of the thousand-petaled lotus is most essential. The one who is warrior must also have in that office the control of power and its uses. There is, then, also the necessity for the priest class as men and women learn to serve at the altar of the sacred fire. This path of ministration you have also embraced as ministering servants. And for the gift of compassion you have known the way of the ruby-ray cross.

There is, then, the path of the perfecting of the soul, always in the heart of hearts of being, as you come to the understanding of that point of communion with the Holy Spirit. And in the Holy Spirit you become the embodiment of the World Teacher. Thus, to teach, to minister, to defend, to hold the flame of justice—these points of the Law are positioned on the interlaced crystalline triangles. And you may observe the one that is essential: the containment of the flame of the Divine Mother.

Beloved ones, the healing arts also have their positioning. We would speak, therefore, of the great hexagon of Light, the crystal that must be polished, and well-cut before it can be polished, that you might understand the power of the three-times-three in the place of the heart flame. We come, then, with you, beloved, to present some understanding concerning the Path that many of you are beginning and that many of you have walked for any number of years.

The path of the Great White Brotherhood, conceived by Saint Germain and beloved El Morya for the dispensation of this activity, is for the bringing of souls of Light to the remembrance of their divine *id-entity*, bringing them to the point of integration with the Real by a step-by-step process of choices. Beloved ones, some have not understood that many are called but not all choose to continue in that calling. I would present to you this day a diagram of the Path, that you can see and understand what are the challenges that lie ahead for you and what, indeed, are the wise counsels to be observed.

The pattern of the steps of initiation from my office and that of my beloved twin flame follows the cycle of fourteen known as the stations of the cross.[2] In this case it is a cosmic cross of white fire to which the soul decides to be fastened—not as crucifixion but as initiation, which may become the experience of crucifixion if one has not learned the art of receding into the white fire core of the heart and the secret chamber thereof. For when all the world of thy karma turns about thee, truly safety is in the very eye of the vortex of Light which thou art becoming, which vortex is also a purging and an accelerating Light.

Thus, beloved, when you determine to enter the Path, at some point from your first contact with the Teachings of the Ascended Masters to the day of your responsibility for that Teaching, there is the beginning of the spiral whereby you yourself begin to walk, year upon year, these fourteen stations. This is why the earlier Teachings of the Messenger on this Path must be put together and set forth.

For the more that is understood in the physical sense as well as esoterically, as well as according to astrology, of the twelve hierarchies of the Sun and also of the lines of the chakras, the quadrants of Matter and the four lower bodies, the more the chela who would become the disciple and the bodhisattva may proceed with eyes opened, fully aware of the protection of each hierarchy as well as of the lessons to be learned, the karma which one must confront with all due courage, selflessness and a desiring for God, including a certain savvy regarding the fallen ones and the manner in which they manipulate personal and planetary karma against the one who is fulfilling this Path.

Beloved ones, your initiation under my office cannot take any less than fourteen years. Fourteen years as a student and on the Path signifies a certain cycle complete. Please understand that this is indeed a very short period of time. And it is given and was given as a dispensation in the very earliest beginnings when the first Pearls of Wisdom were dictated to the Messenger Mark in 1958.

So it is important, then, to realize that the cycle of twelve is one circle of initiation under the twelve hierarchies of the Sun. And these twelve visitations into the 'houses' of these solar hierarchies must be understood as the initiations which Jesus Christ and the avatars of all ages, as well as the [representatives of the] Divine Mother, have faced on earth in this and previous ages.

You know these stations by the description of Jesus from the moment of his condemnation to his being laid in the tomb. The first twelve around the circle, then, is for the balancing of forces, the clearing of the four lower bodies by the violet flame and by this clearing to reestablish the action of the Trinity, the threefold flame and its functioning through each of the four lower bodies as the light is readjusted, regulated, and balanced in the chakras and in the action of the Divine Mother from the base to the crown.

We desire to see a course of study so outlined that those who may leave the Path for ignorance—whether for an inability to perceive or understand the initiations, for something left undone, for some nonawareness or even a neglect of caring for the delicate chemistry of the body and all that is needed to function at the optimum level of Christ attunement—may have this course to fall back on in time of karmic trouble.

So let the Path be made known. Let it be made plain, that those who come here may see that the Ascended Masters' University, the universities of the Spirit and Maitreya's Mystery School, has as its foundation this fourteen-point cycle. The sealing of that cycle occurs at the conclusion of the twelve lines—the threading of the eye of the needle through the center of the clock, wrapping around the six o'clock line in a figure-eight spiral and returning to the twelve.

Beloved ones, at a certain point on the Path, which may be on any line of the clock, the individual will confront a more than ordinary portion of his dweller on the threshold,³ depending on the point of his original departure from the office of the Guru, which I have held in the beginning in the Garden of Eden and now hold in the ending in this hour at the Mystery School at the Inner Retreat.

These confrontations must be observed by the mentors, by the teachers at Summit University, by counselors and fellow disciples on the Path. It is essential that there be an awakening and a quickening of the inner Christ Self of everyone in the Community in order that the signs of duress and distress and burden and of the challenges of the individual's untransmuted dweller be recognized for what they are before the disciple, not understanding his plight, may lose his balance on this tightrope walk to the heart of the Sun.

Thus, beloved, though some lines are more difficult than others, such as the three o'clock line of the pride and ambition, the conceit as well as the deceit of the human ego, the line that is above all most challenging, where many lose the way, is the six o'clock line, which is the seat both of the Mother and of the Guru Sanat Kumara.

This point of encounter, when experienced by the individual, is always the challenge of the astral body, the electronic belt, and the personified dweller. At that point the disciple must come into the love of the Buddha, whose being, multiplied through Gautama, myself, and Lord Jesus, may be known through the love for the Trinity on the twelve o'clock, the nine, and the three. It is the love of the Buddha as the Lord of the World, the Saviour of mankind, and the Ancient of Days, who gave himself to this calling, that anchors the forces, the primary forces of the soul, to the Trinity above and to the threefold flame.

This devotion to the Buddha and the path of the Buddha enables the soul to stand on the six o'clock line and to begin to externalize the flame of the Mother in love for her children and her service as well as in the purification of the chakras from the base to the crown. On this line it is very important to give the exercise of the Buddhist mantras as well as the Sanskrit syllables⁴ that evoke the presence in expression of the divine Shakti.

One must be mindful, then, also of one's age, of one's own years in embodiment. Thus, at the age of six and of eighteen and so forth, the cycle of the six o'clock line repeats itself with measured challenge to the individual. Beloved ones, all of earth has been at that point of confrontation with the Divine Mother and with the Guru Sanat Kumara, whose seat of authority is on that line of the Divine Mother.

Thus, the loss of the feminine ray and the descent of that Light makes this line one that is a particular pitfall. It is a line, beloved, where initiation takes place and where in most lifestreams in this outer evolution on the surface of the earth there is the least attainment; for it [the failure on this line] involves the squandering of the light of the chakras and especially the lower chakras.

And so, beloved, according to the fourteen stations there are two journeys to the six o'clock line—one coming in the first turn [on the outer circle] from the twelve to the six and then finally at the end [in the inner circle] of the figure-eight sealing from the twelve through the center to the six and back again to the twelve. So understand that all of the gain and the attainment that the individual acquires on the outer rim of the clock must then be sealed as one lays upon the altar of Alpha and Omega that attainment that must then become the gift of individual Christhood by the bodhisattva on the Path.

Though the goal be set [by the Guru with the chela] that the light is given for the selflessness of the disciple in order that in the end the disciple may give that light on the altar of humanity, the conclusion of the lines of the thirteen and the fourteen must prove what is the commitment of the soul and whether the vow to use that light for universal healing and planetary elevation will be kept.

So we see, beloved, that at the conclusion of the twelve points of the clock, which would represent twelve years of service, there is a primary initiation at what is called the Y—whether now, with that apparent attainment and adjustment and oneness with the Brotherhood, a certain degree of self-proof and excellence, the mounting of Light [in the ascension coil and the Deathless Solar Body abuilding in, through, and around the chakras], having transmuted by the violet flame much debris, that individual will choose, then, to go his way and enjoy the fruits of that experience privately and unto himself, using that attainment for another round of success or of the getting of wealth or of the getting of advantage in family situations and so forth, or whether he will take all of this attainment and mount the intensity necessary to seal it on the right-handed path through the two wings of Mercury, fastening Alpha and Omega to the point of the third eye.

Beloved ones, along the way of the eighth and the ninth years, the tenth to the twelfth to the fourteenth, there are very serious encounters that disciples must face. I would point out to you some of the problems that arise.

First of all, let me point out that after seven years on the Path, individuals begin to feel a certain amount of self-satisfaction, a sense that they "know their way around" the Great White Brotherhood and the Masters. And so they have adapted the Path to their way of life and often so much so that the adaptability of the soul is not there—its flexibility.

But rather they have seen the Teaching itself. They have seen its ramifications. And they arrange the Path around themselves instead of themselves around the center of the central sun of Being. They have not realized that in the center of this clock of Maitreya are the God and Goddess Meru representing the heart of the feminine ray that is the sign of the coming of Sanat Kumara. And beyond the God and Goddess Meru are Helios and Vesta.

It is beneath this canopy and tradition of hierarchs that we come, bearing well our love for Lord Himalaya, Vaivasvata Manu, and the Great Divine Director. It is through these hierarchs, Meru, and the Father/Mother God of this solar system that these Messengers are assigned to lead you in the path of overcoming.

Thus, there may come upon the disciple a certain sense of self-satisfaction, a certain sense of ritual and routine that whereas he may continue to serve and to give the decrees and to take [to himself] the dictations, there is not in fact an apparent inner increase of the rings of the causal body of Light that ought to be forming themselves as interlaced halos around the four lower bodies.

The reason this does not take place is that the individual comes to the point where he no longer surrenders each day and hour and year another layer of the tree, the human tree of life, of the electronic belt. But he has reached instead a point of accommodation, a point of a false sense of equilibrium where he has learned to balance, so he thinks, "the best of both worlds." Because the light illumines his whole house and he appears to be in the joy of the Path, it is difficult to discern that such a one has in fact stopped the flow of progress.

Thus, it takes not only soul-searching and wise observation but the direct counsel that we give through the Messenger to understand whether one's inner progress has come to a standstill because of this false perception that the circle of Life itself and of the cosmic clock is a treadmill and not a mounting spiral. And therefore, by true perception of this circle of Life, every day takes one higher in vibration and on the Path.

Now, the goal of the Path must clearly be seen. It is re-union with God. It is the becoming of the Great God Self and the dissolution of the lesser self. If the individual has entered the Path without this desire but rather to attain a certain comfort and aura for the human self and the lower self, it will literally balk when it comes to the point of having to shed the self for which all the while it has sought the glory.

This is why the Path comes to an end for many even before the seventh year. For there is a great fear and anxiety of the loss of the outer identity, an unwillingness to experience the divine interchange with Maitreya—which interchange must come, beloved, if you desire to be Real as I AM. For in the interchange I place my Electronic Presence over you as a sustaining, holding presence while portions of the lesser self, then, are received over the figure-eight flow by me. And all the while the light returning to you is building the true identity of yourself with your full cooperation and co-creativity as you lower into manifestation the elements of your own Cosmic Christhood, for which my causal body and Electronic Presence provides the blueprint and the pattern.

So you see, beloved, there is the necessity of the trust and the reliance upon the light to let go and know that in letting go one will not lose but gain. This has been said before. But it is said again because individuals in this Community are yet passing through this experience with truly no desire to let go of that over-self-concern that is the sign, sure enough, of a diminished threefold flame—one that has gone below the level of sufficiency to sustain a calm confidence in oneself as a disciple moving toward the Sun and a calm confidence that the threefold flame of Gautama Buddha, the God and Goddess Meru, and Helios and Vesta will be the sufficiency in the hour of the dark night of the soul and the soul's testing.

Beloved ones, there is a self-imposed roadblock where all of one's life becomes a concern with one's care for one's self, one's insurance, one's preparation for medical emergencies and any manner of need that could be possibly foreseen in an entire lifetime. The anxiety concerning one's physical body, one's wants and creature comforts becomes so great at this point that the individual cannot see beyond this to the challenge that he is facing as he approaches a test of the six o'clock line, no matter what line of the clock he may be on.

For you know that each line of the clock has in and of itself its own twelve lines in the sixty minutes that go round. And therefore the wheels within wheels[5] portend all twelve initiations and the fourteen on every line of this fourteen-step path to the heart of the One.

So there comes the moment when the individual must go forth to satisfy this desire to be in command of all possibilities and probabilities that the human creature could face in lifetimes upon earth. Unless the individual is able to slay that fearsome fear of the dweller on the threshold, he has no alternative but to leave the Path and follow this desiring. This solution may be the best one for such an individual. But I would point out its cause and its cure to those who, in so having this desire, may be able to make the leap to my heart.

Beloved ones, if the four-footed and furry creatures and the birds of the air and those larger ones of the jungles can leap to nestle themselves around me or around Saint Francis or Gautama and Jesus, do you not think that your soul can also make the leap into my lap in that very moment of self-nongivingness which ought to be self-forgivingness?

Beloved ones, we approach, then, the problem of the diminished threefold flame. There are those who love the Path because they were part of it long, long ago. They retain the memory and they know that the Ascended Masters' way and Teaching is correct and the true religion that they must espouse. Yet they have not quite enough magnet of the threefold flame in their hearts to sustain that Omega focus whereby they are in the figure-eight flow with the divine Alpha of the Guru or the I AM Presence or the Christ Self.

Thus, their fears overtake them. They become inundated and surfeited on each line of the clock with the planetary and personal momentums of karma which challenge them. It is exactly these individuals whom we would address with this understanding. You, above all, have the greatest need for physical contact with the physical Messenger and representative of the inner Gurus. You desire to take the hand of Jesus as Peter did when he did not have the balanced threefold flame or the raised Mother Light to sustain himself in walking on the waters of the astral sea. As he began to sink beneath those astral waves (which confront you as you enter the third quadrant of the clock), it was necessary for him to take the outstretched hand of the Master in order to be saved.[6]

This is a step of free will. But some, by their impoverished sense of self through the threefold flame not being expanded enough in this age, do not stretch forth the hand, do fabricate within themselves all type of reasoning and rationalization as to why they do not go directly either to the Messenger or to the heart of their I AM Presence or to the heart of one of the

Ascended Masters or the archangels who would speak directly to them—whether through the dictations, whether through the publications, or whether through the Messenger's own word.

Thus, the crisis of the undeveloped threefold flame is the one which we would avert, beloved. The first step is to trustingly place one's hand in the hand of the Messenger. The second is to understand that that hand can be held only so long as there is obedience to the Word and to the Light. Thus, Jesus said, "If you love me, keep my commandments—obey my Word."[7] For this is simply a definition of the polarity of Alpha and Omega, who are one in the current and flow.

There is a plugging in to the Guru by the chela, who is the feminine counterpart. And, beloved ones, by that plugging in, the flow from the mighty heart of the I AM Presence and Christ Self and from the outer attainment of the Messenger is instantaneously established, even as one might receive a blood transfusion or be placed upon a modern machine for resuscitation or for transfer of oxygen, which the body may require to continue to function.

Having this assistance, it has been seen that the body and the heart and the functions may be restored for many years. But if the assistance is not given and received successfully, the individual may pass from the screen of life almost instantaneously. And so it is at that moment of faltering when the devotee, through a misunderstanding of who he is as the lower self as compared to the inner self and the highest I AM Presence, may thus deprive himself of a victory.

You see, beloved ones, in the Teaching and in the affirmation of the Word we do stress and confirm that at inner levels, through Christ who is your divine Mediator, you can confirm and claim your divine Sonship. But this claim does not mean that you necessarily have this altogether in manifestation through the four lower bodies and through a developed heart chakra. Thus, there is a distance to be traveled between the knowledge of the Teaching and the soul's integration with the spirals of the Teaching whereby here below you have a vessel that can contain the Christ of you.

And so, if you are in that mistaken state of consciousness where you imagine a greater attainment than you actually have as the sacred fire of the threefold flame, the balanced chakras and four lower bodies, then you may consider that you do not need the physical support, the sustaining tie of the Messenger whom we have sent for this very purpose.

You may think you do not need the reinforcement just in the very hour when because of a lack of it you may take either a detour or a downward spiral as you come round the clock, going beneath, therefore, the high road of the rising spiral that moves on to the center of Christ in the center of the circle in the path of the fourteen which I am describing.

And so, beloved, the reading is clear on the part of the Messenger. For we do show the quality of heart and developed threefold flame here below. And the mistake often occurs in those who have developed themselves professionally, who are highly efficient, who may be accomplished in a number of areas because of good training, good education, and good upbringing. This is as it should be, for all of culture and civilization has been designed by the Great White Brotherhood to give the individual all of these advantages that through these various areas of development he may now turn his attention fully to the development of the threefold flame, which he then finds can be expressed through the various areas of achievement of his lifestream.

And so, beloved, those who think they have a greater light, those who appear to have a greater light, whom devotees on the Path mistakenly consider to have a higher attainment than they do, are the very ones who can fall so easily because they imagine they have no need for the support of the Guru in the outward, physical sense. And they are also the first to be offended if they are not assigned the most prominent positions in representing the Great White Brotherhood.

Thus, I come to give you the awareness which has been spoken of in dictations in this past year of the tremendous necessity for concentration on the balance of the threefold flame, both by the devotional songs and decrees to the Christ Self, the threefold flame, and the I AM Presence and by the awareness within oneself of those things of karma and personality and underdeveloped chakras that are an actual block, whether to the will of God and its power, whether to the wisdom of God and its practical application or to the love of God and its compassionate, self-sacrificing offering upon the altar.

In each of the four lower bodies and four quadrants, and therefore on each line of the clock, the opposition to the threefold flame takes another characteristic. And so it takes the astute and desiring disciple to see how in the daily changes of the signs and those thirty degrees between each of the lines of the clock there is the gradual changing—even as the sunlight changes in the heavens from the dawn to the sunset—of those vibrations of things that oppose the Light in manifestation.

Now, beloved, it is therefore necessary to realize that until you reach a certain level of carving your way through the literal chunks of coal and darkness and hardened substance, as hardened molasses, of this burden of the electronic belt around the heart—until you pass through these blocks in this fourteen-year spiral, it is very important to stay close to the heart of the Messenger whom we have sent. Her most important responsibility to you personally is to represent in true justice and compassion and wisdom the Ascended Masters who are your Gurus, to represent your Holy Christ Self and I AM Presence when you cannot pass through the hardened rock of this cave of your karma to have the direct interpretation of immediate events and initiations.

Now understand that when you see this, when you understand it, and when you adjust yourself in humility to a recognition of your need, you have entered an area of safety whereby, though your attainment be lacking, you are firmly and staunchly sustained through the Messenger by the entire Spirit of the Great White Brotherhood.

This sustaining action comes through your commitment to Saint Germain in the Keepers of the Flame Fraternity and that which the Brotherhood has determined to do for mankind through the Fraternity. The sustaining of your path is reinforced many times over as you become a communicant of the Church Universal and Triumphant, whose vows, therefore, that you take are an increasing self-discipline and desire for the purity of the path of the six-pointed star.

Now we come to the understanding, beloved, that those having either an insufficiency of threefold flame or no flame at all, for they have lost the divine spark, may function very well as chelas on the Path with this reinforcing presence of the Brotherhood. You have heard the message of the Lord Jesus Christ this Christmas. You have heard that the Light and the option for divine Sonship is given through the Messenger to all people, [this dispensation] going beyond the circle of the firstfruits to whom it is offered to all beings and lifewaves of this system of worlds.[8]

Thus, the absence of a threefold flame does not disqualify anyone from the Path as long as the requirements of the Guru/ Chela relationship are met. Some having the threefold flame yet fall back into patterns of rote and mechanization which they had long ago. This does not mean they do not have the threefold flame; it means that the four lower bodies and the human consciousness must be held in God-control by the soul, one with Christ.

Thus, fear not. For the human animal in everyone has its mechanization concepts and its rote performances. These will be rebuked fiercely where seen so that you may quickly choose to become the co-creator and co-worker with the living Christ.

Beloved ones, there is of necessity a fundamental requirement. As I mentioned, it is the stretching forth of one's hand to receive help and knowing that in the taking of the hand of the Messenger you take my hand. And in taking my hand there flows to you a Light. To receive this Light there must be the quality and the ability of obedience, the quality and the ability to bend the knee and confess the LORD—the LORD God Almighty in the Central Sun, the LORD [the I AM THAT I AM] of Elohim, of Sanat Kumara and the entire hierarchy of Light down to the nearest angel to your heart, who does happen to be our Messengers.

Beloved ones, you have seen the gross attempts of doctors and scientists to establish heart transplants and other transplants in those cases where they have not worked. There is the case, then, when we desire to transfer a portion of our heart and light through the clasped hand with a chela. There comes, then, the realization of nonreceptivity, the inability to receive that which is called the "engrafted Word."[9] And the transfer does not take.

This inability is based upon the unwillingness of the individual to obey the Christ-commands in the simplest matters, the unwillingness to establish a priority of the tasks assigned, which are always a series of disciplines given only to test the individual's ability to obey the outer representative of that Christ in order that he might be trusted to obey the inner Christ Self and the peace-commanding voice of the I AM Presence and of myself.

Therefore, in all of his wisdom, beloved El Morya, in counsel with Saint Germain and others of the Darjeeling Council, devised this Community and organization with many responsibilities and departments that could afford all types of lifestreams an assignment, a joyous path of contribution whereby they might also receive the testing of their souls of this ability to clasp the hand of the living Gurus, to be obedient to the impulsations of the Light from our heart—to receive that impulsation and to allow one's human heartbeat to now take on the heartbeat of Maitreya by establishing the rhythm of the receiving of the request, the direction, the suggestion or the command and fulfilling it not once but in a daily ritual of performance.

El Morya has engineered into all departments and services the room for creativity whereby in the very process of obedience one has a space and a time also to engage in co-creativity and by free will to determine the rung of the ladder of responsibility. Thus, each individual has determined what responsibility he could take for myself and Morya or for the Work of the Messengers.

In the determination of how much effort of creativity will be applied to the assigned task, how much giving of comfort, how much responsibility to be that pillar at that post, the individual has freedom and leeway to determine just how rapidly he will develop the threefold flame and how much more of the Light of our being he may receive.

Thus, we come to the place where the individual is in one sense of the word his own guru, setting his pace, determining what he can do and what he will not. We have heard many to say, "I will go this far but no farther. I will only do so much and then I draw the line."

This, of course, is your privilege. Sometimes it is wise, as you have assessed your potential and the limits even of your ability to function within the givens of time and space, karma, and the body itself. However, the stretching of that ability through the assignments and the demands of the Brotherhood is that which gives you the opportunity to expand the threefold flame. For the threefold flame can expand only by an exercise of free will and co-creativity based upon a *loving* obedience.

I trust you will study these words well and come to the realization that the rote obedience which establishes a certain rhythm of life is that which enables you to mirror the heart of the Guru. But the mirror may only reflect and not in fact embody. To move from being the mirror of the Guru to become the Guru's own creative self demands the firing of the three plumes—the love of the Will of God, the love of the Wisdom, the love of Love for Love's own sake, the love of co-creativity, the love of engaging oneself in adding to and embroidering upon the nucleus of the blueprint that is given.

And so it is a wondrous Path. And we see this Path in the West in those nations that are yet free and freest from the beast of socialism or totalitarianism or the various types of enslavement of the people.

Now, beloved ones, where the individual declares, "I cannot bend the knee. I do not know how. I do not know how to obey. I am not able to translate a communication that enters my ear and heart into an action that fulfills the word"—where we do not have this fundamental ability of the lifestream, the hand cannot retain the clasp. Maitreya must let go. The chela also has let go by his own nonalignment.

This is the sign of the individual's inability to receive the engrafted Word. This is a word that is very important—the *engrafting*. When there is not the Word or the Flame, the Guru must give you a path and a course where he will graft to your being that portion of his own until your system totally receives it and you have become that portion and extension of Gautama Buddha.

Now, you have been taught that the Lord of the World does sustain the threefold flame in the evolutions of earth by a filigree light extending from his heart. This, then, is the bypassing of the individual's karma whereby there is so much blackness around the heart that the spiritual arteries or the crystal cord have been cut off.

The comparison of this is seen when the arteries in the physical body become so clogged with debris that the area of the flow of blood becomes greatly diminished until it becomes a point of insufficiency and the heart can no longer sustain life. This is comparable to what has happened on the astral plane.

So Sanat Kumara came to earth to keep the flame of Life. And so does Gautama Buddha keep the flame, the threefold flame at Shamballa, and is a part of every living heart. Therefore, as the disciple approaches the path of this fourteen-year spiral, he understands that its goal is to come to the place where the threefold flame is developed enough here below that indeed, with or without the filigree thread from the heart of Gautama Buddha, he is able to sustain Life and soul and consciousness and the initiatic path.

Beloved ones, this step in itself is indeed an accomplishment which few upon this planet have attained to. You have no idea how you would feel or be or behave if Gautama Buddha withdrew that support of the filigree thread and the momentum of his own heartbeat and threefold flame. Most people, especially the youth, do not take into consideration what is the Life that they experience in exuberance and joy.

Because of the sustaining presence of the great Lord Gautama, it is not always clear who has attainment and who does not since all line up with a certain base equality in his sponsorship and all can perform at a certain level. But then when the darkness becomes greater in the earth and the stresses increase, we can see that those who have the developed threefold flame from many past ages are the ones who are enabled to endure.

Now, beloved ones, moving along on this spiral, sometimes nearing the end of the fourteen years—but, as I have said, it may occur at any place on the lines of the clock, depending where the individual left off from that inner walk with the representative of the Cosmic Christ—there does come the day when the dweller on the threshold stands there in all of its misrepresentation of the LORD's Christ. That initiation comes, and it comes irrespective of the individual's development of the light of the rings of the causal body around the lower self.

Thus, it may come to pass in an accelerated and intensive encounter with the Messenger, myself through her, that you will see exactly what that dweller is and know that you are even now at that threshold where you must slay it, else you may become the internalization of that one. In other words, you may become the embodiment of your dweller on the threshold rather than the embodiment of your Christ Self!

This is a moment of serious crisis for the disciple on the Path. The dweller is an all-consuming presence. Alas, beloved ones, not all make it beyond this point. They do not seem to be able to figure out that it is a moment for a tremendous cry of help for the intercession of the archangels, of casting oneself upon the Rock of Christ in the Great White Brotherhood and in the embodied Messenger.

Beloved ones, it is an hour and a time for understanding "I of mine own self can do nothing. It is the Father in me that doeth the work." [10] At that point you are like a patient and your life is in the hands of the cosmic surgeon, the Lord Christ. If you do all those things that the divine physician tells you to do and do them precisely so, you will survive this operation. You will become an assistant in it. And you will be able, through the power of the Great White Brotherhood, to bind the anti-self even before you have fully developed here below your own Christhood.

And when you stand bereft of the dweller because you have determined to stand, the angels and we ourselves, the ascended host, will place our Electronic Presence with you, providing that Christ presence until you have fulfilled and filled in the matrix of your own.

I must repeat that through all of this, if you can only keep the basic requirement of obedience and the bending of the knee, you will survive. But through various mechanisms of the carnal mind there is a self-defeating process so that even when there is the desire to be obedient, the ability to sustain the matrix is lacking.

In preparation, then, for the day of your encounter with Maitreya and the dweller—and perhaps the Messenger as the instrument [facilitator] of both encounters—you, then, beloved, ought to be practicing your scales in the octaves of your being:

(1) of becoming the internalization of your Christ Self and threefold flame and (2) of developing skills of communication, translating from the word received to practical action by a system of obedient love.

This is why the path taught by Maria Montessori is so important for children. For they learn to obey the "inner man of the heart"[11] as well as that which is the precise formula for the use of the equipment, the right way of doing things and that which is the wrong way. This is why we do not encourage random use of the equipment but that the child must be taught that there is a step-by-step procedure in these disciplines.

The step-by-step procedure actually follows the fourteen lines of the clock and develops in the child in the first seven years a momentum of divine order where the communication within from the inner teacher and the communication from the outer teacher become as one voice. And the child, independent as a co-creator with the inner self, is truly prepared for the path of initiation with myself.

This is why we counsel parents to study these works of Montessori, to become a part of the classroom, to place themselves through these steps and stages with their own developing children when it is most interesting to them because they are a part of every smile and move and advancement of the newborn child. Therefore, they themselves can be reborn through their own children and the Manchild in their hearts and come to the point of dissolving anxiety and fear and hardness of heart that cuts them off in the hour of maximum opportunity of initiation with Maitreya.

You can, therefore, see and define the path of the betrayers of the Word, those who have left off their service at the altar. Some who have seen coming down the road the day of the encounter with Maitreya and the dweller on the threshold have set themselves and set their teeth to a path of mechanization and rote performance and [false] sacrifice. And they have gone about this with a great intensity. And they have missed the path of obedient love. They have missed the path of submersion—this baptism by submersion in the waters of the Christ Mind. This is the meaning of the word *baptism by submersion.*

Thus, understand, beloved, they have said with Cain, "We will walk this path *our way.* We will demand that Maitreya accept us for what we do as sacrifice, and we will show that we do not have to bend the knee, that we will enter in by our own way."[12] When these have come to the day of encounter, many have dropped from exhaustion. Their machine method was unable to pass through the nexus from the twelve to the six and back again as the crossing from the twelve to the thirteen to the fourteen stations.

Therefore, beloved, they have slunk away into the night. They have lost all that they failed to gain. And that which was upon them as the mantle of the Messenger was stripped from them. And they were once more as they were before they entered the Path, except they have become worse off—ten times more the Darkness, for now they have indeed become the full embodiment of their dweller on the threshold whereas when they entered the Path they had not yet gone through this transition.

Thus, instead of accepting the engrafted Word, they accepted the engrafting fully of the dweller. And there was unto them, therefore, no separation between the dweller and the soul, as when the cancer fastens itself to an organ or the inner walls of the body and the original body tissue or organ of the individual cannot be separated out from the malignancy. Therefore, the entire organ must be removed if the larger organism is to survive at all.

When the individual becomes the embodiment of his dweller on the threshold, there is the wedding—not of the soul as the bride of Christ to her Lord but the wedding of the soul to the lower nature completely. Once this is accomplished, beloved ones, it is seen and was told by Jesus to the apostles that following this marriage there is no more looking to the path of the ascension but only to the fire of judgment. [13]

This is the process and the outcome of the Path. Thus, it is told to you that you might see that the fourteen-year course is bringing you through fourteen thousand years of your own choices. This most recent fourteen thousand years of your karma, as you know, is also based on prior fourteen-thousand-year cycles. Fourteen thousand years ago you were recently on Lemuria and Atlantis. You have had those experiences.

Now, in each year you go through all of the cycles on that line of the clock, both the positive ones where you have been victors and the darker ones where you have taken the wrong road. If you can understand this and read our dictations and see how we have made reference to the clearing of the records of Atlantis and the clearing of the records of Lemuria, you can now understand that beloved El Morya has been attentive to this, [14] keenly so, so that you might have every advantage in meeting that which have been your past sowings. Thus, it is always wise to call forth from your causal body of Light the most positive momentums of your being and to call to the causal bodies of the ascended hosts of Light for reinforcement.

I have spoken on this subject which in itself may be tedious for you, especially if you do not have full background and cannot visualize these stations or are not familiar with that which they entail. I have presented it to you so that you could understand more clearly the path of Maitreya.

It is, above all, our concern to see you through these fourteen years coming out on the other side with that measure of Christhood, that you may enter the Mystery School not totally dependent, then, upon the Messenger but dependent only in certain areas where you are moving toward an inner and outer sonship whereby you become examples in the Community of true shepherds who have earned your shepherd's crook. And its sign is truly the sign of these fourteen stations and fourteen years.

I trust that the goal of my message to you this day, which is an alert to endure to the end[15] and truly understand your lines of the clock, shall have been satisfied by your attentiveness, your receptive hearts, and the love of the Great White Brotherhood who have sent me here.

I trust you realize that there are other cycles, such as personal and world astrology, the dark cycles affecting the planet, and especially the association of your astrology with that of your embodied Messenger. For the clasping of hands is also made less difficult by a harmonious union of the charts of Guru and chela. And where the charts are not so compatible, the chela, then, may pursue transmutation on those lines of the birth chart as the cycles appear and request the intercession of the calls of the Messenger.

We are here, then, to make plain a Path, to hope, beloved, that in your understanding of this Path you may see that it is difficult for anyone to pass through a fourteen-year program in the Mystery School, that you will not only set an example but also be watchful with a new understanding of what it is to remain the watchman of the night[16]—and that is to be the guardian, the keeper of the flame who watches those new on the Path and helps them so carefully with the profound understanding of Saint John of the Cross of what it means to approach nearer and dearer to the Holy of Holies of the Bridegroom, the Holy Christ Self, Lord Gautama, Sanat Kumara, Jesus, Kuthumi, and my own heart so directly involved with your soul's ascent.

In gratitude to the Messengers who have made themselves available on a continuing basis that this Path might be outlined to you in this hour and physically set forth for those to come, we seal you in an eager and equal gratitude for your receptivity to the Teaching given. By your sustaining of this Guru/Chela relationship, you do form the nucleus of the Great Central Sun Magnet that is truly our foundation of the Inner Retreat and the Mystery School.

In the name of the Light to which all mankind have recourse, I seal you in the joy of the clean white page of the new year in the privilege accorded me to be the first of the Brotherhood to write on that page of your Book of Life.

It is my prayer that I have helped you and shed some vision on the Path. For though the old year and its difficulties have passed, you must expect increasingly difficult hurdles in order that you might attain to the point of the bodhisattva that is appointed unto you.

In the name of my beloved Jesus the Christ, the blessed Saint Issa, I bid you love and truth and peace and freedom.

"The Summit Lighthouse Sheds Its Radiance O'er All the World to Manifest as Pearls of Wisdom." This dictation by Lord Maitreya was **delivered** through the Messenger of the Great White Brotherhood Elizabeth Clare Prophet on **Wednesday afternoon, January 1, 1986,** during the 5-day New Year's conference, *Teachings from the Mystery School,* held at Camelot. (1) See Lord Maitreya, December 31, 1985, "I Draw the Line!" 1986 *Pearls of Wisdom,* vol. 29, no. 19, p. 161. (2) The **stations of the cross** and their initiations on the lines of the Cosmic Clock are listed in next week's Pearl of Wisdom, no. 23, p. 218. See also Elizabeth Clare Prophet, "The Personal and Planetary Initiation of the Crucifixion of Christ: The Fourteen Stations of the Cross," on 6-cassette album *The Second Coming of Christ I* (A7836), $37.50 postpaid; also available separately on cassettes B7840, B7841, $6.50 ea. postpaid. (3) **Dweller on the threshold.** See 1985 *Pearls of Wisdom,* vol. 28, no. 26, p. 350, n. 10; and 1983 *Pearls of Wisdom,* vol. 26: Jesus Christ, March 13, 1983, "The Awakening of the Dweller on the Threshold," no. 36, pp. 383–91; Elizabeth Clare Prophet, "Christ and the Dweller," no. 38, pp. 429–54. (4) See "Bija Mantras to the Feminine Deities," "Buddhist Mantras," and "Bija Mantras for Chakra Meditation," in *Mantras of the Ascended Masters for the Initiation of the Chakras,* Summit University Press, pp. 4, 14, 17, $1.00 postpaid. Recorded on 5-cassette set (B85135–B85139), $32.50 postpaid; single cassettes also available (B85135, B85136, B85137), $6.50 ea. postpaid. (5) Ezek. 1:16; 10:9, 10. (6) Matt. 14:22–33. (7) John 14:15, 21, 23, 24; 15:10. (8) See Jesus Christ, December 25, 1985, "Rise, Peter: Kill and Eat!" 1986 *Pearls of Wisdom,* vol. 29, no. 14, pp. 112–15. (9) James 1:21. (10) John 5:17, 19, 20, 26, 30; 14:10. (11) Eph. 3:16, 17; I Pet. 3:4. (12) Gen. 4:1–15. (13) Heb. 10:26, 27; II Pet. 2:4–22; Jude 3–19. (14) **Clearing of the records of Lemuria and Atlantis.** See 1985 *Pearls of Wisdom,* vol. 28: El Morya, July 19, 1985, "The Inner Temple Work of Serapis Bey," no. 43, pp. 521–26; Sanat Kumara and Lady Master Venus, July 21, 1985, "Our Mission in the Earth," no. 44, p. 530; Archangel Chamuel and Charity, October 10, 1985, "The Light Is Gone Forth and the Light Shall Prevail," no. 46, pp. 549–57; Saint Germain, October 13, 1985, "The Sword of Sanat Kumara: The Judgment of the Rulers in the Earth Who Have Utterly Betrayed Their God and Their People," no. 50, p. 594. And 1986 *Pearls of Wisdom,* vol. 29: Lady Master Nada, November 3, 1985, "The Empowerment of Love," no. 2, p. 9; and Archangel Michael, December 6, 1985, "Archangel Michael Dedicates an Altar and a Sanctuary," no. 9, p. 57. (15) Matt. 10:22; 24:13; Mark 13:13. (16) See Saint Germain, November 22, 1980, "The Watchman of the Night," 1980 *Pearls of Wisdom,* vol. 23, no. 48, pp. 325–34.

Pearls of Wisdom®

published by The Summit Lighthouse

| Vol. 29 No. 23 | *Beloved Lord Maitreya* | *June 8, 1986* |

Teachings from the Mystery School
XIV
Self-Determination in the Real Self

We have come and we have tarried with the Lightbearers here. We have meditated upon your hearts—these disciples who came with me in the golden, shining splendor of the sign of Victory.[1]

Therefore, there is created a oneness, an inner reverberation of harmony, heart to heart, and a determination and a pledge from these disciples to work together with you to fulfill those plans of Saint Germain that he holds so dear in his heart and especially to work with the souls of Light who are so ready for the Path.

Beloved, it is a year when I would be close to you, when I would come to your heart. Do not neglect the key, then, that we have made so plain.

A step backward from civilization is needed. I have pin-pointed a universal problem among chelas of the sacred fire, which is the problem of sugar, refined and processed in any form, and of refined wheat and products that deprive the body of nutrients.[2] These problems that result whether in hypoglycemia or diabetes are more prevalent among those of greater and greater Light because of the problem of the chemistry between these substances and the acceleration of the Light simultaneously in the cells.

My statements to you, then, set forth what I consider to be an earnest and well-thought requirement for chelaship with myself and my beloved twin flame. Please know that when you make the call and give those inserts so named (which sheets

must certainly be duplicated for each and every one of your
decree books concerning all of the factors of the enemy of sugar,
drugs, alcohol, and nicotine) and when you will daily work with
them [these decree inserts] until you have conquered them [these
conditions], you will find that you will be exorcising yourself,
your loved ones, and your families of those conditions most
causative of the ups and downs of moods that result in the
failure of tests, as we have already discussed.

Beloved, I am taking you up the mountain as swiftly as you
choose to run. I am taking you to the place where you desire to
be, where you have desired [to go] all of this life and at least all of
your years of acquaintance with the Ascended Masters. Somehow
you feel that you have not quite made it, that you have not quite
become the master you desire to be. And when you look at those
things that have not been conquered, I tell you, a high percentage
are connected to the body chemistry and the interference in that
chemistry by these entities so named.

Beloved ones, can you imagine an embodied Master who is
still prey to the manipulation by discarnate entities? It cannot
be. Thus, let the chelas of Maitreya prove to the world that this
is indeed a path of physical mastery.

It is my desire in this moment to transfer to you an initiation
of the sacred fire that is for your strengthening, for your healing,
and for the elevation of your soul by a transfer and holding action
from my heart that the soul might be at a place of greater self-
determination in the True Self that is the reality of thy being.

I come in a year that promises to be one of many challenges
of the unreal—this unreality mounting in a frenzy of revenge,
retaliation, resentment, envy, jealousy, and ignorance coming
through that Dark Cycle this spring,[3] whose shadow already
casts itself upon the pages of the new year.

Beloved ones, look to those closest to you and look to the
planet as a whole. Be a lover of souls, trusting and compassionate. But never trust the force that attacks the souls whom you
love. For those whom you love may be under the greatest attack
[designed by the sinister force in order] that they might become
the instrument of moving against yourself.

Beloved ones, we know the ways of the sinister force. Therefore, I have come to initiate a spiral of self-determination in the
Real Self.

I desire to have you focus your attention now on the reality of
your Real Self. This reality is championed by the most beloved
Great Divine Director. I would ask you, therefore, to sing two

songs as you come in line [to receive this initiation of the sacred fire]—the song to the Great Divine Director that is composed to his decree and the song that you call "God's Real in Me."

Beloved ones, bring these words with you. And as you come in line to receive our touch, know that I, Maitreya, stand nigh the physical octave before you through the Messenger. And as she places her hand upon your third eye, know that I am transferring to you the impetus of your soul's desiring to fulfill all of the Love wherewith you descended to earth to become the champion of the poor and of the Lightbearer and of the homeless and of the rejects of life.

Beloved, my words are brief yet they are emphatic. But my greatest statement to you in this hour is the light of my Love. I embrace you and I give you my hand, strong and firm. I shall never fail to answer your call.

Therefore, let all come forward now.

[The congregation passed before the Messenger to receive the blessing of Maitreya while singing alternately "God's Real in Me," number 797, and "Divine Director, Come!" number 418, in *The Summit Lighthouse Book of Songs* (nos. 102 and 33 in *Mantras of the Ascended Masters for the Initiation of the Chakras*, pp. 34 and 9).]

"**The Summit Lighthouse Sheds Its Radiance O'er All the World to Manifest as Pearls of Wisdom.**" This dictation by Lord Maitreya was the concluding address **delivered** through the Messenger of the Great White Brotherhood Elizabeth Clare Prophet on **Wednesday evening, January 1, 1986,** during the 5-day New Year's conference, *Teachings from the Mystery School,* held at Camelot. (1) See Lord Maitreya, January 1, 1986, "The Lord of the World's Path of the Six-Pointed Star," 1986 *Pearls of Wisdom,* vol. 29, no. 22, p. 195. (2) See 1986 *Pearls of Wisdom,* vol. 29, no. 19, p. 164, n. 1. (3) **Dark Cycle.** See *Kuthumi on Selfhood—Consciousness: The Doorway to Reality* (1969 *Pearls of Wisdom,* vol. 12), pp. xi–xii, 10, 30, 246–54, 263–66. On April 23, 1986, the Dark Cycle will enter its eighteenth year, commencing the initiations of personal and planetary karma accrued on the five o'clock line of the Cosmic Clock under the solar hierarchy of Gemini. The flame of God-Wisdom on this line may be misqualified through envy, jealousy, ignorance of the law, spiritual blindness, and mental density. The five o'clock line polarizes with the eleven o'clock line of God-Victory under the hierarchy of Sagittarius. God's energy may be misqualified on this line through resentment, revenge, retaliation, and idolatry. In his December 28, 1985 dictation—"The Descent of the Mighty Blue Sphere: A Fourteen-Month Cycle in the First Ray of the Will of God"—Serapis Bey warned that in the Dark Cycle of Gemini/Sagittarius, earth would face the backlash of the dark ones "for all of the Light that has gone forth in the last twelve cycles of the clock." He said that beginning April 23, 1986, "you ought to expect the revenge of the fallen angels against the Light and the Lightbearer. And you must understand that the wall of blue flame and the sphere of blue flame is given unto you [in order] that when the Darkness comes it may instantaneously be deflected and go back to its source. . . . Do not underestimate the meaning of the Dark Cycle of the returning of mankind's karma and of the karma of the fallen angels, who have in this hour great envy and jealousy of the Lightbearers and the sweet children of Light. And their momentum of revenge has been smoldering as resentment for aeons." For more information on the **Cosmic Clock,** see Elizabeth Clare Prophet, "The Cosmic Clock: Psychology for the Aquarian Man and Woman," in *The Great White Brotherhood in the Culture, History, and Religion of America,* Summit University Press, pp. 173–206, $8.95 postpaid (also on 8-cassette album *Shasta 1975,* cassettes B7528, B7529, $6.50 ea. postpaid); *The ABC's of Your Psychology on the Cosmic Clock: Charting the Cycles of Karma and Initiation,* 8-cassette album (A85056), 12 lectures, $50.00 postpaid; "Charting the Cycles of Your Family According to the Cosmic Clock," on 8-cassette album *Family Designs for the Golden Age* (A7440), $50.00 postpaid, single cassette MTG7421, $6.50 postpaid; and "Childhood Stages of Development: Karma, Christhood, and the Cosmic Clock," on 4-cassette album *The Freedom of the Child* (A83131), $33.00 postpaid.

THE STATIONS OF THE CROSS

	STATION	INITIATION	LINE ON THE COSMIC CLOCK
1	Jesus is condemned to death	God-Power	12:00
2	Jesus is made to bear his cross	God-Love	1:00
3	Jesus falls the first time	God-Mastery	2:00
4	Jesus meets his afflicted mother	God-Control	3:00
5	Simon the Cyrenian helps Jesus bear his cross	God-Obedience	4:00
6	Veronica wipes the face of Jesus	God-Wisdom	5:00
7	Jesus falls the second time	God-Harmony	6:00
8	Jesus consoles the holy women	God-Gratitude	7:00
9	Jesus falls the third time	God-Justice	8:00
10	Jesus is stripped of his garments	God-Reality	9:00
11	Jesus is nailed to the cross	God-Vision	10:00
12	Jesus dies on the cross	God-Victory	11:00
13	Jesus is taken down from the cross	God-Power	12:00
14	Jesus is laid in the sepulchre	God-Harmony	6:00

Pearls of Wisdom, published weekly by The Summit Lighthouse for Church Universal and Triumphant, come to you under the auspices of the Darjeeling Council of the Great White Brotherhood. These are presently dictated by the Ascended Masters to their Messenger Elizabeth Clare Prophet. The international headquarters of this nonprofit, nondenominational activity is located in Los Angeles, California. All communications and freewill contributions should be addressed to The Summit Lighthouse, Box A, Malibu, CA 90265. Pearls of Wisdom are sent weekly throughout the USA via third-class mail to all who support the Church with a minimum yearly love offering of $40. First-class and international postage rates available upon request. Notice of change of address should be received three weeks prior to the effective date. Third-class mail is not forwarded by the post office.

Pearls of Wisdom®

published by The Summit Lighthouse

| Vol. 29 No. 24 | Beloved Sanat Kumara | June 9, 1986 |

The Ancient Mantle Is Restored

Helios and Vesta, I am come, the servant of Light, Sanat Kumara, and the Holy Kumaras with me.

And may I introduce the twin flames, the mighty Snow King and the Snow Queen, whose Light has graced in ancient time the land known as Greenland, beloved ones. And thus they ruled there in an era when all was tropical and beautiful, and therefore the name remained.

Beloved hearts, dwelling in the white fire core of the holy purpose of this ancient civilization, these twin flames release in this hour the light of a cosmic snow which comes upon earth as a cloud of infinite energy such as you call forth according to the alchemy and ritual of Saint Germain.[1]

Therefore, beloved, know that this light of cosmic snow has the same absorptive quality of the cloud of infinite energy. It comes to earth, then, in a release of light, clearing the debris for the descent further and further into the physical octave of the etheric body of Light, the swaddling garment given to earth thirteen months ago.[2]

Blessed ones, this cosmic snow is to absorb ten thousand times the weight of each particle in human creation and substance of the astral plane. Such is the quality of this light. Throughout the world, then, a new purity of light goes forth and a clearing action that comes in answer to your calls to the violet flame.

For the Great Central Sun Magnet of the violet flame, made known to you by Lanello this Christmas Eve past,[3] is surely a triumphant light, beloved hearts. It is the action for the demagnetization and transmutation of great darkness that has covered the land. And now in its wake, in its clearing action, there is a way made clear for the descent of the light of purity. May you celebrate the presence of purity in my own twin flame, Lady Master Venus, keeping the flame of the Inner Retreat of the Divine Mother—that City of Light established over this place from ancient times and now revealed.[4]

Beloved ones, may you receive the purity of Light from the Queen of Light, the Goddess of Light, the Goddess of Purity, archangels and angels serving, then, this frequency of Light— Gabriel and Hope, legions of Elohim Purity and Astrea, legions of Serapis Bey and seraphim. For all gather to amplify this hour.

It is a cosmic moment always when a planetary home may receive this release of cosmic snow, always passed from Solar Logoi through these reigning hierarchs, the Snow King and Queen. May you receive them and the fairy wonderland they bring, as elemental life rejoice, and breathe in this cosmic radiance, radioactive with the light of the Central Sun, which when absorbed is for the healing of disease and the consuming of those diseases which beset the earth in these last plagues.[5]

Therefore, you who are burdened in heart, for your bodies have been burdened even unto the death, we say to each and every one of you, you have not lived in vain. For by your presence, by your life lived with God-determination and sacrifice, dispensations may come forth such as these, which when amplified in the dynamic decrees of the student body can mean the turning back of these plagues of viruses of many kinds.

Blessed ones, take heart, then, for earth has been host to aliens who have permeated its atmosphere and the bodies of people and the animal kingdom alike with those substances working against the light of the centrosome of every cell in the body. Beloved hearts, the age of heart, of Aquarius, of expansion of the heart flame is the pushing back of this darkness.

May your threefold flame be balanced. May the Light push out this darkness and consume it. May the Light of your heart as a sun radiance, O beloved, now greet the pressing in of this cosmic snow. And may the patterns of rays from your heart be open channels whereby the light of the cosmic snow may enter your being as an immunization, then, from this darkness moving, then, from the astral to the physical plane.

We have placed the armour of Light, the blue sphere in the fourteen-month cycle; and you have been admonished to call for the golden chain mail established by the God and Goddess Meru many years ago.[6]

These actions of the sacred fire taken by the cosmic hosts, beloved ones, are for your appropriation. And this is the reason why you have the dynamic decree—to affirm and confirm our Word that comes out of the highest octaves of Light through the etheric plane. From the etheric plane down through the mental, astral, and physical is your responsibility to invoke it, to establish the highways of our God[7] that the light may pass through for the purging, yea, and the acceleration of matter molecules until this earth not only reflects the Light but becomes that Light in every cell and particle and grain of sand!

Therefore, beloved, we come with legions of Light. And I AM Karttikeya, known of old as the leader of the armies of heaven. We come for the defense of Light in this heart and your heart and every heart on earth yet to be contacted by Morya's thread of contact.

O beloved ones, as you have decreed it, so the Great Law then affirms that we may answer that call. And we come to defend the right of the Great White Brotherhood to be in the physical octave. This is the drawing of the light of the hosts of heaven down to the very base of the pyramid of Life. Thus, in the cities, in the streets, in the professions, in the businesses and marts of commerce, let the light of the Great White Brotherhood permeate and penetrate through!

Let life be a circle of oneness and not of separation. Let there not be, beloved, the separation of the arts and culture and music from government or from religion. Let not life be compartmentalized, beloved! Let it not be that one is a specialist in this area and suffers, then, the nondevelopment of all other areas and chakras.

Let the religion of Almighty God—the stretching forth of his mighty hand finding the soul, turning the soul back to the original Central Sun—be, then, the set of the sail of every endeavor. Let every attitude of life, every beatitude of love therefore be the encompassing of the understanding of the I AM THAT I AM.

Let this Chart given to you by Saint Germain become a great stained glass window, that the light of the sun may play upon these spheres of light and all may see, as with the passing of the cycles of the hours and centuries, how different qualities of the flames are seen and the hues of light increase and decrease.

Thus, all in his time, every man and every woman must become on the stage of life, then, prominent for the quality of Light he may deliver that is uniquely required to save his nation, his people, and the idea itself of Love and the universal religion of the Universal Christ.

Beloved ones, when the Sun shines through the crystal of your being and the fire is so intense that the world is fairly blinded for the light, it is your hour and not the power of darkness[8] but the power of the light of your causal body descending! So let it be that this light may flow through your auras and the rings of the auric field and the chakras. So let it be that you are prepared additionally, then, by the gift of the cosmic snow, which you may call forth and amplify in any hour by this power of the Great Central Sun Magnet of the violet flame.

Oh, we intensify the release of Light! Oh, we come for the confounding of those fallen ones who have set their teeth and, in so setting their teeth against the Light, have then become those for whom the outer darkness is the weeping and the gnashing of teeth.[9] Therefore, beloved ones, they are ground to powder[10] and the Light itself is all that remains. And the identity that has denied the Light is no longer. It is cosmic law.

And you are in embodiment for one purpose—that the wheels of your chakras might accelerate to amplify and increase that cosmic law of Light! Light! Light! Light of purity descending now for the fulfillment of the vow of every lifestream upon this earth—lifestreams in India and China and Tibet and throughout this planet who have maintained their tie to the Great White Brotherhood through adversities and persecutions and eras of darkness.

Light! Light! Light! go forth now from the Central Sun by the power of the secret rays in this cosmic snow! And let these souls of Light receive our assistance. And let this trial be the statement of the Victory of every saint and martyr and everyone who has stood for Light and has fallen for want of the defense of this Community of the Holy Spirit.

I, Sanat Kumara, stand in the City of Light above and below here with you. And I say with Lady Master Venus, our gift to Saint Germain and Portia is to extend the Light, to penetrate through, to clear the way for the drawing of these souls under the canopy of the Great White Brotherhood for bringing these souls to the path homeward, to reestablish the Light and contact with the Great White Brotherhood and to let them know that they are not alone.

No matter what their path or element of devotion, there is a oneness worldwide in this new year of 1986 of all those who consider themselves a part of the forces of Light of all cosmos. This oneness we secure at inner levels. You, then, may secure it on the outer and have our full support, beloved. Oh, will you do it with our fervor now? ["Yes!" applause]

The ancient mantle is restored—the mantle worn by this Messenger at inner levels before the world was, in the heart of the Great Central Sun. This mantle, being retained at the level of the Christ Self at inner levels of Light, does drop, then, upon the physical shoulders of the physical Messenger. And therefore, the full authority of her divine being is reestablished this day in the physical octave.

Beloved ones, understand the meaning of the Path. All have gone forth into the Matter spheres. And in the making of karma and in the entangling alliances with the fallen ones, there has been a separation of the inner being and the outer. When the initiations are sufficiently passed, when the 100 percent of the karma is balanced, when the God-Control is shown in the face of adversity, then the inner mantle may be restored and returned.

Blessed ones, whether or not you have realized it, you are all striving for the mantle of your Holy Christ Self and the highest attainment of your being which you knew with your twin flame in the beginning and which you also earned in the service of the hierarchy of angels, of Ascended Masters, Elohim, and elemental life.

Thus, beloved ones, this mantle is the mantle of the angelic hierarchy. For your Messengers began their evolution as angels of Light and came descending into form, walking in the way of the sons and daughters of God and earning therefore that individual Christhood. Thus, from the bands of angels and legions of Light whence they descended comes this ceremony at inner levels, and now on the outer, of the reinstatement of that mantle.

Now, if she shall wield it in the full power of its origin in the heart of the Word, you will see that it becomes a canopy and a call and a sustaining presence to all similarly aligned in this wavelength of Light and hierarchy of service. It is an infinite hierarchy of Light, beloved ones. And therefore know that as you are chelas of Sanat Kumara through this Messenger, you also increase, you also expand and abound in Light through this mantle which you touch and have in this figure-eight flow.

Therefore I say again, as the fiat of the beloved Father unto her: The ancient mantle is restored, my own beloved. Go forth in confidence. For the light and the authority of the mantle of the Great White Brotherhood is indeed multiplied by the full attainment now of thy causal body.

I say it, beloved ones, as a fiat and as a message to the sinister force, who have taken full advantage of the condition of the flesh and the lowliness of the physical octave in which ye all have been bound and separated from the Holy of Holies. And they have enticed and entranced from the least unto the greatest of Light-bearers. And therefore, they have feared the hour and the coming of the restoration of the mantle. And they have tried at every hand and in every way to delay its manifestation through the passing of the plots to create more and more karma and therefore to sustain the separation.

Beloved ones, this is the value of the path of chelaship through Lanello and El Morya given to your Messenger, which she does strive daily and hourly to give to you that you might realize that any condition of density or stubbornness or division within your members does postpone the very day of the return of your own mantle of grace and authority in the hierarchy of the Godhead whence you descended to this world, coming desiring to save the children of the Light yet not always remembering your highest calling and the honor of it in word and deed and company.

And I mention the word *company*, beloved ones. Let your company, then, be with angels and souls of Light. Guard well your company that you do not absorb the darkness and the lethal emanations of fallen ones. Be free to consort with Divinity and his offspring but do not consider this freedom as license to do or to be any thing. For thereby you may discover yourselves once again entangled in the ways of the fallen angels who lurk to take you from your highest attunement.

Therefore, to you and to all upon this earth I say, the ancient mantle of the Divine Mother *is* reinstated, *is* restored. Therefore let the Light prevail. Let the Darkness wane. And let those criminal elements in every land receive the judgment of that mantle.

Thus far and no farther! You shall not cross the line of this mantle of Light. And we, the emissaries of the Great White Brotherhood, we who express and carry the authority of the Guru, of the Great God—we, Sanat Kumara, Holy Kumaras and the Lady Master Venus—take our stand for the rolling back of the entire force of dark ones in all galaxies and systems who have set themselves against the Light of Almighty God in embodiment in you, each and every one who is an extension of ourselves, and in the Witnesses[11] and all who have gone before.

Beloved ones, this is the hour of the turning around of Darkness on planet earth. What we face, then, as the equation, beloved hearts, is that the momentum of Darkness in the individual lives of the people and their ignorance of this dispensation may cause them to experience that slip twixt the cup and the lip whereby, because they do not know of the turning around of Darkness and the turning of the Light against that Darkness, they may allow themselves to be once again beset by that Darkness.

Therefore let the fiat go forth. Let it ring throughout the planetary body. The Darkness this day is turned back! It shall not stand! And the dark ones have no defense, no access to the Light of the Divine Mother! And the mantle of the LORD God upon the Messenger does drive back these fallen ones. And they must receive their judgment in answer to the call of the children of Sanat Kumara, the children of the Mother and the sons and daughters of God with her on a planetary scale.

Beloved ones, the hour is come for a tremendous reinforcement of positive victory within your hearts! That this action of Light decreed become physical, we have come. For as you know, the confirmation of this dispensation of the Central Sun may be in the earth only by your affirmation.

Well done, thou good and faithful servant. Thou hast been faithful in a few things, I will make thee ruler over many.[12] Thus may it be spoken of you, beloved, as it is spoken here this day.

Go forth in triumph, for the Light does prevail! The Light does triumph! And I AM in the Spirit of the cosmic forces of Victory who assemble in your behalf, in behalf of the entire Spirit of the Great White Brotherhood on earth in this hour.

I salute you. I extend to you from my heart the light of peace and the embrace of heaven unto earth.

Be healed, O beloved, for thy soul does ascend to God.

"The Summit Lighthouse Sheds Its Radiance O'er All the World to Manifest as Pearls of Wisdom." This dictation by Sanat Kumara was **delivered** through the Messenger of the Great White Brotherhood Elizabeth Clare Prophet on **Sunday, January 26, 1986,** at Deer Park Chapel, Royal Teton Ranch, Montana. (**1**) **The Cloud**. In his book *Intermediate Studies in Alchemy*, Saint Germain teaches how to magnetize millions of "focal points of light" into a brilliant pulsating 'cloud' of infinite energy that can then be directed into specific personal and planetary conditions for the healing of disease, pollution, crime, and war. See Saint Germain, *Intermediate Studies in Alchemy*, Summit University Press, pp. 38–87, $3.95 postpaid; also published in *Saint Germain On Alchemy: For the Adept in the Aquarian Age*, Summit University Press, pp. 191–251, $4.95 postpaid. (**2**) See Sanat Kumara, December 31, 1984, "The Turning Point of Life on Earth: A Dispensation of the Solar Logoi," 1985 *Pearls of Wisdom*, vol. 28, no. 6, pp. 60–61. (**3**) See Lanello, December 25, 1985, "A Report from the Darjeeling Council," 1986 *Pearls of Wisdom*, vol. 29, no. 11, pp. 79–80, 82–83. (**4**) See Sanat Kumara, December 15, 1985, "The Retreat of the Divine Mother at the Royal Teton Ranch," 1986 *Pearls of Wisdom*, vol. 29, no. 10, pp. 70–72. (**5**) Rev. 15:1, 5–8; 16; 21:9. (**6**) See Serapis Bey, December 28, 1985, "The Descent of the Mighty Blue Sphere: A Fourteen-Month Cycle in the First Ray of the Will of God," and God Meru, July 26, 1964, "The Coat of Golden Chain Mail," 1986 *Pearls of Wisdom*, vol. 29, no. 15, pp. 125–32. (**7**) Isa. 40:3. (**8**) Luke 22:53. (**9**) **Weeping and gnashing of teeth.** Matt. 8:12; 13:40–42, 47–50; 22:13; 24:50, 51; 25:30; Luke 13:28. (**10**) **"Grind him to powder."** Matt. 21:44; Luke 20:18. (**11**) Rev. 11. (**12**) **The faithful servant.** Matt. 25:21, 23; Luke 12:42–48; 19:11–27.

The Acceptance of the Mantle and the Mission

O Spirit of the Great White Brotherhood, Lord Sanat Kumara, beloved Father, I raise the sword of the sacred fire, and with the mantle that is my own and the mantle of the Great White Brotherhood, I divide the waters of Jordan. I cleave asunder the Real from the unreal. I AM the binding of all forces of Darkness assailing the Light of God in his people on earth.

Let the mantle of Light descend and the power of Moses and Elijah, the Lord Christ and Sanat Kumara. Now, therefore, O God, fulfill in us by the power of thy office with us this day the divine plan for this Inner Retreat that we might be in position according to the grid of Light and the will of God, January 1, 1987.

Let all Darkness that assails the Great White Brotherhood be confounded, bound, and turned back. I decree it by the authority of the Light of God with me and within each and every one of the chelas of the will of God worldwide. Wherever they may be, I call upon their causal body of Light, the mantle of their own Christ. Let it descend, O God! For this earth is the LORD's, and the fullness thereof, the sea, and all they that dwell therein.

O God, we are one. In the name of the Father, the Son, the Holy Spirit, and the Mother, we accept thy call, we accept thy light, thy cosmic snow and secret rays. We accept our mantle, O God. We wield it in thy name to thy holy purpose.

(In the name of Jesus Christ, let us kneel before the altar of Sanat Kumara.)

Beloved Father, we are thy sons and daughters, thy angelic emissaries of Light. Let us go before thee and before thy name, even as thy presence dost always go before us for the Victory of the Light.

Even so, Lord Jesus Christ, come quickly into our temple by thy Holy Spirit! Let the power of the three-times-three swiftly bring in the great golden age. Let walls of light and of the ruby ray seal this endeavor, seal this place and our hearts from that darkness which may come upon the people for their karma and the karma of the earth. Therefore we say to it, "Thus far and no farther!" God has decreed this day: the Darkness is turned back.

In the name of Sanat Kumara, we accept thy blessing, intercession, and initiation of Light, O God. May this that is unto us be laid upon the heart's altar of Saint Germain and Portia for the Victory of the Aquarian age. Amen.

In the name of the Father, the Son, the Holy Spirit, and the Mother, it is done.

Pearls of Wisdom, published weekly by The Summit Lighthouse for Church Universal and Triumphant, come to you under the auspices of the Darjeeling Council of the Great White Brotherhood. These are presently dictated by the Ascended Masters to their Messenger Elizabeth Clare Prophet. The international headquarters of this nonprofit, nondenominational activity is located in Los Angeles, California. All communications and freewill contributions should be addressed to The Summit Lighthouse, Box A, Malibu, CA 90265. Pearls of Wisdom are sent weekly throughout the USA via third-class mail to all who support the Church with a minimum yearly love offering of $40. First-class and international postage rates available upon request. Notice of change of address should be received three weeks prior to the effective date. Third-class mail is not forwarded by the post office.

Pearls of Wisdom®
published by The Summit Lighthouse

| Vol. 29 No. 25 | *The Beloved Messenger* | June 10, 1986 |

The Healing Power of Angels
The Reestablishment of the Electromagnetic Field of the Aura

I
The Path of Twin Flames
through the Mighty I AM Presence
and the Science of the Spoken Word

As we come together this evening, some of us are perhaps seeking solutions or resolutions to burdens we bear, problems we may have, a sense of incompleteness. Something makes us pursue the Self beyond the self and the greater Light. Something goads us, and usually it is our extremity, our need, even if it be but a sense of emptiness, of desiring to be filled with the love of the Holy Spirit.

I do not profess in any way to have human solutions to human problems. They are like the bottomless pit. If we don't have problems, we manage to create them. We embroider upon our woes and continue in our discords and diseases, our worries and concerns.

And so, I am not an expert in solving the problems of soul mates and twin flames by psychology, by all kinds of human improvement courses, positive thinking, and so forth. There are so many counselors who are experts in these areas. If you have need of them, I bid you go to them.

What I offer you is not this, but it is the walk with God, your Mighty I AM Presence, that lifts you above that human scene and all of its relativity and all of its goodness and badness.

And sometimes it's very easy to see how human good or evil is only the flip side of the same coin. And it doesn't really seem to matter because, you know, when you are surfeited in human goodness, it is just as bad as human badness, because what it lacks is the reality of your divinity, the expansion of that spark within you. It lacks the light of eternal Life, of Reality with a capital R, which is God. And so, beyond human pleasure and pain, neither of which can surely satisfy us, what we are seeking is divine bliss.

The path of twin flames which we seek and practice here is realized through the science of the spoken Word. It is through our ultimate devotion to the one true God that we reenter the Love which gave us birth in the beginning. And we know that in Him we live and move and have our being. And in that being, in that divinity, we discover who is the I AM THAT I AM where we are—who and what is Real.

We are so often fooled by the human or human relationships. We, so weary of the round of relationships, are seeking for something that is the beautiful bliss of God which we knew in the beginning with our twin flame. Some have forgotten that the bliss of God is quickly spent unless there is always that threesome of twin flames united through the Universal Light or the Universal Christ. The bliss, then, of the return to God is a parallel path of seeking and finding our Wholeness, first in God and then in the Beloved.

We remember the magnificent words of Jesus Christ. He gave us the formula for finding God and the twin flame all in one. He said, **And I, if I be lifted up, will draw all men unto me.**[1] And the "I" that is lifted up is the I AM THAT I AM. It is the sacred fire. It is raised in you from the base of the spine unto the crown through seven planes of being called the seven chakras.

This I AM that we lift up is also the Mighty I AM Presence that you see in the Chart behind me, the magnificent spheres of Light—rainbow spheres within spheres. That depiction is of your causal body. It is a replica of the Great Central Sun.

This entire Spirit/Matter cosmos has a Great Central Sun, which is the point of your origin, conceived in liberty by God—the Alpha, the Omega, the yin and the yang, the masculine and the feminine. Once the Divine Whole separated into the twain as twin spheres of these causal bodies—two spirit sparks, twin flames descending for the purpose of evolution in the Matter cosmos as they had evolved in the Spirit cosmos, which is that causal body of Light.

And so we went forth to be the manifestation of our Father/Mother God, sons and daughters who could put on more and more of those spheres of Light which we call God consciousness. So it is in this God consciousness that we live and move and have our being. This we must not forget.

Veils of illusion surround us now. We are separated by time and space, but they are not. As surely as we are here and now, we are still in that Central Sun. We are in the beginning and we are in the ending. We do not have to get anywhere—we have to know who we are now. This absolute immaculate concept of our identity is the foundation of every quest and pursuit.

If you do not understand that you are the Holy Grail, the chalice for God's Light now, you will never find the Holy Grail. You cannot find what is not in yourself. That is why it is absolutely certain that you will find your twin flame—because your twin flame is inside of you, in that great causal body of Light, in the middle figure in the Chart who is your Holy Christ Self. In every heartbeat the other half of the Divine Whole is present.

Going forth, then, from the highest octaves of Light, we begin a scenario of descent into relativity, into karma, causes and effects we have set in motion. And karma is certainly the inexorable, immovable force. Karma is a law so perfect, so just, so loving as to teach us by our reapings what we are sowing and to show us how to transmute those causes.

Karma is inescapable, and yet it is a challenge, it is a joy. We wake with God-determination to slay that dweller on the threshold of our karma. We rejoice that God has given us the opportunity to meet our destiny, a destiny we have forged right or wrong—as the Divine Absolute or as relative good and evil.

What makes this challenge so wonderful, so enjoyable is the day-by-day victory that we gain—the mastery of self. And we see how through personal or planetary karma God shows us a way of self-mastery. We gain independence and creativity. We have to have ingenuity to see how we are going to jump through that hoop of fire or walk on the hot coals of the world's hatred or condemnation—how we are going to make it through the labyrinth of the astral plane when we know at the other side standing before us, waiting for us, is the beloved Bridegroom, the eternal Christ, beloved of our souls, and the twin flame.

So the quest for Love must never be seen as a sorrowful way. You must never think of yourself as burdened, bowed down, having problems, but as a spirit spark who has descended into this Matter cosmos with the eternal partner, who is somewhere working as hard as we should be working for our joint victory.

And what is the purpose of seeking and finding the twin flame? It is because the two halves are needed. The twin causal bodies need to be present. There needs to be a consonance and a divine harmony in order for us to fulfill our reason for being, whatever that reason is. The divine interchange of that Light between the causal bodies above enables us here below—whether we are acquainted or introduced or halfway around the world from each other—to do that which we must do.

We all saw the tent posts tonight, and we saw the wind and the rain moving against the tent. And we wondered if the water would be so heavy as to perhaps come through on our heads. It's a very good analogy because, you see, each one of us is a pillar holding up the mighty tent of the LORD. It is a very vast tent and it has many pillars. If you pull out a few, the tent will still stand, but if you pull out too many, there is no longer a tent. So there are many vacancies on the planet earth today, and that's why a lot of things are not getting done in the nations.

We see a mismanagement of money and the economy. We see things we would like to improve in our schools, our educational systems. So many people have the right solution. They truly have become messengers of God in this or that field. They know what should be done. Then they go to Washington, they get into the Senate or the House or on a committee or in the great bureaucracy that is there, and they suddenly find out that nothing moves.

They can't get the solution to the problem to the point of action. There are too many blocks, there are too many forces, there are crosscurrents. Not everyone has the same goal of freedom and liberty for all peoples. Not everyone has the same vision for the people of

Light in America and the world to be champions of freedom and peace and full enlightenment.

So, many go away discouraged. They resign out of protest from those situations where the divine solutions are blocked. People in some areas are without hope because of this. And others do not accept hopelessness, but they continue to understand that if they work hard and they try their best and they keep on trying, somehow good will come out of it and Good will triumph over Evil.

The forces we encounter in our subconscious and in daily life are like the blocks we see. Somehow the whole world wants peace, yet war is everywhere. A hopeless, helpless state results from the absence of contact with our Mighty I AM Presence and from an absence of union, at least at inner levels, with our twin flame.

We need to get back to the position of the brightness, the Light, the heaven world, the power we had with God in the beginning. And we need to bring it all down to this point of action, to this grid of time and space created for us as the means of the testing of our souls and the learning of the lessons that at one point in life we refused to learn in any other way.

This seminar on the healing power of the mighty angels of the LORD shows us how we can enlist the archangels and their hosts of the seven rays and bring them into action through our seven chakras for the clearing of those chakras, for the clearing of our four lower bodies so that we can get into alignment with the Presence of God, with the Presence of the twin flame, and access that Light and bring it into action in the streets of life.

We have wars that we must fight, such as the war on drugs. We have wars to fight for the salvation of our children and our youth, whether it is from psychological manipulation or indoctrination or chemicals or drugs or what is portrayed to them from such an early age through television and the motion-picture industry. There are many areas where, united with our twin flame, we are a vital force for Good, where we can make a cosmic difference in what will be the future of this nation and this planet.

Archangel Chamuel and Charity of Love's Third Ray

I would like to introduce you to Archangel Chamuel, mighty Archangel of Love of the third ray. His divine complement and twin flame is the Archeia Charity. Charity, sweet Charity, is her name. And concerning charity we have the magnificent writing of the apostle Paul.[2]

Charity is the epitome of Love. It is self-giving love that gives oneself with the gift—not as a bestowal, but as a transfer of knowledge of how to use and wield the flaming sword of Love. It is a transfer of the education of the heart, of skills, of the means to restore dignity to the poor and the impoverished.

I heard someone say over and over again in the past week or so that sympathy, like charity, is never enough. And I wanted to cry out and say, **Charity never faileth! Charity is the bliss of God!**

Charity is the infilling of ourselves with a tremendous love. Charity, then, again, is the emptying of the cup of love, the giving with a purpose—not to demean, not to control, not to possess but to raise up because we transfer our flame of profound respect, a sense of honor, a sense of coequality with those with whom we share our love.

Not systems of redistribution of wealth mandated by a powerful federal or world government but the expansion and the God-mastery of the flame within the heart—this is the divine way of sharing, so that those who have the mastery of multiplying abundance in all levels and all fields may share it by offering the challenge of independence, individuality and self-mastery to those who need our love, that they, too, might keep the flame of Life: the respectability and the responsibility of personhood in God.

So charity begins at home. And we begin this seminar with Chamuel and Charity for the understanding of the transmutation of a limited human love by the fulfillment of Divine Love. As you know, there are many forms of love. Human love can be used to possess, manipulate, control, belittle, to program and psychologically harm people. Divine Love is liberating. It is the caring enough to stand guard, to watch over but not to do for others, especially our children and the ones we love most, what only they can do for themselves.

Charity is a love so great that when we see all of the world suffering and all of the great need, we understand why Jesus, who had the great commission of the Cosmic Christ these two thousand years, left home at a very young age and went to the Himalayas for seventeen years to study, to learn, to increase his self-mastery.[3] He put himself beneath the greatest teachers on the way. Though filled with the Christ Spirit, he set the example of being God-taught before he would show forth the fullness of that masterful Presence for all the world to see. He was the Word incarnate, but he demonstrated for us a path of discipleship, a love so great that said, I must show the way of proving the Law step by step—how that Christhood is won whereby each disciple of the living Word may lay down his life for his friends.[4]

Haven't you thought it a great pity when you see the struggles in Ireland and young men and women starving themselves to death or other protests by Buddhists in Vietnam setting themselves on fire? There is a human sacrifice that availeth nothing, but there is a divine sacrifice that availeth all when the Christed one lays down his life, not by dying but by living, and gives the full cup of his Light that millions might live.

We are not here to die as martyrs; we are here to live as Christed ones, anointed ones,* to pick up the path of the Ascended Master Jesus Christ, to find his Lost Teachings and to apply them. This we will teach and compress into our sessions as much as we can throughout this weekend retreat on the healing power of angels.

Each one of the seven rays and the archangels who serve on those rays focuses an entirely different vibration and initiation. You need to make friends with the archangels. They are already your friends. And the legions who serve under them are your very personal brothers and sisters. They move with you, they do all they can do for you. And what prevents their total and complete giving of themselves to you is the absence of your understanding of the Call—calling the archangels and their legions of Light into action to assist you on your path of personal Christhood, to cut you free, to help you.

*The word *Christ* is derived from the Greek *Christos,* meaning "anointed," from *chriein,* "to anoint."

We have such a desire, all of us gathered here, to serve God and man and to help this planet through her dark night. I know why you are here and that this is the reason—it is the desire to help others and somehow feeling that as much as you would help, you cannot do enough, that the world is careening at breakneck speed, wobbling with the weight of planetary karma in these end times. We want to make more of a dent on the darkness and the burdens of people. And this is precisely what the archangels are teaching us to do.

So I would like to invite you to come into the vibration of beloved Chamuel and Charity. The pink flame that they bear goes from the softest petal pink, almost white, into the deep rose and ruby color. A ruby ray is a very intense action of Love. It is purging. There is such a thing as a ruby sword that is wielded by legions of the third ray. There is such a being called the Buddha of the Ruby Ray, meaning he has the Buddhic mastery of this intense action of Divine Love.

Love is sometimes a very difficult thing for people to handle. And because it is the sacred fire, when Love enters one's being it can upset, it can cause a chemicalization. You can actually become sick from the Divine Love entering your being before you have purged the four lower bodies of toxins, from records of karma on the lower astral plane, which is the plane of pollution.

So, you see, in order to have more Light and in order to have the presence of the archangels with us, we need to be emptied so that we can be filled. And actually, this process goes on within us simultaneously. Day by day as we are purged of darkness by the Holy Spirit's violet transmuting flame, we increase our capacity to contain God's Light.

I would like to make an invocation to Chamuel and Charity in your behalf, and then we will sing to "Beloved Chamuel and Charity, Archangel and Archeia of the Third Ray," number 301 in our songbooks:

Beloved Mighty I AM Presence from the heart of God in the Great Central Sun, we call upon Chamuel and Charity in this hour. Blaze thy Light, O angels of the sacred fire, Angels of the LORD, flaming ones of Divine Love, Thou who hast descended from the heart of the Great Central Sun for the confounding of tongues in the judgment of Nimrod and the Nephilim gods in their building of the tower of Babel: come now for the confounding of all ignorance, all illusion that would separate us from the LORD God and our beloved twin flame.

Bind all of this! Let our souls rise in the freedom of the eternal Christ, rise to thy flaming presence in the heart.

Come, angels of the Holy Spirit, angels of Divine Love. Surround us now with infinite Light.

O Helios and Vesta, Alpha and Omega, Lord and Lady Meru, come forth! Thou sponsors of twin flames, let Love now begin to press in and penetrate into the cause and core of disease, all forces of anti-Love burdening those who are gathered here with absolute God-determination to enter the heart of hearts of Divine Love.

Legions of Light, millions of angels of Love from the Central Sun, we welcome you to planet earth. Bring Love to all who need compassion in this hour, the caress of Christ, the kiss of peace. O living flame of Love, be thou the All-in-all. Let perfect Love cast out fear![5]

We accept it done this hour in full power.
In the name I AM THAT I AM, Amen.

> O come, beloved Archangel of Love
> Stand in our midst today
> Beloved Chamuel!
> O Lord of heaven's third ray
> O Lord of heaven's third ray.
>
> O Charity, beloved complement
> Twin flames from heaven sent
> Beloved Charity!
> Pink flame of majesty
> Pink flame of majesty.
>
> O come, flaming cherubim, seraphim
> Who abide in the fires of creation
> Who abide in the fires of creation.
>
> Raise thy flaming sword on high
> Cherubs gather now in the sky
> Our hearts expand with gentle love
> Enfolding love, adoring love
> Holy Spirit, caress with tenderness
> And each one bless.
>
> O come, flaming ones from the
>   Great Central Sun
> Who abide in the fires of creation.
> Who abide in the fires of creation.
>
> Take, O take my hand and heart
> Feel the love I to you impart
> For life is love and love alone
> And for mortal error it doth atone
> And raise you in redemption's name
> Out of the realm of human pain
> To behold once again the Light of God
> And His true love!
> All this I AM—All this ye shall be!
>
> Ye shall be Love! Ye shall be Light!
> Ye shall be Life! It is done!

Knowledge of the Call and Friendship with the Angels

We discover, then, that Charity is more than a virtue. Charity is a divine being, an angel of the feminine ray who in answer to our call comes into our hearts. The knowledge of the call is the greatest key to your victory in life. This is a simple call you can make:

Beloved Mighty I AM Presence, beloved Father, send to my side, to my right and to my left, right now, Archangel Chamuel,

**Archeia Charity. Send them to me, O God, and raise up thy
mighty Spirit of Love within me.**
I ask it and I call it forth with all of my heart.
In the name of Jesus Christ, Amen.

This is a very simple way to compose a call, calling in the name of
your Mighty I AM Presence to the heart of the Father to send his
angels to your side and to do so in the name of the Son of God. You
needn't have it written down. It comes spontaneously from your heart
wherever you see need. You can make this call for your children, for
your family, for strangers in distress.

What is the key to God's heart? What opens the channels between
heaven and earth? It is your devotion, your purest devotion and love
for Christ, for God, for all the saints in heaven, for all of the millions of
angels who serve at the throne of grace, for one another and especially
for yourself.

If you do not love yourself, how can you love your twin flame?
And Jesus said, if you do not love your neighbor whom you have seen,
how can you love God the Father whom you have not seen?[6]

So we seek attunement with our Father. We seek the full power of
Light. We seek to be one not only with the virtues of God but with
those whom he has called to embody those virtues—our divine Teachers. This is the reason for being of the mighty archangels. They come
to teach us, to inspire us, and to show us how to draw into our own
aura, our own dynamic forcefield, into the electronic field of Light
around our bodies, the qualities of heaven, the love of God, the
wisdom, the will of God, his purity.

All these things are ours naturally by divine inheritance, but when
we move through the world and its density, somehow they are
absorbed. And so we have to daily renew our momentum, because we
always want to have so that we may give.

Devotion, then, is a very important part of seeking and finding
God's helpers and working together with them for world peace and
freedom. It has been my greatest desire for many years that the whole
world should know the friendship of the angels.

I would like to invite you to sing the words of the apostle Paul
which he wrote down to Charity (number 289 in our songbooks).
Many of you know these words by heart. You can take them as a song,
a meditation, and a psalm of praise. Meditate on the beauty of Love,
then go by that ray of Love to the heart of the most magnificent
heavenly angel that you can picture in your mind—an archeia of Love
whose aura is filled with the pink and the rose emanation, smiling at
you, one you have known for ages.

You all know the angels and the archangels. You have known
them from the beginning. They have accompanied you in your descent
to earth. When you pass from the screen of life they greet you and take
you to the higher octaves and prepare you for your next assignment.
You will never see an angel that you don't know!

So here is beloved Charity who longs to send you the full-gathered
momentum of her love. And as you are desirous and pray in your heart
of hearts to Almighty God to deliver you through this angel, it is done.
For you are sons and daughters of God, you have free will, and the call

to God, when it harms no man, when it is in keeping with the will of God, is always answered.

When you make a call to God to send his angels, remember this saying: **The Call compels the answer!** You believe it, you know it—not alone by faith but by the science of Being.

Therefore, O God, I say in the name of thy Son, send Chamuel and Charity now to expand and expand and expand thy Light within our heart chakra. Let Love expand, O God. Let millions of angels descend to earth to sustain thy Love and Grace.

Chamuel and Charity, place your Electronic Presence to the right, to the left of each one here. Be with us forever, O God.

O God, come into my temple quickly.

O Jesus, come quickly into my temple now.

Charity

Though I speak with the tongues of men
   and of angels, and have not Charity,
I am become as sounding brass
   or a tinkling cymbal.

And though I have the gift of prophecy
   and understand all mysteries
   and all knowledge;
And though I have all Faith,
   so that I could remove mountains,
   and have not Charity,
   I am nothing.

And though I bestow all my goods
   to feed the poor,
And though I give my body to be burned,
And have not Charity,
   it profiteth me nothing.

Charity suffereth long, and is kind;
Charity envieth not;
Charity vaunteth not itself,
   is not puffed up,

Doth not behave itself unseemly,
   seeketh not her own,
   is not easily provoked,
   thinketh no evil;

Rejoiceth not in iniquity,
   but rejoiceth in the truth;
Beareth all things, believeth all things,
   hopeth all things, endureth all things.
Charity never faileth, never faileth
Charity never faileth.

But whether there be prophecies,
   they shall fail;
Whether there be tongues,
   they shall cease;

Whether there be knowledge,
it shall vanish away.

For we know in part
and we prophesy in part.
But when that which is perfect is come,
Then that which is in part
shall be done away.

When I was a child, I spake as a child,
I understood as a child,
I thought as a child:
But when I became a man,
I put away childish things.

For now we see through a glass, darkly;
But then face to face:
Now I know in part;
but then shall I know
even as also I am known.

And now abideth Faith,
And now abideth Hope,
And now abideth Charity,
these three;
But the greatest of these is Charity!
Charity! Charity!   *I Corinthians 13*

The path and the teaching of Divine Love taught by the
Ascended Masters is very, very practical. When you leave here this
evening you will have in your hand effective tools for the raising up of
your spirit, for the solving of problems in human relationships, in your
marriage, with your children by the only means possible—the sacred
fire of the Holy Spirit.

So I would like to show you these techniques if you will take your
Stump booklet.[7]

Saint Germain and the Ascended Masters

Today is a day when we experience great love for Saint Germain.
Saint Germain is the Master whose portrait hangs to my left who
complements the presence of Jesus to my right. Saint Germain was
embodied as Saint Joseph and as the prophet Samuel and other
illustrious figures beyond Atlantis and Lemuria many thousands of
years ago and even up to the present era as Francis Bacon.

Today he is an Ascended Master. Tomorrow you may be an
Ascended Master, because that is the path that he teaches, that is the
path he has showed to us.

The definition of the term *Ascended* Master is a Master who has
ascended: one who has mastered the flame of Love, the light of God, in
all of the seven chakras of being—who has brought those sacred centers
into balance, who has taken God control of his own consciousness,
being, and world, who has balanced 51 percent of his karma, fulfilled
his divine plan and merged with the consciousness and flame of God.
This flame of the ascension, which is the white fire of the Divine

Mother, begins to accelerate the very atoms and cells of the body whereby the soul is filled with Light—no longer, therefore, a candidate for reincarnation in these bodies we wear but a candidate for heavenly octaves in bodies celestial.

As Paul the apostle was taught directly from the heart of Jesus, so he wrote that there are bodies terrestrial and bodies celestial.[8] You have an Ascended Master light body above you in vibration. It is the body of your Higher Self that you enter. You become one with it. And it is the only means of dwelling forever in the presence of God with the saints in heaven. The ascension is the goal of your life.

The Ascension and the Threefold Flame

The ascension is therefore the process, the ritual, the sacred adventure of accelerating all that we are. Saint Germain teaches this, explaining the mission and the Lost Teachings of our Saviour Jesus Christ. Jesus, of course, does not remain silent. He also teaches us by the Holy Spirit this path of the violet flame.

One day a number of years ago—in fact, in 1962—Saint Germain wrote to his students around the world a valentine. And through this valentine he explained the greatest gift of Life to us—the threefold flame of our hearts, the divine spark. I would like to read it to you as the sweet offering of his heart to you. He dictated this to my late husband, Mark Prophet, whose picture you see to your right. Mark Prophet lived and served as a Messenger for the Great White Brotherhood in this century and he passed on in 1973, fulfilling the teachings of the Ascended Masters that he taught, through the ritual of the ascension.

The ascension is not so far from you. It is capable of being entered into through Christ the Lord. The reason it is not a popular teaching or a known teaching is that the real Teachings of Jesus Christ have been lost or stolen from us. And they are being restored today by the Holy Spirit to the hearts of millions.

The purpose of our twin flames—of Mark and me—is to bring that Teaching together: to write it into books and to deliver it in the spoken Word so that all may have it and use it. It is the lost Word and the lost chord of the fullness of your being and your reunion with your twin flame. This we will unfold in this seminar.

So here is the valentine poem as Saint Germain gave it to Mark and as Mark wrote it down.

A Call to Hearts of Gold

Methought I would compose a sonnet
Valued by the world,
A poem with light of Love upon it—
A challenge to be hurled.

The "spear" I "shake"
And now do make,
A "Willing" of "I AM,"*
To be the break
That all may take
O lovely God, I AM.

* Will-i-am Shake-speare

For thou hast sought
And to men brought
Opportunity and plan,
But men have thought
And oft been caught
By delusions in a jam.

Now if the power
Of Truth this hour
Earth's freedom course must chart,
There must be men,
O valiant men,
To rally from the start—

To see behind
The shams of men
The fraud they have created,
Attacking Truth
And Sons of Light
Whom they have oft berated.

Now, I might add
This "not so bad"
Assessment of our friends
Is bad enough
Through lacking Love—
How they have underrated!

But we who've been
A part of earth
And felt the lash
Of tyrants bold—
For freedom's sake
We now do make
A call to hearts of gold.

Stand stalwart, then,
And let your heart
Be framed by fragrant flowers,
Not earthly substance
That will fade—
Choose immortelles
From heaven's bowers.

And see thy heart
As altar chalice,
Loved by God and man,
And holding forth forevermore
Tripartite Flame
. . . 'Twill exalt the plan.

You are never alone
But always one
With us who love you now,

> And as all came
> From Central Sun
> Our Love's eternal, vowed.

May I, on this occasion, speak of the heart to those of you who are perhaps familiar with the subject. And at the same time, inasmuch as many new souls are joining the ranks of those who read and love the Pearls of Wisdom, may I say to all that your heart is indeed one of the choicest gifts of God.

Within it there is a central chamber surrounded by such light and protection as that which we call a "cosmic interval." It is a chamber separated from Matter, and no probing could ever discover it. It occupies simultaneously not only the third and fourth dimensions but also other dimensions unknown to man. It is thus the connecting point of the mighty silver cord of light that descends from your divine God Presence to sustain the beating of your physical heart, giving you life, purpose, and cosmic integration.

I urge all men to treasure this point of contact that they have with Life by paying conscious recognition to it. You do not need to understand by sophisticated language or scientific postulation the how, why, and wherefore of this activity.

Be content to know that God is there and that there is within you a point of contact with the Divine, a spark of fire from the Creator's own heart which is called the Threefold Flame of Life. There it burns as the triune essence of Love, Wisdom, and Power.

Each acknowledgment paid daily to the flame within your heart will amplify the power and illumination of Love within your being. Each such attention will produce a new sense of dimension for you, if not outwardly apparent then subconsciously manifest within the folds of your inner thoughts.

Neglect not, then, your heart as the altar of God. Neglect it not as the sun of your manifest being. Draw from God the power of Love and amplify it within your heart. Then send it out into the world at large as the bulwark of that which shall overcome the darkness of the planet, saying:

> **I AM the Light of the heart**
> **Shining in the darkness of being**
> **And changing all into the golden treasury**
> **Of the Mind of Christ.**
>
> **I AM projecting my Love**
> **Out into the world**
> **To erase all errors**
> **And to break down all barriers.**
>
> **I AM the power of infinite Love,**
> **Amplifying Itself**
> **Until It is victorious,**
> **World without end!**

With this gift of infinite freedom from God's own heart this Valentine season, I close this epistle with a never-ending promise to assist you to find your immortal freedom as you determine never to give up and never to turn back. Remember that as long as you face the Light, the shadows are always behind. And the Light is there, too, to transmute them all.

Keep your gaze toward "the City" and be not overcome of evil but overcome evil with Good.

For the freedom of all mankind,

Lovingly, I AM

Saint Germain

The Power of the Name of God I AM THAT I AM

This is a very profound teaching. It is a teaching of the third ray of Love. Your heart is the chalice of this third ray and of Love. It is through your heart that you receive the blessings, the healing, and the initiations of the Archangel Chamuel and Charity.

This gift of a prayer, which is called a mantra, from Saint Germain, is to be found in this booklet. So we can give it together now. It is number 19 on page 5.

When you see the word "I AM" capitalized, you know you are pronouncing the name of God. I AM THAT I AM was the name of God given by God, and by the angel of the LORD who stood in his presence, to Moses[9]—Moses, our leader, Moses, who has liberated us from Egyptian bondage.

Can you not feel yourself present at the Red Sea in Egypt and then moving toward the Promised Land? Can you not identify with Moses and the moment of the Ten Commandments and this tremendous contact with Almighty God who, when he gave his name to Moses, gave it to him for us and said, "This is my name forever and my memorial to all generations"? "All generations"—that means you and me and all of the generations of our consciousness since then, before then, and till now.

When you say **I AM THAT I AM** you are saying, **Where I stand, there God is. I could not exist if God were not where I am. He is a living flame of Love, Wisdom, and Power in my heart. He gave to me the divine spark. He feeds that spark, that unfed flame, over the silver cord which connects me to his living Presence through the Universal Christ.**

You see this diagrammed on the Chart behind me—the I AM THAT I AM above; the Universal Christ, your Real Self, in the center; and the lower figure, yourself as you are seated here. You are the temple of the Holy Spirit, as Jesus and the apostles have taught you.[10] And therefore the flame of the Holy Spirit can be seen by you and called forth as the violet flame which is depicted on this Chart.

So when you look at this decree it says, **I AM the Light of the heart.** What it is saying is **God in me, the I AM THAT I AM, is the Light of my heart.** It is an affirmation. When you affirm the Light of the I AM THAT I AM here below through the power of the spoken Word, which is the power to create, so it is done. So it does manifest.

Our entire reason for being, for being born into these bodies, is to access the Light of the Spirit of the I AM THAT I AM and to draw it down into every cell and atom of these lower vehicles we wear until they become all Light; and therefore, no longer subject to time and space, they accelerate and there is no longer any difference between us and our Divine Reality above.

It is the Light in our hearts expanded to fill all of our house that collapses time and space—the grid of karma and mortality. And when you pass from the screen of life you are intended to *ascend* to that Presence—to *transcend,* vibrationally, these veils of death. And the reason your soul has taken embodiment this time is because you didn't contain enough Light in your bodies, in your members, at the conclusion of your last life, so you had to come back again.

And why didn't you contain enough Light? Because you had karma. Because you also had mortal desire and unfinished business to tend to. And because you didn't know how to call forth the Light of your Mighty I AM Presence and to accelerate God's Consciousness in your chakras. This is why you didn't make your ascension in your last life.

"I Must Work the Works of Him That Sent Me"

So God sends us forth again and again to finish the work—his Work on earth. **I must work the works of Him that sent me.**[11] Isn't that a wonderful mantra of Jesus? He said it. And that's why you are here. God sent you to work his Work. And the way to do it better is to increase the Light by his name, by his Word, by the use of the mantra. So you take Jesus' mantra and you say, **In the name of my Mighty I AM Presence, in the name of the Son of God and beloved Jesus Christ,**

**I AM working the works of Him that sent me—
right now today!
I AM working the works of Him that sent me—
in God's own way!
I AM working the works of Him that sent me—
by Love's consuming sacred fire!
I AM working the works of Him that sent me—
by Christ's own God-desire!**

The mantra is a worded formula expressing devotion to God; it is an energy matrix that sustains the qualities invoked by the science of sound and rhythm. It is a prayer, but it is also a dynamic decree. It is also an affirmation. The prayer contains the pattern of that which you desire to manifest on earth by the authority of your God-given free will, by this divine spark in your heart, and by your beloved I AM Presence.

Therefore, with all of the love of your heart, all of the faith, all of the knowledge of the science of Being, won't you offer Saint Germain's prayer—a prayer of love to your God and to the God of your twin flame.

I AM the Light of the Heart

**I AM the Light of the heart
Shining in the darkness of being
And changing all into the golden treasury
Of the Mind of Christ.**

I AM projecting my Love
Out into the world
To erase all errors
And to break down all barriers.

I AM the power of infinite Love,
Amplifying Itself
Until It is victorious,
World without end!

(given three times)

The Exercise of the Spoken Word

There is a great deal of understanding that must precede the exercise of the spoken Word in prayer, in mantra, in decree. The science of this Word is both simple and vast. Usually I spend two or three hours teaching the fundamentals before we even begin to say a decree. If you are interested in studying and mastering these principles, I have a number of lectures on videotape and audio cassettes; above all, I recommend that you read our book *The Science of the Spoken Word*[12] from cover to cover and give the decrees that are in it with your whole heart.

I am trusting that you who are here recognize the power of prayer and of the spoken Word and understand that it is a profound communion with God. What you need to know is that you have a river of Life which is called the silver cord, and that it descends from the heart of the Father through the heart of the Son to your own heart chakra.

This is your natural spiritual resource. It is the energy you use to live and move and have being—to put your ideas into action, to express your love, to do everything you do in a lifetime. Your spiritual resources may be used by you according to your free will because you have a divine spark—because when God gave you that threefold flame, he gave you the gift of Himself, the gift of his power to create.

The threefold flame (which is also called the Holy Christ Flame) is the focus in you of the consciousness of the Trinity—Father, Son and Holy Spirit. By that sacred fire of God burning in your breast, you are endowed with the Universal Mind, you are a son of God and a co-creator with Him.

A decree, then, is an expression of your joy in God's flame in your heart. It is your joyous response to your Creator, affirming His Being where you are. For when you decree, you are the instrument of God's Word. By the power of that Word you draw down the infinite Light that is sealed in your I AM Presence.

You will notice that this decree says, "I AM the Light of the heart shining in the darkness of being and changing all. . . " The word *change* is the sign of the age of Aquarius we are entering. It's the name of the game of the seventh ray. It is called *transmutation,* or purification. It means that if we have sent out hatred or even mild dislike in our lifetime, we have bound others by that energy and that energy will cycle back to us and bind us.

We become enlightened by our love for Jesus Christ and all of the saints of God. Our profound love for him makes us suddenly aware that this hatred or mild dislike is a wrong for which we are responsible

(to be continued)

and ultimately accountable. One day we will pay the price; and if we do not do so willingly, on our own initiative, the Law will exact it. This is the explanation for sudden calamity and cataclysm and cancer and the woes coming upon the earth. Karma. We cannot hate any part of Life, which is God, with impunity. Therefore, the perversion of the third ray of Divine Love is hatred, and we see that that energy of hatred must be *transmuted* by Love through the violet flame.

Now, we may have an accumulation of that karma of hatred from previous embodiments. Sometimes you meet someone and you have an instantaneous dislike for that person but you don't really know why. It might be that you had an altercation in a past life, and the sense of injustice and the energies tied up in it are unresolved. So we don't want to hate, and hate again, and pour out dislike again. We want to release this balm of Gilead—the power of God's Love—for change, for transmutation, for the dissolution by the sacred fire of this record, this knot in our subconscious, or astral body.

We understand that energy is neither created nor destroyed. It goes somewhere, but it may be transformed. So what we must really understand is that hatred is a thing that we create—an overlay of negative vibration which we impose upon God's pure energy. Because we are God's children and his sons and daughters, he gave us the power to be co-creators with Him. We have made the mess we have made of our world. We have also created the bliss. We have made our choices and we live in the realms of our own creating. We can undo our past hatreds, discords and dislikes *before* they return to our doorstep for our undoing.

To that end, this evening is devoted to the third ray, to the ray of Divine Love. And this slide illustrates the heart chakra, which corresponds to that ray. It has twelve petals. You can visualize it as a pink flower having twelve petals with a threefold flame in the center.

The Violet Flame for Personal and Planetary Transmutation

Now, the action of change is brought about by the violet flame, which is the flame of the seventh ray and the seventh age of Aquarius. It is violet in color. Its purpose is transmutation. By the authority of the I AM Presence, the Holy Christ Self and the threefold flame within us, we can give a decree that calls forth the violet flame from the heart of God and sends it into the cause and core of all conditions known or unknown, conscious or unconscious, of hatred and the psychology of its nonresolution, arguments, anger—any and all problems we have ever had with people. Or perhaps we've even been angry at God because we don't think our life has panned out the way it should.

So everything from mild dislike to irritation to fear, which is also a perversion of Love—all of this burdens the heart. It causes heart disease. It weighs down the chakra. The chakra doesn't spin with the Christ Light. If we don't have a functioning heart in the physical octave, we leave this octave, don't we? We can't make it without a heart, physically. And the truth is we can't make it spiritually without an expanded heart flame, without Divine Love blazing from us as the great central sun of our being.

So what do we do now?—now that we've discovered we've mis-qualified the flame of Love. Well, we have to call forth the violet flame from the Person of the Holy Spirit, who both forgives our sin and transmutes the misqualified energy that is the product, or precipitate, of the consciousness and the act of sin.

This violet flame is the promise of God spoken by the prophets of the Old Testament. Jeremiah said:

> After those days, saith the LORD, I will put my law in their inward parts, and write it in their hearts; and will be their God, and they shall be my people. And they shall teach no more every man his neighbor, and every man his brother, saying, Know the LORD: for they shall all know me, from the least of them unto the greatest of them, saith the LORD: for *I will forgive their iniquity, and I will remember their sin no more.* [13]

The alchemy of the violet flame is described by Isaiah, who spoke for the LORD:

> Though your sins be as scarlet, I will make them white as snow. Though they be red like crimson, I will make them as wool. [14]

That's a promise which is being fulfilled in the end times, now today in the seventh age.

Saint Germain is referred to as the seventh angel in the Book of Revelation, chapter 10. It is written:

> But in the days of the voice of the seventh angel, when he shall begin to sound, the mystery of God should be finished, as he hath declared to his servants the prophets. [15]

These are indeed the days of the voice of Saint Germain when he is speaking through his Messengers the prophecy of the seventh age, sounding and intoning the sound of the violet flame; and the mystery of God is being finished through his sponsorship together with the entire Spirit of the Great White Brotherhood (the saints robed in white, their souls and auras and chakras purified by the white light; see Revelation 3:4, 5; 4:4; 6:9–11; 7:9, 13–15; 15:6; 19:7, 8, 14).

And this mystery of the Word is being fulfilled in us through that "little book" which the angel gave to John the Revelator, who found when he "ate it up" that it was in his mouth sweet as honey, but bitter in the belly. [16]

Today the message of this little book has been set forth by Saint Germain and published by us under the title *Saint Germain On Alchemy: For the Adept in the Aquarian Age.* [17] This is your handbook for the Coming Revolution in Higher Consciousness. When you take it and eat it up, you will know the fundamental laws governing your fiery destiny in this life. And if you diligently apply them, you will fulfill that destiny and your reason for being—and no man shall take thy crown. [18] For the LORD Thy God has decreed it. And it is so!

The violet flame, whose alchemy produces the sweet and the bitter chemicalization as it contacts the substance of good and bad karma in our system, is the greatest revelation and the greatest gift to all mankind in the twentieth century next to that of the threefold flame itself.

Now, there is a mantra for the calling forth of the violet flame into your heart, which is found on page 3, number 5, of your Stump booklet.

I am going to show you how to make a simple call to the heart of God for the violet flame to come into your heart physically, mentally, spiritually, through all of the various layers of your being, even to the subconscious levels, to purge you of the records and momentums of these burdens that I have named.

I want you to be recalling in your heart incidents in which you may have in any way misused Divine Love in this life—human possessiveness, factors of control, et cetera, et cetera. I think we all know the whole litany of ways Love can be compromised to the detriment of all.

Beloved Mighty I AM Presence, beloved Father, in the name of thy Son, by the full power and presence of thy Holy Spirit with us and beloved Archangel Chamuel and Charity, we invoke the intense action of the violet flame from the heart of Jesus Christ and Saint Germain.

Legions of Zadkiel and Holy Amethyst, angels of the violet flame, come forth! Release now in answer to our call an intense action of the violet flame into our hearts and into our heart chakras.

In the name I AM THAT I AM, we command the sacred fires of the Holy Spirit to transmute now the cause and core of sin, all habits of the habitual misuse of Divine Love in fear and doubt, human questioning of our LORD, in hate and hate creation and disease, every form of death and dying, even the perversion of Love in the practice of witchcraft, voodoo, black magic, and the perversion of the sound and rhythm of the Word.

Almighty God, deliver us. For by thy Holy Spirit we would have the purification, the transmutation *now* of that which burdens our heart as well as the heart of our beloved twin flame, all family and Community members, all Lightbearers throughout the world, all whom we have ever wronged and all who have ever wronged us.

Almighty God, answer now our call! Enter our hearts through the Father and the Son in this Holy Spirit action of the violet flame.

We offer now in silent prayer to Thee, O God, our confession of the misuse of Love and our deep desire to have this transmutation take place in this hour. Therefore, in Jesus' name we enter into silent prayer for the purging of our hearts.

[pause for personal prayer]

Therefore, O God, desiring to be delivered of all these things and to retain only thy flame of perfect charity, we offer this decree in the name of Jesus Christ:

> **Violet Fire, thou Love divine,**
> **Blaze within this heart of mine!**
> **Thou art Mercy forever true,**
> **Keep me always in tune with you.**
>
> (given 12 times)

Now, what we are doing is calling for the action of the Light that descends over the silver cord. It is a crystal-clear river of Life which, as John saw it, proceeds "out of the throne of God [your I AM Presence] and of the Lamb [your Holy Christ Self]."[19]

This "pure river of water of life" has no qualification. It is God's pristine energy that has not had the stamp of creation placed upon it. When it reaches your temple, it passes through the top of the head (the soft spot on the baby's head that you see pulsating at birth, which is later covered over). The 'lifestream' descends to the heart, where the threefold-flame fountain receives this light stream of its source.

The author of Proverbs says, "Keep thy heart with all diligence; for out of it are the issues of life."[20] All that we do issues from the meditation of our heart and our communion through our heart with our Lord.

Here, then, illustrated in this slide is that threefold flame, the divine spark. By the authority of that divine spark within us we are commanding the Light of God that is descending from his Presence into specific action. We are saying:

O Light of God that never fails, in the name of Jesus Christ, I command you to manifest as the seventh ray of God's violet flame! Go forth from my heart. Purify and purge my heart of all misuses of God's sacred fire of Love. Consume and transmute all hardness of heart, all records of fear, doubt and death, the cause and core of heart disease in my karma and my bad eating habits. Let the violet flame of the Holy Spirit blaze and burn through my heart until I am free from all that is not acceptable in thy sight.

Now, why do we repeat the decree? Why don't we say it only once? Is it not a vain repetition of words? Didn't Jesus warn against the vain repetition of prayer?[21]

Come let us reason together, saith the Lord... You are using the power of the spoken Word, and that Word in you is qualifying this never-ending flow of spiritual energy depicted on the Chart—the crystal-clear light. It's a moving stream. As it passes through the nexus of the mind and heart, it is stamped with your fiat,* or decree. By this act of calling forth the violet flame in giving this decree, you are *coloring* the stream violet and *qualifying* it with the seventh-ray vibration.

You know, if you were standing by a stream, you'd be watching the flow—moment by moment new water is passing by you. Decreeing is like putting some dye in a stream—it colors the water violet, but that stream keeps moving. So if you want the whole stream to be violet, you have to qualify the next water and the next.

So the crystal water of life is descending like a Niagara Falls. The more we decree, the more we are charging the energy flowing over the silver cord with the violet flame. First this violet-flame stream charges our whole body and mind with the transmutative healing power of the seventh ray. Then it flows from us through our chakras, which it purifies on the way, blessing all whom we meet. This explains Jesus' Eastern teaching: "He that believeth on me, as the scripture hath said, out of his belly [the solar plexus and seat-of-the-soul chakras] shall flow rivers of living water."[22]

So, then, our 'lifestream' is stamped with the violet flame every

---

* *fiat* [Latin, "let it be done," from *fieri,* to become, be done]: a command or act of will that creates something without, or as if without, further effort; an authoritative decision of consciousness; an order or decree. A short dynamic invocation or decree usually using the name of God, I AM, as in *I AM the Way! I AM the Truth! I AM the Resurrection and the Life!* Fiats are exclamations of Christ-power, Christ-wisdom, and Christ-love consciously affirmed and accepted in the here and now.

time we decree. The repetition of the dynamic decree is for the intensi-
fication and the acceleration of God's light scientifically within us,
qualifying our spiritual resources with the vibration and the purity of
the Holy Spirit for the blessing of all life.

You see, this is not vain repetition but prayer with a purpose: the
re-creation of ourselves and our world in the image and likeness of
God. Because the decree is expressing our will to confirm God's will
"on earth as it is in heaven," the qualification of our energy and consciousness continues after the decree is given—so long as we hold the
desire, the harmony, and the free will to have it so in our lives.

Now, you can hear the decree accelerate. You can hear it become
fiery and intense because a decree is a command. And God said to us,
Command ye me—"Ask me of things to come concerning my sons, and
concerning the work of my hands *command ye me.*"[23] And the work of
God's hands is everything that's happening in the physical universe.
And the reason our souls descended into this physicality is to "work the
works of Him that sent me." We are not only the handiwork of God,
we are the instruments of God's work. John Kennedy captured this
idea when he said, "On earth God's work must truly be our own."

God told us to take dominion over the earth and to subdue it.
What's more, He gave us the free will to make it his kingdom. Creation is
always by free will and by the spoken Word. God said in the beginning,
"Let there be light." And it is written in Genesis, "and there was light."[24]
He gave the spoken command and the physical cosmos was created
through all manifestations of himself—Elohim, archangels, and all the
heavenly host.

But you yourself also have a world. It is your "little world," your
microcosm. You make the same fiat, **Let there be Light!** You are tired
of the void of darkness and human nonsense in your four lower bodies.
You're tired of disease or being accident-prone or having problems
with your job or your family. You want it all to be consumed by the
fire of God's will, so you make that creative fiat, **Let there be Light!**
And you are so determined in your heart and in your soul and in your
being that it becomes a command both upon the force of Nature and
your causal body, and the Light descends and you are filled with that
Light. And, by the way, when you say *Light* with a capital L, you mean
Christ—that Christ who personifies in you and precipitates all of the
light, energy, and consciousness of God in your being and aura.

The Bible and all scriptures of the world are filled with fiats of
God, decrees of God. And the Father intended us to repeat them, to
affirm them. The Psalms contain the fiats of God.

So this decree manifests through you as an effect. You are the
receiver of the Light. The real decreer, the one who is really decreeing,
is your own Holy Christ Self, who is your Real Self—the individual
manifestation of that Universal Christ where you are. So when you let
yourself be the instrument of the decree, rather than trying to take *it*
over, the Light *itself,* as Christ in you, accelerates and increases *its*
power over you!

I didn't increase the speed of that decree. It's the power and presence of the Holy Spirit. It picks you right up and it carries you wherever
it wills, and it goes through your whole body. You can feel the love of

God and the happiness and joy of the violet flame when you give this. So we're going to give it again and I am going to make another call.

Beloved Mighty I AM Presence, O beloved Father, receive us now into your Heart of hearts. Come, now, and let our heart be your own. Deliver us from all miseries of the past by the flaming presence of the Holy Ghost, by the sacred fire of the violet flame.

Come, O Christ, into my heart. Heal me! Purge me! Cleanse and purify me now. Therefore, in thy name I AM THAT I AM, we decree.

Heart, Head, and Hand Decree

Heart

Violet Fire, thou Love divine,
Blaze within this heart of mine!
Thou art Mercy forever true,
Keep me always in tune with you.

(given 15 times)

So we are carried by the Word, even as we are carriers of It, and the Holy Spirit picks us up and takes us where we know not. It picks up our vibrations, that's what the Holy Spirit does. It picks us up in joy.

Now, there are a number of very important decrees and affirmations you can give from this Stump booklet, and I want to give a couple of them with you for this heart action, but first let's complete the threefold action of the threefold flame—heart, head, and hand:

Head

I AM Light, thou Christ in me,
Set my mind forever free;
Violet Fire, forever shine
Deep within this mind of mine.

God who gives my daily bread
With Violet Fire fill my head
Till thy radiance heavenlike
Makes my mind a mind of Light.

Hand

I AM the hand of God in action,
Gaining Victory every day;
My pure soul's great satisfaction
Is to walk the Middle Way.

Your heart is the seat of Christ in you. When you call to the Universal Christ, when you say, O Jesus, come into my temple! the Son of God takes up his abode in you, *in your heart.* And you can journey to your heart and greet your Lord there.

You have a manifestation of Christ's presence above you, as we mentioned. It's called your Holy Christ Self. When Jesus comes into your heart, so your Holy Christ Self also comes into your heart because they are one. There is really only one Christ, one Universal Light, one only begotten Son of God who was embodied in the son of man Jesus and who is intended to embody in the son of man, or *mani*festation—you! You are sons and daughters of God following your elder brother, who is also the manifestation of the Master, the Lord, and the Saviour. He has shown the way of the incarnate Word. Now it is your time to draw down this Light into your temple.

I AM the Christ in Action Here

So we have an affirmation, **I AM the Christ in action here.** This is for the expansion of the heart flame. I'd like to invite you to sing it, because singing is another way of decreeing. It's on page 20, number 76.

Now is the time to offer in your heart, in silent prayer, your personal prayer to Christ—Jesus Christ, your Holy Christ Self, God the Father, the Holy Spirit, the Universal Light. When you've made your personal prayer, that becomes the *matrix,* or pattern, into which the Light descends when you sing. Whatever you pray for, whatever you pray that shall happen upon earth, submitting it to God's will, that, then, becomes the cup of your desire into which the Father pours his Light. And into that matrix you pour the devotion of your song to Him.

Listen to the words you are singing and accept them as a divine decree that is happening now right where you are and right where your twin flame is anywhere in the universe. Wherever your twin flame is, affirm this and pray for the same action. Things equal to the same thing are equal to each other. When you give your prayers and calls for your twin flame as well as for yourself, you are establishing between your souls a reverberation, a consonance of harmony—Alpha/Omega, the positive/negative spirals of the Godhead.

When you and your twin flame are one in vibration, you cannot be separate. You are one in that vibration. And every word you couple with I AM, or I AM THAT I AM as the name of God, is released and multiplied by the power of his Sacred Name and Presence in your life.

So now we will sing this decree for the Universal Christ to come into action in our lives to the music of Excelsior.

Christ I AM—with Light surround me
Christ within and all around me
From above God's love enfolds me
I AM the Christ in action here.

Grace I AM—with grace surround me
Grace within and all around me
From above God's love enfolds me
I AM the grace of Mary here.

Michael, come, with faith surround me
Blaze thy pow'r of faith around me
From above God's love enfolds me
I AM thy full protection here.

Violet fire, come now, surround me
Blaze thy mighty pow'r around me
Saint Germain's great love enfolds me
I AM the flame of freedom here.

Jesus, raise thy Light around me
Resurrect thy Light within me
May thy star of peace e'er hold me
I AM the peace of Jesus here.
(given three times)

Now accept the peace of Jesus in the name of God, and dwell within it forevermore.

The Holy Christ Flame

The archangels and their archeiai are the great Teachers of mankind, and they have called me to conduct this retreat on the healing power of angels so that they might teach you what is the power of God that is available to you through their intercession. So I am not the Teacher (the I AM in me *and* you is the Teacher), but I am the messenger of the archangels.

Therefore, in each of the seven scheduled sessions, beginning with this evening, the archangels will dictate their words through me to you by the authority of the Lord Christ and his Holy Spirit. And so, in offering dynamic decrees and devotional songs you are preparing your body temple as a chalice to receive this Light and Teaching. We are going to consecrate our energies in a few more songs and decrees for the clearing of the heart chakra so that you may receive not only the archangels but, through their clearing action, the presence of your Lord, Jesus Christ and your beloved Holy Christ Self.

A very sweet prayer that we have to the Holy Christ Flame is also sung and it's on page 20. It is number 74. Through this prayer you can pour your heart to your beloved Holy Christ Self. This Holy Christ presence is referred to as the guardian angel, the presence just above you who protects and directs you. And when you obey this voice of your Lord you are always on the right path.

The first verse is your call to the Holy Christ Flame, and the second is the answer. Won't you now in your heart offer this prayer on behalf of your soul, the soul of your twin flame, your families, children, loved ones, and everyone you know, or don't know, in the whole world:

Thou Holy Christ Flame within my heart
　　Help me to manifest all thou art
Teach me to see thyself in all
　　Help me to show men how to call
All of thy glory from the Sun
　　'Til earth's great victory is won
I AM we love thee, thou art our all!
　　I AM we love thee, hear our call!

I hear thy call, my children dear
　　I AM thy heart, so never fear
I AM your mind, your body, too
　　I AM in every cell of you.
I AM thy earth and sea and sky
　　And not one soul shall I pass by
I AM in thee, thou art in me
　　I AM, I AM thy victory.

Now we'll sing the "Introit to the Holy Christ Flame," the next song on page 20. Let us first chant the AUM (OM). It is the sound we learn from the Eastern Masters for the intoning of the Word:
AUM AUM AUM

1. Holy Christ Self above me
    Thou balance of my soul
    Let thy blessed radiance
    Descend and make me Whole.

Refrain:
    Thy Flame within me ever blazes
    Thy Peace about me ever raises
    Thy Love protects and holds me
    Thy dazzling Light enfolds me.
    I AM thy threefold radiance
    I AM thy living Presence
    Expanding, expanding, expanding now.

2. Holy Christ Flame within me
    Come, expand thy triune Light
    Flood my being with the essence
    Of the pink, blue, gold, and white.

3. Holy lifeline to my Presence
    Friend and brother ever dear
    Let me keep thy holy vigil
    Be thyself in action here.

Decrees for Freedom's Holy Light and More Violet Fire

We would like to give some additional decrees to the violet flame to prepare our hearts for the gift of Chamuel and Charity. Won't you turn to page 5, the "Decree for Freedom's Holy Light."

Another name for the violet flame is freedom, is liberty, is mercy, is justice. All of these are qualities of the Holy Spirit's seventh ray. All of this is what creates the Holy Spirit's action of transmutation. So listen to this wonderful fiat as we give it now.

In the name of our Mighty I AM Presence, in the name of the LORD God Almighty, let this Mighty Cosmic Light of Freedom's Flame penetrate and saturate and burn right through all that is unreal about us and our beloved twin flame, all unreality that burdens our homes, our families, our consciousness, our minds, our work.

Purge and purify us, O Holy Spirit of God. Come into our temple now. So, as Above so below, I and my Father are one, I and my Mother are one, I and my twin flame are one.

In Jesus Christ, we say together the "Decree for Freedom's Holy Light":

Mighty Cosmic Light!
My own I AM Presence bright,
    Proclaim Freedom everywhere—
In Order and by God Control
I AM making all things whole!

Mighty Cosmic Light!
Stop the lawless hordes of night,
     Proclaim Freedom everywhere—
In Justice and in Service true
I AM coming, God, to you!

Mighty Cosmic Light!
I AM Law's prevailing might,
     Proclaim Freedom everywhere—
In magnifying all goodwill
I AM Freedom living still!

Mighty Cosmic Light!
Now make all things right,
     Proclaim Freedom everywhere—
In Love's Victory all shall go,
I AM the Wisdom all shall know!

I AM Freedom's holy Light
     Nevermore despairing!
I AM Freedom's holy Light
     Evermore I'm sharing!
Freedom, Freedom, Freedom!
     Expand, expand, expand!
     I AM, I AM, I AM
Forevermore I AM Freedom!

Now we'll take the decree "More Violet Fire," on page 6. Together.

Lovely God Presence, I AM in me,
Hear me now I do decree:
Bring to pass each blessing for which I call
Upon the Holy Christ Self of each and all.

Let Violet Fire of Freedom roll
Round the world to make all whole;
Saturate the earth and its people, too,
With increasing Christ-radiance shining through.

I AM this action from God above,
Sustained by the hand of heaven's Love,
Transmuting the causes of discord here,
Removing the cores so that none do fear.

I AM, I AM, I AM
The full power of Freedom's Love
Raising all earth to heaven above.
Violet Fire now blazing bright,
In living beauty is God's own Light

Which right now and forever
Sets the world, myself, and all life
Eternally free in Ascended Master Perfection.
Almighty I AM! Almighty I AM! Almighty I AM!

Now let us affirm the violet flame by the power of God's I AM name. Page 5, number 18. Now, this is going to be a decree that you give with all the authority of the God flame within you, all the Christ-determination you can muster. So I am going to ask you to stand for this. "Where I AM is the flame of God." Try saying that.

> Where I AM is the flame of God!
> Where I AM is the flame of God!
> Where I AM is the flame of God!

"Here I AM, so help me God!"

> Here I AM, so help me God!
> Here I AM, so help me God!
> Here I AM, so help me God!

"Take me, O Lord, to thy heart."

> Take me, O Lord, to thy heart.
> Take me, O Lord, to thy heart.
> Take me, O Lord, to thy heart.

I AM the Violet Flame

In Jesus' name I call upon the Holy Spirit. I call, therefore, to the Father in the name of the Son to send the twelve legions of angels from his heart who are under the dominion of Jesus Christ to come to our aid. Come, holy angels, for our healing. Come for the healing of Love. Come now, O violet flame, perfect our hearts that we might know thee as thou art.

O Almighty God, let thy dispensation of mercy come that our twin flame might be cut free to ascend to thee in this hour—to see thee face to face, to work thy works on earth. According to thy will, O God, let us work together hand in hand for the victory of thy kingdom, thy divine plan, thy Word manifest in us.

In the name of the entire Spirit of the Great White Brotherhood, who are the saints robed in white in heaven, having risen from every race and nation and religion, we joyfully invoke thy violet flame.

The name of this decree is "I AM the Violet Flame."

> I AM the Violet Flame
> In action in me now
> I AM the Violet Flame
> To Light alone I bow
> I AM the Violet Flame
> In mighty Cosmic Power
> I AM the Light of God
> Shining every hour
> I AM the Violet Flame
> Blazing like a sun
> I AM God's sacred power
> Freeing every one
> (given six times)

This decree, then, becomes a fiat—a fiat of your will one with God's will. With the deep desiring of your heart, when you send forth this call, it does manifest. You must watch for the signs of God's answer to your call in little things, in great things. Above all, you will see it in a new joy and peace that is ever with you.

Now, this fiat that is so powerful when you give it this way becomes a lilting lullaby when you sing it to the three-quarter time that corresponds to the rhythm of your heart chakra and your threefold flame. So these words can receive and empower—by God's Word—your spirit, your desiring, your own creativity.

No one individual is quite like any other. You may say the same words as your neighbor, but the entire momentum of *your* faith, *your* love, *your* devotion is poured into the chalice of the worded pattern or matrix. The words form a crystal chalice. You pour into that chalice the gift of your heart to God, to all the hosts of heaven, and to your beloved, and it is very special, very personal and private between you and God. ["I AM the Violet Flame," sung three times.]

Jesus' I AM Lord's Prayer

As we prepare for the dictation of Chamuel and Charity, we are going to sing a hymn. Welcoming the hosts of the LORD in the person and presence of Chamuel and Charity, let us sing Jesus' I AM Lord's Prayer. It is on page 13, number 49.

Remember, when you say "I AM," you're saying, God is where I AM and God in me is "Thy Kingdom come, Thy Will being done," etc.

> **Our Father who art in heaven,**
> **Hallowed be Thy name, I AM.**
> **I AM Thy Kingdom come**
> **I AM Thy Will being done**
> **I AM on earth even as I AM in heaven**
> **I AM giving this day daily bread to all**
> **I AM forgiving all Life this day even as**
> **I AM also all Life forgiving me**
> **I AM leading all men away from temptation**
> **I AM delivering all men from every evil condition**
> **I AM the Kingdom**
> **I AM the Power and**
> **I AM the Glory of God in eternal, immortal**
> **manifestation—**
> **All this I AM.**

"The Summit Lighthouse Sheds Its Radiance O'er All the World to Manifest as Pearls of Wisdom." This Pearl is taken from the introductory lecture on twin flames given by the Messenger of the Great White Brotherhood Elizabeth Clare Prophet on **Valentine's Day, Friday, February 14, 1986,** at the weekend seminar *The Healing Power of Angels,* held at Camelot. (1) John 12:32. (2) I Cor. 13. (3) See Elizabeth Clare Prophet, *The Lost Years of Jesus,* Summit University Press, $12.95 postpaid. (4) John 15:13. (5) I John 4:18. (6) I John 4:20. (7) *Mantras of the Ascended Masters for the Initiation of the Chakras,* Summit University Press, $1.40 postpaid USA and Canada. All other internationals, $2.15 airmail postpaid. Also published on 5-cassette set (B85135–B85139), $35.10 postpaid USA and Canada. All other internationals, $37.35 airmail postpaid. (8) I Cor. 15:40. (9) Exod. 3:1–15. (10) **The temple of the Holy Spirit.** I Cor. 3:16, 17; 6:19; II Cor. 6:16; II Tim. 1:14. (11) John 9:4. (12) Mark L. Prophet and Elizabeth Clare Prophet, *The Science of the Spoken Word,* Summit University Press, $5.95 postpaid. (13) Jer. 31:33, 34. (14) Isa. 1:18. (15) Rev. 10:7. (16) Rev. 10:2, 8–10. (17) *Saint Germain On Alchemy: For the Adept in the Aquarian Age,* Summit University Press, $4.95 postpaid. (18) Rev. 3:11. (19) Rev. 22:1. (20) Prov. 4:23. (21) Matt. 6:7. (22) John 7:38. (23) Isa. 45:11. (24) Gen. 1:3.

Pearls of Wisdom®
published by The Summit Lighthouse

| *Vol. 29 No. 26* | *Beloved Archangel Chamuel and Charity* | *June 11, 1986* |

The Healing Power of Angels
The Reestablishment of the Electromagnetic Field of the Aura
II
Keys to the Twelve Gates of the Celestial City
The Weaving of the Deathless Solar Body

Salutations from the Central Sun unto the Sons and Daughters of God Seeking the Way of Perfect Love!

Enter now if ye would, O children of the Sun, the heart of hearts of very Love. For we are Chamuel and Charity, angels of the LORD who stand in the presence of God.

Beloved ones, this means literally that the archangels do attend the throne of grace. Standing in the presence of God, we are therefore one with your own Mighty I AM Presence. For God individualized is yet one LORD and one Presence.

Thus we are called, one and all, angels of the LORD, which means messengers of the I AM THAT I AM. We bring not only good tidings of great joy to all people but also the Light-emanation of this point of the Word from the beginning unto the ending of your rounds in these lower planes of life.

Beloved hearts of the infinite God, we are grateful to speak to you directly, for so many of you have come to our own retreat, and that in the etheric octave. For though you do not retain the memory, yet, beloved, your souls take leave of that physical envelope you wear at night; and while the body sleeps, you journey in garments of light to the etheric plane, otherwise known in scripture as the heaven world.

This plane of heaven is truly the place where your soul does meet the Lord Christ in the air, as they say. It is the point where you find the descent of the Lord Christ in the full power of the resurrection. Therefore, to meet your Christ you yourself must be capable of rising to that plane and vibration.

Thus, though this take place at inner levels with the assistance of guardian angels, you are now in the stage of your evolution on earth where you must learn consciously the way of Love and Love's self-mastery and thus, not only in sleep but consciously, journey in the power of the heart and the mind to upper octaves. These octaves of heaven are a transition plane whereby you then are taken by the Lord Christ to the very throne of grace whence we have come this night, as has been said, trailing clouds of glory and glorious love.

Thus, we inaugurate a spiral of seven rays which correlate with seven planes of heaven that you will also find in the etheric octave prior to your return and immersion in that absolute Spirit that is the sacred fire even beyond the heaven world. Thus, as you might realize, we come, then, from the third plane of heaven. And we come for a very important mission, which is to bring into alignment now the chalice of your heart, that this chakra and its twelve petals might receive from our own hearts, by the magnetism of Love, a realignment, a balancing of twelve vibrations.

Do you know, beloved ones, that God so loved the world that he sent his Son, this Lord Christ, who does also manifest above you in that personal presence of the Christ Self. And he so loved you that he gave to you twelve petals of the heart chakra, signifying twelve unique vibrations that are as keys to the twelve gates of the celestial city—right here in your heart, beloved one.

Thus, hear our call and understand the true meaning of the call of Jesus: "The kingdom of God is within you." God has placed himself inside of you, else you would be vacant—vacuous beings without soul or mind or righteousness or sense of what are the moral requirements of the hour.

Blessed ones, a fire does burn in your heart and it does intensify. For you are indeed in the presence of Christ and of mighty archangels who come as your servants and truly bow before the divine spark because it is the Person of God.

Understand, then, that this heart is truly the seat and throne of Christ and his grace in your temple and that he does receive you daily through one of these gates of the Holy City, through one of the petals. How do you enter in and approach him—he who sits in the center of that City Foursquare, he who stands to receive you and take your hand as a friend, as a brother and a sister, as a disciple of Love?

His is the way of Love and the way of perfect Love that

always casts out fear. For Love is a burning fire, an all-consuming fire, as Moses discovered. And it is the consuming fire of Love that is your deliverance. And we come to transfer it to you this night.

Beloved ones, how then do you approach one of the gates of the celestial city? You see, your heart and soul, then, must come into the vibration that is in accord with the vibration of that single petal of the heart chakra and the single door. When you knock at the door, you are received if you have the key. And the key is the vibration. Vibration, then, opens the door. It is as though you had a combination for a safe—the combination of vibrations keying by the sounding of the Word.

Why is it, then, that this is the requirement? Beloved ones, within the celestial City Foursquare the light is very great. Those who enter there must be protected by having a prior sheath of light around them. This is the meaning of the parable of the wedding feast.

Thus, all who are called and bidden may enter. But one does enter without the wedding garment, which is the name of the etheric garment of the soul. Thus, the master of the house does say unto him, "Friend, how camest thou in without a wedding garment?" And he says to his servants, who are the angels, "Bind him and cast him into outer darkness."

The meaning is so clear when you understand the wedding is no ordinary wedding. It is the wedding of your soul to Christ—the goal of Love's mystical union and the Path that has ever been of all saints of East and West.

Thus, when you knock at one door and seek to enter by one petal of the heart chakra, you must have that wedding garment which does correspond to that path, that initiation, that door. And when you have the wedding garment and you enter into that bridal chamber, the all-consuming flame of Love will not devour you, for you are already clothed upon with the singular and unique vibration of that chamber.

Thus understand, those who intone the Word for the balancing of the chakras find that they come into consonance with the Lord Christ step by step, or petal by petal, as we say. The Law will not require of you more than your capacity in a given day. Heaven's schoolroom is not more harsh than earthly schoolrooms.

Understand the compassion of the Holy Spirit, who is not only Teacher but Comforter—who does comfort your soul, beloved, as He does teach you. Thus, this presence of God, acting through whether angels or Ascended Masters or friends of Light, does provide you with an understanding of how to sow seeds of righteousness—righteousness, as you have been told, being the right use of God's laws.

Day by day, then, by right application of the Light in your being, you are weaving that wedding garment. And layer upon layer it does become complete until, when you carry the twelve vibrations of the twelve petals and have tarried in each of the twelve bridal chambers with Christ, the initiator of your soul, you then have upon you what is known as the Deathless Solar Body.

This weaving of the Deathless Solar Body is the mighty work of the ages, has ever been the goal of the saints. But these Teachings have been held—held in the inner retreats of the Brotherhood of Light, held there for those who would not profane them or misuse them.

Thus, all who have ascended from earth, when they have been ready for the call of Love, have come apart first at inner levels, as I have described the soul's journey at night, and there attended classes in the retreats of the Masters and angels of the Great White Brotherhood.

Thus, much of this work is accomplished at inner levels. And those who are working out their salvation in this scientific manner taught by Christ, as the apostle wrote, "with fear and trembling," they, then, in the outer sense, when they are again in the physical form, become seekers of Truth, going here and there until they hear the same voice that they have heard at inner levels—the voice of Christ. And thus they journey sometimes around the world to find someone who can give them a single key to understand this sweet mystery of Life.

You have come because you seek. This is always the case of those who arrive here in the Sanctuary of the Holy Grail. Therefore, it is our opportunity given to us by the LORD to give to you in your outer mind that which you already know at inner levels, that you might find a union and a communion with your Higher Self and know yourself as you truly are—a sevenfold being of whom the lower self is the one encased in the greatest density and bodies of density as you wear.

At inner levels you are God-free beings. On earth you are yet bound by karma manifesting through heredity and environment and situation. But, beloved ones, that condition of your birth is a springboard, which when taken may become the giant leap into the arms of Victory—a mighty angel of Light whose name is Victory, who leads other legions of Victory all dressed in a golden flame of illumination. These legions of Light champion the victory of your soul and of your twin flame.

You see, beloved, while you sleep at night you do journey to our etheric retreat in the etheric octave over Saint Louis. There we have the focus of the heart of the United States. And there you come and there you meet your twin flame.

You are not apart. Trust in the Law of Love. You work together at inner levels and then return to your circumstance in embodiment, there with a drive and a creativity and a determination to do the job that you are assigned to do by God, knowing that the fulfillment of all promises by yourself and the balancing of every jot and tittle of the Law—the law of karma, which is the Law of Love—will truly lead you to the complete union with the beloved, not only then at inner spiritual levels but in outer physical manifestation.

The goal, then, of union becomes as the pot at the end of the rainbow for some and for others a very immediate encounter. For the cycles turn and opportunity comes to those who have earned opportunity by giving it to others. But the rainbow itself, which is the path to the prize for which we all run—that rainbow is the sign that on seven rays of God's being you must find the perfecting of the Law.

Thus, it is the seven rays and the seven petals of the heart chakra which correspond thereto which is your first assignment on the path of self-mastery in Love. Your first lessons on these rays are taken at the recently opened universities of the Spirit conducted by the Seven Chohans (or lords) of the Rays.

These Masters, one and all, have ascended from earth's schoolrooms. They are sons and daughters of God like yourselves who have seen the equation of life, have separated the Real from the unreal and determined to become one with God and therefore through that union to be in a position to bless and heal all life.

Thus, you may think of the Masters of the seven rays as your elder brothers on the Path—the Masters most closely associated with your immediate needs for transmutation, purification, the discovery of your sacred labor, which you may or may not have already manifested or expanded. It is your profession or life's calling, the work that you are set to do.

Now, then, beloved ones, we, the archangels, perform a very special service. We have come for the healing wherever possible, as directed by the great Law of Love—for the healing of concentric rings which compose the auric sheath and envelope. Called sometimes the "electromagnetic sheath," this presence of the aura does reflect the condition of your soul and your four lower bodies. In higher octaves it is of the spiritual light and purity, but in lower octaves and in the condition you are in, it has the colorations of your vibrations, impressions of your karma, the recording of the condition of the body, of disease, and many, many records of many, many lifetimes.

Thus, we cannot interfere in all ways. But we may assist as you make yourselves available by being with us through this weekend and as you avail yourselves of our presence. Thus, each time you go through a session of decrees to the violet flame and songs of praise and prayers of heartfelt sincerity, the angels may take from your auras some of the burdens, some of the problems.

If you invite us, we will come home with you. We will help you with your family members. We will help you with situations of your neighbors, your relatives, or whatever is most burdensome to your heart.

We must have the call and the permission to enter your life. For we are respectful of the circle of your free will and of your own human creation, for it also is the expression of your free will. Until you determine that that will shall be God's will on earth in you, we will not in any way rearrange or dismantle your life. And when called upon, we are still under the constraints of cosmic law, which says that that which you have created you must uncreate.

You have begun this evening to understand the science of the spoken Word and the use of the violet flame—the most powerful and the most essential tools to work constructive and positive change in your life. Now, then, as you apply this Teaching, we may day by day become more a part of your life. Thus, it is for the healing and the sealing of this electromagnetic field consisting of ring upon ring and layer upon layer in egg formation of emanations coming from the Central Sun of your own heart chakra.

Some of you have scars and rents in this garment of light, as you have suffered trauma in this and previous embodiments. All these things can be healed by the Holy Spirit's violet flame and by all of the seven rays in consonance together, which when accelerated produce the white fire—the sacred fire, which is the robe and the righteousness of the saints.

Now, then, beloved, you have come as you are. You have been bathed in light. We see at this moment the exact person (and the soul's place in or out of embodiment) who is your twin flame. The service of archangels, then, is a transfer of light. Our light is an energy and a flame that now begins to flow from our heart to your heart, and through your heart, by your consent, to the heart of your twin flame. This flame begins as a delicate petal pink, an intense fire and ray, and will deepen in color and in intensity in the physical vibration.

The highest spiritual intensity is the white light. But in the Matter universe that white light becomes intense in its coloration as the seven rays express that light and penetrate the sheaths of planet earth, which as you know are fraught with density and heaviness and karmic weight. In the center of the ray is the pure white fire and surrounding it is the shaft of the intense colorations. Thus the ray contains the Alpha and the Omega of its expression from the heart of the Central Sun.

Our release of love is the love of the Holy Spirit and the reminder to you, therefore, that unless you have love you will not succeed in the quest for Truth or justice or even your own divinity. Love is forgiveness. Love is without criticism and condemnation of the friend, the marriage partner, the child, the employer or the employee. Love is a giving of light and this intensity which we give to you, which will be as a mighty sword cleaving asunder the Real from the unreal, consuming the unreal and therefore liberating all life to do the will of God in perfect Love.

"That ye love one another as I have loved you" is the word of your own Christ Self spoken unto you and to your twin flame. For painful as it might be, beloved ones, I tell you, you are separated from your twin flame for one reason and one alone: You have not loved one another as Christ has loved you individually, and therefore the karma has produced the separation.

Let perfect Love cast out the fear of aloneness and separation and parting. Let the violet flame invoked by you be said with the promise, "O God, never again may I injure or hurt or defile or speak unkindly to my beloved."

But if the beloved be not at your side—oh, listen, sons and daughters of God—how can you atone for the sins of anti-Love? Christ Jesus gave you also the understanding, "Inasmuch as you have done it unto one of the least of these my brethren, you have done it unto me."

Therefore, if you love one another as Christ has loved you forever, so it will be counted unto you as the expression of love for your twin flame. For life is one and God is one. And souls of Light and Love are one. And therefore bless all life. Love all life free and, you see, you will balance every injustice that has separated from you the beloved of your heart.

Now, beloved ones, you may be together and not recognize one another, or you may. And even in recognizing one another you may not have maintained the self-mastery of Love to refrain from all discord and inharmony. Thus, you must learn how Love is a two-edged sword and how you suffer, then, for the absence of God-control and harmony. This suffering can only cease when you determine to cease from suffering and to engage in those causes of suffering which are in your own world.

Yes, the kingdom of God is within you and within your twin flame. But that kingdom of God must come into expression by your determination. Thus, neither prayers or mantras, success courses, counseling or any other means can help you unless your free will be tethered to the true solution that you may discover wherever—for anyone may be a messenger of Love to you.

So, beloved, with all of thy getting, get the understanding of Love that the experience of true Love rests upon your free will, your determination in God to be all that you are intended to be and all that has been given to you from the beginning by Almighty God, who created you out of his very being and sacred fire—you and your beloved. Take responsibility for your wants and lacks and fill the void with devotion and prayer and ascend the scale of being until you are ready for the trials and the triumphs of a perfect Love.

There is no relationship in this world this side of heaven that can be sustained merely by the romantic love and its union. A relationship is sustained by hard work and striving, giving of the self and expecting nothing in return. Expect nothing and you will never be disappointed. Be the giver and find how soon you receive the gift of love in return.

The lessons of life are very basic. You know them well, but you are surrounded by a society and a media that tells you the opposite of heaven's laws by which you ought to live. Thus you expect that which cannot be expected. And you defy a law that you know not. And you squander an energy that you have never understood. And you are dissatisfied and sometimes chagrined and disappointed and sometimes angry.

Now come, let us reason together. For perfect Love can be yours and the bliss of union with God through the crown chakra. But, beloved, you are the one who determines what happens in your life.

Do you know the sign of a fallen angel? Do you know the sign of those who fail in life? I will tell you the single sign to look for. Look for it in yourself and root it out. Look for it in others and know that they will surely not win the prize until they change.

And that single trait, beloved, is the unwillingness to take full responsibility for their lives, their actions, their words, their deeds, and all that surrounds them. Instead they blame their society, their condition, their karma, their friends, their family and those they love most for all things that befall them—every crisis, every sorrow. Everything that comes upon them they have an explanation about some cause or set of circumstances or accident outside of themselves.

From within, O beloved, from the point of Light in the center of the heart is the kingdom of God spun as a cocoon of light around you. Call it forth and it is done. But until it manifest, you must clear that space, clear that aura. Pour into it the violet flame through your devotions to God.

Do you see, beloved? As the LORD told the great prophet, you must first tear down before you can build. You must first level until you can raise the edifice that is truly the Holy Grail.

I have said much. And my Teaching has come to sustain your attention locked in the vibration of the third ray and the archangel and the archeia thereof, that by our word and presence and aura surrounding you now we might transmit to you this blessing of the altering and the reestablishment of the electromagnetic field—this in the wavelength of Love. Each of our cohorts who follow will add unto this the adjustment according to their ray and the chakra.

Thus, beloved, your cups are full. Be silent now as we complete our work. [chant in angelic tongues, 26 seconds]

Cherubim of God, in his name we command thee descend! Descend upon this planet for poor humanity's sake. Deliver thy people, O God.

Cherubim, cherubim, come forth. So, covering cherubim, keep the way of the Tree of Life and its future initiations unto these hearts.

O Lord of the World, we have come. We bow before thy grace and before the heart of God in the Great Central Sun, to whose heart we return and return again on the morrow. For we will attend as our cohorts deliver the liberating Word of the sacred fire. [chant, 18 seconds]

Messenger's Candle-Lighting Invocation before the Dictation:

O bright and burnished sword of Chamuel and Charity, mighty two-edged sword of Divine Love, cleave asunder now within us the Real from the unreal. O angels of the sacred fire of Love, Chamuel and Charity, come forth in this hour of world need.

By the love of the cloven tongues of the Holy Spirit of our twin flames, we summon Elohim of Love, Heros and Amora. Blaze thy triumphant light of the Universal Love of the Divine Manchild, who does wield the sword of Love in this hour for the binding of the seed of the wicked who tempt the little ones, the holy innocents, the children of the Sun and of the Light.

O hosts of the Lord of the Ruby Ray of Sanat Kumara, we summon thee from the Great Central Sun and from far-off worlds. Hosts of Light, bind now the hordes of darkness and war in the earth. Burn through, O living Light of the Holy Spirit! Purge and purify our souls that we might enter the heart of Christ's own Love. Seal us there, O God. Guard us. Send thy flaming cherubim who guard the ark of the covenant of our Maker and our souls.

O divine Law of Love, eternal commandments of Love whereby we are bound to Thee and whereby we do bind every corruption of perfect Love—come forth. Come forth, O Keeper of the Scrolls. Come forth, our Father Enoch.

O mighty angel with the flaming sword of Love, thou who dost keep the way of the Tree of Life, hear our call now and answer for the sealing of this union of our hearts in the Mystical Body of God, in this Church Universal and Triumphant. Let Love and only Love prevail.

O angels of the sacred fire, by thy flaming sword, purge us that we, too, might enter in with him, the Bridegroom of our Love, the eternal Christ, the Word. O God, Thou who art the only Guru, rescue us now. Part the veil. Deliver us from all illusion.

In the name of thy Holy Spirit, we call forth the fourteen archangels and their archeiai. Twin pillars of the sacred fire of God, descend from the heart of the Great Central Sun. Burn brightly.

O angels of the sacred fire, tend this altar of the Holy Grail. Tend the altar of our heart's union with Thee, O God. Wherever I AM THAT I AM, let the altar of our oneness be. In the streets of the cities, in the darkest places of Death and Hell, let the altar of the LORD God Almighty, the I AM THAT I AM, be the purifying and purging Light, be the victory of the God flame.

Unto Thee, O God I AM THAT I AM, I lift up my heart and my prayer.

Seven Mighty Archangels, Seven Beloved Archeiai, come now for the wedding of our souls to the Divine Light.

O Love, O perfect Love of our being and our becoming, Thou who wast with us in the beginning, we are grateful for thy presence in the everlasting Word, that we might be here on earth and in heaven as one, that in the very midst of this flame of the ark of the covenant time and space are not. That which was in the beginning, O Alpha, is in the ending, O beloved Omega.

Now, therefore, in the secret chamber of the heart, in the sacred fire of all, let time and space collapse. Let the eternal Presence *be!*

Angels of the sacred fire of Zarathustra, hear our call and deliver us, O God.

In the name of our Lord and Saviour, Jesus Christ, Amen.

Messenger's Invocation following the Dictation:

The assimilation of the Word is now your joy. As you take your leave and go to rest, affirm and pray that your very inner soul will receive now and receive throughout the night the penetration and the absorption of the tremendous Love of God brought to us by the archangels.

I make this call for you so that you may make it for yourself:

In the name of the beloved Mighty I AM Presence, the LORD God Almighty, we summon angels of Light to take us this night to the etheric retreat of beloved Chamuel and Charity that we might study the path of Love and be perfected in the Love of the Lord Christ.

O Jesus, we thank you for saving our souls for the path of Christhood, which you have walked and proved and demonstrated before us. Therefore in thy name we go to our teachers, the archangels of Love, that we might become the expression of thy Love, O Christ.

In the name of the Father, the Son, the Holy Spirit, and the Mother, Amen.

This dictation by Archangel Chamuel and Charity was **delivered** through the Messenger of the Great White Brotherhood Elizabeth Clare Prophet on **Friday, February 14, 1986,** during the weekend seminar *The Healing Power of Angels,* held at Camelot.

Pearls of Wisdom®

published by The Summit Lighthouse

| *Vol. 29 No. 27* | *The Beloved Messenger* | *June 12, 1986* |

The Healing Power of Angels
The Reestablishment of the Electromagnetic Field of the Aura
III
The LORD Will Be Magnified!

So the Word of the LORD came unto the prophet Malachi. And this Word of the LORD is for the judgment of those who profane the worship of God.

The burden of the Word of the LORD to Israel by Malachi.

I have loved you, saith the LORD. Yet ye say, Wherein hast thou loved us? Was not Esau Jacob's brother? saith the LORD: yet I loved Jacob, and I hated Esau, and laid his mountains and his heritage waste for the dragons of the wilderness.

Whereas Edom saith, We are impoverished, but we will return and build the desolate places; thus saith the LORD of hosts, They shall build, but I will throw down; and they shall call them, The border of wickedness, and, The people against whom the LORD hath indignation for ever.

And your eyes shall see, and ye shall say, The LORD will be magnified from the border of Israel.

The LORD will be magnified from the border of Israel!
The LORD will be magnified from the border of Israel!
The LORD will be magnified from the border of Israel!

A son honoureth his father, and a servant his master: if then I be a father, where is mine honour? and if I be a master, where is my fear? saith the LORD of hosts unto you, O priests, that despise my name. And ye say, Wherein have we despised thy name?

Ye offer polluted bread upon mine altar; and ye say, Wherein have we polluted thee? In that ye say, The table of the LORD is contemptible.

And if ye offer the blind for sacrifice, is it not evil? and if ye offer the lame and sick, is it not evil? offer it now unto thy governor; will he be pleased with thee, or accept thy person? saith the Lord of hosts. (Mal. 1:1–8)

Malachi, a prophet of the mid-fifth century B.C., is speaking to the Jewish community almost a century after the return from the Babylonian exile. The original enthusiasm and expectation of the tiny remnant who did return had by now turned into frustration and depression. The people had lost faith in God's love for them and had become lax in their worship—conditions which Malachi lays at the feet of the clergy.

So the corrupt priests in Israel, instead of taking the best offering of their flocks, took the lame and the deformed and put that upon the altar, even though the law as stated in Deuteronomy required that animals fit for sacrifice had to be perfect—they could not be blind, lame or have any "ill blemish."[1] The whole idea of sacrifice—that the offering to God is something of value that the giver is willing to give up in order to prove his sincerity—was being mocked by these priests.

The term "governor" refers to the governor appointed by the Persians, who ruled the land at that time. The implication is that the priests wouldn't even treat their foreign rulers with as much disrespect as they have treated their God.

Thus, it is a teaching that if we would be priests and priestesses of the sacred fire under the Order of Melchizedek, we must give the sacrifice upon the altar of the firstfruits of our Christhood—not of our human creation, not of that which is dispensable which we desire to be rid of. We must place the very best of ourselves, even as Jesus Christ did set the example of giving his Christhood for the salvation of the whole world.

Therefore, the priesthood in Israel was condemned by God for their misuse of the light of the Holy of Holies and, in the performing of their offices, the defilement of the table of sacrifice. The word *table* as used here means the altar.

Understand that these priests are in the world today. They are a tribe of fallen ones—some reincarnated and others who are of the same ilk. And thus they function as leaders of the people in Church and in State but they do not offer the acceptable offering before the hearts of the people, before the Mighty I AM Presence. They pretend to officiate and to bear the burden of the Lord as they sit in their seats of authority. And yet they do not.

Archangel Michael has called me to read to you from sacred scripture the judgment upon those who hold an office in the name of the people and in the name of God and yet defile the mantle of that office.

The high priest is the Lord Christ, your own beloved Christ Self. And you also have a mantle. It is the mantle of the disciple. Let it not, then, be trailed in the dust of darkness. Let the mantle remain pure and unsullied. And let your office be upheld; for it is the office that was once held by our brother Jesus Christ when he was a disciple on the Path proving the way of his Christhood.

We understand that the judgment and the power of God's judgment as it is written in scripture goes forth again when it is read from the high altar. And all that follows in this vein as the response of the congregation of the righteous (those who in the LORD's righteousness lawfully exercise the power of His Word) is the means of the implementation of the judgment through Archangel Michael, as you have invoked the decree dictated by Jesus Christ—"They Shall Not Pass!"

Thus, in the understanding of the betrayal of the office of priest by some of the Levites—descendants of Levi, the son of Jacob, who were consecrated as the priestly order in ancient Israel—realize that that judgment is sustained until the individual turns away from his sin. Realize that as it was then, so it is today: those who betray the divine calling, whatever their profession or sacred labor, must give accounting under their own I AM Presence.

And now, I pray you, beseech God that he will be gracious unto us: this hath been by your means: will he regard your persons? saith the LORD of hosts.

Who is there even among you that would shut the doors for nought? neither do ye kindle fire on mine altar for nought. I have no pleasure in you, saith the LORD of hosts, neither will I accept an offering at your hand. (Mal. 1:9–10)

The Jerusalem Bible translation illumines the meaning of this passage: "Oh, is there no one among you who will shut the doors and stop you from lighting useless fires on my altar?" In other words, it would be better to close the temple doors and stop sacrificing than to carry on this sham.

Thus, the defilement of the mantle renders null and void your spiritual inheritance—your divine heirship under the laws of Almighty God. If the mantle has been defiled, we are also defiled; therefore let us bring it—and ourselves—to the altar. Let us pray unto the LORD that Archangel Zadkiel will send his violet-flame angels to our side that we might be restored by the mercy of God and by the commitment of our souls to that holy calling to which we were called from the beginning.

From the rising of the sun even unto the going down of the same my name shall be great among the Gentiles; and in every place incense shall be offered unto my name, and a pure offering:

for my name shall be great among the heathen, saith the LORD of hosts. (Mal. 1:11)

Thus, as it was given to Jesus Christ and to the apostles, the offering of the Mighty I AM Presence profaned by the priests of the tribe of Levi was then given to all others who are the inheritors of the seed of Light (of the Mighty I AM Presence) throughout the world. And this name I AM THAT I AM, which we do pronounce in great joy, therefore rings from every cathedral, every temple and mosque; for in pronouncing it as the flame of Emmanuel, our God with us, we do take up the fallen mantle.

And **from the rising of the sun** *of the Mighty I AM Presence* **even unto the going down of the same my name** *I AM THAT I AM, Yahweh, Elohim,* **shall be great among the Gentiles; and in every place incense shall be offered unto my name**—the incense of the sweetness of our love for God offered up in dynamic decrees. The violet flame is the incense of the ritual of our freedom that we offer, together with the frankincense of our surrender to God's will that brings us to the very heart of the three wise men—**and a pure offering** (and that pure offering and that only acceptable offering of our Christhood): **for my name** *I AM THAT I AM* **shall be great among the heathen, saith the LORD of hosts.**

But ye have profaned it, in that ye say, The table of the LORD is polluted; and the fruit thereof, even his meat, is contemptible.

Ye said also, Behold, what a weariness is it! and ye have snuffed at it, saith the LORD of hosts; and ye brought that which was torn, and the lame, and the sick; thus ye brought an offering: should I accept this of your hand? saith the LORD.

But cursed be the deceiver, which hath in his flock a male, and voweth, and sacrificeth unto the Lord a corrupt thing.

The "weariness" refers to the boredom of the priests in routinely carrying out their rituals. The last verse is directed to the layman, "the deceiver" who sacrifices a blemished animal after he has voluntarily vowed to sacrifice a male from his flock.

For I am a great King, saith the LORD of hosts, and my name is dreadful among the heathen. (Mal. 1:12–14)

The LORD will be magnified from the border of Israel! (4x)
The LORD I AM THAT I AM will be magnified
   in the United States of America! (4x)
The LORD I AM THAT I AM will be magnified
   in the Church Universal and Triumphant! (4x)

Pearls of Wisdom®

published by The Summit Lighthouse

| Vol. 29 No. 28 | Beloved Archangel Michael | June 13, 1986 |

The Healing Power of Angels
The Reestablishment of the Electromagnetic Field of the Aura
IV
My Word Shall Not Be Defiled!

Children of the Light of the Sun,

I AM come and I AM Michael! And the cosmic being Faith with me does ensoul in you the power of the Almighty One.

Blessed Light of all ages, hear, then, the release of sacred fire! Hear, then, that release, for none shall now reduce the Light and the Power of this Word going forth!

Therefore, hear me! For the Power of the Word does now reach every atom and molecule of your being, for you have indeed prepared this chalice to receive of my heart.

I AM the outpouring of the heart of the Universal Mother. I AM the confounding of the tongue of the seed of the wicked. I AM the confounding of the Liar and the lie and the murderous intent.

Therefore, ye who are called of God as God's people, welcome to the heart and the ranks of the archangels. So, in the name I AM THAT I AM, be seated.

The full power of the Holy Spirit be upon you and the seven rays of God now penetrating the seven planes of the chakras of your beings. I AM blazing the Light into manifest action! And I AM binding the very force itself of all attempts to reduce the impact of this mighty Word in every nation on this planet and in the very depths of the sea!

And you, therefore, shall give accounting this day, you fallen ones across the earth who have attempted to silence the saints and priests of Melchizedek, the messengers and the prophets, those who have come in the name of this Word. You will no longer silence them, for I AM speaking through the very heart of these my own. I AM speaking unto the very source of being!

And I say to you: Resist not the intensity of Truth, for Truth shall and can speak through you if you will seek and desire with all of your heart that calling of the Holy Spirit. For it is the Holy Spirit of the mighty archangels that is for the conversion of earth in this hour. And this is the turning around of the downward course of civilization, which you have seen with your very eyes.

Now therefore, beloved, stand fast and behold the salvation of your God![1] And behold the judgment of the fallen ones who have arrayed themselves against the person of the Divine Mother in every nation. For in every nation the Divine Feminine is raised up in men and women and in children. And all have begun to speak in the name of the Mother, but not all have brought the desired Teaching of the Mother.

Therefore, O hearts of living Flame, be purged. For the purifying, then, of the sons of the priesthood and the daughters of Melchizedek must come in this hour. And you may be purified and tried and made white[2] if you no longer resist, then, the winds of change and the power of the violet flame that does come to you.

Therefore, beloved ones, the line is drawn and there is a great liberation in the power of the first ray and the judgment of the Lord Christ through us. For, you see, when evil is bound, as when you root out the weeds of a garden, so the flowers blossom and they come forth in joy and in a new freedom, for they are not choked off by the binding roots of materialism and the seed of sinfulness devouring itself in a cancer that is preying upon the bodies of the world this day.

I AM Archangel Michael of the first ray and I say to you, my presence here and now is also for the shattering of forcefields within you that have lingered too long from ancient Atlantis when you were drawn into the cults of the fallen angels and the gods and their evil and their wickedness in their animal forms and miscreations.

Beloved ones, the cults of Satan have had their day upon this planet and that day is done! And the Light of Almighty God does descend for the purging! And the raising up of the seed of Light is come. Therefore, let the records of the entanglement of the children of the Sun with these cults of the fallen ones be purged in this moment from your auras, from your mind and consciousness.

I AM that way of the sacred fire! I AM that mighty deliverance! And I AM releasing the fire of God, the sacred fire, as that
wrath of God that does consume that recalcitrance, that resistance that does come from old and knotty records of compromise
and being involved in these very cults.

No wonder they have gone forth to accuse the Lightbearers
of their "cults," for they themselves are the ones who originated
the only cults that have ever existed on this planet—which are
the cults of Satan, the cults of materialism and the [cults of the]
misuse of the sacred fire.

Let these, then, be exposed—and all of their promoters in
the public schools and in the media and throughout the field of
psychology and even religion. And let the false priests within the
Church be cast down! Let those fallen ones who have defiled the
Church of Christ be bound! And let those who know, who are the
hierarchs of these churches, now receive the judgment, for they
have failed to challenge the very corruption of the altar of God.

And therefore, a corrupt altar is no altar. And we will take
in preference the altar of the heart of the children of the Sun.
We will take the altar prepared and the place in the wilderness.
We will take the humble abode of the pure in heart and we will
say, "Here is the vicar of Christ! Here is Christ's representative in
each and every one of these little ones who have kept the purity of
the flame of the tabernacle of the Light of the Holy of Holies!"

So let purity abound. And where purity doth abound, so let
the Spirit of the LORD be. And where the Spirit of the LORD is,
there is liberty[3] and there is the liberty to set those captives free!
And they are set free by the power of the Word that I do speak
to you now.

And this Church Universal and Triumphant is set free
from the gates of Death and Hell who would torment and defile
and tear down. Their day is done and their cults of infamy are
exposed! And their vibration shall be no more! And you will
stand and see the salvation of our God, and you will know that
once and for all the Teachings of the saints of heaven, the hosts
of the LORD, and of Jesus Christ himself shall prevail in their
totality in the fullness of the cup of Communion which he gave
to drink.

Thus, Drink ye all of it.[4] These are the words of Christ.

Do not turn back, blessed ones of Light. Do not turn back
when you see the day approach that demands of thee something
that God has required of thee and will require of thee unto the
end of thy incarnations ere the resurrection be attained. Beloved

ones, what are all these things when the power of God is offered
to you in the sharing and blessing of Communion this day?

Beloved ones of the living flame of Light, I AM Archangel
Michael and I serve to you Communion in this hour. Let everyone drink, then, and understand the drinking in of the wine of
the Spirit of the Lord Christ. Let everyone know that assimilation of the Body of God in this earth.

I transfer to you, then, building upon the mighty work of
Chamuel and Charity, the borders of faith, the sealing of that
electromagnetic field by this mighty sphere of blue descending
from the heart of Serapis Bey, descending from the heart of the
Great Central Sun.

And my spirit, saith the LORD, will not always strive with
flesh.[5] Beware, then, ye who come in the service of the Holy of
Holies. Wash, then, and be cleansed in the river Jordan.[6] Be
cleansed wholly. And know that thy service must accelerate into
the heart of Victory.

Know, not I but God in me is the Word. Know this law of
thy Being. Know the fullness of rejoicing in the Spirit and the
Body, in the Blood of Christ. Know the transforming Power.
Know that the pathway of divinity was set and is set forevermore
in the Universal Christ, who always has been your Advocate
before the throne of grace.

For before Abraham was, I AM THAT I AM.[7] And I AM
in that Spirit on the LORD's day.[8] And that Spirit here and now
is the Holy Spirit come upon you.

Receive, then, the Holy Ghost. Receive the Holy Ghost in
the name of your Lord. And know that God desires to empower
ye who resist not, ye who understand how the self-qualification
process must proceed—how you must absorb and internalize the
Word and how that Word will go forth from you when you have
prepared the way in your innermost recesses of being.

Blaze the Light through now, O seraphim of God! Blaze
the Light of the blue-lightning angels! Blaze the Light of the
Great Central Sun Magnet!

Lo, I AM that Light and that Fire! Lo, I AM that Light
and that Fire! Lo, I AM that Light and that Fire of Alpha and
Omega here and now!

I AM in the Victory of the God Flame. And I AM Archangel
Michael. And I AM clothing our Messenger with that Flame of
Victory. And I AM clothing you with your Flame of Victory now.

And it is God's Victory. And that Victory will not be denied
in your life unless you yourself deny it, beloved ones. And indeed

by free will you can deny the Victory. And therefore I say, watch and pray that in every act and word and thought and deed you therefore affirm the Power of God-Victory and you deny the power of all defeat and defeatism and death and cynicism.

Blaze the Light of the Great Central Sun Magnet! Blaze the Light of the Great Central Sun Magnet! By the power of my flame, I am extending to you my right hand and my left hand as the pillars of Alpha and Omega. And the cosmic being Faith does extend the power of the feminine ray in the right hand and in the left hand now.

And there is a mighty figure-eight flow as these twin pillars are also established here. And you will see in the very heart of the earth a holding of the balance in this city of Los Angeles. And that balance is held. And that balance is for the Power of the Mighty Threefold Flame that is borne.

And you shall see, then, the transformation of your world. For you have been this day, beloved ones, in the presence of the archangels who come, beloved hearts, flaming from the Central Sun and bear to you an extraordinary Light which, if you will use It, beloved ones, and not lose It, you will come to the day of your salvation.

And you will see and know that in this life you can be transformed! And you can enter into the fiery coil of the ascension as was prophesied to you, as was demonstrated to you, as was revealed to you in the life of Jesus Christ and of Enoch and of those who have gone before. Thus, the saints robed in white in heaven are the testimony of the path of the ascension.

And, beloved ones, will you wait for another round to pass from the screen of life, to be on the other side to recognize that you have once again, due to the false pastors, missed the course of your ascension and your resurrection? I say to you, give answer this day before the LORD God Almighty! Will you or will you not take your Victory in this hour and receive it of me? I ask you and I demand the answer! ["Yes!"]

Beloved ones, I give it to you as God has given it to me—as surely as God gave to me his full flaming Presence for the deliverance of your souls when many of you were embodied as the children of Israel, as you were therefore bound to the Egyptian slavery of death and materialism and bondage to the outer self of the fallen angels, the pharaohs.

Beloved ones of Light, understand, as surely as I was the instrument of the LORD's deliverance all the way to that Promised Land and as I have been the instrument of your deliverance all the way to the United States of America, I say to you now, I AM your deliverance and the LORD's instrument thereof of the transfer of Light for your own ascension! You have only to go out in this hour to win it, to prove it, to manifest the glory of God day unto day and night unto night[9] until your round is finished. And the Lords of Karma have decreed unto you a certain round which you are capable of fulfilling.

And sometimes when you are weary, the step of Saint Germain at your right hand and the words of comfort "Keep on keeping on" are the only thing that you can see when you face the adversary or the burden of your own karma. Beloved ones, keep on keeping on! Put your right foot and then your left and move forward and take those steps and we will do the rest.

We will be there before the Court of the Sacred Fire and in the courts of the world! We will be there as the witness of the Light and the Victory, but you must play your part! You must speak the Truth where Truth must be a sword that cleaves asunder the Real from the unreal. Therefore, do not withhold the word of Truth wherever you are, beloved ones from out the heart of the Great Central Sun.

I AM delivering unto your hearts now a flame that does rise, a flame that does come to the center of the throat chakra, the will of God, the sixteen-petaled chakra therefore centered. Beloved ones of the Central Sun, I AM THAT I AM. I AM in the presence of your Mighty I AM Presence, who sends forth to you this day a clear ray of light for the quickening of the Power of the Word within you by that Holy Spirit.

I come to you now in the magnificence of the God Flame. Woe to the evolutions of mankind who reject, therefore, the intercession of the archangels! For I tell you, the day will come when you will need us—all of us—in the hour of world transition; when you will be grateful that you have learned to call upon the name of the LORD and to call upon the names of the LORD's angels; when you will know that we will also move heaven and earth to rescue you, comfort you, protect you, and seal you.

Beloved ones, it is well in preparing for the storms of life to build and gather a momentum of the whirlwind of the sacred fire. It is well to walk with God in the days of gladness, in the days of peace, that thy God with thee might succor thee in the days of death and destruction and of war.

Pray God these will not manifest physically. But even the manifestation on the astral plane is sufficient to tear down many a weak and faint heart who may thrive in the presence of a stronger lifestream but does not fare well for want of momentum in the aloneness of the desert—which every true disciple of Christ will face, as Jesus did also. [10]

It is your victory to pass the tests of the tempter at every hand. It is your joy to learn the way. It is learning and achieving. It is coming to understand where you have failed in the past and what were the mistakes—getting up and moving again, moving on, then, and saying:

This time I understand all the rules of the game and the strategies of these fallen ones. This time I understand the philosophy of the tempters and the serpents. This time I have learned from the Divine Mother all of their evil ways and I will not be moved! I will not be fooled! I will not be set aside from my path of the glorying in the Lord.

I AM the blazing action of the Great Central Sun Magnet. I AM the fury* of the Elohim of God! I AM the will of God made manifest! I AM that Light descending and that heavenly Light now! And I AM the purging, therefore, of the priesthood of Melchizedek of those false priests who are the betrayers of the Word and who do not come to build but to defile.

Therefore, my Word shall not be defiled, saith the Lord— neither in Church nor in State. The Word of God shall not be defiled. The Word of God shall not be defiled. The Word of God shall not be defiled.

Thus I stamp my mantra with Mighty Victory upon every grain of sand and erg of energy on planet earth. [11] My Word shall not be defiled, saith the Lord. My Word shall not be defiled.

Therefore, let the sacred fire be raised up. Let the All-Seeing Eye of God be opened. Let discernment and discernment of spirits and discrimination be the gift of the sons and daughters of God by that Holy Spirit, [12] that you might have your inner sight opened, that you might see the Light and Darkness and know that though the dark ones pronounce the same words, yet *their vibration is their judgment.* Their evil intent and motive is their judgment. Their desiring, lusting after the Light of the sons and daughters of God is their judgment now! And that pure Word spoken by the little child in your midst is the power of that judgment, beloved ones.

So, I have come. Let the nations give attention, for I stand in every nation upon earth. I stand for the shaking of the bastions of tyrants and the tumbling down of the betrayers of the people. Let them fall! Do not preserve your idols! Let them fall. And let the very vacuum of leadership be the opportunity for the sons and

* an avenging spirit; extreme fierceness; a state of inspired exaltation

daughters of God to rise up and take dominion over the earth.

Lo, I AM that sacred fire! Lo, and none shall calculate the decibels of my Word and therefore attempt to tamper with it. None shall turn it back! None shall stand in the way of the full Power of my being reaching every heart and mind and soul! For the very physical atoms do quiver with the vibration of the Word of the sons of God and of archangels and of Elohim and of the Great White Brotherhood.

Therefore, beloved children of the Sun, send forth the Word! Send it forth now for the binding of tyrants and injustice in every nation! So it is done in the Philippines. So it is done in America. So it is done in Russia and in China, in every nation of Africa. So it is done! So it is done! So it is done!

Let the tyrants be bound in the name of Saint Germain, in the name of the dispensations of the Cosmic Council. And let the sons and daughters of God prepare the children of the Light and educate them properly for their responsibilities as true representatives and world servers. And therefore, let not there be a vacuum, but let there be the filling in by the Lightbearers of every nation who have been called once again to the divine government of the Mother—the Mother in Lemuria, the Mother Omega, the Universal Light of Mary.

May you bear the Light of the Mother. May you be the Light of the Mother. May you have recourse to Mother Mary. May you have recourse to beloved Helios and Vesta. May the circle of fire be drawn. May the seraphim of God and fiery salamanders seal! seal! seal! this city and let it become a city of Light.

And let Darkness flee. And let those who flee, then, be bound by a mighty cordon and ring of angels—blue-lightning angels of Astrea, blue-lightning angels of my bands. So they surround the city now and they bind those demons and discarnates who would flee the very wrath of God and the coming of the hosts of the LORD.

And they are bound. And they are removed from this planetary home. For I, Archangel Michael, give forth the Word in the name of the Lord Christ: They are bound and they are purged in this hour.

Therefore, let the vacuum that is left by the infestations of these hordes be filled by the preaching of the Word, by the Holy Spirit of the Lord Jesus Christ and Saint Germain. Let it blaze forth and let there be teachers who will teach and enlighten the children and youth and all people as to the advocacy of their souls by the entire Spirit of the Great White Brotherhood who is now assembled and who does now stand with Saint Germain.

For Saint Germain has sent forth the call for his dispensations to descend for the swallowing up of that Darkness and for his message to go forth. And therefore, the Cosmic Council has been petitioned and Saint Germain has been granted that dispensation for the covering of the earth with his own Teaching, with the path of the seventh ray, and with the Everlasting Gospel.

And as the dispensation is granted, so it is granted to every child of God's heart who will take the mantle, who will call forth the mantle of Elijah, who will call forth the mantle of Lanello and Moses, of Christ and Buddha, who will go forth and who will fearlessly proclaim that Word.

Beloved ones, it is the enlightenment of the Holy Spirit and the teaching of Charity that is the only hope for the avoidance of planetary darkness and karma. Therefore, go forth in the mighty Word of the LORD and proclaim the Coming Revolution in Higher Consciousness.

And I, Michael, shall be with you! And I will stand and I will not leave you! For I am with you in the name of Saint Germain and Portia, in the name of the Lords of Karma, in the name of the Lord Christ, in the name of the Holy Christ Self of all and in the name of every Lightbearer on earth sent from God who in this hour *must* be awakened, *must* be shakened to the realization of God, *must* be brought into the knowledge of his own I AM Presence. And therefore we go with you.

Let therefore the souls of Light qualify themselves and be not consumed of Evil but overcome Evil by the all-consuming fire of Love. The all-consuming fire of Love, then, does go forth, beloved hearts. It is the sacred fire of the ruby ray. Thus, call upon the LORD and he will answer you. And I will deliver that answer in person.

Beloved ones, run then for the Victory! Run for the Sun and be one. For the oneness of your Love is truly a chalice unbroken and the seamless garment. Therefore, the seamless garment of the entire Spirit of the Great White Brotherhood be upon you.

In the name of holy Faith, I seal you. I blaze the Light now and I AM the encirclement now of your chakras, of your aura. And the Power of God is released for the mending of the flaws.

We will mend the flaws! We will mend the flaws! We will mend the flaws! So it is done.

In the name of the Great Divine Director, it is sealed.

"The Summit Lighthouse Sheds Its Radiance O'er All the World to Manifest as Pearls of Wisdom." This dictation by Archangel Michael was **delivered** through the Messenger of the Great White Brotherhood Elizabeth Clare Prophet on **Saturday, February 15, 1986,** during the weekend seminar *The Healing Power of Angels,* held at Camelot. In the service to Archangel Michael which preceded the dictation, the Messenger delivered a sermon on Malachi 1. Teaching taken from this sermon is contained in Pearl no. 27. (**1**) Exod. 14:13; II Chron. 20:17. (**2**) Dan. 12:10. (**3**) Isa. 61:1; II Cor. 3:17. (**4**) Matt. 26:27. (**5**) Gen. 6:3. (**6**) II Kings 5:10–14; Matt. 3:13–17. (**7**) John 8:58. (**8**) **The LORD's day.** Isa. 2:10–22; 13:6–16; 34:1–8; 61:1, 2; 63:4; Rev. 1:10. (**9**) Ps. 19:2. (**10**) Matt. 4:1–11; Luke 4:1–13. (**11**) **"Victory" on every grain of sand.** In a dictation given January 3, 1971, Mighty Victory told us the fiat by which he invokes the angels: "The earth is the LORD's, and the fullness thereof!" "As I spoke these words," he explained, "every grain of sand upon the planet recorded them . . . . Every grain of sand, every drop of water, every portion of *all* substance has recorded my words tonight because I speak with the authority of God. And I have delivered unto the world this, my fiat: 'Victory, Victory, Victory, Victory, Victory!'—billions and billions of times written upon the sands of the planet. You cannot handle a grain of sand or substance from now on without knowing that the word 'Victory' is upon it." See Mighty Victory, "Indomitable Greetings of Cosmic Victory," 1976 *Pearls of Wisdom,* vol. 19, no. 45, pp. 221–22. Also on 2-cassette album *Victory in the Holy City* (A7710), $12.95 postpaid; single cassette B7710, $6.50 postpaid. Affirmations taken from this dictation are published as decree 22.03 in *Prayers, Meditations, and Dynamic Decrees for the Coming Revolution in Higher Consciousness* (Section II), Summit University Press. Sections I, II, and III each $2.95 postpaid. (**12**) I Cor. 12:10.

ERRATUM: There is a printed error on the 1986 Sun and Moon Sign Chart which needs to be corrected on your personal copies. The full moon currently listed for October 19 occurs October 17. (The time as noted is accurate.) Please correct your charts accordingly.

Pearls of Wisdom, published weekly by The Summit Lighthouse for Church Universal and Triumphant, come to you under the auspices of the Darjeeling Council of the Great White Brotherhood. These are presently dictated by the Ascended Masters to their Messenger Elizabeth Clare Prophet. The international headquarters of this nonprofit, nondenominational activity is located in Los Angeles, California. All communications and freewill contributions should be addressed to The Summit Lighthouse, Box A, Malibu, CA 90265. Pearls of Wisdom are sent weekly throughout the USA via third-class mail to all who support the Church with a minimum yearly love offering of $40. First-class and international postage rates available upon request. Notice of change of address should be received three weeks prior to the effective date. Third-class mail is not forwarded by the post office.

Pearls of Wisdom®
published by The Summit Lighthouse

| Vol. 29 No. 29 | The Beloved Messenger | June 14, 1986 |

The Healing Power of Angels
The Reestablishment of the Electromagnetic Field of the Aura
V
Christ the High Priest

Holiness unto the LORD. Holiness unto the LORD. Holiness unto the LORD. Holiness unto the LORD where I AM THAT I AM!

Holiness unto the LORD. Holiness unto the LORD. Holiness unto the LORD where I AM THAT I AM!

Holiness unto the LORD. Holiness unto the LORD. Holiness unto the LORD where I AM THAT I AM!

Holiness unto the LORD. Holiness unto the LORD. Holiness unto the LORD where I AM THAT I AM!

The higher the cosmic being, the greater the fierceness of Light which descends through him for the rebuke of that state of consciousness which is unlike God, which is out of alignment with the will and the harmony and the wisdom of God. This force that has made its way through the Matter cosmos is called the force of the anti-Self or the anti-Christ—that which opposes as anti-Matter the universal Light within every cell and molecule of your being.

We have not so much in modern time understood the message of the prophets. We must realize that they were pillars of fire, extensions of the Presence of God. And by their word and the Word of this LORD spoken through them, the power of the spoken Word brought judgment and karma upon the individuals who had sinned rather than a general karma where all people should bear the burden for those who were their oppressors.

Thus, the archangels have requested that I read to you from the Book of Malachi, which we began earlier today, that you might hear the Word of the LORD as the judgment which comes as the result of our desiring to approach the altar. So it is out of the Flame of the ark of the covenant that the Mighty I AM Presence speaks to us, and it comes for the rebuke of that which is not of the Light in those who represent the Light or who would serve that Light.

You see, the return of God's presence to us when we pray, desiring to serve his holiness, is that he comes with that two-edged sword of judgment. He separates the Real from the unreal within us—shows us on the one hand our error, shows us on the other our righteousness, which can only be God's righteousness. And then he says, as Joshua said: Choose ye this day whom you will serve.[1] If you will now forsake your ways that are out of keeping with the Law of Love, you may return and be restored to that point of Christ-perfection.

The judgment is not something we fear. We run to greet the Lord Christ, who occupies the office of Judge as well as Healer and Burden-Bearer and Saviour. For we know that only by his just judgments can we survive, can the Light within ourselves be extricated from the entangling threads of Darkness.

Listen to this prophecy of judgment with the realization that as the Word is spoken and as you read scripture, it is happening now. Such is the Power of the Word.

And now, O ye priests, this commandment is for you.

If ye will not hear, and if ye will not lay it to heart, to give glory unto my name—*I AM THAT I AM*—saith the LORD of hosts—*the YOD HE VAU HE*—I will even send a curse upon you, and I will curse your blessings: yea, I have cursed them already, because ye do not lay it to heart.

The term *curse* is interpreted as the judgment, the binding by the Law of God of their ways of infamy in the misuse of the blessings of the altar. Scholars have interpreted "blessings" in this verse to mean the privileges enjoyed by the priests or their levitical revenue.

Behold, I will corrupt your seed, and spread dung upon your faces, even the dung of your solemn feasts; and one shall take you away with it. This is the prophecy of the instantaneous return of karma. **And ye shall know that I have sent this commandment unto you, that my covenant might be with Levi, saith the LORD of hosts—*Sanat Kumara, the Ancient of Days.***

My covenant was with him of life and peace; and I gave them to him for the fear wherewith he feared me, and was afraid before my name.

**The law of truth was in his mouth, and iniquity was not
found in his lips: he walked with me in peace and equity, and
did turn many away from iniquity.** (Mal. 2:1–6)

Robert C. Dentan, in his exegesis on Malachi in *The Interpreter's Bible,* tells us that "all through this section the name 'Levi'
is to be understood as a vivid personification of the priestly order,
not as a reference to the Hebrew patriarch. . . . The particular
duty which is mentioned is not that of performing the ritual of
sacrifice, but rather that of giving true instruction."[2]

**For the priest's lips should keep knowledge, and they
should seek the law at his mouth: for he is the messenger of the
LORD of hosts.** (Mal. 2:7)

This is the definition of the office of priesthood. Dentan
further comments that "Malachi revitalizes this whole conception of the priest as teacher by relating it to religious and ethical
attitudes rather than to the minutiae of liturgical practice. Ideal-
izing the past in typical homiletic fashion, he pictures the priests
of former days as animated wholly by a spirit of true devotion
and as powerful influences for sustaining the moral life of the
community."[3] Verse 7, he says, "contains both the noblest statement of the function of priesthood to be found in the Old Testament and the highest estimate of its dignity. The priest is the
messenger of the LORD of hosts and thus takes over the office
formerly filled by the prophets."[4]

The Christ of each one of you is the high priest. Those who
are called to the priesthood of Melchizedek, the priesthood of
the order of the sacred fire and of Lord Zadkiel, must understand that your calling is to be a messenger of the LORD of hosts.
The LORD of hosts is Sanat Kumara and Karttikeya, the Ancient
of Days whom Daniel knew.[5] It is He that sitteth upon the great
white throne.[6] Thus the words of your mouth, the meditations
of your heart come forth to deliver his Word.

This is your calling in life. This is why you love the LORD and
his prayers and his sayings. This is why you tarry in the temple
longer perhaps than those of any other religion in the world. You
are of the ancient ones of the seventh ray—the ray of ritual before
the temple of God. And in your heart you understand that as you
serve at this altar with your prayers and your fastings, you are
counting for millions upon earth who go about their ordinary
business and the challenges of life.

There are some who come to this world knowing that the
Flame must be kept at the altar of God. This is why the archangels desire you to know what it means to keep the Sabbath

and to keep it holy[7] and to understand the integration with the Flame of the ark of the covenant.

The ark was that in which they carried the tablets of the Law, understanding that as the Law is written, so the very writing of the Law is power. So they bore the tablets of the Ten Commandments as the focus of their altar. And out of that Flame of the ark, guarded by covering cherubim, the voice of God spake from above the mercy seat (the "lid" of the ark).[8]

And so the Flame, the Flame of the sacred fire, burned. And a mighty cloud surrounded Moses whenever he was in the tent (which is called the tabernacle) communing with the LORD God. And the people would wait when they saw the mighty cloud surrounding him for the Word of God that he would speak to them.[9]

Moses was a messenger of the I AM Presence and of the Ancient of Days. And this is the true office of the priesthood of Melchizedek to which you aspire—the seventh-ray priesthood that, as I have told you, was entered into by Jesus Christ and Saint Germain as they were initiated by the Archangel Zadkiel in his retreat of the seventh ray and the violet flame in the Caribbean, now in the etheric octave. This occurred long ago on Atlantis. And so, Melchizedek was there and present when Jesus was initiated and the words were pronounced upon him, "Thou art a priest forever after the Order of Melchizedek."[10]

There was a very amazing occurrence in Washington, D.C., when we were there and I was being trained as a Messenger by beloved El Morya under Mark Prophet. On January 1, 1962, at the New Year's Class which was held at the Theosophical Hall in Washington, D.C., a great being of Light spoke. It was Diana, Goddess of Fire, with Saint Germain.

This beloved servant of the Most High embodies the God consciousness of the sacred fire with her twin flame, Prince Oromasis, on behalf of elemental life. They are the ascended hierarchs of the kingdom of fire who direct the fire elementals, called salamanders. (As you know, there are ascended twin flames who are the hierarchs of the kingdoms of air, water and earth who direct the services to mankind of the sylphs, undines and gnomes.)

Now, at this service there was a venerable white-haired gentleman in attendance whom we scarcely knew. His outstanding feature was his fiery blue eyes. Well, it happened that during the dictation Beloved Diana called Mr. Chagnon to the front of the room and through Mark she addressed him thus:

O son of Heliopolis,[11] the blessing of the Most High be upon thee. Thy priesthood of love and light at inner levels is beauteous, is glorious. And I, Diana, in the name of Almighty God, say that thou art a priest of the sacred fire forever. Will you turn now and face these people? And everyone, please join hands with this blessed soul. Form a circle.

Omri-Tas, Ruler of the Violet Planet, blaze thy transmutative substance through these lifestreams and let them by the fire element find the blessing of Almighty God bearing forth the sacred fire I am releasing this day. Let them carry it and be firebearers throughout the earth, and let the earth find, even from this nucleus and those at inner levels, that the power of Light eternal shall free this earth in the name of Almighty God.

I, Diana, have spoken.

Then Saint Germain addressed the students and Mr. Chagnon with the following words:

Precious ones of the unfailing Light of God, lest you think these moments strange, let me tell you this: this Messenger did not know when he took this platform what the plan was for this meeting any more than individuals who open their eyes on a certain day will know what the events of that day will be until they have taken place. You do not know even now the full meaning or significance of this act.

Melchizedek, priest of the Most High God, without father and without mother, was an ancient member of the sacred-fire priesthood. I wish to call to the attention of those of you here that the historical knowledge of the mankind of earth is so muted and lacking in substance of truth that it has given a very perverted concept to mankind. Unfortunately they think in terms of one thousand, five thousand, ten thousand, or a million years. Aeons and aeons and aeons of time have passed and shall continue to pass.

The priesthood of Melchizedek and the glorious civilizations on other systems of worlds are unknown in the annals of humanity. And so here in this room today is a mixture (and I smile as I speak it), for here is a cross-section of many evolutions, root races, planetary beings from various systems of worlds. Even in your physical forms you are not all alike. And therefore it is not always strange as it may seem, for you have heard it said that truth is stranger than fiction. And I think this is true.

And, blessed ones, be at peace. The purpose of this may not even be known to your outer self. But I, Saint Germain, will tell you—if you do not know, beloved Mr. Chagnon—exactly why this has taken place when you either make your ascension or shall meet me. If you wish and desire it enough, at inner levels, even while your body sleeps, you may be able to come to the knowledge of what this really means.

So Mr. Chagnon, "Chag" as we all called him, became a Keeper of the Flame and we knew him for many years, even after we moved our headquarters to Colorado Springs. And I became aware of his passing after Mark's ascension. And a number of years thereafter, Mark, whom we call the Ascended Master Lanello, escorted this one, this soul, to the sanctuary in Pasadena to present him to me as a newly ascended Master. And there he was—he had made his ascension from inner levels, this one who had come to that very small room in Washington and received the immediate recognition of Beloved Diana and Saint Germain.

And then on June 30, 1978, beloved Ascended Master Kuthumi, who was embodied as the blessed Saint Francis, made reference to these events in his dictation:

. . . I bow before Melchizedek and I say, "Hail, I AM THAT I AM. Hail, thou priest! Hail, Melchizedek! Hail, thou holy one. Hail, thou holy one of God." Measure for measure, then, so now drink in that light. So it was spoken of the Lord Jesus Christ, "Thou art a priest forever after the Order of Melchizedek."

Beloved ones, there is one Keeper of the Flame who, in the very early days of the movement in the nation's capital, came to be a part of this activity and was promised his ascension; and this one had followed in the lineage and the descent and in the path of initiation under this order.

And therefore, there comes with Melchizedek this day your own beloved Lanello and this one chela of the Light who has ascended in very recent months—one known to some of you as Leon E. A. Chagnon, to whom the LORD God has given this anointing.

This going before of one from among this body is the

opening of the way of the dispensation [of the Melchize-
dekian Order]. This individual had endured many thousands of years in pursuit of that Path. Now there comes to
you the bequeathing of a causal body, not of someone
remote as a great cosmic being, but of one of your own
members, a member of the body and the cell of God
among you, bequeathing what you might call an "ordinary causal body," as you would consider your own; and
yet I say, that causal body is extraordinary as yours too
can become, for it is supercharged with the white light of
that holy order.

Not by signs and wonders and outer signs are the
souls of devotees known, but by the clear recording of the
Law itself, of the great computer of the Mind of God, of
the very flow of the heart's devotion.

Beloved ones, this blessed soul stood at the marriage of
your own beloved Messengers [March 16, 1963]; and therefore, a very intimate friendship transpired over many years,
even after the ascension of your beloved Mark.

Do you see, then, that the realization that you can
reach out and touch a friend of Light, one who has
walked among you, enables you to translate that realization to know that you may also reach out with your hand
in this very moment and clasp the hand of Lanello and of
this [newly Ascended Master] Leon, and of many others
whose names are not known to you.

To this priesthood you must aspire—to this calling. For the
seventh ray is the open door to the return to the holiness of
God—Holiness unto the LORD. And the prophecy is that in that
day of the return of the true Israel and the remnant, which is
prophesied to take place here in this Promised Land, here in
America, there shall be upon the bells of the horses HOLINESS
UNTO THE LORD; and the pots in the LORD's house shall be
like the bowls before the altar.

Yea, every pot in Jerusalem and in Judah shall be holiness
unto the LORD of hosts. And they will all be engraven with this
mantra, HOLINESS UNTO THE LORD. And all they that
sacrifice shall come and take of them, and seethe therein: and
in that day there shall be no more the Canaanite in the house of
the LORD of hosts. (Zech. 14:20, 21) And the name *Canaanite* is
symbolical of the fallen angels and their godless genetically
engineered race of "giants" who have walked the earth.

This is the day of the seventh age when there has permeated

the consciousness of all Lightbearers—those who have come out of every nation and people and religion and are called *Israel*—the realization that all things are holy. And they shall have this reverence for life, even to the very pots and the bridles of the horses; and they shall engrave thereon the words HOLINESS UNTO THE LORD.

They shall have transcended this period of the judgment of the false priests. And the false priests, as we have been taught, have entered positions of authority and leadership in Church and State. Not only are they the false pastors or the false rabbis and the false ministers, but they are also those who profess to represent the people in every field—in education, science, technology, and the economy.

For this reason, then, the archangels come in this weekend. For this reason the presence of the LORD God of hosts in the person of Gautama Buddha does release this particular judgment of the LORD God. For unless the false hierarchy be judged and bound by the hosts of the LORD, the true hierarchy of Light cannot come into manifestation as the angels of God, as the sons and daughters of God to take up Light's dominion once again in the earth.

And so, **the priest's lips should keep knowledge, and they should seek the law at his mouth: for he is the messenger of the LORD of hosts.** (Mal. 2:7)

May you never forget that you are the messenger of the LORD of hosts wherever you are and that there is engraven upon the miter across your forehead HOLINESS UNTO THE LORD[12] for the sealing of the third eye, that you might immaculately behold the Christ of every person you meet. For this is your office, beloved who are the true seed of the Ancient of Days through Abraham.

And you know that the beloved Ascended Master El Morya was embodied as the patriarch Abraham, and you who are his ardent chelas (disciples) today are called of him because of your spiritual descent in Christ. But unto those who have not kept the Spirit of their divine calling, the LORD Sanat Kumara spoke long ago, and the message of the judgment goes forth today:

But ye are departed out of the way; ye have caused many to stumble at the law; ye have corrupted the covenant of Levi, saith the LORD of hosts.

Therefore have I also made you contemptible and base before all the people, according as ye have not kept my ways, but have been partial in the law. (Mal. 2:8, 9)

So, have we not lost our respect for many of our leaders in Church and State because of the bribery, the favoritism, the prejudice, the scandal, the politicking and the misuse of power and of money? So it has come to pass that because of their partiality for the human consciousness rather than their deference for divine justice, they have lost their mantle, if indeed they ever had it in the first place.

Have we not all one father? hath not one God created us? why do we deal treacherously every man against his brother, by profaning the covenant of our fathers?

Judah hath dealt treacherously, and an abomination is committed in Israel and in Jerusalem; for Judah hath profaned the holiness of the LORD—*the Mighty I AM Presence*—which he loved, and hath married the daughter of a strange god. (Mal. 2:10, 11)

We wed ourselves to false gods, philosophies, materialism, attachments to the human condition, excluding God from our daily deeds. This is the marriage to the unlawful self instead of the marriage to the Universal Christ.

The LORD—*the Mighty I AM Presence*—will cut off the man that doeth this, the master and the scholar, out of the tabernacles of Jacob, and him that offereth an offering unto the LORD of hosts.

And this have ye done again, covering the altar of the LORD with tears, with weeping, and with crying out, insomuch that he regardeth not the offering any more, or receiveth it with good will at your hand. (Mal. 2:12, 13)

The corrupted offering may not reach the I AM Presence. It is *disallowed* by the Universal Christ in the person of your Holy Christ Self, who says, "Thus far and no farther. Your impure vibrations shall not pass. They are the unacceptable offering."

Yet ye say, Wherefore? Because the LORD hath been witness between thee and the wife of thy youth, against whom thou hast dealt treacherously: yet is she thy companion, and the wife of thy covenant.

And did not he make one? Yet had he the residue of the spirit. And wherefore one? That he might seek a godly seed.

One must be wed to the Christ to produce the seed of Christ. One must not divorce oneself from this Christ in order to follow the ways of the world. One must not compromise. The marriage is the fastening of one's energy to the living Word within. It is a mystical union of the soul with her Bridegroom.

Therefore take heed to your spirit, and let none deal treacherously against the wife of his youth.

For the LORD, the God of Israel, saith that he hateth putting away: for one covereth violence with his garment, saith the LORD of hosts: therefore take heed to your spirit, that ye deal not treacherously.

Ye have wearied the LORD with your words. Yet ye say, Wherein have we wearied him? When ye say, Every one that doeth evil is good in the sight of the LORD, and he delighteth in them; or, Where is the God of judgment? (Mal. 2:14-17)

In the full knowledge of this Law, David, King of Israel (c.1013-c.973 B.C.), prayed unto the Mighty I AM Presence: Let the words of my mouth, and the meditation of my heart, be acceptable in thy sight, O LORD, my strength, and my Redeemer. (Ps. 19:14) So may you, beloved, as the redeemed priesthood of the LORD, say this prayer each morning as you awaken to a new day of *HOLINESS UNTO THE LORD!*

Let us welcome beloved Archangel Jophiel as we sing his song. [song 300, "Beloved Jophiel and Christine"]

"The Summit Lighthouse Sheds Its Radiance O'er All the World to Manifest as Pearls of Wisdom." This Pearl is taken from a sermon **delivered** by the Messenger of the Great White Brotherhood Elizabeth Clare Prophet on **Saturday, February 15, 1986,** at the weekend seminar *The Healing Power of Angels,* held at Camelot. (1) Josh. 24:15. (2) Robert C. Dentan, Exegesis on Malachi, *The Interpreter's Bible,* 12 vols. (Nashville: Abington Press, 1956), 6:1132. (3) Ibid. (4) Ibid., pp. 1132-33. (5) Dan. 7:9, 13, 22. (6) Rev. 20:11. (7) **Keep the Sabbath.** Exod. 16:23-30; 20:8-11; 31:12-17; 35:2; Lev. 19:3, 30; 23:3. (8) **Ark of the covenant.** Exod. 25:10-22; 30:6; 37:1-9; 40:20, 21; Deut. 10:1-5; Heb. 9:2-5. (9) **The cloud and the tabernacle.** Exod. 33:7-11; Lev. 16:2; Num. 7:89; 9:15-23; 12:4-10. (10) **"Thou art a priest forever. . ."** Gen. 14:18; Ps. 110:4; Heb. 5:5-10; 6:20; 7. (11) **Heliopolis.** 1. Biblical city of On (see Gen. 41:45, 50; 46:20): Ancient ruined holy city northeast of modern Cairo, Egypt, dedicated to the worship of the sun god, Ra. 2. Ancient Egyptian city south of Cairo, said to be of the late Stone Age, destroyed c.5000 B.C. 3. Ancient "City of the Sun" in Lebanon, now Baalbek. (12) Exod. 28:36-38; 39:30, 31.

Pearls of Wisdom, published weekly by The Summit Lighthouse for Church Universal and Triumphant, come to you under the auspices of the Darjeeling Council of the Great White Brotherhood. These are presently dictated by the Ascended Masters to their Messenger Elizabeth Clare Prophet. The international headquarters of this nonprofit, nondenominational activity is located in Los Angeles, California. All communications and freewill contributions should be addressed to The Summit Lighthouse, Box A, Malibu, CA 90265. Pearls of Wisdom are sent weekly throughout the USA via third-class mail to all who support the Church with a minimum yearly love offering of $40. First-class and international postage rates available upon request. Notice of change of address should be received three weeks prior to the effective date. Third-class mail is not forwarded by the post office.

The Healing Power of Angels
The Reestablishment of the Electromagnetic Field of the Aura
VI
Slippers of the Ancient Guru

Legions of the Central Sun, we are come! We are in the oneness of the universal Light of Christ. And Christine, my beloved, does impart the initiation of that Word to you in this hour, beloved. For the feminine ray is raised up in you and it is renewed as the fountain of Light.

So let the Mother and let the cosmic virgins who are the archeiai be received by yourselves, who come in grace and, if you will, as the Shakti of the archangels. Know, then, the feminine power of the archeiai of God. Know them through the presence of Wisdom's Mother and Mother flame.

Now, beloved, as you are seated, golden flames form the seat of the Buddha. Thus, in the coolness of illumination's fire, so be seated in this our love—the loving presence of many angels of the sacred fire weaving in and amongst you that filigree light and garlands of flowers fastened as though to a latticework.

But this latticework is as angel hair. So it is that God would then interpenetrate the Matter spheres on the wavelength of your mantra, the portion of heaven that brings fragrance and unity with the etheric octave.

Wisdom's flame shall have her perfect work as wise dominion in your being takes command. Fear not, then, for the Mother of Wisdom stands to defend the Buddhas and the bodhisattvas, the disciples and the bhikkhus.

Dear hearts of living fire, the solar ring in this hour through our presence now is become yellow fire-rings surrounding cities and this place, this county and nation, and goes beyond this octave to ancient records. Millions of rings of yellow fire now upon the earth are set in motion for the piercing of the veil and as an outer corona signifying that the Great Central Sun Magnet in all of the holiness of illumination's flame pouring out of the Mind of God is truly focused in the heart of the earth.

And dancing around these rings are angels of Light and also nature spirits. And you may join them also. For ring upon ring of Light—this becomes circles of fire and the dance of Shiva: Shiva as the Holy Spirit, Shiva as the purging and the judging Light.

Thus these rings move. And each turning, then, of Life within this wheel of the Law does consecrate space and time, collapsing the evil that has ensconced itself therein. For evil is an energy veil; and when time and space collapse, so evil itself must collapse together with illusion. This may take place first in the mind and the heart of the devotee, beloved ones, then in the hearts of many as nature and the four lower bodies of the earth become purified, as the ether itself penetrates the four elements and as the five secret rays once again have expression.

Beloved ones, illumination for the path of Light is that which we bring, and the understanding of the Inner Retreat. As you know, there are a certain number of retreats of the Great White Brotherhood in the etheric octave devoted to Wisdom's flame, else under the direction of hierarchs who have attained on the second ray. Your own Royal Teton Retreat at the Grand Teton is a center of Cosmic Christ illumination so dedicated by Lord Gautama, the Lords of Karma and Mighty Victory, so dedicated by Lord Lanto and Confucius.

There is a turning of worlds. And as you have heard of the exchange of the poles,[1] so you may contemplate the interchange of the hemispheres whereby East and West reverse roles and the wisdom of God and the spirituality and the holiness now does become the principal thing[2] for those rising from the heap of materialism to the pinnacle of praise, having been so surfeited in all these things that they desire only union with God, whereas the impoverished masses and peoples of the East, having not had the abundance of material things, now enter the age of the worship of the gods of materialism and the forsaking of the ancient Teachings of their fathers. And thus, products come inundating the West out of the East, goods of all sorts as well as goods of mechanization and scientific precision.

Beloved ones, the precipitation flame that burns in the Grand Teton is a mighty living fire. We have drawn to the

West, therefore, the souls of Light who may easily dispense with material things, for they have enjoyed the abundant life and seek now to lay it upon the altar of humanity and to claim the highest gifts of Christhood and Buddhahood. See then, therefore, that the religions of the world must complement one another until all embody equally the paths that lead to the God-mastery of the seven chakras.

Christine comes now. And with the delicate ones who accompany her, there is an arranging now of silken garment of sacred fire, of golden flame. Beloved ones, there is a draping of your bodies as though you were monks in an ancient Buddhist temple, else among the Essenes or of the mystics of Zarathustra.

Have you not meditated on the Word before? Have you not become the Word? Are you not a part of the moving stream of the Word and the eternal sound? Aye, and I have known you forever and a day also.

I AM Jophiel. And I desire that you should go back now, back to the ages of glory and golden ages of China where you served under those Masters who have long ascended, leaving a vacuum for you to step into their shoes. But some have lost the memory of where the Master has placed his shoes—under the bed or in a cave or in some lost field or beneath the earth.

It is not so easy to find that which is lost, beloved ones. It is not so easy to discover and reconnect. But the thread of contact is reestablished through the devotion of Kuan Yin and beloved El Morya, who also ruled in ancient China. Therefore the Lord of the First Ray does know indeed the path of Wisdom with Kuthumi. And the World Teachers, Jesus and his own Kuthumi, have gone north and south and east and west establishing grids of light and illumination's flame.

Beloved ones, how important it is for Truth to be established and for the perversions of the Flame and of Wisdom and of Light to be bound and judged that they not encroach upon the true golden flowers of the crown chakra. Thus Lord Himalaya and the God and Goddess Meru, thus focuses around the world established by the Wisdom Masters have set the open door for the banishment of the darkness of ignorance.

Beloved ones, illumination [illumined action] is king; wisdom [wise dominion] is queen. Understand that this flame, when it seizes the mind of the sincere, those who try to be just and pure in all their doings, will guide and reform and convert souls—souls by the millions who know the Truth because they have been illumined and enlightened by that Truth.

Understand that Truth is a quality of seeing. By the All-Seeing Eye of God one may see the Truth. But to know the Truth one must have the infusion of illumination's flame for the understanding of that which one has seen.

Therefore, simply because Truth parades in the marts of commerce—or should the Ascended Masters walk down the streets of New York City—does not guarantee that Truth will be recognized. And it has often come to pass that Truth has been despised by those indoctrinated by error.

Indeed, this has always been the ploy—the anticipation by the adepts of the left-handed path of the coming of Truth. Therefore the setting up of councils of error and erroneous doctrine, misinformation, disinformation, manipulation of the press and the media so that a whole nation may believe a lie[3] concerning this or that situation and reject the Truth and mock it when beloved Pallas Athena comes.

Therefore, beloved, wrapped in beautiful silken robes, seated in the lotus of the Buddha, you come now. It is well to restore and know the peace of ancient times. It is well to be in the heart of hearts of God.

This is the meaning of the Inner Retreat. This is why we call you apart and say, establish your base of operation. Let it be practical in every way. Insure your economic as well as your spiritual survival. And then do not spend all of your days in retreat, but go forth in the "Ritual of the Atom"[4] from the center of that sun to the periphery, desiring to minister unto life until you are spent and have given all light and must retreat once again to the etheric plane that is so evident, so there at our Royal Teton Ranch.

Blessed ones, the inner City of Light, the Retreat of the Divine Mother,[5] is a place called Home by many souls. It is a veritable city, and the light is a golden light upon its streets. And hosannas are come and the restoration of the Divine Woman clothed with the Sun, who is the Divine Mother of whom you are a part, whose messengers you are, whose expression you manifest in all poetic tenderness and in all sternness of the cutting edge of the sword of Shiva.

Thus, it is well to enjoy grace and beauty, the presence of the Mother. And it is well to realize that the Mother in all of her beauty and wisdom must also don the armour, the shield and the sword to go forth as Kali to rescue her children in the name of Christ.

I AM THAT I AM Jophiel. I AM THAT I AM Christine. We are now accelerating the wavelengths of the crown chakra in each one of you as we are able. And we have secured the dispensation of the restoration to you from your own causal body of that which you were abuilding in former golden ages which has heretofore been sealed in that second band of your causal body, beloved ones. For, precious hearts, you realize that your own Christ Self would not release to you the fruits of the spirit of the crown chakra while you were embodied in dark ages, beset by degeneracy and degeneration spirals.

Thus, with all due consideration of your desiring to serve and in consultation with your Holy Christ Self, there is restored to you at the etheric-body level and at the level of your chakras on the etheric plane those portions of light of golden illumination's flame that might serve you well, taken from your own treasury and storehouse of your causal body.

I counsel you, then, that you understand this is sealed also by your Christ Self, that not by folly or tomfoolery there should in any way be the squandering or misuse of this Light. But as you show yourself capable of using Wisdom's flame with equanimity, peace, justice, and impartiality, more will be added unto you, immediately accessible, then, in the plane of the Christ Mind.

Beloved ones, to increase illumination, as we have said before, by only one percent or three—to increase the threefold flame and wisdom—can make the difference between Darkness and Light, between success and failure, between joy and self-denial. The wisdom of God is a most precious oil of gladness and a nectar from the crown chakra.

May the filling in of the outline of the petals of the crown chakra be for you a daily joy. When you cannot feel the Light pulsating through the head, rising on the altar of the spine, remember it is lawful to fast and pray. Remember it is lawful to abstain from excessive uses of the sacred fire in other chakras, to withdraw one's energies from squandering in the world and from being tied to the world through the media. It is lawful to come apart even for three hours or one or a day in some manner to find the renewal and the sealing of the figure-eight flow within you.

I tell you, those who have this Teaching ought to be concerned when they do not feel the fire of the Mind of Christ with them in the upper chakras. And they should take necessary steps to use the mantras and the systems of purification and devotion to reestablish this communion. It is a goal to be sought, a prize to be won. And when it is won, it is to be cherished.

Thus, above all things, to this Higher Self and Light be true. And this Trust and this Truth established in thee will see to it that thou canst not be false to any part of Life, or God. Unless some determine to conserve the sacred fire in order to be world teachers, millions will remain in darkness and in ignorance.

Contemplate thy reason for being. Do not respond to me from an outer anxiety or even an outer or mental rigidity. Do not respond from the human level of desperation or of fear or doubt or even of guilt. Put all these things aside, beloved ones. These are not suitable responses to an archangel's call.

The call from my heart is to your heart and to your soul. I have infinite patience. I am long-suffering and peaceful. I desire you to come to the Light only when you are ready not only for the Light but for the persecution that its bearers must indeed bear.

Therefore, beloved ones, though cycles turn swiftly, the world karma is oncoming and very impatient. I am patient. And you must also be patient with yourselves.

We release, then, the matrix and thoughtform of the divine architect and the blueprint of the entire Inner Retreat, the Royal Teton Ranch and its auxiliary lands and manifestations. Beloved ones, a portion of this grid is intended to be lowered into manifestation in this year—a very key year of the release of the intensity of the sacred fire. Let those who have learned the path of the Buddha as builders hear, then, the call and identify with their inner calling and reason for being.

The weather and the cycles and the months turn. And soon it will be a period of great acceleration. Let those who are there prepare for many who must come. For by the end of the year and this time in 1987, that which is etheric must become physical as a certain portion of this divine blueprint fulfilled.

From the heart of Alpha it is set—in the earth, in the ground, in the mountain, in the lands, in the hearts of those around the world who also contain the blueprint and feel the magnet of that retreat.

You must be able to serve in health and in abundance, recharged by the fire in the heart of the earth. Thus, we have set a place for your victory and for your going forth therefrom periodically and cyclically as bodhisattvas caring for the suffering and those who are lost who have not found the slippers of their ancient Guru. Go after them. Wash their feet. Place upon them the slippers of their ancient path.

O Bodhidharma, precious one now ascended, thou art a part of every chela of the will of God. We have not forgot thy devotion, thy sternness with the beast of the lower self, thy determination to be the best example of Teacher on the Path.

O Maitreya, O Confucius, Lanto, Lao-tzu, Gautama, Padma Sambhava, thy feet have left footprints of sacred fire. Now will you not uncover a bit the hiding place of your slippers? For many must find the way.

[Mudras performed for 1 minute, 10 seconds.]

Peace forevermore in the flame of Buddha.

Thus the electromagnetic field is sealed with a heightened flame of illumination.

"The Summit Lighthouse Sheds Its Radiance O'er All the World to Manifest as Pearls of Wisdom." This dictation by Archangel Jophiel was **delivered** through the Messenger of the Great White Brotherhood Elizabeth Clare Prophet on **Saturday, February 15, 1986,** during the weekend seminar *The Healing Power of Angels,* held at Camelot. In the service preceding the dictation, the Messenger read and preached on Malachi 2 at the request of the Archangels. Teaching taken from this sermon is included in Pearl no. 29. **(1) Exchange of the poles.** The study of paleomagnetism (the magnetism residual in rocks) has provided evidence that the earth's magnetic field has reversed direction every few hundred thousand years—i.e., the north and south poles have switched polarity. Some scientists as well as psychics predict this phenomenon as occurring in the near geological future. **(2)** Prov. 4:7. **(3)** II Thess. 2:11, 12. **(4) Ritual of the Atom.** A meditation taught at Summit University for the expansion of God-awareness. In this ritual, one visualizes an electron spiraling from the nucleus of God-identity in the center of the circle to the circumference and back again in a continual flow for initiation under each of the twelve solar hierarchies. See "The Ritual of the Atom" on *The ABC's of Your Psychology on the Cosmic Clock,* 8-cassette album (A85056), $50.00 postpaid, single cassette B85063, $6.50 postpaid; or *Mother's Chakra Meditations and the Science of the Spoken Word,* 8-cassette album (A82162), $50.00 postpaid, single cassette B82169, $6.50 postpaid. **(5)** See Sanat Kumara, December 15, 1985, "The Retreat of the Divine Mother at the Royal Teton Ranch," 1986 *Pearls of Wisdom,* vol. 29, no. 10, pp. 70–72.

Messenger's Candle-Lighting Invocation before the Dictation:

In the name I AM THAT I AM Jesus Christ, I invoke the entire Spirit of the Great White Brotherhood. Legions of Cosmic Light from the heart of God in the Great Central Sun, twelve legions of angels at the command of the Lord Jesus, come to our aid in this hour of world need.

O Jophiel Archangel, we welcome thee and beloved Christine in the fullness of the Mind of God, in the fullness of the thousand-petal lotus.

O Ancient of Days, Alpha and Omega, let all the world be bright with illumination's flame in this the hour of Christ's conquest over Death and Hell. Let the brilliance of the Great Central Sun purge and purify, renew and revivify this earth. Oh, let those who have lost their way, O God, beloved Father—let them come to know Thee as Thou art in the very midst of the blue lotus, in the very midst of illumination's flame. In the heart of Himalaya, in the heart of Lake Titicaca, let thy brilliance shine forth.

O instrumentation of the Divine, holy angels of illumination's flame, we are grateful to consort with thee as we are yet veiled in these veils of flesh. Yet, by thy grace and presence, which is the LORD's, we may enter in to that portion of heaven which our God has allowed. And in his allowing, we therefore, touching the hem of his garment, may bring to earth some measure of joy, some measure of the quickening, O God.

We are grateful in this hour for all great beings of Light who have tarried with our planet—beloved God and Goddess Meru, Vaivasvata Manu and the Great Divine Director, beloved Saint Germain, each and every angel and Ascended Master who has brought to us the touch of Light, the inspiration, the realization of our Divine Reality, as we are pilgrims journeying upon this distant star making our way to the throne of grace with a very special mission to alleviate suffering, to illumine where there is ignorance, to proclaim liberty to the captives.

O Light of eternal Freedom, thou Light so essential to the victory of planet earth, we summon you in the name of the legions of the seventh ray. Let this earth be free this hour, beloved Jophiel, by illumination's flame. Let ignorance be banished and let it be accomplished by the raising up of the Mother flame within us, from the base unto the crown.

Thus, with Chamuel, with Michael, come, Jophiel, come, Faith, Hope and Charity, to complete the balancing action of the threefold flame within our hearts.

In the name of the Father, the Son, the Holy Spirit, in the name of Gautama Buddha, Padma Sambhava, Maitreya, Avalokiteśvara, in the name of Kuan Yin, Amen.

Pearls of Wisdom®

published by The Summit Lighthouse

| *Vol. 29 No. 31* | *Beloved Archangel Gabriel* | *June 22, 1986* |

The Healing Power of Angels
The Reestablishment of the Electromagnetic Field of the Aura
VII
The Judgment of Love
The Coming of the Messenger ~ The Dividing of the Way

The Word of the LORD unto the prophet Malachi.

Behold, I will send my messenger, and he shall prepare the way before me: and the Lord, whom ye seek, shall suddenly come to his temple, even the messenger of the covenant, whom ye delight in: behold, he shall come, saith the LORD of hosts.

But who may abide the day of his coming? and who shall stand when he appeareth? for he is like a refiner's fire, and like fullers' soap:

And he shall sit as a refiner and purifier of silver: and he shall purify the sons of Levi, and purge them as gold and silver, that they may offer unto the LORD an offering in righteousness.

Then shall the offering of Judah and Jerusalem be pleasant unto the LORD, as in the days of old, and as in former years.

And I will come near to you to judgment; and I will be a swift witness against the sorcerers, and against the adulterers, and against false swearers, and against those that oppress the hireling in his wages, the widow, and the fatherless, and that turn aside the stranger from his right, and fear not me, saith the LORD of hosts.

For I AM the LORD, I change not; therefore ye sons of Jacob are not consumed.

Even from the days of your fathers ye are gone away from mine ordinances, and have not kept them. Return unto me, and I will return unto you, saith the Lord of hosts. But ye said, Wherein shall we return?

Will a man rob God? Yet ye have robbed me. But ye say, Wherein have we robbed thee? In tithes and offerings.

Ye are cursed with a curse: for ye have robbed me, even this whole nation.

Bring ye all the tithes into the storehouse, that there may be meat in mine house, and prove me now herewith, saith the Lord of hosts, if I will not open you the windows of heaven, and pour you out a blessing, that there shall not be room enough to receive it.

And I will rebuke the devourer for your sakes, and he shall not destroy the fruits of your ground; neither shall your vine cast her fruit before the time in the field, saith the Lord of hosts.

And all nations shall call you blessed: for ye shall be a delightsome land, saith the Lord of hosts.

Your words have been stout against me, saith the Lord. Yet ye say, What have we spoken so much against thee?

Ye have said, It is vain to serve God: and what profit is it that we have kept his ordinance, and that we have walked mournfully before the Lord of hosts?

And now we call the proud happy; yea, they that work wickedness are set up; yea, they that tempt God are even delivered.

Then they that feared the Lord spake often one to another: and the Lord hearkened, and heard it, and a book of remembrance was written before him for them that feared the Lord, and that thought upon his name.

And they shall be mine, saith the Lord of hosts, in that day when I make up my jewels; and I will spare them, as a man spareth his own son that serveth him.

Then shall ye return, and discern between the righteous and the wicked, between him that serveth God and him that serveth him not.

Malachi 3

And so, my beloved, I am Gabriel which stand in the presence of God.[1] I, too, am the angel of the LORD. And so my cohorts of Light—Archangel Jophiel, Archangel Chamuel, and Archangel Michael—have spoken to you in the midst of the flame that does consume all that is not of the Light. And you have gathered because you have yearned to be in the presence of angels, in the very center of the eye of their healing power.

And I say, the Light has called you. And world karma and plague have chased you. And therefore you have been pulled by the heart and pushed by the winds of adversity. And therefore you find yourselves in the lap of the Divine Mother as though you had entered a new octave of Light. For so is the forcefield established by the mantra of the Word.

Enter ye, then, at the strait gate. For there is a broad and a narrow way: There is a broad way that leadeth to destruction, and there is the narrow way of the disciplines of the path of discipleship.[2]

Come, then, unto me as unto the LORD Christ, for I speak to you as one who does succor the weary, heal those who mourn, quicken those who have been dead, and return joy to those who have been sorrowful too long. Beloved hearts, we see and we know and we understand the burden. And by Love, burdens can be healed.

Remember, then, that there is a partnership to be had with the archangels of God—that there is a cooperation and a working together shoulder to shoulder for the Victory. There are things which must be done, beloved, by you—which only you can do. But these things are not an hard saying. They are, in the purity of the Word, that which all can follow; for they come by the Holy Spirit.

And that sharper-than-the-two-edged-sword[3] comes to you, beloved, by my hand. For I, too, stand to cut you free with the Divine Mother from those unseen forces, entities, and discarnates that invade the body with disease and the mind with all forms of insanity. Beloved ones, all things are not the mere product of chemistry or biochemistry within the body, but there do come to pass in the lives of individuals those effects of past causes set in motion.

Thus, the LORD God spoke to Malachi. And it was I, the Archangel Gabriel, who came to him to deliver that word of the judgment and of the coming of the messenger John the Baptist who would go before the LORD Christ.

You are also messengers of your God Presence. And we have sent to you that Messenger to remind you of the inner calling of the priesthood of Melchizedek. Thus there is the dividing of the way of those who wait upon the LORD and those who do not. And in their failure and in their absence they are not content to leave well enough alone but they must persecute, they must gainsay, they must put down those who have become the devotees of Love.

It has always been thus, beloved ones. For the ruby ray does go forth and those who are confounded by their own anger against the Light or their own dishonesty or wickedness—these, beloved hearts, receive returned unto themselves tenfold the judgment of their evil words and works.

This judgment of God, as the law of karma, is written [on] page after page of scripture in the Old and New Testament. But because the word *karma* is not used, thus they deny the universal law of reciprocity, the universal law of retribution, and the universal law of the resurrection of the sons and daughters of God.

But the LORD has pronounced it. And he has sent me on missions from the Great Central Sun to many homes of Light and systems of worlds where I have come to speak to evolutions concerning their going out of the way of the central light of the I AM THAT I AM.

It is with a cyclic regularity, by the progressions of the sun centers of these systems, that the archangels return to the scene of their [the evolutions'] incarnations. We descend from the Central Sun and we deliver, therefore, to lifewaves the mandate of the will of God, of purposeful living in the ways of righteousness.

And through prophets and messengers and avatars and saints, we have proclaimed a path of the resurrection by the ascension flame, by the spirit of the resurrection, and by the raising up of the Divine Mother. Thus, to honor the feminine ray of God is to salute the Shekinah glory that is radiating even now from the flame of the ark of the covenant.

Hear, then, the Word of Yahweh unto the false priests and pastors and those who do not try* justice in the marts and courts of the world. Let the flame of the sword of the angel—the angel with the flaming sword[4]—be thrust now into the very ground of this planetary home! And the Lightbearers do rally for the Light. And let those who would turn the tide toward darkness be stopped in their way by this flaming sword ere civilizations and continents face the conditions of earthquake and darkness that have been predicted.

It is self-predicted by mankind's karma, who have refused to accept accountability. Nevertheless, the ignorance of the Law is no help but rather the hindrance on the path to union with God.

*prove

Beloved ones, there are experts in all fields of human knowledge. But there are many across the board who consider themselves already "experts" in the path of that true religion that does restore man's relationship to God through the Mediator of the Universal Christ. Therefore, inasmuch as there are so many experts in the fields of theology, philosophy, and psychology, let me come to clear, then, the jungle and the babble of voices to tell you that the most direct route and the only route to the very center of the heart of God is by the path of the ruby ray, by the path of Love—the love that first embodies the cup of kindness, of compassion, and of charity and moves on to a love of discipleship and self-discipline that can hold the balance to be the friend of Christ on earth.

Beloved ones, many fail the test of being the friend of Christ. For to know him as friend is to know him in the intimate contact of the day-to-day manifestations of ordinary life. All who wear the human form must go through the human condition. This is no detraction from sainthood. Nor is it, therefore, the mark of the sinner. But all who pass through this octave must be reduced to the same common denominator of the body of flesh—[and] inherent in it, its desires and basic needs. Beloved ones, all begin at the beginning with this base and common factor. Yet some rise and some fall by the burdens that beset them.

Beloved ones, not because of but in spite of and beyond the lesser self is the transcendent Life known. Yet, so long as the soul has need of the body, so then all walk as "men" and "women" until the hour of the transfiguration. And when that transfiguration is come, then the Son of man contains an extraordinary light that is the power of the etheric body and of the I AM Presence.

And thus, the mortal is being put off and the soul is putting on the garments of immortality.[5] And therefore, those who climb the highest mountain and mount the spiral staircase are found often betwixt and between their mortality and their immortality.

And this, too, is no crime. Nor is it a crime when mistakes are made or errors entered into and there is a stepping back a step down the rung of the ladder to retake those lessons and the testings of the soul that one might find strength and equilibrium and a new balance of the heart chakra to mount again what has been known as a most treacherous path to the heart of Himalaya.

Beloved ones, what matters is that the heart is pure. God does judge by the heart and not by the outer mechanizations of the form. So many engage in rote and rituals in life and seeming niceties. But within, either there is no character or no spirit or there is only the ticking of the inner time bomb to the moment when, turned inside out, that individual becomes enraged in the very presence of God manifest in the person of his prophets.

So look to the ancient prophets of Israel and see how they were scorned and spat upon and separated. And, remaining apart from the community, going into the desert, beloved ones, they were ostracized. And when they did not preach a popular word, they were condemned by Church and State alike, who demanded that they make proclamations that were pleasing to the ear.

Thus, what have you come to hear from me and from the LORD God this day? You have come to hear of the healing power. Beloved ones, this healing power of an archangel can be with you, but you must play your part. Our emphasis in this seminar has been the science of the spoken Word, for by its use you gain swift strides on the path of Light.

Beloved ones, from out of the Great Central Sun the LORD God does send a ray of Light. It is a ray of purification passing through your auras now. And by the Holy Spirit there is a sacred fire that does burn and consume within you those forces and forcefields that are detrimental to the will of God, to the divine blueprint, to the purest expression of your soul. Therefore, feel the intensity of the Holy Spirit now that comes by the flaming presence of my beloved Hope, archeia and feminine light of the fourth ray of the archeiai of God.

O legions of the Central Sun, seraphim of the sacred fire, Justinius, now come with the legions of the fourth ray! And therefore, the mighty action of the demagnetization of darkness from the aura and the binding of the discarnate entities is accomplished by Astrea and Purity, by the seraphim of God who place themselves in answer to your call congruent now with your form.

So they bear a chalice of immortal light and sacred fire. And so they encourage you to put off the old man and the old woman and to put on the new[6]—the new manifestation that is born in Christ, and out of Christ a new creature,[7] a creature rising toward the sun of the I AM Presence.

All this you are and all this you can be, beloved ones. Therefore, there is a piercing sword that I now use for the exorcism of those conditions that prevent you in this hour and in this life from fulfilling the fullness of your divine plan.

Beloved ones, I am Gabriel and I announce to you the very present possibility of your ascension in the Light. And this is the goal of life. And on pain of the same ostracization, there is going forth from this Messenger that word that does give the word of Saint Germain of the promise that those who use the violet flame and remain faithful to their God wherever they may be, in whatever faith or church or organization, may rise to the new heights of the sun [Son] and greet Archangel Uriel—truly the archangel of the resurrection and of the judgment who does come in the name of the LORD Christ.

And therefore, there is the very present possibility for you to intensify your stand and to settle into the very work of the ages—that mighty work of which we have spoken—to balance your karma in this life and to move on with the solar winds and the Central Sun.

Beloved ones, no matter what you have been taught otherwise, it must concern you that you are lifestreams who have been sojourning on this planet and reincarnating for want of the key, the very key that unlocks the door to that path of Christhood. And by the dispensation of Saint Germain and Portia, beloved ones, this Teaching, the knowledge of this Path, is set before you.

Those who love the search and the quest for the sake of the quest but are confounded in finding the Truth will not be happy to hear that the message of the violet flame, the message of Saint Germain, does provide you with all that is necessary for the balancing of your karma, for the healing of your diseases. It is a knowledge that is no longer withheld. It is a knowledge that is set forth and is yours for the asking, beloved ones.

In the course of this Path you will surely be tried and tested. And that testing has naught to do with this Messenger but is between you and your God and your own Christ Self and the archangels who intercede in the name of the LORD.

Therefore, go after the prize of this high calling.[8] For it is an opening of ages and a turning of ages when many souls may be caught up in the resurrected Son of God and in his Second Coming, which is occurring daily to souls who have the eye to see him, the ear to know his voice, the commitment to run with him to the farthest reaches of impelling stars of Light.

O seraphim of God, in answer to the call of those here and now who desire healing for themselves and for their loved ones, let the power of seraphim be known. I, Gabriel, summon you in the name of Justinius! Place your electronic forcefield over these sons and daughters of God. Let their auras be saturated in the sacred fire of seraphim, that they may see and know that the LORD God of Israel is with his people and that the LORD Christ is both Saviour and Healer and Friend of Light.

Blessed ones, I send light now into the cause and core of war upon earth and all inequity and all injustice. We release that which is sent by God, measured and sent in the very cups of angels—ministering angels of the ascension flame. They are cup-bearers, beloved ones. And they bring those portions of sacred fire from the Central Sun that may come to earth without disruption of the ordinary course of the turning of worlds and the signs of the seasons.

Thus God does pour into the earth by the instrumentation of his angelic host that quotient of sacred fire that the earth can contain, that may be for the judgment of the seed of the wicked and the liberation of these little ones and yet not turn the tables toward destruction by planetary karma or personal karma.

Beloved ones, understand the great balance of forces in a planet where returning karma does accelerate, where Light-bearers make the choice, when awakened, to serve God—and where fallen ones, when awakened to the Light, do make their freewill choice to turn their back on the proffered gift of the Messenger of the Lord.[9]

So it is and so it has always been. The Light has gone forth. The sword is thrust into the earth. And all may choose what is their perspective, what is their relationship, what is their positioning to this flaming sword that no eye hath ever seen, save in the etheric octave. But now every eye shall see it and know that the archangel of the Lord has thrust his sword into the ground as a challenge to all forces of Death and Hell in the earth.

Let them respond, beloved ones! Within a fortnight you will see the judgment of the Lord God Almighty. You will see the right hand of the Buddha Gautama. And you will see the driving back of those who have sought to take the Light where the Light has been ensconced, of those who have sought to tear down that true religion where it has been planted, of those who have sought to seize governments of nations unlawfully.[10]

Look, then, to the fortnight and understand the coming of the sign of Archangel Gabriel. For I AM here, and I AM the Archangel of the Fourth Ray. And I do not intend to leave this place until the Lord God has accomplished that holy thing to which he has sent me.

Therefore, know that I stand and I still stand. And my right hand is raised, even as the hand of Moses was raised and even as that hand was held up.[11] For I stood and overshadowed, therefore, the prophet and the messenger of God. And therefore were the fallen ones turned back.

Thus, beloved ones, understand the meaning of the sacred fire. Understand your oneness and integration with archangels of Light. And so see how the LORD God will intercede to deliver every Christed one and every little one of his heart.

There is no turning back of the Light in the earth. Therefore maintain your vigil as watchmen of the night, for the night is all they have left. And when the night is far spent and has divested itself of all of its schemes and strategies of darkness, the dawn shall appear.

And the angel of the dawn, Archangel Uriel, will then take his post, as I will pass therefore the rod to him. And he shall stand in that dawning day, Archangel Uriel, with the proclamation of the sons and daughters of God that shall never, never, never again be turned back.

Beloved ones, as I stand here, I stand in the very presence of the cathedrals, mosques, synagogues, churches, and places of worship throughout the entire planet. And my Electronic Presence is placed there. Therefore, let those who speak the lie find justification. They will not find justification in God. And thus the lie will be turned against them. And their defilement of the altar shall be no more. And the hosts of Light shall withdraw from those temples where the LORD God Almighty and his archangels are not welcomed.

Beloved ones, see to it that in your heart is the burning, all-consuming Love of the flame of the ark of the covenant, for to this all must have recourse. All must know that the resource of the flaming presence of the Buddha of the Ruby Ray and of the sacred fire thereof is the alternative to that which is unreal, that which is false and untrue, that which is dishonorable and disrespectful before the living presence of his Word.

I AM Gabriel in the heart of the Sun. I AM in the heart of Hope. And Hope is in the heart of me. Therefore we are one. And therefore our flaming presence, as Alpha unto Omega, does form the mighty spheres of Light. And therefore, we send forth now the angelic tongues for the cleansing and for the purging and for the changing of the water into wine.

[angelic tongues chanted 15 seconds]

Therefore there does come forth from the heart of the universal Word the sounding of the eternal tone. [tone chanted 6 seconds] And the Divine Mother has sent forth and Sarasvati has sent forth and Lakshmi has sent forth and Durga has sent forth and the eternal Word of Kali has sent forth!

And therefore the keying of the Light by the sound of the Ma-Ray, by the sound of the eternal Word, by the AUM, is the intoning now of Matter spheres, is the clearing of that darkness, and is the binding of the hordes that assail the Divine Mother as the demons and discarnates on the astral plane.

Therefore [angelic tongues chanted 20 seconds] there is now come, beloved, sent from the Sun, the messenger of Sanat Kumara. And that messenger from the Sun does stand and does hold, therefore, this proclamation of the sons and daughters of God. And it is held, therefore, as the focus and the power and prayer of the pledge of the sons and daughters of God in the earth which shall be made known to you in that hour so designated.

And in the flaming presence of God, I, Archangel Gabriel, do declare before you: So it is the flame of the Divine Mother! So it is the flame of the living Word! So it is now, by the power of the angels and seraphic bands. It is done in the name of the living Word. It is done in the name of the LORD Christ.

Helios and Vesta, Helios and Vesta, Helios and Vesta, let thy presence descend! Let thy judgments descend in the flaming light of the ruby ray! So the Divine Mother Mary does attend, so Raphael does attend for the coming on the morrow of the archangel, the archeia of the fifth ray.

Beloved ones of the Light, I salute you by the power of the flaming light of Hope. And I seal you in the heart of hearts of the immaculate concept of your own conception in the heart of God. By the light of Alpha, by the light of Omega, it is done.

"The Summit Lighthouse Sheds Its Radiance O'er All the World to Manifest as Pearls of Wisdom." This dictation by Archangel Gabriel was **delivered** through the Messenger of the Great White Brotherhood Elizabeth Clare Prophet on **Saturday, February 15, 1986,** during the weekend seminar *The Healing Power of Angels,* held at Camelot. (1) Luke 1:19. (2) Matt. 7:13, 14; Luke 13:24. (3) Ps. 149:6; Heb. 4:12; Rev. 1:16. (4) Gen. 3:24. (5) I Cor. 15:53, 54. (6) Eph. 4:22–24; Col. 3:9–11. (7) **Born again, a new creature in Christ.** John 3:1–8; II Cor. 5:17; Gal. 6:15; I Pet. 1:23. (8) Phil. 3:14. (9) Dan. 12. (10) In November 1985, Philippine President Ferdinand E. Marcos, in ill health and besieged by criticism at home and abroad for corruption and cronyism, announced that he would call a special election to prove his popular support. Marcos' political opposition, which was not unified at the time, did not seem to pose a threat to his reelection. His announcement came in the midst of increasing U.S. pressure for economic, political, and military reforms to eliminate the corruption that had been fueling a growing Communist insurgency. In the election, held February 7, 1986, Marcos was challenged by Corazon (Cory) Aquino, widow of opposition leader Benigno S. Aquino, Jr., whose assassination in 1983 had shocked the country and intensified anti-Marcos sentiment. (continued in next week's Pearl) (11) Exod. 17:8–14.

Pearls of Wisdom®

published by The Summit Lighthouse

| *Vol. 29 No. 32* | *Beloved Archangel Raphael* | *June 29, 1986* |

The Healing Power of Angels
The Reestablishment of the Electromagnetic Field of the Aura
VIII
The Day of the Coming of the LORD's Angel
Healing, Karma, and the Path

For, behold, the day cometh, that shall burn as an oven; and all the proud, yea, and all that do wickedly, shall be stubble: and the day that cometh shall burn them up, saith the LORD of hosts, that it shall leave them neither root nor branch.

But unto you that fear my name shall the Sun of righteousness arise with healing in his wings; and ye shall go forth, and grow up as calves of the stall.

And ye shall tread down the wicked; for they shall be ashes under the soles of your feet in the day that I shall do this, saith the LORD of hosts.

Remember ye the law of Moses my servant, which I commanded unto him in Horeb for all Israel, with the statutes and judgments.

Behold, I will send you Elijah the prophet before the coming of the great and dreadful day of the LORD:

And he shall turn the heart of the fathers to the children, and the heart of the children to their fathers, lest I come and smite the earth with a curse.

Malachi 4

Pilgrims on the Path Journeying
  to the Shrine of Christ Healing,

Come into the center of the One and into the heart of Mary, whose healing flame abounds, as my own does also make the rounds of your four lower bodies as together we build a figure-eight flow, demagnetizing your auras from those things which ought not to be and which should never have been.

Beloved ones, we have been a part of your auras for these hours of service, preparing your receptivity for our release, through the spoken Word, of this healing light and the healing thoughtform[1] that may be anchored now by your Christ Self above you. Do indeed, then, appeal to God, to Christ, and to us as their servants to transfer to you throughout this day healing light and restoration of the inner blueprint [in order] that the healing light might coalesce not around distortion but around vibration that corresponds to the higher being that is your own in the Central Sun.

By the amethyst jewel, by the jade and the diamond, so we release that fire that is most necessary to you. Angels of Light with the power of master surgeons—healing angels who use laser technology that is beyond the physical as an emerald ray, a crystal ray, and a ruby ray, beloved ones—may penetrate to the very core of a cell or its circumference and seal that cell in the healing thoughtform and expand the violet flame from within.

Thus, in joy, in relaxation and freedom, as you go forth from this dictation, breathe a prayer to us, and unto God for us, that will allow us to enter your life and help you to become all that you really are through the mending of the vessel—the chalices*—and those things which have gone out of the way according to the inferior design of the matrix of the imperfect mind.

Having so said, won't you, beloved, be seated.

Some of you may remember the establishment of the healing focus at La Tourelle which was to be a forcefield of great light and healing and a mecca such as Lourdes or Fátima. Beloved ones, this property being no longer useful to our activity, these forcefields have been withdrawn. And for the duration of this established Camelot, we come to Los Angeles and we place a ring of light over this land that does establish here that same healing matrix and shrine.

Beloved ones, it is the great desiring of the heart of my beloved Mother Mary to draw souls of Light in this city—those acutely in need of healing in all levels—to this Path and Teaching: a path through her sacred heart that comes indeed through

---
*the soul, the four lower bodies, and the chakras

the individual's exercise of the science of the spoken Word, especially the use of the violet flame and the healing flame and thoughtform.

Beloved ones, therefore the one whom you have called the Blessed Virgin does come to you and is present in this hour, choosing the Great Silence this day from whence to direct to your forms a cycle and a spiral of Light for the reversing of degeneracy, old age, disease and death that besets earth's evolutions because of the condition of the absence of Light and the frequency of Light that makes for buoyant Life, renewal and the ever-renewing cycles of youth.

Healing angels of Mother Mary—these have answered the call. Let those who truly keep the flame without compromise or backbiting, wherever upon earth there are Keepers of the Flame and Lightbearers pure in heart, loving of the presence of angels— let them receive the radiation of my heart, our heart, let it now also reach them from this place.

Let filigree lines of force now be established. Let angels of the fifth ray, angels of the immaculate conception, angels of birth, angels of the Holy Spirit tend Life on earth. And let those of all nations having the highest vibration, no matter what their course of devotion or study, be the ones to whom it is given, having sealed within them these frequencies of Light.

They, then, beloved hearts, may be electrodes. They may carry now the rays of force that connect all of the retreats of the archangels. And thus, around the world the connection of these retreats and the reinforcement by Elohim makes possible, ever increasingly so, the accessibility of embodied souls and souls in inner planes to the Light, to the fountain, to the inner knowledge and to the practice of the precepts of heaven.

Such is the karma of many of earth's evolutions, beloved ones, that our intercession is not possible without their exercise of the science of the spoken Word. Many could achieve freedom from bondage through the use of the decrees, so perfectly outlined by El Morya in these booklets that are for Saint Germain's Stump to the nations.[2] These mantras and decrees, when used with great love and devotion and constancy of daily application, may result, then, in miracles of grace and healing.

Karma, beloved, is something that few understand. And many can hardly believe its science. Many will hardly understand how karma plays such a key role in whether or not a diseased situation may respond to the best of natural cures or those offered by medical science.

The x factor of the equation as to whether or not an individual will attain healing and wholeness or pass from the screen of life is this karmic circumstance. When the Law decrees that karma must be balanced and it must be balanced now, if the individual has not prepared a literal fountain of light through a momentum of devotion and light sustained in the aura, when he is bereft of that joy of service unto God, he may find himself having not enough of the light of God to consume the darkness that suddenly and swiftly is outcropping in the physical body. And before the soul can even regain composure or balance, that soul finds itself in other octaves, having passed from the screen of life, for the body was no longer able to sustain light adequate for physical life.

Beloved ones, these are facts of life on earth. And, after all, you are also wise and may not need the presence of an archangel to tell you that this is so. It is more my interpretation and explanation of the passing scene that may shed some light as to the prudence, even the wisdom, of preparing—as you also prepare so fastidiously on this planet for old age by setting aside funds and properties and all sorts of situations to guard against poverty or want.

Beloved ones, is it not also well to prepare for the day of urgent need by building up the light in the body temple and by balancing karma while you are able to work? This is the true meaning of "work while you have the Light,"³ which Jesus told to his disciples. The meaning is: balance your karma while you have the strength of the light in your being to perform those services, that sacred labor and the holy application of prayer and affirmation that can make a change in the karmic equation.

The pattern which the Karmic Board desires to give to the majority of lifestreams is opportunity for joy and happiness in youth, which opportunity is given whereby parents may train children to follow the precepts of God, obey the commandments, worship and keep on the path of Light, get their education, have their livelihood and profession, be established and capable of meeting the needs of life before those situations of karma that become serious and challenging do set in.

Now, those who are not properly trained to prepare for adulthood and the full maturity which comes (and when it comes must give to the individual the severe tests of karma) find themselves unprepared at that hour when past the twenties they enter the age and decade of the thirties and forties and fifties and in those years discover that calamity, disease, and challenges of all kinds have not escaped them.

Some face these with poise and the equanimity of the Spirit, having been taught from the knees of their fathers and mothers the way to go in righteousness. Others, however, imitate their parents' squandering of light. And these parents often pass on at an early age. And thus the children see the futility of it all but they never had the example of inner discipline to follow a course whereby they could stand, face, and conquer, remain in embodiment and keep on keeping on.

Thus, there is a period when the challenges of life and facing karma become the major portion of one's day. Livelihood, childbearing, getting ahead while one is young and all the things that come into this circumstance are a part of this karma. The diseases which manifest, of course you understand, can be avoided through the understanding of natural remedies and what God has placed in the earth in pure food, light, water, air, and so many of those healing aids of which you have availed yourselves.

Those who practice, then, a pure life in this manner and take care of their bodies are also staying the hand of karma, that when it come they are able to meet the challenge. The Lords of Karma, then, intend that those who successfully face these challenges, come what may, may have the fruits of the Spirit and of their lives in the latter years and use them for the spiritual path that is understood to be the way in the East.

Beloved ones, when the cycles of life are taken as they are given, then, you see, the karma which is meted out need not be so heavy as to take one from the screen of life. Now, if these teachings are practiced from the earliest childhood days and the light of the aura does expand and the children are becoming in the path of perfect Christhood chalices of the Light, you see that almost every karmic condition can be transmuted, saving those rare exceptions where in the course of sainthood one must lay down his life in what seems to be an untimely manner.

It has been said before but I say it again that many are called to this Path because they specifically need these techniques to avoid the calamity of oncoming years. We have seen time and again over the centuries and in this activity that those who have neglected the opportunity or turned their back upon the discipline because it is sometimes a hard saying,[4] sometimes painful, sometimes demanding amazing resources and stamina will realize that having left off of the course of the most valiant and noble discipleship they do come to the place where the diseases that set in render them no longer capable of either dealing with the disease or of invoking the Light that could consume it.

Having so said, beloved ones, our admonishment to you who have faced struggle and pain and suffering is to realize that I am the angel—the Angel Raphael—who have come this day for "the troubling of the waters,"[5] which means I am troubling with my vibration the aura of this entire property. And I place in it and around it healing light and energy, that all who may come may avail themselves and be inundated and flooded with this light of healing.

This shall be sustained by my healing angels and renewed by me from time to time. In addition, the healing focus is also placed here that was once at La Tourelle. You may see now in the upper atmosphere a giant healing thoughtform. Through this thoughtform and your giving whether of Mother Mary's Rosary or Archangel Michael's Rosary, you will send forth those rays of light whereby those souls who indeed have need of this form of help may come and find the Helper as the Holy Spirit, which our twin flames release uniquely and specifically for this world's evolutions.

Beloved ones, I speak, then, of those whose karma especially entails the necessity of self-help and self-application. You have come to a place where you may meet brothers and sisters on the Path who have practiced and demonstrated the techniques which indeed you may also practice. Here you will find reinforcement and advice and knowledge of other sources and resources around the world where you can go and study—or go for healing itself or for learning to become a practitioner of one kind or another in the healing arts.

Remember, beloved ones, what is right for one may not be so for another—not because the rightness is not right but because the cycles of another lifestream may involve other opportunities or obligations. Thus, there are many churches, many schools, many paths of healing and religion. What is most important for your discernment in deciding your chosen way and that which will be the acceleration of your life is to determine what is the greatest need of your soul and your four lower bodies, what is the weakest link in the chain of being of your lifestream, then to find the teacher and the teaching, the path and the system, whether of prayer and fasting or any kind of remedies that may be from the highest source that would be the ones that would help you most to attain a greater integrity and a greater wholeness.

Let the goal, then, of thy life be wholeness, knowing full well that the sphere of wholeness becomes the divine magnet for every good thing from God to the twin flame and all in between. Then, knowing that wholeness is the goal, observe through the eyes and heart of Mother Mary that portion of yourself requiring the greatest attention. Go after this. Bring the spirit of Light and the dynamic decree to it. Approach it from all of the four lower bodies and the chakras.

Bring up, therefore, the lowest vibrating frequencies of your being. And if you do not know what these are, ask. Knock, and it shall be answered.[6] Call unto the LORD Christ. We are his servants and we will deliver to you that word of the magnificent God-free being who helps you now in this very hour, even the Ascended Master Jesus Christ.

Blessed ones of the noble lineage of the house of David, you who are the seed of that ancient Light, come now and understand that not only individual wholeness but wholeness of the cells in the Body of God makes for a greater wholeness in the entire Mystical Body. Thus, we seek spheres of light that may interconnect and form therefore a surface of light, a body of light, a magnet of healing.

See what will contribute to the greatest good for your inner integrity, but do not stop there. Look what will contribute to the greatest good of the integrity of the Community. Then see how the Community itself may help more and more on the Path who struggle, are burdened, are bowed down and still fall beneath the weight of the cross of personal karma.

Have compassion for life in the ultimate sense. And let this love be the love of the scientist who has learned the ways of the emerald ray and the emerald crystal and the fifth ray of the holiness unto God.[7] Understand the meaning of the third eye and the immaculate concept and learn that way. Study the 'eye magic' that is taught by the Messengers in *Climb the Highest Mountain.*[8]

Know that you have the power to see through the window of the third-eye chakra, to outline perfection on behalf of yourself or any part of your body, on behalf of loved ones, and to visualize that organ, that eye, that heart filled with light, called back to the heart of the healing thoughtform and blazing with the violet flame.

That which you desire to be you must see and visualize at least once a day. You must hold the thoughtform in mind as something you are not only approaching but you are also filling in with light.

Thus, goal-fitting is for goal-establishing. Take out a notebook at the nearest possible opportunity. Write down the most important goals in life, both spiritual and physical. Decide, after all is said and done, what is the most important physical goal, what is the most practical physical goal that can lead you to the attainment of the most important spiritual goal.

You should not be nebulous in that which you desire to achieve in this life. And if in the course of achieving your goal—which is God's direction to you within your heart—you realize that your physical body or any one of your four lower bodies is not adequate to the task as a vessel of strength and light, then, you see, the moment of decision has come—whether to say, "I give up. I can't. I am not able," or to say, "In the name of my God, I will and I shall overcome!"

Therefore, in that God-determination you lay down the life of the lesser self and all of its indulgences—not only a part thereof. You determine to forge a perfect union of the four lower bodies that can be the LORD's vessel at any hour of the day or night, and then you move on to that conquest of self and that attainment of the goal.

The science of Being is taught by the fifth-ray Healing Masters. We have given so much Teaching and so much is here. The practical application of it is most easily done when reinforcement is present in a Community such as this one. Therefore, the archangels have always sponsored spiritual communities of brothers and sisters who have walked a path and have loved one another and reinforced one another to come apart and accelerate on this homeward journey.

Beloved ones, the nucleus of brothers and sisters and families forms the heart of any church, whether Christian or Buddhist, Moslem, Hindu. Beyond this fire core of those who keep the flame of a religion are happy families and individuals who take the crumb of the Bread of Life from the Master's table, who take Communion and find great strength and inspiration and go forth to live their lives, to sort out their karma, to have those experiences which they may only have outside of such a Community and its white fire core.

Let all realize that each one is called according to his anointing in the Great Central Sun, according to his appointing by his own heart and Christ Self of the mission of twin flames. Realize, then, that everyone may be in his right place, whatever rung or positioning is decreed, even as one does not criticize the positioning of the stars in the heavens, the galaxies, or even the comets in their courses. There is a divine plan and a network. And the interconnecting forcefields show that the balance of Light and Light-holders is achieved through a vast pattern that may reach across the earth and beyond.

Let none, then, consider that another may not be as well off because of a supposed absence of dedication. Leave off from judging the service of anyone in this entire organization, for no one may know the dedication and love of a heart save God and the holy angels. Do not try to read or anticipate, but let the discerning Holy Spirit tell you what you must know in the avoidance of danger or the knowledge necessary to keep the flame with all due vigilance.

Beloved ones, all of the archangels give freedom and peace to any and all who may come to drink of this fountain. Freely you have received, freely give[9]—this is the science of the figure-eight flow of the fifth ray.

Beloved ones of the healing light, Mother Mary and I now seal the electromagnetic field upon each one of you, building upon the action of the dictations of the archangels who have gone before us. If you have come newly to this seminar, by listening to those previous dictations in order you may also receive the blessing through the spoken Word of that which is described and therefore have the mending of the flaws according to the cosmic conception of the Divine Mother.

In the name of Alpha, in the name of Omega, we are Raphael and Mary. We have accomplished our purpose, the end to which we have come.

Therefore, from the beginning unto the ending, I AM Alpha and Omega.

HUM

"The Summit Lighthouse Sheds Its Radiance O'er All the World to Manifest as Pearls of Wisdom." This dictation by Archangel Raphael was **delivered** through the Messenger of the Great White Brotherhood Elizabeth Clare Prophet on **Sunday, February 16, 1986,** during the weekend seminar *The Healing Power of Angels,* held at Camelot. (1) See Archangel Raphael, March 28, 1964, "The Healing Thoughtform: The Crystalline Star of Understanding," 1982 *Pearls of Wisdom,* vol. 25, no. 49, pp. 461–65; and Mark L. Prophet and Elizabeth Clare Prophet, "My Visualization for the Healing Thoughtform," in *The Science of the Spoken Word,* Summit University Press, pp. 144–49, $6.80 postpaid. (2) *Mantras of the Ascended Masters for the Initiation of the Chakras* ("Stump Booklet"), Summit University Press, $1.40 postpaid USA and Canada. All other internationals, $2.15 airmail postpaid. The mantras, songs, and dynamic decrees contained in the Stump Booklet are recorded on a 5-cassette set (B85135–B85139), $35.10 postpaid USA and Canada. All other internationals, $37.35 airmail postpaid. Or order singly at $7.20 ea. postpaid USA and Canada. All other internationals $8.20 airmail postpaid. (3) John 9:4, 5; 12:35, 36. (4) John 6:60. (5) John 5:4. (6) **Knock and it shall be answered.** Matt. 7:7–11;

21:22; Luke 11:9–13; John 16:23, 24. **(7) Holiness unto the LORD.** Exod. 28:36; 39:30; Zech. 14:20, 21. **(8) Eye magic** ('I-magic', image): the transforming power of visualization through the inner eye. See Mark and Elizabeth Prophet, *Climb the Highest Mountain, The Path of the Higher Self, The Everlasting Gospel,* Book 1, Summit University Press, pp. 38–39. **(9)** Matt. 10:8.

Footnote 10 from Pearl 31 by Archangel Gabriel continued:

In the campaign, Cory Aquino emerged as the leader of a new, surprisingly powerful grass-roots movement, soon to be known as "People Power." During the election, Marcos supporters engaged in widespread fraud and violence which involved vote buying, intimidation, falsification of voter registration lists, assaults on ballot-box guards, murder, and tampering with election returns. On February 15, the National Assembly declared Marcos the winner, according to the official count. Aquino also claimed victory, based on the tallies of the National Citizens Movement for Free Elections. She called for a nonviolent protest campaign by the people, which was endorsed by the bishops of the Roman Catholic Church. On February 22, two key Marcos officials—Defense Minister Juan Ponce Enrile and deputy military chief of staff Lt. Gen. Fidel V. Ramos—denounced Marcos, demanded his resignation, and pledged to support Aquino. Enrile, Ramos, and 300 soldiers seized Camp Aguinaldo and Camp Crame, which they made their headquarters, and called upon the remainder of the president's cabinet and the 200,000-man armed forces to defect. Jaime Cardinal Sin, archbishop of Manila, summoned the clergy to use their "spiritual power" to bring their parishioners into the streets to form human barricades protecting Enrile and Ramos from possible military retaliation by the Marcos regime. Marcos threatened to "let the blood flow" and to use force to "wipe out" the rebellion, but tens of thousands of Filipinos flooded the streets of Manila in an unprecedented three-day peaceful revolution that turned back even tanks and troops. Nuns fasted and prayed for three days and nights and exposed the Holy Sacrament in their monastery. Statues and other images of the Blessed Virgin were set up at key positions. In a remarkable act on February 24, rebel forces, largely civilians including nuns and priests, seized the government-run television station, Channel 4, cutting Marcos off in mid-sentence during a press conference in which he was declaring a state of emergency. The same day, President Reagan asked Marcos to step down and indicated he would grant him U.S. asylum. On February 25, in two separate ceremonies, Aquino and Marcos both took the presidential oath of office. The same evening, after vowing he would never abandon the Philippines or his office, Marcos fled the country with his family, ending a tyrannical and corrupt reign that had spanned two decades. Corazon Aquino became the new president of the Philippines, just ten days after the judgment pronounced by Archangel Gabriel. In the words of Cardinal Sin, "The force of the Filipino people stormed heaven with prayer and got answered with a miracle." As the *Los Angeles Times* (27 Feb. 1986) commented, "One of the world's longest-serving dictators had fallen with relatively little bloodshed."

Pearls of Wisdom®

published by The Summit Lighthouse

| Vol. 29 No. 33 | Beloved Archangel Uriel | July 6, 1986 |

The Healing Power of Angels
The Reestablishment of the Electromagnetic Field of the Aura

IX

The LORD's Vindication of the Divine Mother

Unto the Son I vow my flame.

O beloved of the Light, Uriel and Aurora greet you this night in the joy, the purest joy of His presence.

Oh, the name I AM THAT I AM, oh, the name of Christ Jesus before which every tongue should confess, every knee should bow;[1] for herein lies the road—the royal road to reintegration with the Universal Light.

Herein, therefore, is the return to godliness and godhood, set aside so long ago that the children of the Sun scarcely can believe upon awakening from the long sleep of a dark night, upon rubbing their eyes and seeing the presence of the Lord of the World, that they, too, were once endued with such power and wisdom and love that, therefore, because it was in the beginning, it shall be in the ending.

Thus, the return to God and godly manifestation is the subject of our instruction and our teaching. It is the way made plain. And it is for you not a mere regression to a former state but a reintegration with the high estate of perfect man, perfect woman in the causal body of Elohim.

Blessed ones, seek, then, penetration to the superconscious plane. Never look back, never go back. For it does not matter. It does not matter!

Only God is real where I AM. I AM the Lightbearer, and in bearing that Light, beloved, I have gone to the darkest places to expose, therefore, the fallen ones in their lair and those who have spread the lie of the force of the anti-God. You see, I trace their course by the moving finger that writes. And the finger of God does find out, therefore, that which is said in secret which will now be shouted from the housetops.²

Let the judgment of God appear! For it is the hour in 1986 for my return, for my vindication of the sons and daughters of God and the LORD's vindication of the path of the Divine Mother in the person of the Woman clothed with the Sun. Nearer and dearer to your heart does this cosmic being descend until all the world is filled with the glory of the Divine Mother and her sign is seen as effect in every area of life, every compartment of knowledge.

Beloved ones, ere this become the reality in the physical octave, there must be the binding of the force of the anti-Woman. This has naught to do with the feminist movement but everything to do with the divine incarnation of the Motherhood of God in all who wear the feminine ray in this life, as well as in those who hold the masculine flame and therefore as Buddhic warriors and Christian pilgrims do hold with absolute adoration the 'womb-manifestation', the portal of the birth of the Eternal Christ.

Beloved ones of the Sun, therefore to this end are we come. In the name of the Lord and Saviour Jesus Christ and the Sun behind the sun and the Cosmic Christ thereof, we say, Let the tormentors of Woman and her seed go down by the flaming sword of Elohim of Peace! Let them go down in this hour! For they have not sought to destroy a religion or a place of worship or even a Community of the Holy Spirit. It is Woman herself whom they determine to put down, even the very joy of Omega in millions of hearts.

Recognize, then, this opposition to Light for what it is. For the personification of Mother within you is indeed the rising ascension flame personified in the Kundalini fire. Thus, all of the hosts of Darkness have assailed the Mother in the sons and daughters of God to deter that rising flame, to strike it down at every hand!

I say, then, sent from the heart of God in the Great Central Sun, I AM come! We are one! And the intensity of the Light does probe and penetrate, then, the reasons behind the reasons of those who assail not alone this Messenger but all men and women of the Spirit who have taken up the sword of the Divine Mother in the name of her children.

This, you might say, is the incidental crossroads of Armageddon. Where one is assailed, the many will not rise above that level. Thus, without the victory of the Mother in this hour, beloved ones—very personally in your circumstance and everywhere on earth—others who come on the path of initiation will rise no higher than the level of that defeat.

Thus, in all areas—in education, in the field of abortion, and in the lives of little children—let the Divine Mother be defended that she might defend her own. For to strike the Divine Mother is, as the saying goes, to "smite the shepherd and the sheep are scattered."[3] Therefore, destroy the image, the purity, and the office of the Holy Mother in every family and you have indeed smitten the Holy Child. And the child without the blessedness and the holiness of Mother can only become, then, that human one and that human "I" or mortal form.

Blessed ones of the Central Sun, legions of Victory, descend in the name of Helios and Vesta and let the masks be torn from the oppressors who come in the name of justice. Justice is not their cause, for they worship the money beast. Greed is in their hearts and more—the desire to destroy, then, the image of Woman here and there and everywhere. And at inner levels they are linked on the astral plane to everything from pornography to the denial of the divine right of Woman to be, then, the inspiration and the point of aspiration of all society.

Blessed ones, I am the angel who does implement the judgments of God. In this hour, then, I bid you call with me, for I, too, stand with Gabriel. And I stand and I still stand. And by the power of the cosmic cross of white fire it shall come to pass that Truth as Pallas Athena is vindicated, that Justice as Portia is vindicated, that Mercy as Kuan Yin is vindicated, that Liberty as the Goddess of Liberty is vindicated, and that Love as Nada is vindicated.

Let all saints and Lady Masters of heaven who have expanded the great God flame come nigh to thee in the presence of archangels now. For in the perfect Electronic Presence of the holy virtues and the virgins who ensoul them—blessed archeiai of the Sun—there is, then, in the earth the perfect presence of the peers of the Divine Mother who stand as the witness unto the integrity, the integration of the Path and the manifestation of that Truth in the fullness of time and space. Time and space are not, for the sacred fire does blaze from the altar.

Let the Four and Twenty Elders, then, speak. Let them speak and resound their Word through your heart. Let the Logos be known. Let it be known in the reverberations as the Central Sun does press out.

Beloved ones, Aurora, as the dawn, does bring the dawn of a new age. Let elemental life adjust, then, the earth—with all due consideration of the mercy of the Law as well as of karmic cycles that must be rectified.

Adjustments must come. May you be found in the perfect poise of the Prince of Peace where I AM always the I AM THAT I AM.

I AM with you, beloved. And I place now the light of my energy upon your electromagnetic field, once again for the healing of the aura. If you give me leave by silent assent in this moment, I am touching and balancing the petals of the solar plexus. I raise my hand and I conduct now the "place of the sun" and upon it a great sun disc. I AM the sealing, I AM the healing, I AM the balancing of the ten petals of the Law. Lo, I AM THAT I AM.

And the judgment of the sixth ray is the parting of the way of anger. If you give me leave, I enter now your electronic belt for the binding of the core of those demons of anger that have tormented you and your lifestream and your home and family. Beloved ones of the Light, let the anger of hell be exorcised from you—you who have kept the vigil in this hour who desire to be free with the saints of God. I say, it has no longer any power over you.

Take dominion now in the plane of the sun, in the heart of Helios and Vesta. For I have assisted, but you must have the victory over the beast.[4] To you belongs this trial and this victory. Beloved ones, the testing of your soul for the exorcism of foul spirits must be your own conquest. For by that strengthening, you see, they will not return to an empty house to enter again.

Beloved ones of the Sun, know that the purging of [by] the God flame, the purging of the body of God in the earth, is a sacred-fire action. And it is a strengthening action. And by that strengthening you are also made pillars of fire that become electrodes to transmit the flame of God's justice and judgment, even as my angels perform this service.

Therefore, they become as pillars of fire throughout this city and county. And they remain standing as sentinels of God's justice. And you will see changes taking place, first at inner levels and then on the outer. For we seek the turning around of the downward spiral in this city and the acceleration of the upward movement, rising back to the heart of the Sun.

May lifewaves who are worthy of the calling receive, then, the cosmic spin in this healing power of the resurrection flame borne by millions of angels who plant now the resurrection flame of the Lord Christ and his victory over Death and Hell.

We are sealing this city in Light. We are binding, then, the
bottom ten percent of the evil forces who assail it. And they are
bound on the astral plane, and this city is also swept clean by
elemental life of fire, air, water, and earth. And there is a purging, and the purging is for the prevention of cataclysm.

Therefore, know the LORD. Therefore, understand his judgment. Therefore, understand that mighty sword that does stand
in the very heart of hearts of that focal point of Light.

I AM the placing of the sword and my presence, then, where
all ought to be for the victory of the Light. I AM in the center of
the flaming presence of the Lords of Karma. I AM for God-
Justice. And I AM bringing to naught those who are the tempters
and the tormentors and those who would destroy the Woman and
her seed as the Guru/chela relationship in every octave of Light.

Thus, Sanat Kumara descends. He descends in the wake of
the mighty archangels and he does place his Electronic Presence
with the Seven Holy Kumaras for God-Justice in all seven points
of the Law. And you may see them now—the defenders who are
the eternal youth who come, then, empowered by the Divine
Mother for the victory over the forces of evil that have assailed
the youth of the entire world through that which has gone forth
out of this city.

Beloved ones, there is no area of life where evil spawned has
not become an avant-garde movement out of the fads and fancies
of individuals in this city who are not of the Light. And therefore
they have polluted the matrix of the seat-of-the-soul chakra.

And Saint Germain and Portia stand to give the acceleration of that chakra now. And they are blazing forth the light and
establishing that matrix for the descent of Lord Zadkiel, who
does come now to speak to you for the mighty sealing action of
this judgment of the Lord Christ in the sixth ray.

Beloved ones, we remain and we still remain until the hour
is fulfilled, until the God-Justice does appear, until the judgment
is known and the victory of the Light is won.

Hail, Mighty Victory! Hail, Mighty Victory! Hail, Mighty
Victory! I, Uriel, with Aurora, salute thee, thou God from the Sun.

Messenger's Invocation before the Dictation:

LORD God Almighty, we stand with great joy, thy Spirit of Liberty, and thy God-determination to face the forces that move against freedom in America and in every nation. Therefore, we summon the hosts of the LORD in the name of Jesus Christ to drive back the hordes of Darkness, the demons out of Death and Hell, and the fallen angels that would tear from us and any and all people of God upon earth their God-ordained, Christ-confirmed right to complete freedom of religion and conscience and freedom of speech to voice the fruit of the inner communion— freedom of assembly for the congregation of the righteous and all people to choose to assemble, to speak out, no matter what their condition or rank; freedom of the press, that we might publish the word of truth and that all might publish their point of view regarding events.

We demand the turning back of all forces of Darkness, organized or not, in or out of embodiment, pitted against the light of this freedom and especially the light that we bear in the Church Universal and Triumphant and all religions and churches, all political groups, all those who would form their associations for the cause of the advancement of their ideas or their persons.

In the name of the living Word, we champion the right of the Goddess of Liberty and her legions to stand in this land and everywhere upon this planet to defend this flame of Liberty.

O mighty threefold flame of Life, come forth. And now, by the right hand of Lord Gautama Buddha, beloved Mother Mary, Helios and Vesta, in the name of Jesus Christ, we say: Hosts of Light, turn them back, confute and confound them now, and raise up the banner of thy living Word unto all people. Let religious and political fanaticism and the demons and discarnates thereof go down! Let those who have made themselves the policemen and women of others' faith and conscience and others' way of life also be bound by the hosts of the LORD. Let the bells of freedom ring! Let the Light shine forth, O God.

Hear my call, beloved Father, beloved Son, beloved Holy Spirit. O eternal Mother, come to our aid in this hour. Let Light prevail, and let every child of God coming to this planet be guaranteed this freedom to grow and to prosper with life and liberty and the pursuit of happiness.

O Jesus Christ, let thy twelve legions of angels at thy command descend now from the heart of the Father to defend the twelve gates of the City Foursquare that all who would might enter in and know thee as thou art—the true and living witness of our Christhood.

Therefore in thy name I AM THAT I AM, we rejoice in Thy Victory through us.

"The Summit Lighthouse Sheds Its Radiance O'er All the World to Manifest as Pearls of Wisdom." This dictation by Archangel Uriel was **delivered** through the Messenger of the Great White Brotherhood Elizabeth Clare Prophet on **Sunday, February 16, 1986,** during the weekend seminar *The Healing Power of Angels,* held at Camelot, Los Angeles County, California. **(1) "Every tongue should confess..."** Isa. 45:23; Rom. 14:11; Phil. 2:10, 11. **(2)** Luke 12:2, 3. **(3) "Smite the shepherd..."** Zech. 13:7; Matt. 26:31; Mark 14:27. **(4)** Rev. 15:2.

Pearls of Wisdom®
published by The Summit Lighthouse

| Vol. 29 No. 34 | *Beloved Archangel Zadkiel* | *July 13, 1986* |

The Healing Power of Angels
The Reestablishment of the Electromagnetic Field of the Aura
X
The Liberation of the Woman in Church and State
The Seventh Ray for the Implementation of the LORD's Judgment

Friends of God-Freedom Worldwide,

We, the angels of the seventh ray, appeal in this hour of world need to you to hearken unto Uriel and to understand that the seventh ray is for the implementation of the LORD's judgment in the physical octave.

Turn, then, your attention to the gross injustice which has been done against the woman in the Philippines who has lawfully secured the support of Light and of the people and whose victory has been stolen by one entrenched who has sought to tear the crown from the Divine Mother in this election. Realize, beloved ones, that the attack upon the Mother is upon the entire lifewave of the Philippines and upon the children and the families and the economy of the nation, which is a shambles as a result of the manipulation of one called Marcos and his wife.[1]

Beloved ones, I come to anchor the judgment of these two. And I declare it gladly in the physical octave that all the world might know that Zadkiel has not forsaken the nations or the flame of freedom in this hour—that Holy Amethyst comes in full support of dispensations given to Saint Germain and Portia since that New Year's conference. And therefore, we go before him with all of the love of our causal bodies for the clearing of the way of Saint Germain's dominion in the plane of the seventh ray and in the earth for the support of God-government once again.

And therefore we say, They shall not pass! Their karma is delivered unto them this night. And the people shall prevail when they remain in the heart of God. Therefore, let them stand guard. And let the Keepers of the Flame summon the elect from the very streets to recite Archangel Michael's Rosary round the clock until God-freedom is won. For at that level and that nation, this freedom must be won.

And I charge the members of the government of the United States, from the president through the Cabinet to the State Department and the Congress, that they shall speak openly and with God-determination and forcefully to challenge with one voice the infamy of the stolen vote and the stolen victory.

These fallen ones shall not pass! Will you confirm that word and stand upon your feet and say with me now: *They shall not pass! They shall not pass! They shall not pass!*

Therefore, while you have breath and life, understand that the threat to Mother Liberty is a desecration of the Goddess of Liberty. The threat to Mother Liberty in every nation is a threat to your own heart and threefold flame. There is a time to act. There is a time for the swelling of the ranks. There is a time to let the representatives of a free people know that this nation must stand for God's righteousness where it is assailed anywhere and everywhere on earth.

Thus, beloved ones, the shower of freedom's flame does descend. Following, then, the ray of Light from the heart of God, let the people be vindicated.

I call to you, Archangel Michael, for the absolute God-protection of the woman who has dared to defy this tyrant and ancient serpent-foe of the people. Beloved one of God, let your legions be assigned to her protection and all supporting her. And let her not fall as her husband fell.

O angels of the LORD, hear the voice of Keepers of the Flame and go forth in answer to their call. For I tell you from the heart of my retreat of freedom my report to all angelic bands: that if freedom is to prevail upon earth, freedom must have the full protection of the entire Spirit of the Great White Brotherhood and especially the mighty archangels and those in embodiment.

At every hand where there is the battle line drawn, where the light of freedom meets the darkness of totalitarian movements and tyrants, there must be the vigil, there must be the All-Seeing Eye of God. There must be played in this very sanctuary films showing the misbehavior of these fallen ones. Let us no longer tarry while the earth is consumed by tyrants and entire generations [are] compromised who have been born to sing the anthem of the free.

I AM Zadkiel. And I AM here for the liberation of this Messenger from all attempt to stop her voice and the Teaching of God through this very mouth, to curtail it in the name of every fantasy and accusation and claim against this Teaching and its supposed harmful effects, psychologically and otherwise, upon those who may freely come and go at will.

Blessed ones, do you understand that this trial has to do with the stopping of the mouth and the Messenger herself? Do you understand that if found guilty, it will mean that no minister or spokesman for the LORD is free to speak that which is upon his heart, even as every parishioner and follower is free to reject or accept that which is spoken? This is the real issue—the stopping of the mouth to speak in freedom by the inspiration of the Holy Spirit.

Must it come to pass that prophets and messengers and disciples of God in this nation must fear to release the full power and fury of the presence of God for those who come into their midst with secret tape recorders to take evidence with them to show the fanaticism or the nature of the so-called cult? Beloved ones, in one's home and sanctuary one ought to be able to speak without surveillance and persecution, whether by one's government or by private citizens.

Beloved ones, understand the meaning of freedom and do not let your freedom to be who you are be encroached upon in this hour or in any other situation. We view with deep concern the rising tide of fanaticism worldwide. And therefore, if you will be seated, we will explain to you just what is this psychology of fanaticism.

Apart from the fallen ones and the devils who roam about knowing that their time is short, there is the psychology of the children of the Light themselves who are not accepting of the Path and the responsibility of karma and reincarnation nor of all of the Lost Teachings of Jesus which freely flow from this fount sponsored also by Saint Germain.

Therefore, beloved ones, throughout the earth at the subconscious level there is an extreme anxiety on the part of the children of God who themselves ought to take dominion and follow the lead of their Teachers in the person of the archangels. This anxiety causes a preoccupation with the minutiae of life, avoiding the direct encounter with the real issues of our time, nation by nation.

And they become embroiled in personal lawsuits, accusations, blames, arguments, gossip, and all types of minor nit-picking in which they therefore have their clubs, their occupations, their entertainment, and their causes célèbres (which do not even amount to a molehill), while skipping and looking over the gross injustice that covers the land in the basic issues of drugs, poor education, poverty, manipulation of labor unions by organized crime, and manipulation of the money system.

These glaring, overpowering—seemingly overpowering—conditions so frighten those who do not have recourse to us that they avoid the entire contact with this reality and engage in attacking one another and finding one who will become the scapegoat for all of their own personal neglect and all of their fancied, fanatical evils and demons that exist all around them in their imagination.

Thus, to find one individual who is the worst and most evil of all and to rid the world of that individual has become the way of escape for generations, but never more so than in this hour. Are people looking for Christ? I tell you, they look more for Antichrist—to see who is the most horrible, who is the worst of world leaders and to fear some prophecy or psychic prediction, real or imagined, of what great powers such an individual will have to destroy mankind or the nations.

Beloved ones, all of this is put to naught by mature sons and daughters of God who have entered the fullness of the LORD's Spirit and do not fear and do not have the necessity to condemn. For they realize that whether truth or error be spoken, the fruits of either will be seen. And by those fruits, by the results, by consequences and actions people may choose the better way.

Are they concerned with bringing up their children in the right-usefulness of the Law, in peace and self-confidence? They spread fear. They teach their children to lie. They teach their children to point the finger as though it were the Dark Ages and these freedoms had not been won.

Beloved ones, witness the fanaticism of a group of individuals who for year upon year have spread the maligning of gossip in the press concerning this organization, with the full cooperation of that press, never even concerning themselves that the word of truth spoken by its members should have equal voice or count. They simply accept the assumption that all [members] are mindless, brainwashed individuals who can only be expected to parrot the word of the central evil force, which they have attributed to this Messenger.

Beloved ones, it is an insanity based on internal insecurity. When this is achieved by fallen ones, their insecurity is the impending judgment. When it is achieved by those who are truly the brainwashed children of God, then it becomes their anxiety concerning returning world karma and their own—which they sense but do not admit, for their false pastors tell them that karmic accountability does not exist. I can tell you, beloved ones, you would be anxious also if all that is coming upon the earth and all that you have had to face you had to deal with without the Great White Brotherhood, this Teaching, and the archangels.

Therefore, we say that the psychology of madness is in full swing upon planet earth. And this madness feeds upon itself. And world condemnation does abound. And I know. And I know that the Liar is enthroned and is allowed to take the reins of power in the Philippines for the moment. And the only salvation unto this people is the intercession of the mighty archangels.

Beloved ones, millions of people of Light—a sweet and cherished people in that land, as many lifestreams throughout Asia are—are about to be swallowed up in the controversy of that nation, which could easily become a conflagration by those who hoard power, who then employ troops and military forces to put down the people. This can accelerate or it can decelerate. And the difference will be achieved by the armies of the LORD's host only in answer to your call.

You, beloved ones, if called, if you knew it would help, would gladly join the armed forces of this or any nation to fight for freedom. But you have seen the folly of it all, as those who plan military campaigns or those who are the politicians never seem quite to arrive at the point of the struggle or what is real or who is of the Light or what cause or what side they should be on.

Understand, beloved, you need not join the forces of the world. But you must join the army of heaven. You must be our instrument. You must be our Word, our sharper-than-the-two-edged-sword going forth.[2] If you can imagine what arrays itself out of the pits of Death and Hell in a last stand led by the Fourth Horseman, Death—if you could realize that the victory of the Light will mean the binding and exorcism from that nation, the Philippines, of millions of hordes of Darkness and the taking of many members of the false hierarchy who are today ensconced as the cronies of Marcos and as an entire machine that is so vast as to defy interference by the people and has thus far defied intervention by the representatives of the United States, would you not act?

Beloved ones, you know that such conditions are the very forcefields which attract chaos, anarchy, and then, on its wake, the entering in of the forces of a new totalitarian regime of World Communism. We have seen it happen in nation by nation. Let us not see it happen again in the Philippines. Somewhere the world must rise up and say, "We will not allow the tyrants to stand!" Let it be in Manila. Let it be throughout that nation.

Beloved ones, let it be here in Los Angeles. And nation by nation let the Feminine Ray rise. For she is the sword of Kali in the hand of Shiva. And he will slay those tyrants. He will slay their envy. He will slay their criticism and condemnation and their greed and lust for the Light, refusing to bend the knee before that Light.

Let it come to pass, therefore, that the rallying of forces, that the message of the Ascended Masters through this Messenger and everyone here who is also a messenger of God in the preaching of that Word—let it come to pass that the judgment which has descended and the light which has been released in this weekend will be the impetus for men and women of the Spirit in every walk of life to say: Nothing is worth more than individual freedom and that freedom won here and now on every issue where compromise steals the cutting edge of liberty and where tyranny would swallow it up.

I, Zadkiel, with Holy Amethyst, now come bearing with angels of Light crystal-jeweled amethyst, massive forms of this crystalline substance. It is being carried about these rooms for the purification and demagnetization of the auric envelope as we and our violet-flame angels place upon you the final blessing and clearing of the auric field.

Into the Body of God we distribute this light. Therefore, beloved ones, let these hands so blessed with our Electronic Presence touch you lightly as you pass quickly before the Messenger and we may make physical contact with your physical auric field.

Beloved ones of the Light, following this blessing there will be silence, and you will return to the heart of God as you place your body to rest and go to the inner temples.

Therefore we, the Seven Archangels, pledge our light and love to the defense of this Holy Church and its vicar and all communicants. We pledge our support to maintain the ongoing movement and revolution in Higher Consciousness, to help every soul who sincerely desires to be divested of the unreal.

We stand and we are determined that God shall have the Victory. May it be had in His way in answer to your call.

The victory also lies in the shuttle of your attention and devotion and in the decisions of your heart. For in this octave it is you in God who must prevail.

Therefore, receive us as we receive you in love now, and go forth champions of freedom.

[The congregation passed before the Messenger to receive the blessing of Archangel Zadkiel and Holy Amethyst.]

Messenger's Sealing Invocation:

Almighty God, we thank you for the presence here of your beloved emissaries, the archangels, their archeiai, the hosts of Light. We are so appreciative—and I know I speak for every heart here—for the blessings received, the Teaching, the Light, and all that you have given us.

Beloved Father, beloved Alpha, we greet you in the joy of your victory here on earth as in heaven. We thank you for this opportunity to serve, for this wondrous Church and Community that you have so blessed and given to us. We thank you for these wonderful souls of Light, our brothers and sisters, for the beautiful children, families, and marriages, and the joys that we have shared on the Path together. We thank you for our Royal Teton Ranch. We thank you for all who have come together.

It is our prayer that through whatever adversity we may pass, or trial—that as the result of our oneness and our effort and our victory, the walls of bigotry and prejudice and ignorance may come tumbling down, so that all souls of Light who truly need this Teaching may receive it freely and go forth with it freely and use it as they see fit.

Therefore, we commend these souls, O God, to thy keeping, and to the keeping of their own conscience, which is thine own. We commend them into the care of the archangels. And we charge you, holy ones of God, for the protection of each individual member, each one who does come to this table of Communion. We charge you for the protection of all Lightbearers to come, all who will ascend in this life, the forces of freedom in every nation, all who have taken up the cause of Saint Germain.

In the gratitude of the entire Spirit of the Great White Brotherhood, we say with one heart and voice:

Hear, O universe, I AM grateful!

Hear, O universe, I AM grateful!

Hear, O universe, I AM grateful!

"The Summit Lighthouse Sheds Its Radiance O'er All the World to Manifest as Pearls of Wisdom." This dictation by Archangel Zadkiel was **delivered** through the Messenger of the Great White Brotherhood Elizabeth Clare Prophet on **Sunday, February 16, 1986,** during the weekend seminar *The Healing Power of Angels,* held at Camelot. **(1) Philippine economy.** Since the fall from power of Philippine President Ferdinand E. Marcos (see *Pearls of Wisdom,* vol. 29, nos. 31 and 32, pp. 306, 316, n. 10), Marcos and his wife, Imelda, have been living in exile in Hawaii and face numerous charges of mismanaging billions of government dollars. The Aquino government is suing Marcos for the return of $5 billion to $10 billion he allegedly plundered from the government treasury during his 20-year reign. As a result of corruption, economic favoritism (known in the Philippines as "crony capitalism") and mismanagement, the nation, once regarded as an Asian boom country, has been in a prolonged slump and is in its worst shape in decades. Rather than concentrating on industrial and agricultural development, the Marcoses spent billions of government dollars building luxury hotels, ultramodern convention and cultural centers, casinos, a never-used nuclear power plant, monuments and statues of themselves, and lavish mansions and private palaces for their family. When the Marcoses fled the country, Imelda left behind in the presidential palace 37 clothes racks holding more than 1,000 gowns and mink stoles, over 2,600 pairs of shoes, hundreds of imported leather purses, and boxloads of jewelry, gold coins, and art treasures. One elderly woman who subsequently toured the palace lamented, "That is all the money of the Filipino people that she spent on all these clothes. She forgot about us—her people." In 1985 the nation's per capita income dropped to about $600 a year—the second-lowest in the Asia-Pacific region—and the economic growth rate declined to –3.5 percent. The foreign debt currently exceeds $26 billion, and unemployment affects almost half of the nation's 21 million workers at least part of the year. As Father Mariano Saraos, a priest in Marcos' birthplace of Sarrat, put it: "Most of the people here are poor—only the top government officials are rich." Though the nation has the agricultural resources to feed its people 10 times over, there is widespread malnutrition, extreme poverty in the countryside, and vast slums around Manila. After the 1983 assassination of opposition leader Benigno S. Aquino, many middle- and upper-class Filipinos left the nation taking with them millions of dollars that could otherwise have been used as capital for industrial development. The growing armed Communist insurgency, with an estimated 15,000 members, has increased in power and influence fueled by the problem of corruption and the nation's devastated economy. In response to an appeal from the Aquino administration for additional aid, President Reagan has pledged to increase U.S. economic aid to the Philippines by $150 million, thus raising his proposed aid package to $500 million for the fiscal year. **(2)** Heb. 4:12; Rev. 1:16; 2:12.

Pearls of Wisdom®
published by The Summit Lighthouse

Vol. 29 No. 35	Beloved Godfre	July 20, 1986

A New Definition of Freedom of Religion

Heart Friends of Freedom, Most Gracious Ladies and Gentlemen,
Sons and Daughters of Liberty and Children of the Light,
   I, Godfre, salute you in this hour of the victory of our Lord.
For 'tis the season, then, of Pisces. And the two-thousand-year
dispensation of Jesus Christ is fulfilled in this hour through every
one of you who does understand that the culmination of that
mission and the fullness of that cup is to go all the way in the
stand for freedom.
   In the name of Lanello, who also conquered in this sign[1] by
which the LORD graced me in my embodiment as George Washington, I say to you, be seated in the flame of cosmic glory.
   For it is indeed a glorious day—a day of opportunity to take
the stand for religious freedom and freedom of conscience, freedom to worship in this nation and upon this soil where each and
every one is free to worship his own God, to sit under his own
vine and fig tree,[2] and to know the LORD. For these prophecies of
the ancient prophets, beloved hearts, are fulfilled in this century.
   When we were there in the early days of this nation's history,
beloved ones, realize that all perceived God out of the Judeo-
Christian dispensation. All understood the One, and the One who
was found in the Masonic order, as the presence of the All-Seeing
Eye of God that blessed our undertaking and that did fulfill in us,
as Masons building the pyramid of Life, the reason for our being.
   Today, beloved ones, two hundred years have passed.
Beloved hearts of Victory, know, then, that the perception of the
one God in the peoples who have gathered in this nation is representative of every belief and belief system held on earth. Each
one may determine his own religion or non.

Thus, the individual's conception of life and love and peace has many rainbowed rays. It is indeed the hour of the fulfillment of the promise "They shall all know me—all of them—from the least unto the greatest."[3]

Thus it is the new dispensation of Aquarius. Thus it is understood that there must be a new definition of freedom of religion. There must be a new understanding by those who founded this nation and have moved forward in their Protestant-ism, in their Catholicism, and in their Judaism that in this hour none may have a monopoly on the path of religious freedom, that the way made plain must be acknowledged to be made plain by the one God and the I AM Presence of that individual and the beloved Holy Christ Self.

This Higher Mind, beloved ones, does lead the soul into all Truth step by step in the seven rainbow rays. Thus, the paths of enlightenment by the Holy Spirit in this age, prophesied by the Lord Christ, come unto the individual, each one according to his need, his ancient karma, his preparation in the school of life, his initiations of spiritual fire that have taken place in the inner retreats of the Great White Brotherhood.

And this assessment of souls by guardian angels and World Teachers is also according to the age of the soul. For the souls have passed through many ages and have come forth in what are known as root races—souls who have descended with a mission to embody one of the seven rays and a holy calling. These root races have come to many planetary homes, solar systems, and galaxies. And as you are well aware, earth has become the crossroads and the gathering place of many evolutions.

Thus, in this age of the ripening of the fruit of each man's tree of life, it remains to be seen, when the fruit is ready to be plucked, what sort of fruit has come from each man's philosophy and each man's actions. One may taste the fruits of the orchards of life—sweet and sour, bitter, dry, or filled with the juice and nectar of the Buddha, the Christ. Beloved ones, one accepts or rejects by the senses of the soul. Tasting, then, the offering, one concludes what is the best philosophy by the fruit that that tree of life has produced.

Where there must be choice and free will in the marketplace of ideas, all offerings must be present, from the least to the greatest, from left to right, those that may be anti-Life or pro-Life, in order that individuals, children, nations might exercise the scrutiny of the soul, the sword of the Spirit, the testing by the heart in order to come to the conclusion of what is right.

God has entrusted every man and woman with an inner standard. Thus, you are called to be standard-bearers. And the Path is that thou might go to the heart and determine what is the divine standard, what is the human standard—in what way shall I walk.

The unerring voice of God and the inner conscience does make known to every soul that which is approved by the living Word and that which is not approved. Some men have therefore neutralized their sensitivity to the voice of God and conscience, for they desire not the living Truth. They desire not the living Truth, beloved ones, because they prefer their ways. They prefer the Darkness to the Light, for their deeds are evil.[4]

Thus, this is the searing of conscience as with a hot iron,[5] as the apostle said. And they no longer respond to the voice within. Therefore, they make their own rules, regulations, and laws. They have become a law unto themselves and raised on high the banner of their human standards of right and wrong.

Thus, beloved, let the whole stream of ideas, actions and the consequences thereof be examined. Because Elohim trust in the divinity within each individual, they do not interfere with the learning process, the experimentation when the children of Light experiment with this or that activity and then hopefully draw early the conclusion that the way of Light—the fullness of Life, not Death—is the chosen way.

Let all take the example from the LORD God Almighty, who is the great sifter of men's hearts, that those in whom there dwells the divine spark, those in whom the I AM Presence does yet live, will find their way to Truth and to the summit of their own Divine Being.

Therefore, beloved ones, when the choice for God's right is made and human error is seen by the flame of the heart, you, then, champion of God's right, must call to the Lord Christ for the binding and the judgment of the forces of Evil who embody the philosophies of Death and Hell. Let the angelic hosts separate the tares and the wheat.[6] Let not men interfere to dash the cup of Life of some man's religion, to tear from him that which is precious. For if it not be true, the LORD God himself will reveal it unto him.

Only God can guarantee freedom of religion. Only God can champion the right of free men and women to worship. And so it is with the other basic freedoms you cherish. Only God can guarantee freedom, for freedom is a living flame of God. It cannot be defined by some men's concepts of what is religion.

Therefore, beloved, see that it is a spiritual victory that you are about—and we with you. See, beloved ones, that you must push back the barriers that heretofore have defined the context of religious freedom.

Many have set themselves as authorities as to what is the true religion of Jesus or of Gautama or of Moses. They have banded together and they have said, "All other theories are null and void." And therefore the council of churches, who call themselves Christian, have denied fellowship to all who may differ in the doctrine of Christ's love.

You realize, then, beloved, that the denial of religious freedom began in this vein long before the more recent movement raised its head to call anything not similar to its own belief system a dangerous cult of indoctrination, mind control, and the complete turning around of the inner and outer life of an individual.

Beloved ones, the nature of the true religious experience *is* a conversion, *is* a turning around of the soul to face the Son of God. Now, beloved, [following this conversion] religious freedom as a flame must fill the void. It must penetrate where old thought systems sought to limit this divine experience between a man and his God. It must fill the space of the babble of voices and the many who have written their scholarly works defining what is a dangerous cult and what is not.

Thus, with a laundry list of definitions, they go out and prepare their cases and seek to draw parallels in the Teachings of the Ascended Masters and this Path to the dangerous cults which they say exist here and abroad. Beloved ones, there are always dangerous conditions in every field and undertaking. The education of children and adults must be to beware always of the forces of Darkness that attempt to thwart the real, the true, the lasting Light in any endeavor or educational system or system of government or religion.

Thus, beloved, you live in a century of clichés, assisted by tens of thousands of advertisements seen and flashed before the mind. Not able to present their case by the reason of the Logos, they must transfer to you by some implant—or band-aid on the surface—a cliché that will now govern your actions to go out and purchase this product.

Religions are also sold with clichés. And clichés are groups of words that have come to mean certain things to certain people. Thus, if these clichés can now be pasted upon this or that movement according to the laundry list of definitions, they therefore conclude that this organization must be a cult and its leader must be a hypnotist.

Beloved ones, the Holy Spirit is the power, the wisdom, and the love of God to draw men's souls back to the Real. This turning around and this elevation of life must be the duty of every messenger of God in every pulpit, in every house of worship worldwide. Our testing of the righteousness of any movement is the presence and power and purity of the Holy Ghost upon its leadership, its membership or student body.

Beloved ones, once they have used the freedom of the press dangerously and irresponsibly to brand any man's religion as a cult or a dangerous doctrine, you can see how difficult it is to undo the impression, for the clichés have made their way as the poisoning of men's minds.

But the Lord Christ has said, "This is my cup. Drink ye all of it."[7] Why, then, must you face this battle? It is because religious freedom must find a new definition, a complete and absolute freedom, stopping only at that which becomes illegal—the very danger to physical life itself.

Beloved ones, houses of worship, as institutions of learning and all public places, must have doors opened where people may enter if they choose and leave if they choose. As the Archangel Gabriel has said, it is the responsibility of parents and teachers to teach children how to think, how to reason, how to draw a series of conclusions from premises at hand but not to indoctrinate them, not to point the finger and prejudice their minds from early youth. Those who are free and independent beneath their own vine and fig tree, their own Holy Christ Self and Mighty I AM Presence—these cannot stray from the everlasting Reality.

Thus, build upon the sound foundations of the lives—the lives and how they have been lived—of the prophets of East and West and the saints and avatars. For the life [of the soul], by definition, becomes a road map. One will never know by dos and don'ts and a list of regulations how to make choices, how to decide this or that at any point in the crossroads of a difficult karma. Life cannot be reduced to a set of rules or dogma.

When you study the great heroes, the heroines of East and West, you come to realize that they faced the human equation. Many fell beneath the cross of personal and planetary karma, as did Christ the Lord himself. This is to teach that the least unto the greatest may err, may make mistakes, may receive help in bearing their burdens from friends, disciples, and communities of Light.

Beloved ones, it is important that you make the effort to rise again beneath the seemingly unsurmountable weight of your personal karma or the portion of planetary karma you bear with this Messenger. It is important to have faith that if you cannot, another will come to your aid. And if there is no one in sight, angels of the LORD will succor you and uphold you and feed you and help you.

"Keep on keeping on" is the way of the cosmic cross of white fire. Thus, when discernment is needed, when a difficult decision is to be made which you have placed upon the altar of God, look then to the lives of the greatest of heroes and those who have ascended. Study their right choices and understand the rightness of choice by the fruit of that action. Understand [human] errors and be spared of pitfalls because [you understand how] saints who have gone before you have also temporarily fallen into the traps of the seed of the wicked.

Realize, beloved, that every succeeding test of Divine Love will call for you to sacrifice, [sometimes] even to sacrifice "morality" or what is the acceptable human standard in that time frame. The purity of heart and the motive of your soul and that which impels you to lay down your life for the friend may be an overriding concern that is also one with the heart of God.

The tests are spiritual ones. They leave the moorings and the support systems of all of the rules and regulations of the world and they bring you directly to the heart of Christ—not *what* he would do, but what *did* he do. There are abundant examples. And from isolated examples, not taking all into consideration, men have arrived at warped doctrine, half-truths, an inability to understand the application of Love in all circumstances.

Considering Jesus to be the Prince of Peace and the embodiment of perfect Love, let all of you consider, episode by episode of his life, how he wielded the sharp sword of Love and how that Love was expressed, whether as compassion or rebuke, chastisement and judgment, healing or the raising of the dead. For in the many-faceted jewel of the ruby ray, you will discover how to pass through this labyrinth of maya and illusion and astral denizens at every hand—how, then, to outsmart every form of error with many applications of the emerald crystal of Truth.

Thus, I come before you with the proposition of this case, this lawsuit that faces you. And I must explain to you, beloved, that in this nation the tyranny of what has been called the anti-cult movement against unorthodox religions must be broken— not by human will or might but by the Spirit of the LORD,[8] by the entire Spirit of the Great White Brotherhood manifesting in you.

The tyranny of so-called fundamentalists who themselves do not know the fundamental teachings of the Lord Christ, for these have been taken from them and are not fully contained in approved scripture—these, then, have said, "We know the truth. We know the way. Therefore, all deviations must go down."

Their prayers of malintent, their false pastors, insofar as they attempt to encroach upon others' freedom, must also be broken. Thus, if necessary, this cause must be championed all the way to the Supreme Court of the United States of America. Whether at the level of the present court or beyond, you must realize that this cup is given to you to drink to break once and for all the insidious cancer that has moved through the houses of worship, through the associations of psychologists and those with degrees who are "authorities" on what they consider to be mind control.

Beloved ones, this nation will not be safe for any new idea, for any revolutionary of the Spirit, for anyone whom we might send into the midst of Darkness to bear the present message of the present dispensation of Saint Germain and Portia and the Aquarian age unless these forces receive the absolute word that they may not interfere with any man's religious freedom.

Therefore, beloved ones, do not consider this cause something that should occupy your peripheral attention or a small percentage of your time. It is *the* cause of the hour that must be espoused by every Keeper of the Flame. For the flame which you keep is the flame of Liberty.

And the highest liberty that must be guaranteed on earth is the liberty of the sons and daughters of God to commune with the Almighty and to deliver the fruits of their communion to the children of the Light. This must not be gainsaid by the hordes of the astral plane, by the fallen angels in embodiment and their godless creation. They have amassed the armies and the prophets of Baal. And therefore, let Israel and the light of Israel come into union. Let not the Keepers of the Flame place other priorities and other gods in the midst of this trial.

You must look squarely at the reality that if your freedom to embody the flame—the flame of Love and Peace and Light and Life—is denied you; if the power of the dynamic decree should become forbidden, as could easily occur in a totalitarian state, so that it would be a crime to open your mouth and give a session of Astreas; if any part or portion of the Ascended Masters' Teaching should be denied you and prohibited as church councils have done in past ages; if the Messenger should not have freedom from fear to be the instrument of whatever we may say concerning personal and planetary conditions—then, beloved, your loss of a part of this freedom becomes the loss of the whole.

Only the whole wafer can make you free. Only the whole body of the mystical Teachings of the Lord Christ is sufficient. There is a completeness and a wholeness waiting to be fully delivered as the Everlasting Gospel.

Some men in past ages have in their cowardice and compromise been content to surrender a portion—some of their land, some of their income, some of their control over their personal lives, some of the controls of their employment and their stations. At each and every hand when any liberty has been conceded, the forces of tyranny have never been satisfied. For they will never be satisfied until the Light and every Lightbearer on earth is stamped out.

Thus, beloved, see then how all religions and representatives thereof are brought to America from around the world, that through the path of their calling and their birth they may come to the Maypole itself. They may come to the pole of being and the polestar of their Mighty I AM Presence. They may trace the thread of contact as the ribbon of Light all the way to the Source. And when they do, they may find defined the Mighty I AM Presence, the God of Israel that is the God of all peoples and nations and kindreds and tongues.

This is the reason for the founding of America—that when it was time for these white stones to reach the apex they might have the place to graduate from the exercise of physical freedoms to the consummate spiritual freedom, the right to ascend to God, the right to earn that ascension and to receive it by the grace of the Son of God, and the right to preach this path to all children of God and to all peoples.

For the promises are given to Jew and Gentile alike, to any and all evolutions who have come to earth. None are excepted if they will bend the knee and confess that Light as the Universal Christ. They may receive the engrafting of the Word.[9] They may be endowed with a divine spark.

Beloved ones, if any portion of religious freedom be denied, then we shall have lost the entire reason for being of Saint Germain's dispensation in America and his full dispensation for the Aquarian age. For I tell you, what is given here, which is limited because of the force of Darkness moving against this Church and this Messenger, is the foundation Teaching, as the

Founding Fathers set the Declaration of Independence and the Constitution as a guide to build upon.

In order to disseminate many of the mysteries that should follow from the inner retreats, there must be a guarantee of the protection of life to all who espouse those truths. There must be a guarantee of the freedom of the press to publish them, of people to assemble to practice them, of the soundness, beloved ones, of the individual right to free speech—that either the one isolated or the many may speak his mind without being mobbed, killed or maimed.

Therefore, beloved, it is a profound calling to come to this sanctuary and keep a prayer vigil, not only for the victory in a lawsuit but for the binding by the path of the ruby ray of those forces of Darkness and tyranny that have much more as their goal—the destruction of the ways of eternal Life at every stage in every house of worship.

For the majority of religions preach eternal Life and the path thereto. And if the adherents thereof would follow that path and that way, they would all come to the place of the entering in at the strait gate[10] where the initiations of the Lord Christ unto them personally begin.

Beloved ones, I am personally asking you to come to this Holy Grail to keep the vigil for the Goddess of Liberty. For in a military, political, and economic sense, America cannot move forward in her destiny until this hatred and madness of the anti-God, anti-cult movements is put down.

It is a pity that more do not see the handwriting on the wall. The Lightbearers of all ages have been called to carry a banner, which in many times the masses of the people have not understood. And they have won victories on behalf of those not yet born or not yet educated to perceive that they also had need of that victory and that freedom.

Thus, my own beloved twin flame passed through the judgments of this world all the way to the Supreme Court, finally to have this persecution overturned.[11] That was in 1940, beloved ones—a year after the birth of this Messenger.

Other pioneers of religion in America have had to fight for their freedom to be, including Mary Baker Eddy.[12] You will remember the trial by press of Aimee Semple McPherson.[13] And you will remember the persecution of the Mormons and more recently of the new-age activities. You will realize that every ground that is won guarantees that that point of the law has become precedent, at least in the higher court.

Children of the Sun,* I summon you to the calling of the protection of the Light of that Sun—its ability to shine through a free people who have championed the cause of freedom and therefore may allow that Sun to shine through them as they so choose.

I am asking you to drink this cup—this cup which you now see passed from Jesus to Saint Germain. For in one sense, though it is watered down woefully, Christianity has gained a right to religious freedom. But those who dare say there is more, those who dare take mankind all the way to Golgotha and Bethany's hill—these must be protected.

Beloved ones, your right to pursue your mission fully (as your calling is to disseminate this Word, else you would not be here) will be prevented if this victory is not won. I ask you to gather, then, for the flame of Life itself which you have committed to bear, following this service and continuing until the opportunity for the fullest descent of the great wisdom of the causal body of your beloved Lanello is fully guaranteed and you yourself as a spokesman for this Path may not be inhibited or interfered with by any court or fanatic or private citizen who suddenly may decide to sue you as responsible for all of his woes and karma.

The sons and daughters of God must have the right to call the judgment and the justice upon the fallen angels, without these fallen angels turning to rend them in the courts to tie up their lives, their money, and their mission and path.

Beloved ones, when you see these fallen ones turn and rend you—who hate the Light because the Light through you has been their judgment—it is time to realize that this calling of the Lord Christ to give the decree "They Shall Not Pass!" must be protected and protected again through Archangel Michael's Rosary.

Thus realize that protection comes to you when the whole man is made whole through harmony, through obedience to *all* of God's laws. I can tell you, beloved, if you have not sinned against that Law, they will fabricate their lies out of the whole cloth and attempt to trap you to convince a court that you have indeed sinned. Thus, keep yourselves unspotted from the world.[14] For those who accept that cup this day will not be without persecution in this lifetime.

You must learn to wield the sword of the Spirit and be fearless. And you will see what new territory of the Mind of God you shall claim for evolutions of earth today and those unborn, those of the new root races and beings of Light who can only be born where they are free to be.

*the Great Central Sun

I seal you in this hour in the presence of our twin flames and Lanello.

Let those who desire the full cup of our calling as Messengers come forward now and receive communion at the appropriate stations. For I, Godfre, in the spirit of the LORD on the LORD's day,[15] do charge the whole wafer and the fullness of the cup of the wine with the power and the presence of God to pass this test and initiation, that you might bring home to God and to his children the fullness of the Spirit of Liberty.

Lo, you are come to set at liberty the captives in Christ's name![16] I send you as the patriots of a far country who have come to claim all who are born of the Spirit of Liberty.

In the name of Saint Germain and Jesus Christ, in the name of Mighty Victory, I serve. [standing ovation]

"The Summit Lighthouse Sheds Its Radiance O'er All the World to Manifest as Pearls of Wisdom." This dictation by Godfre was **delivered** through the Messenger of the Great White Brotherhood Elizabeth Clare Prophet on **Sunday, February 23, 1986**, at Camelot. In her sermon before the dictation, the Messenger read I Kings 18 and 19—"Elijah's Challenge to the Prophets of Baal"— and George Washington's inaugural address. (**1**) Under the sign of Pisces, George Washington was born February 22, 1732, and the Messenger Mark L. Prophet made his ascension February 26, 1973. (**2**) I Kings 4:25; Mic. 4:4; Zech. 3:10. (**3**) Jer. 31:34; Heb. 8:11. (**4**) John 3:19. (**5**) I Tim. 4:1, 2. (**6**) Matt. 13:24–30, 36–43. (**7**) Matt. 26:27. (**8**) Zech. 4:6. (**9**) James 1:21. See Jesus Christ, December 25, 1985, "Rise, Peter: Kill and Eat!" 1986 *Pearls of Wisdom*, vol. 29, no. 14, pp. 112–15; and Lord Maitreya, January 1, 1986, "The Lord of the World's Path of the Six-Pointed Star," 1986 *Pearls of Wisdom*, vol. 29, no. 22, pp. 206–12. (**10**) Matt. 7:13, 14; Luke 13:24. (**11**) *United States vs. Ballard.* The Ascended Master Godfre and his divine complement, Lotus, were embodied as Guy and Edna Ballard, Saint Germain's Messengers, through whom he founded the I AM activity in the early 1930s. In Los Angeles in 1940 (the year following Godfre's ascension), federal criminal indictments were brought against Mrs. Ballard, her son, Donald, and others in the activity for fraudulent solicitation of funds through the mail. Despite strenuous objections by the defendents' attorney, a jury was in effect given the task of deciding whether the Ballards really believed what they taught and wrote about their Messengership and the Ascended Masters. Over a period of six years, *United States vs. Ballard* went through two trials and an extended series of appeals, during which Mrs. Ballard was at one point convicted and sentenced to a year in prison and fined $8000, although the prison sentence was later suspended. Soon thereafter the Post Office Department issued an order denying use of the mail to the I AM activity. In the face of adverse media coverage and extreme prejudice within the criminal justice system, Mrs. Ballard and her students fought on and their efforts culminated in the U.S. Supreme Court throwing out the conviction in 1946 on the grounds that women were improperly excluded from the jury. Dictum (the written opinion) from the case has often been cited in subsequent First Amendment litigation to prohibit judicial inquiry into the truth or falsity of religious beliefs. **(12) Mary Baker Eddy** (1821–1910), who founded the Christian Science Church in the latter nineteenth century, was beset in the early years by a series of court cases which stirred public controversy and raised questions concerning her doctrine, organization, and followers. Some of the litigation was vengefully initiated by former associates who had defected from the movement, and some by Mrs. Eddy herself in defense of her teachings. Although she was vilified in the press, for the most part she emerged victorious from each case. As she wrote in her book *Science and Health with Key to the Scriptures,* "Trials are proofs of God's care." Mary Baker Eddy is now the Ascended Lady Master Theosophia, upholding the office of the Goddess of Wisdom. **(13) Evangelist Aimee Semple McPherson** (1890–1944), founder of the International Church of the Foursquare Gospel, mysteriously disappeared from a California beach on May 18, 1926. After thirty-six days during which thousands searched for her, she reappeared in the Mexican border town of Agua Prieta and recounted how she had been kidnapped, taken to a desert shack, and finally escaped. Los Angeles District Attorney Asa Keyes launched a full-scale grand jury investigation into the incident. While charges of conspiracy were being leveled against Aimee and her mother for allegedly misappropriating church funds and staging a phony kidnapping, the newspapers spread rumors that Aimee had been seen with the married operator of her radio station, Kenneth Ormiston, during her five-week absence. "Though unbelievable and wildly inconsistent, so persistent were these stories," Aimee later recalled, "that some people who did not know me or know my life could not be blamed for believing this absurd, paper-selling propaganda." Keyes, who had intended to go on with criminal proceedings, conceded on January 10, 1927, that there was insufficient evidence for the case to be "prosecuted with honor or with any reasonable hope of success." The court agreed and the charges were dropped. Aimee declared that "a case as rotten as the Tower of Babel" had collapsed. Aimee Semple McPherson, who was also embodied as Mary Magdalene, is known and loved today as the Ascended Lady Master Magda, twin flame of Jesus Christ. **(14)** James 1:27. **(15)** Isa. 2:10–22; 61:1, 2; Rev. 1:10. **(16)** Isa. 61:1.

Pearls of Wisdom, published weekly by The Summit Lighthouse for Church Universal and Triumphant, come to you under the auspices of the Darjeeling Council of the Great White Brotherhood. These are presently dictated by the Ascended Masters to their Messenger Elizabeth Clare Prophet. The international headquarters of this nonprofit, nondenominational activity is located in Los Angeles, California. All communications and freewill contributions should be addressed to The Summit Lighthouse, Box A, Malibu, CA 90265. Pearls of Wisdom are sent weekly throughout the USA via third-class mail to all who support the Church with a minimum yearly love offering of $40. First-class and international postage rates available upon request. Notice of change of address should be received three weeks prior to the effective date. Third-class mail is not forwarded by the post office.

Pearls of Wisdom®
published by The Summit Lighthouse

| Vol. 29 No. 36 | Beloved Lanello | July 27, 1986 |

Teachings from the Mystery School

Mysteries of the Violet Flame in the Heart of Buddha
Ascension Day Address, Thirteenth Anniversary 1986

Hid with Christ in God, I am in the heart of Gautama Buddha. Ensconced in the lotus flame of his desiring to be with thee tonight, my beloved, I am one in Buddha—and we [are one] with thine own heart, buoyant in the violet flame as though you had prepared a violet-flame nest carefully woven of flames of crystal of light. Thus, within the within—the I, the Thou, the Buddha and I.

Blessed sons and daughters of God, I speak, then, from a new plane of my causal body. For you have not known me in this heart of hearts of the five secret rays. I establish, therefore, the filigree thread of light with thy heart through the Buddhic heart and mind to the very heart of Cosmos.

Thus, beloved, we shall overcome all things according to the cosmic cycles. And even then we shall accelerate the release of light of cosmic cycles. Let the days of injustice be shortened for the elect of God who have elected to do his will.

So, my beloved, the shortening of the days must come by the violet flame with Cosmos' secret rays. And all Buddhist mantras are also in the secret rays. There are secret rays in the heart of every chakra—secret rays, therefore, as the nucleus in the heart of the white fire and the white-fire rod in the center of every ray. What magnanimity is released, what piercing light from the heart of the flame of God!

You know me in this hour in the mighty emerald sphere,[1] and it is so. But I release now from these seven rays the unique quality of the ray when it is multiplied by the five secret rays, and not always in the same manner.

Calculate, then, how many combinations of five numbers there can be and then these multiplied by the infinite combinations of numerical order of each of the seven rays of God, and you will see how the symphony of words and sound and music and vibration may proceed therefrom, touching everything in every octave of the Matter cosmos—therefore touching those things that have been brought to the threshold of your being through this particular lawsuit.

Realize, beloved, that the Mother is surrounded by rings of fire and the inundation of waves of light—waves of light and waves of the cosmic sea. And the tides of the sea bring to the circumference of the aura of the Mother the light of the Great Central Sun as well as the momentums in the Matter cosmos.

Thus, trust all things, believe all things, hope all things, have faith in all things,[2] but center thyself in this Love of the heart of Buddha. Secret rays, beloved, five secret rays in the heart of the ruby ray—and in the heart thereof, the Buddha of the Ruby Ray.

I bring thought, your own, in the interior light, preparing visualization and the inner sense of the going to the heart of nirvana. So understand, beloved, thou must also go within to bring forth the Light, to greet the inundations of the wave of the Central Sun that must also bear with it burdens of karma of galaxies and dark cycles.

Greet the wave, then, with the wave coming forth from the center of thy heart. Circular circles of light, waves of the sea that come from the inner sea of the cosmic rays now go forth in the rhythm of the heartbeat of Gautama, as that heartbeat now does release the ocean of light from the point of bliss in the center of the One where thou art.

Now see how the perfect circular waves go forth, and they greet the wave oncoming from without. In the meeting of these waves, beloved, there is a leaping of the foam of light and cosmic energy. And in the leaping thereof, the light of thy heart that is the light of Gautama does bear a rod, a cone, a sacred fire of transmutation—violet flame. And the violet flame, then, pierced by Cosmos' secret rays, does release also its secret powers. For the secret powers of every ray lie in the secret rays themselves, these five.

Therefore, understand the jeweled light. Understand the power behind the ray. Thou canst not enter this point of Light or release it without certain attainment, beloved. But thou shalt have from this night on recourse to me as thy advocate and Ever-Present Guru who does stand before the Lord of the World, Gautama Buddha.

Therefore, by my call to him made in thy name, as thou dost call to me and to the Lord of the World, that Lord of the World shall release [that Light] through my heart, whether through your own heart and chakras or bypassing them, to the very cause and core behind this lawsuit and all other darkness or the dark ones that may ever assail thee or this activity of the Great White Brotherhood.

Beloved ones, understand that when thou art centered in the heart of Buddha this light may pass through thee. But in its absence, in the absence of equanimity, fail not to make the call. For I shall place my Electronic Presence with all of my chakras focused where thou art or in the positioning of the point of darkness itself to release this light of the secret rays from the heart of Gautama Buddha.

Thus, the incoming light of the Central Sun will also help thee, as it does bear to thee obligation, dharma, responsibility—not necessarily thine own karma, beloved. But Maitreya, Maitreya does say in this hour, "O initiates of the Mystery School, greet every proud wave of the fallen ones with a clap of the hand, a joyous shout, and the release of the ring of light from the heart!"

Then, beloved, know that thou dost fulfill in us and we do fulfill in thee this release from the heart of Gautama, Lord of the World, for transmutation, resolution, God-harmony everywhere and violet-flame dispensations from the causal bodies of many Buddhas who have stepped forth from nirvana in this hour to keep the vigil for thy Victory.

They release, one and all, the violet flame and the Great Central Sun Magnet of the violet flame multiplied by their attainment of the Buddhic Light in the five secret rays. Thus, accept the spirals. Accept the shortening of the days of injustice for the elect. Accept it, O beloved. Become it. Internalize this Word of Light that I bring to you.

Yes, I am Lanello. And do you know, my beloved ones, I speak to you from the heart of the potential Buddha thou art, from the heart of the potential Divine Mother thou art. This potential is the sphere of Light surrounding thy Mighty I AM Presence.

Thus, know that thou canst cross the abyss. Thou canst be victorious over the astral plane and all that is in it. Beloved, it is not alone for the proving of thy soul by Maitreya but because you have volunteered.

physical embodiment in the taking of the dictations. And I hold this heart as a focus of all dictations that I ever took from the hour when I received it and it became the lodestone of the altar.

Imagine the molecules of this heart, a mere heart of stone containing, as recorded in the nucleus thereof, these words that have passed through me. Then think to yourself and say, "I have a heart of flesh. And I have a heart of gold, of Spirit. Cannot my heart also record on spindles of light in the nucleus of every atom of every molecule even the words of the Almighty One through the beings of Light now passed to the Blessed Mother and our Messenger?"

And it is of a truth thine own right. Thus, visualize the white heart as the receptacle and receptor, the receiving station, and survive in all octaves by that living Word sealed within.

My beloved, I have brought to you a very special light and a very special message. These things are of the holiness of God, and mysteries beyond mysteries lie awaiting thy meditation upon these words. I have given to you a thread of contact with the heart of Gautama in the secret rays. I have given you keys of teaching. This is because you have given your hearts in such intensity of service, decrees, and song. Faithfulness to us, faithfulness in the Light, beloved—for this we are most grateful and we express our gratitude in this way.

You have taken the key of the science of the spoken Word and now earned the right to open the door. To fulfill that which is beyond the door, you must now move on in this marathon of light, claiming the earth as God's kingdom, as the domain of Freedom, Justice, Light, Peace, Truth, and Love.

Oh, the Principle of the Mind of God! Oh, the wonders of his Love!

Let the ruby ray and the ruby-ray angels and the Buddha of the Ruby Ray dissolve now all Darkness pitted against the Church Universal and Triumphant!

Let this be your fiat and mantra, as I have just said it, beloved. So hold up the right hand. And in holding it up with this fiat, visualize the white heart as you do say it. For, beloved, it is the perpetual call of the hour and the victory of the five-pointed star that you are about.

We are interested in you learning the ritual of Victory, defeating the forces of fallen ones who have plotted, I tell you, more than a million years for this hour when they think they shall have the victory. And we shall see what Keepers of the Flame will make of their challenge, of their denial of the Light of the Great White Brotherhood.

Beloved ones, the ball is in your court for the Victory in this hour. Make the most of it. For the world awaits your stepping forth from the secret chambers of the heart to the housetops, to the mountains through the systems of communication with the Word for which they have been waiting.

I say, therefore, let the entire momentum of anti-God, anti-religion, anti-the-culture-of-the-Mother-on-earth go down before the legions of Light encamped on the horizons of the world.

Thus, legions of Uriel march with the dawn. Legions of Michael, Gabriel, Jophiel, Chamuel, legions of Raphael, Zadkiel, Uzziel all march in the earth for the binding of the fallen ones who have denied God in the little children, in the sons and daughters, in the holy Church.

Therefore, we affirm from the heart of hearts of Gautama Buddha and confirm the fall of tyrants[4] and all enemies of the Light: Stand fast, beloved, and see the salvation of your God!

Let all study this my message and apply it immediately. For the Light awaits the proper channels. And when the proper channels are established, the Light! Light! Light! will have her perfect work in thee, in this hall, in this university, in this Church Universal and Triumphant forevermore.

I seal you in the Light of Archangel Michael and Mighty Victory. And I say to you, one and all, in their names:

Charge! Charge! Charge! and let Victory be proclaimed!

The mantle of the thirteenth cycle awaits the qualified chela. I am at your side, ready to bestow it at the moment of the Lord of the World's summoning of thee to this initiation.

In the love of Mother Mary, whom I praise for assisting me through all of the dark hours of my karma and my path on earth, I commend you to her tender care. For she is as close to you physically as I am somewhat removed keeping the flame in the heart of Gautama Buddha in the secret rays where I am hid with Christ in God.[5]

So then shall you be. Come to me, beloved, through the heart of your own beloved Mother Mary and mine.

"The Summit Lighthouse Sheds Its Radiance O'er All the World to Manifest as Pearls of Wisdom." This dictation by Lanello was **delivered** through the Messenger of the Great White Brotherhood Elizabeth Clare Prophet on the thirteenth anniversary of his ascension, **Wednesday, February 26, 1986,** at Camelot. (1) Refers to 40-day cycles of the causal body of Lanello charted since his ascension, February 26, 1973. (2) I Cor. 13:7. (3) Luke 22:53. (4) See Archangel Gabriel, Feb. 15, 1986, and Archangel Zadkiel, Feb. 16, 1986, 1986 *Pearls of Wisdom,* vol. 29, nos. 31 and 34, pp. 304, 306 (n. 10), 323, 324, 328; and Saint Germain, Oct. 13, 1985, "The Sword of Sanat Kumara: The Judgment of the Rulers in the Earth Who Have Utterly Betrayed Their God and Their People," 1985 *Pearls of Wisdom,* vol. 28, no. 50, pp. 589–91. (5) Col. 3:3.

Pearls of Wisdom®

published by The Summit Lighthouse

| *Vol. 29 No. 37* | *Beloved El Morya* | *August 3, 1986* |

Rights of Passage

Chelas of the Will of God,

I am in the center of the forget-me-not of your heart. When you forget me not and give that decree for the Will of God, then I may enter your affairs and the affairs of men. But when you forget, beloved, then I must be the worst of the worst: a spectator in the sport of life. Can you imagine my chelas benching their coach for want of the word and the beckon of the heart?

Thus, indeed it is so that I have come to sponsor this activity through Mark, through Elizabeth. I came confident that through all of the dark night the Lighthouse would still stand. My confidence is great indeed. It is in Almighty God and in the divine spark within you, my chelas.

Beloved ones, when tyrants conspire to destroy the living Word, it is the hour of perpetual prayer. Therefore, I bid you be seated perpetually in the flame-flower of the forget-me-not.

I would speak to you, then, of rights of passage. I would speak to you in this hour, beloved, of the testings that have always come in order that the soul might pass to new dimensions of being.

The usurpers of the seat of authority of the living Christ of you must not be allowed to stand.[1] Sinners midst the congregation of the righteous are these.[2] To gain your right of passage for dominion in this life, you must come to the understanding that at inner levels and on the outer there are those who thoroughly disrupt and set aside your mission. Unseen are they, never to be feared but to be reckoned with by the calculation of the stars.

The science of Being works for those who work for it and with it. Life is indeed a sacred science. And as the Word does go forth, I release the power of Hercules, the wisdom and the astuteness of Archangel Michael, and the very presence of the blue lotus flame of Lord Himalaya.

Vaivasvata, the great Manu, Lawgiver of ages, has stood in his retreat this day and has said, "I shall stand until the victory of the Mother, who does represent the Divine Woman today. I shall stand releasing the blue lightning of the will of God. Morya, go and see who will receive it and who will release it in purity, in perpetual prayer, that the words of their mouths might be the Light-emanation of the Logos given unto me for the root races of the planet."

Thus, I come, beloved. And I tell you, the fallen ones know that this is their last stand. They will stop at nothing, not even the intrusion upon the phones and the holiness and the sacred circle of your very life and Community. You must be vigilant in the understanding of what is at stake—the freedom of this Church Universal and Triumphant to go forth with the banner of Maitreya and the emblem of the Lighthouse to acquaint every soul upon earth with his own God-free being, else the setting aside and the delay of cosmic purpose in ye all.

I tell you, you cannot wait. You cannot afford to part with time and space, for you require all that is allotted unto you and more to be given by the grace of the Lords of Karma for that service of the covering of the earth through all communication means possible with the true message of liberation.

Beloved ones, there are battles that have been fought and won without the [participants'] full outer knowledge of the archangels and the false hierarchies and the fallen ones pitted against the Light. But when the fullness of Armageddon is outplayed physically on this planet, should it come to pass, beloved ones, it is essential, *it is absolutely necessary* that lifestreams have that dynamic decree book in hand and the understanding of how to use the sacred fire.

When all hell breaks loose, as it has in this case against the Messenger and the Teaching, only those who know and practice hourly the sacred science can overcome. Thus it is, as you might say, a foretaste of what the nations must face—your own government, the people of Mother Russia, who one day must overturn their tyrants also as the people of the Philippines have done.

Precious ones, many tests are ahead for the people of every nation. You must win and then go and teach them how to win in their area of knowledge and in their field of operation.

Beloved ones, there is a pass and there is a right that you

must earn to pass over that pass into a new plane of activity and attainment. This is the meaning of the trial and the testing—the testing of the soul. There is no hierarch in heaven or saint of God who has not faced an ultimate encounter in order to move on to the plane that beckons, to the field that waits, and to greater challenges ahead.

Beloved ones, do not think that these individuals who have plotted this destruction by every means of character assassination and strategy of lie upon lie to fabricate an image of this church that is entirely untrue do not have at stake the ultimate. They will stop at nothing to silence our voice.

We have in our hands a movement and a Community, a knowledge dispensed already that can itself dispense with all errors of the world's major religions and restore to all humanity on each of the seven rays the essential knowledge of their oneness with God, their beingness in God, the Presence of the I AM.

False doctrine, false pastors and false gurus are being exposed. The walls of dogma are tumbling down. The Light is piercing, it is penetrating, and the waves that go forth from your calls and publications, your voice and your presence are incomparable and unprecedented in recent history.

Beloved ones, the force of Light of this Community must be sustained. It must be protected. Thus, beloved, we must have your call. This is a perpetual prayer of the hours. It is a marathon that continues unabated. Each and every hour the Light must go forth to devour the increasing intensity of that Darkness that is indeed reinforced by contingents of the astral plane going beyond this system of worlds.

Realize, then, beloved ones, that it is a maximum opportunity to stand for and in the Light and to clean up those who have come out of their holes and trenches to defend the fallen ones. And therefore, by their action, by their word and work, by taking their stand against the Great White Brotherhood they may be judged.

It has been said by the Universal Christ: He who is not for me is against me.[3] This must truly be understood. For in the hour of maximum peril to the incarnate Word on a planetary system, it is not sufficient to be a bystander and say, "I will not take sides. I will not get involved. I will wait and see whether or not the Messenger is truly a Messenger by the result. If there be the victory, then I will believe. But if not, I will go my way."

Beloved ones, happy are ye who take sides in the Great White Brotherhood's stand for freedom. Happy are ye who espouse the cause of this Path and this Teaching and the right of every individual to preach the Word, to retain the power of speech and the freedom thereof to declare his own heart and conscience. Happy are ye who recognize that all of the sacred freedoms are challenged in this hour and that if any minister or representative of any religious body is to be penalized because of someone's reaction to their word, then effectively we will see the muzzling of the mouth of the ox.[4]

There will not be the Word that goes forth when anyone, anytime, may stand and say, "You have caused me untold anxiety, derangement, mental and physical illness, and therefore you must pay for your words." Beloved ones, let us not see these candles snuffed out.

I come to reinforce the message of Godfre. And I come to confirm the heart and the plane of the Buddhic mind, from which point Lanello does release to you increasingly the light of the secret rays.

I ask you to literally camp round about this sanctuary. I ask you to give the calls now perpetually unto the day of Victory. For we would send you and the Messenger around the world. We would build the Inner Retreat. We would be prepared.

Thus, we declare the will of Almighty God that this organization ought to be and shall be cut free by the legions of Light from all entanglements with the fallen ones by lawsuits and any other gossip or darkness and dark deeds that are done, that this sphere of Light that is Community should be sealed in the white fire of the Great Central Sun Magnet as a mother ship of Maitreya, able to move about the world to deliver the Light unencumbered by the false hierarchies and their misstatements and their perpetual war declared against the seed of Sanat Kumara.

It is the will of God that this should take place. And the declaration and the dispensation has gone forth from the heart of the Father. From the heart of Alpha and the Cosmic Council the decree is sent that this woman, this child, this activity, these sons and daughters of God are now free and protected by legions of Archangel Michael and seraphim of God to speak the Word, to preach the Word.

They are sealed in blue lightning. Contingents of angels of the first ray gather for the protection of every true Keeper of the Flame and Lightbearer who has dared to affiliate himself with this Church Universal and Triumphant and to come to the altar for the casting into the sacred fire of his human creation for the refinement of the inner being unto the Divinity made manifest.

The decree is gone forth and the dispensation is given. It is the will of God, beloved. Understand that this will that is the matrix and the Light to cut you free from all of the Darkness and death and hell of it must be implemented and called forth and brought into manifestation by you. The dispensation is given from the heart of the Father for the protection of his own Church and the Church of his Son and of his Holy Spirit and the Church of the Divine Mother on earth.

Beloved ones, those who are of this Mystical Body must receive the dispensation, must call it forth, must give the decrees hour by hour until the City Foursquare in heaven, the New Jerusalem, is truly manifest here below and the North American continent becomes the bastion of Light for all people of earth. Blessed ones, understand that this dispensation comes forth because of the steadiness of purpose and the constancy of Lightbearers and the purity of hearts and the tests that you have passed.

I, your beloved El Morya, could not have gained this dispensation without certain levels of attainment having been reached by yourselves, certain inner communions and groanings of your souls with the Holy Spirit as you have chosen the right way and the higher way and determined to fight over every obstacle within yourself or that is in the world.

Blessed ones, this has been made possible and you have made it possible by your diligence to the calls to Archangel Michael. Truly the rosary is the gift of God through his heart for your own attainment and testing. Thus, beloved, according to the measure of the decree work that is done, you will see that portion of the dispensation that shall come to pass in the name of Mighty Victory.

The rights of passage are to be earned by initiations passed by yourselves. We have cleared the way and prepared you well. Now, beloved, this is your individual solo flight: to each and every one of you it is given now to mount with wings of eagles, to fly to the sun, to bear the sword, to be the incarnate Word, to be one with Maitreya, The Faithful and True,[5] and to know that the dispensation of the Witnesses,[6] the mighty sword of the Word going forth out of the mouth,[7] is indeed the science of the spoken Word.

Thou shalt decree a thing, and it *shall* be established unto thee: and the Light shall shine upon thy ways![8]

With all of our love we support you unto the Victory, beloved. And when it is won, you will know that it is your victory—yes, by the grace of God, but *your* victory, *your* staying power, *your* determination, your having said in your heart, "There is no other cause. For this cause alone shall I give my life in this world and in the next, that the Great White Brotherhood and the Teachings of the Ascended Masters might endure until every little one of this planet and system and galaxy and beyond shall know the LORD and ascend to God whence he came."

This is the vow of all members of the Great White Brotherhood. So count yourself a part of that vow and know that forever, forever and forever, therefore, we are one!

I AM God's Will
by El Morya

In the name of the beloved mighty victorious Presence of God, I AM in me, and my own beloved Holy Christ Self, I call to the heart of the Will of God in the Great Central Sun, beloved Archangel Michael, beloved El Morya, beloved Mighty Hercules, all the legions of blue lightning, and the Brothers of the Diamond Heart, beloved Lanello, the entire Spirit of the Great White Brotherhood and the World Mother, elemental life—fire, air, water, and earth! to fan the flame of the Will of God throughout my four lower bodies and answer this my call infinitely, presently, and forever:

1. I AM God's Will manifest everywhere,
   I AM God's Will perfect beyond compare,
   I AM God's Will so beautiful and fair,
   I AM God's willing bounty everywhere.

Refrain: Come, come, come, O blue-flame Will so true,
   Make and keep me ever radiant like you.
   Blue-flame Will of living Truth,
   Good Will flame of eternal youth,
   Manifest, manifest, manifest in me now!

2. I AM God's Will now taking full command,
   I AM God's Will making all to understand,
   I AM God's Will whose power is supreme,
   I AM God's Will fulfilling heaven's dream.

3. I AM God's Will protecting, blessing here,
   I AM God's Will now casting out all fear,
   I AM God's Will in action here well done,
   I AM God's Will with Victory for each one.

4. I AM blue lightning flashing Freedom's love,
   I AM blue-lightning power from above,
   I AM blue lightning setting all men free,
   I AM blue-flame power flowing good through me.

"The Summit Lighthouse Sheds Its Radiance O'er All the World to Manifest as Pearls of Wisdom." This dictation by El Morya was **delivered** through the Messenger of the Great White Brotherhood Elizabeth Clare Prophet on **Sunday, March 2, 1986,** at Camelot, Los Angeles County, California, USA. (1) Matt. 23:2. (2) Ps. 1:5. (3) Matt. 12:30. (4) Deut. 25:4; I Cor. 9:9; I Tim. 5:18. (5) Rev. 19:11–16. (6) Dan. 12:5; Zech. 4:1–3, 11–14; Rev. 11:3–13. (7) Rev. 1:16; 2:16; 19:15, 21. (8) Job 22:28.

Index of Scripture

See "The Past Is Prologue" in *The Lost Teachings of Jesus I,* pp. xxiii–lxi.
Note: In this index, *pp. 1–10* in italics refer to "The Karma of America" by the Goddess of Liberty.

II Peter
1:10	80
1:19	94
2:4–22	212

I John
4:18	233, 256–57
4:20	234

Jude
3–19	212
4, 12	147, 185

Revelation
1:10	272, 341
1:16	107, 137, 299, 327, 353
2:9	138
2:12	107, 327
2:16	353
3:4, 5	244
3:9	138
3:11	244
3:17	117
4:4	244
4:7	72n.1
6:1–8	46
6:9–11	244
7:9, 13–15	244
10:2, 8–10	244
10:7	244

11	224
11:1, 2	46
11:3–13	36, 353
11:15	32
11:18	54
12:1, 2, 5	2
12:14	110
13:10	6
14:8	116
15:1, 5–8	220
15:2	320
15:6	244
16	220
16:19	116
17:5	116
18	116
19:7, 8, 14	244
19:11–16	74, 137, 353
19:15, 21	353
20:3	82
20:6, 14	149–50
20:11	281
21:8	149–50
21:9	220
21:10–16	256
21:15–17	46
21:27	111
22:1	245–46

Enoch*
7:11–14	55
9:8	55

*References to the Book of Enoch are from the translation by Richard Laurence. This translation along with all the Enoch texts can be found in *Forbidden Mysteries of Enoch: The Untold Story of Men and Angels* by Elizabeth Clare Prophet (Livingston, Mont.: Summit University Press, 1983).

Index

For an alphabetical listing of many of the philosophical and hierarchical terms used in 1986 *Pearls of Wisdom,* see the comprehensive glossary, "The Alchemy of the Word: Stones for the Wise Masterbuilders," in *Saint Germain On Alchemy: For the Adept in the Aquarian Age.* Note: In this index, *pp. 1–10* in italics refer to "The Karma of America" by the Goddess of Liberty.

Abortion, *5, 6.*
(See *Life Begets Life,* 16-audiocassette album A83034; *Abortion Update—Exposé: The Controllers and the Destroyers of the Human Race,* 8-audiocassette album A83135)
Abraham, 98, 140n.10; El Morya was, 66n.7, 286.
(See "Teachings of the Mother on Morya as Abraham" and "The Story of Our Father Abraham and of His Chela and of His Guru" on *In the Heart of the Inner Retreat 1982 I* and *II,* 6-audiocassette albums A82105, A82111)
Abram, 54–55, 57–58
Accidents, 75
Accommodation, most dangerous, 60
Afghanistan, 26
AIDS, 63–64
Akbar, 98
Alchemy, 22–23.
(See *Saint Germain On Alchemy: For the Adept in the Aquarian Age,* paperback, 544 pp.; *Saint Germain on Alchemy,* 2 videocassettes V8607-0)
Alcohol, 216
Aliens, earth has been host to, 220. *See also* Spacecraft
Altar: to Archangel Michael, 57, 59, 65; defilement of the, 305; the Flame must be kept at the, 281
America: battles that must be fought and won in, 61–63; destiny of, *2, 3–4, 6;* guru nation, 190; hatred of, 191; overrun with the Canaanite, 55; physical victory in, 43; a question before, *8–9;* reason for the founding of, 338. *See also* Hemispheres; North America; South America; United States
Americans, of the I AM Race, 62
Amerissis, 193n.6
Amethyst, 328
Andes, retreat in, 193n.6
Angelic hierarchy, 223

Angels: choirs of, 73–74; eclipsed in every world religion, 139; healing, 308, 309; trinity of elementals and men and, 109; will help you, 260; you have known from the beginning, 234. *See also* Archangels; Fallen angel(s); Seraphim.
(See 1986 *Pearls,* nos. 51–57, pp. 459–518; *The Healing Power of Angels* I and II, 12-audiocassette albums A86040, A86055 and 2-videocassette albums V8616-0, V8609-0)
Anger, exorcised, 320. *See also* Wrath
Animal forms, 149
Anxiety, 325–26, 327
Apostles, of Jesus, 98
Apple, 141
Aquarius, 332
Aquino, Corazon, 306n.10, 316, 324
Arabia, 179
Archangels: feet of, 171; footsteps of, 178; great Teachers, 250; intercession of, 274; LORD's emissaries, 137; partnership with, 299; reason for being of, 234; work with and call upon, 138–39; your friends, 231. *See also* Chamuel and Charity; Gabriel, Archangel; Michael, Archangel; Uriel, Archangel; Zadkiel, Archangel.
(See *Vials of the Seven Last Plagues: The Judgments of Almighty God Delivered by the Seven Archangels,* paperback, 206 pp.)
Ark, of the covenant, 282
Armageddon, 350
Arrow Air accident, 74–75, 84n.3
Arthur, King, 98
Ascended Master(s): are applying to embody, 119; def., 236; dictations of, 85–86; hands are tied, 21; Lightbearers introduced to, 175–77; path of, 83; souls come for the first time to knowledge of, 128–29; twin

Economies, 43
Eddy, Mary Baker, 339, 342n.12
Eden, 92n.4
Education, golden-age, *3*.
(See *The Education of the Heart,* 16-audio-cassette album A83095; *Education in the Age of Aquarius,* 8-audiocassette album A7616)
El Morya, 87; as Abram, 54–55; called Mark Prophet to found The Summit Lighthouse, 99–100; devised this Community, 207–8; embodiments of, 98; as Melchior, 97–98, 99–100; ruled in ancient China, 291; souls sent by Saint Germain to, 23–24; was Abraham, 66n.7, 286. *See also* Chohans.
(See *Lords of the Seven Rays: Mirror of Consciousness,* Book One, pp. 21–78, and Book Two, pp. 7–64; *The Sacred Adventure,* hardback, 152 pp.; *Morya: The Darjeeling Master speaks to his chelas on the Quest for the Holy Grail,* paperback, 436 pp.; *The Chela and the Path: Meeting the Challenge of Life in the Twentieth Century,* paperback, 168 pp.; *El Morya: Chohan of the First Ray,* 2-audiocassette album A7626)
Electronic belt(s), 58, 118
Elementals, 109, 282
Elohim, 144, 153.
(*See* 1978 *Pearls,* nos. 8–27, pp. 39–144, 319–445; 1982 *Pearls,* no. 8, pp. 77–86; nos. 10–14, pp. 97–168; *The Seven Elohim in the Power of the Spoken Word,* 4-audiocassette album A7636; *The Class of Elohim,* 8-audiocassette album A8204)
Emerald ray, 108
Enemy, greatest, 27
Energy, 243; qualification of, 246–47
English language, 24, 191–92
Enlightenment, 161, 332
Entities, binding of, 302. *See also* Discarnates
Etheric plane, 255–56
Europe, 3, 9, 14, 60, 61; bring the Stump message to, 181; European continent, 1; European theater, 2–3; final attempt to unite, 193n.8; final opportunity in, 194n.8; Keepers of the Flame in, 8; Messenger's embodiments in, 17
Eve, 84n.13
Evil, 129; collapsing, 290. *See also* Darkness
Evildoer, 143
Eye magic, 313

Fallen angel(s): challenge of, 7; cults of, 270; darkest of, 75; karma-dodging,

128; purvey rock music, 5; revenge of, 127; sign of, 262–63.
(See *Forbidden Mysteries of Enoch: The Untold Story of Men and Angels,* paperback, 516 pp.)
Fallen ones: becoming active in stopping, 22; have attempted to silence the saints, 269–70; plotted for more than a million years for this hour, 347; set their teeth against the Light, 222; strategies of, 275; their day of opportunity is done, 44; their judgment, 225; their last stand, 350; turn and rend you, 340; turned back, 304–5. *See also* Dark ones; Serpents; Wicked One
Fanaticism, 43–44, 325–27
Fast(ing), 8, 113
Fearful followers, 4
First ray, 174. *See also* Blue ray
Fishers, of men, 31–32
Flag, 194n.15; of the I AM Race, 189
Forgiveness, law of, 77
Four Cosmic Forces, 72n.1
Four lower bodies: can be the LORD's vessel, 314; plastic nature of, 82. *See also* Astral body; Bodies; Body; Mental body.
(See *Climb the Highest Mountain: The Path of the Higher Self,* pp. 164–73, 180–82)
Fourteen months, 108; in the blue sphere, 126, 143–44, 220; in the emerald sphere, 121.
(*See* 1984 *Pearls,* no. 56, pp. 483–510)
Fourteen thousand years, 212
Fourteen years, of initiation under Maitreya, 197–214
Freedom, 26; do the most you can for, 28; freedom fighters, 26; individual, 328; loss of, 338; must have protection, 324; only God can guarantee, 333
Freedoms, challenged, 352
Fundamentalists, 337
Future, writing your, 22

Gabriel, Archangel, 128; overshadowed Moses, 304; spoke to Malachi, 299. *See also* Archangels.
(See *Mysteries of the Holy Grail,* paperback, 504 pp.)
Gautama Buddha, 345; light of, 344; love of, 199; in the office of the Calf, 72n.1; sustains the threefold flame, 209; thread of contact with, 347. *See also* Buddha.

Genes, of Lightbearers, 63–64
Germany, 57
Goal-fittedness, 142
Goals, most important, 313–14
God: Godhood, 317; only route to, 301; return to, 317; touch and contact, 124
Goddess of Light, 181, 193n.6
Goddess of Purity, 181, 193n.6
Golden ages, 195–96
Goodness, human, 227
Government, 276; God-government, 78. *See also* Leaders
Grand Teton, 192; precipitation flame in, 290; procession from, 195–96; tapestry in, 190–92. *See also* Royal Teton Retreat
Great Central Sun, 228. *See also* Central Sun
Great Central Sun Magnet, 187, 214; supercharged with the violet ray, 79–80, 109; of violet flame, 80, 89, 153, 219–20, 222, 345
Great Divine Director, 2, 169, 174n.3
Great White Brotherhood: contact with, 222; goals of, 172; mission of, 112; in the physical octave, 221; source and fount of, 154; those taking their stand against, 351; vow of, 354; warfare against the cause of, 180.
Greenland, 219
"Greensleeves," 110, 120n.7
Guru(s): departure from, 199; false, 5; mirror and self of, 208; plugging in to, 204; those who imagine they have no need for, 205

Habit, human, 78
Halley's comet, 128
Hatred, 8, 242–43
Healing(s), 10, 302; of the aura, 259–60; of the four lower bodies, 177–78; healing focus at La Tourelle and Camelot, 308, 312; healing thought-form, 308, 312, 313; karmic equation in, 309–11; many paths of, 312.

59, 119–23, also on 2-audiocassette album A84070 and videocassette V3303-03; "Herbs: You Can Heal Yourself through Nature's Pharmacy," *The Coming Revolution*, Summer 1986, pp. 16–25, 78–79; *Emerald Matrix: The Perfect Light*, 16-audiocassette album A82121; *Maria Treben on Self-Healing through Nature's Pharmacopoeia*, 4-audiocassette album A84184 and videocassette V8601-1; *Dr. Vasant Lad on the Ancient Science of Ayurvedic (Hindu) Medicine*, 4-audiocassette album A84208 and videocassette V8602-1; series of 2-audiocassette albums of healing services; *Homeopathy*, videocassette V8604-1 and audiocassette S86004; *From the Edgar Cayce Readings*, videocassette V8603-1 and audiocassette S86003)
Heart: all-purpose beacon, 101; burden(s) of, 206, 243; clogged arteries of, 209; cosmic interval within your, 239; God does judge by, 301; that is the focus of all dictations Lanello ever took, 346–47. *See also* Chakra(s)
Heaven, planes of, 255–56
Hebrews, those called, 140n.10
Heliopolis, 288n.11
Helios and Vesta, 201
Hemispheres, interchange of, 290
Henry II, King, 146–47, 148n.2
Heroes, 129, 335, 336
Hilarion, 179. *See also* Chohans.
History, repetition of, 1
Holiness: denuded from you, 20; unto the LORD, 285–86
Holy Ghost, Holy Spirit, 335; compassion of, 257–58; descent of, 102.
Homo sapiens, 113
Human creation, 65; slaying of, 114; vise grip of, 56
Hypoglycemia, 215

I AM movement, 193n.8, 341n.11
I AM Presence, 122, 274
I AM Race, 62
I AM THAT I AM, 228, 240–41, 268
Illumination, 31, 131, 293
Immaculate concept, 313
Incarnation, of souls, 5
Initiation(s), 346; fourteen years of, 197–214; from Maitreya, 162, 216–17. *See also* Testing(s); Tests.
Inner Retreat, 39, 69; ascensions from, 180; blueprint of, 294; building

of, 159, 186; City of Light over, 220; of the Divine Mother, 70–71; eye and body of, 187; foundation of, 214; heart of, 171; meaning of, 292; molecule of the first ray at, 151; must be secure, 187; Mystery School at, 199; pilgrimage to, 40; Retreat of the Divine Mother over, 162; securing of, 79, 129–30; summit beacon shining from, 180; understanding of, 290; Western Shamballa over the Heart of, 178; what lies ahead at, 90; you who will build, 158; if you would stand at the gate of, 159; your welcome home to, 71. *See also* Royal Teton Ranch

Intercessor, 135

International capitalist/communist conspiracy, 62–63. (*See* 1987 *Pearls,* no.3, pp. 39–72; *The Psychology of Socialism: The Religion of Hatred, the Cult of Death,* 4-audiocassette album A7892; *The Religious Philosophy of Karl Marx,* 4-audiocassette album A7896; *Mother's Manifesto on the Manipulators of Capitalism and Communism,* 3-audiocassette album A7938; Summit University Forum *Professor Antony C. Sutton on the Capitalist/ Communist Conspiracy,* 2 videocassettes GP87017 and 2 audiocassettes A87054)

Introspection, 122

Israel: children of, 273–74; misinterpreted as the Promised Land, 63; priesthood in, 265–68; reincarnation of the tribes of, 140n.10

Jerusalem: Archangel Uriel walking in, 133; New, 135

Jesus: birth of, 95, 99; called your Messengers to found that Inner Retreat, 39; demonstrated a path of discipleship, 231; held the chohanship of the sixth ray, 8; his example, 83, 266; initiated as a priest, 282; initiations faced by, 198; love of, 199; in the office of the Man, 72n.1; painting of, 190; was Joseph, 191; wielded the sword of Love, 336; in your heart, 248–49. (*See The Lost Years of Jesus,* paperback, 416 pp.; *Prayer and Meditation,* paperback, 360 pp.; *Corona Class Lessons...for those who would teach men the Way,* paperback, 504 pp.)

Joan of Arc, 64

John of the Cross, Saint, 213. (*See Saint John of the Cross on the Living Flame of Love,* 8-audiocassette album A85044)

Joseph, 191

Judgment, 137; acceleration of, 136; of dark ones, 275; electrodes to transmit God's, 320–21; upon the fallen angels, 340; within a fortnight, 304; judgment calls, 155; upon laggard elements throughout the Middle East, 133–35; liberation in, 270; of Marcos and his wife, 323–24; by the power of the ruby ray, 7; in scripture, 266–67; of the seed of the wicked, 5; two-edged sword of, 280

Justice, 19

Karma, *1;* cave of your, 206; of fallen angels, 128; forestalled, 6; and healing, 309–11; inescapable, 229; law of, 146–47, 300; 100 percent balanced, 223; personal and planetary, 198, 335–36; returning, 327; scheduled to descend, 35; story of, *5;* transmuted by the violet flame, 243; between twin flames, 49–50; which you have borne, 182

Karmic Board, 2–3. *See also* Lords of Karma

Keeper(s) of the Flame, 41, 57, 118; Fraternity, 206; play the role of mediator, *9;* shown to Lightbearers at the Grand Teton, 175–77

Kingdom: keys of, 102, 112, 115; of God, 146, 256

Knowledge, gift of, 68

Kundalini, 5

Kuthumi, 77, 99–100. (See *Prayer and Meditation,* paperback, 360 pp.; *Understanding Yourself: Opening the Door to the Superconscious Mind,* paperback, 182 pp.; *Studies of the Human Aura,* 172 pp.; *Corona Class Lessons...for those who would teach men the Way,* paperback, 504 pp.)

La Tourelle, 72, 308, 312

Laggard evolutions, 154–55; in the Middle East, 37, 133–38

Lanello, 65, 175; with Abram, 54–55; causal body of, 110; is everywhere, 177; presents a newly ascended Master, 284; recourse to, 345; was Lot, 66n.7. *See also* Messenger(s); Prophet, Mark L. (See *Incarnations of the Magnanimous Heart of Lanello,* 2-audiocassette album series, including *Aesop* A8200, *Ikhnaton* A8243, *John Mark* A8255, *Longfellow* A83000, *Louis XIV* A82170, *Saint Bonaventure* A8220, and *Saladin* A8214)

Lanto, 178. *See also* Chohans.

ancient mantle restored to the, 223–25; anointed, 13, 194n.8; any desire contained by, 170–71; association of your astrology with that of the, 213; the attempt to stop her voice, 325; began their evolution as angels, 223; called to found that Inner Retreat, 39; called to give invocations to cut you free, 56–57; chelas desire to control the, 152; contact with the, 203–4; embodiments in Europe, 17; empowered to read past lives, 19–20; encounter with the, 188; every word uttered through the, 86; fear not the coming of the, 116; fiats made by your, 124; gratitude to, 213–14; of the Great White Brotherhood, 8; has known Saint Germain would be free once again, 182; her experience in this land, 59; her responsibility to you, 206; to intercede for you, 58–59; intercession of the, 213; is not on trial, 116; of Jesus, 112; mantle of, 81, 212; option for divine Sonship through the, 206; Power of the will of God in the, 151; prayers of malintent offered against this, 153; in Rome, 135; shown the quality of heart and developed threefold flame, 205; sustaining action through the, 206; sustaining tie of the, 204–5; taking the hand of the, 207; those who assail this, 318–19; transfer of the threefold flame through the, 114–15; as the Vicar of Christ, 114; voice of the, 186; world karma borne by the, 191; with you, 4. *See also* Lanello; Prophet, Mark L.
(See *The Chela and the Path: Meeting the Challenge of Life in the Twentieth Century,* pp. 115–24; *Prayer and Meditation,* pp. 246–53)
Messenger's invocations, 18, 93–94, 120, 226, 232–33, 245, 246, 248, 251, 253, 263–64, 296, 322, 329
Mexico, earthquake in, 35
Michael, Archangel: altar to, 57, 59, 65; Archangel Michael's Rosary, 73–74, 126, 154, 184, 188, 324, 340; call to march at night with, 37; instrument of the LORD's deliverance, 273; physically present, 65; your diligence to the calls to, 353. *See also* Archangels.
(See 1985 *Pearls,* no. 19, pp. 243–64; *Archangel Michael's Rosary for Armageddon,* 36-page booklet and single audiocassette B85108)
Middle East, 37; decrees for conditions

in, 179; laggard elements in, 133–38; lifestreams in, 154
Mind, of God, 124, 166–69
Minister, 325; penalized, 352. *See also* Pastors; Priests
Ministering servants, 196.
(See 1985 *Pearls,* no. 42, pp. 501–20)
Miracles, 144
Montessori, Maria, 211
More, Thomas, 98
Morya. *See* El Morya
Moses, 240, 282, 304
Mother, *2–3;* ancient mantle of the Divine, 224; assailed, 318–19; aura of, 344; confrontation with the Divine, 199–200; culture of, *4;* Divine, 292, 305–6, 318; four personages of God as, 71; peers of the Divine, 319; Retreat of the Divine, 70–71, 162, 178, 292; what it means to be, 109
Mystery school(s), 161; foundation of, 214; fourteen-year program in, 213; at the Inner Retreat, 199; Maitreya's, 90, 92n.4, 159–60, 198; in the outer octave, 10; two, 158.
(See 1984 *Pearls,* no. 36, pp. 313–26)

Nada, 2, 179. *See also* Chohans.
(See *Lords of the Seven Rays: Mirror of Consciousness,* Book One, pp. 217–35, and Book Two, pp. 211–46)
Napoleon, 193n.8
New-age movements, 41–43
New York, 32
Nicotine, 216
Noblesse oblige, 117
North America, 135

Obedience, 207, 208, 210
Offering, unacceptable, 287
Oil market, and OPEC, 139n.5
Omega, her retreat over La Tourelle, 72
One, Law of the, 145
One-hundred-year cycle, *3*
One-pointedness, 122
One Sent, 150
Only Mark albums, 158
Opportunity, 19
Order of Melchizedek, 346
Order of the Golden Lily, 74, 76
Order of the Great Central Sun Magnet, 80
Oromasis, 282

Padma Sambhava, 8
Parents, 211, 335; and children, 310–11

Round Table, 136
Royal Teton Ranch, 69, 72, 163, 188; blueprint of, 294; one thousand souls cut free to come to, 89; Retreat of the Divine Mother over, 70–71, 178, 292; securing of, 79. *See also* Inner Retreat.
(See *Royal Teton Ranch News*, vols. 1, 2; "Starting a New Life: In a Self-Sufficient Spiritual Community in the Making," *The Coming Revolution: The Magazine for Higher Consciousness*, Summer 1986, pp. 26–31, 79–80)
Royal Teton Retreat: center of Cosmic Christ illumination, 290; fourteen days at, 178; Lightbearers gathered at, 175; make the call to be taken at night to, 47; souls sent by Saint Germain to, 23. *See also* Grand Teton
Ruby fire, 68–69
Ruby ray, 89–90, 232; Buddha of the, 54, 70, 88, 232, 305, 344, 347; judgment by, 7; path of, 301; wall of, 87–89, 111, 163

Sacred labor, 259
Sacrifice, 231, 266
Saint Germain, 32–33, 164, 236; champion of every seeker, 42; chelas presented by Morya to, 24; covering the earth with his Teaching, 277; fourteen days with, 178; having known you for 70,000 years, 25; his burden of incurred karma lifted, 182–83; his gratitude, 183–84; hour of the coming of, 32–33; initiated by Archangel Zadkiel, 282; long series of initiations given to, 193–94n.8; mantle and cape of, 71; message of, 303; painting of, 190; rejected, 4, 14, 191; seventh angel, 244; seventy-two-week vigil for, 33n.1, 194n.8; those who say the world is not ready for, 163–64; valentine of, 237–40; at your right hand, 274. *See also* Chohans.
(See *Lords of the Seven Rays: Mirror of Consciousness*, Book One, pp. 237–75, and Book Two, pp. 247–76; *Saint Germain On Alchemy: For the Adept in the Aquarian Age*, paperback, 544 pp.; *Saint Germain On Prophecy: Coming World Changes*, paperback, 608 pp.; 1977 *Pearls*, nos. 31–52, pp. 143–256; 1978 *Pearls*, nos. 1–7, pp. 1–38; *Saint Germain: Chohan of the Seventh Ray*, 2-audiocassette album A7648)
Saint Germain On Alchemy: For the Adept in the Aquarian Age, 244

Saint Louis, 259
Saints, 27, 336
Sanat Kumara, 199; confrontation with, 199–200; dispensation from, 176; his Electronic Presence for God-Justice, 321; his words to Saint Germain, 186–87; LORD of hosts, 281; messenger of, 306; in the office of the Flying Eagle, 72n.1
Sanskrit syllables, 199
Satan, 61; cults of, 270–71; seed of, 149–50
Satanism, 6
Scapegoat, 326
Science, *4*
Scientists, Atlantean, 150
Secret rays, 343–45, 346, 347, 348; five, 108; Mighty Cosmos', 153–54
Self: conquest of, 314; lesser, 119, 202; marriage to the unlawful, 287; self-concern, 202. *See also* Pseudoself
Seraphim, 185, 303; daily dispatched from Luxor, 124; teaching of Serapis Bey on, 37. *See also* Angels
Serapis Bey, 12, 108–9; was Leonidas, 130n.2. *See also* Chohans.
(See *Lords of the Seven Rays: Mirror of Consciousness*, Book One, pp. 149–81, and Book Two, pp. 135–68; *Dossier on the Ascension: The Story of the Soul's Acceleration into Higher Consciousness on the Path of Initiation*, paperback, 232 pp.; "Welcome to A Retreat on the Ascension" on *A Retreat on the Ascension*, 8-audiocassette album A7953)
Serpents, dividing the people, 3. *See also* Fallen ones
Service, 122; leave off judging anyone's, 315
Seven rays, 178, 259
Seventh ray, 23, 285, 323. *See also* Violet fire
Seventy-two-week vigil, for Saint Germain, 33n.1, 194n.8
Seventy-two weeks, 33
Shepherds, in the Community, 213
Sicily, 193n.6
Silver cord, 239, 240, 242; Light that descends over the, 245–46
Singing, 249
Sirius, Eagle of, 189–90, 192
Six o'clock line, 199–200, 202, 212
Sleep, why you cannot, 27
Snow, cosmic, 219–20, 222
Snow King and Queen, 219, 220
Socialism, 160
Solar hierarchies, 198

To Those Who Seek Initiation on the Path

To be a Keeper of the Flame is to be a torchbearer of the age. To be a Keeper of the Flame is to run with the fires of the resurrection, that all life might be regenerated in the flame of Reality.

The crumbling of the old order and the building of the new take place simultaneously. Some identify with the downward spiral and some with the upward spiral. Keepers of the Flame recognize that this is a time for the gathering of the sheaves of consciousness. This is a time when men must reap the sowings of the past. This is a time when the foundation of a golden age must be built.

The crosscurrents of world karma with individual reckoning of the Law of Life must be reconciled with the oncoming tide of cosmic light that spirals from the central sun of a cosmos throughout all galaxies evolving from the center of the Creative Mind. The Great White Brotherhood summons devotees of the Law of Being—those who recognize that this is an hour when souls and worlds are crying out for salvation. This is an hour when those who have the vision to see the end from the beginning must leave their nets and their lesser causes for the one cause that counts—the cause of freedom. . . .

It is time for men and women mature in judgment, capable in leadership, humble before God, and possessed with a profound vision of the consequences of mankind's turning from their God, to make the decision to come together in the communion of the flame under the aegis of the Great White Brotherhood to sponsor the revolution of the ages— the revolution of Light, Love, and the Victory of the Flame. Keepers of the Flame and those who would be, accept the challenge! For it is nothing less than the reversing of the tide of sin, disease, and death and the arresting of the spirals of disintegration and decay now outpicturing in the mass consciousness of the world.

This is a time when men and women must face their responsibilities or face the consequences. It is a time to accept the challenge! . . .

In memory of all who have overcome the world, all who have set their feet on the path of initiation, I, Saint Germain, stand in this age to receive the Lightbearers as my own.

Saint Germain

KEEPERS OF THE FLAME
A FRATERNITY
Of Sons and Daughters of God
Dedicated to the Freedom and Enlightenment of Humanity

Become a Keeper of the Flame today. Write for a free brochure.

The Summit Lighthouse, Dept. 402, Box A, Livingston, MT 59047-1390 (406) 222-8300.
(Enclose $2.00 postage if you live outside the U.S.A.)

A Pearl of Wisdom *for You*—
Every Week! *"The Pearls of Wisdom are the practical manifestation of the Great White Brotherhood's marvelous blueprint for man's deliverance in this day and age. They show the way out of the human dilemma."*
—Mark L. Prophet

Since 1958 the Ascended Masters have released their teachings through the Messengers Mark and Elizabeth Prophet as Pearls of Wisdom. These weekly letters dictated for students of the sacred mysteries are delivered as a Holy Spirit prophecy from the immortal saints and spiritual revolutionaries of East and West who comprise the spiritual hierarchy known as the Great White Brotherhood.

The Pearls of Wisdom contain both beginning and advanced instruction with a practical application of Cosmic Law to personal and planetary problems. Learn about healing through the violet flame, the Lost Teachings of Jesus, the prophecy of Saint Germain for the Aquarian age, twin flames and soul mates, karma and reincarnation, the science of the spoken Word and the path of initiation.

Discover how you can, through soul travel, journey to the etheric retreats to attend the universities of the Spirit conducted by the Lords of the Seven Rays, who will teach you how to fulfill your divine plan and receive the gifts of the Holy Spirit.

In the Pearls of Wisdom you will find out how to meet the challenges of our time by tapping the spiritual resources of your own Higher Consciousness. And make contact, heart to heart, with the Teacher...

"We write our Pearls of Wisdom out of engrams of light, out of matrices of the Spirit. Paragraph by paragraph, the sacred formula of selfhood unfolds. Man must decipher the formula of life and of living. He must probe. He must read and reread. He must invoke the Holy Spirit in whose flame is to be found the interpretation of the living Word and the multiplication of the loaves and fishes....

"By the alchemy of the Master and the chela [disciple], by the fusion of selfhood as above so below, there emerge from the printed page and from the spoken Word a definition of concepts and the sacred formula that is unique for each individual even while it affirms the universal law of the elements....

"Thus the association of the chela with the Master is unique in each and every case. For every lifestream there is a special oneness all its own, and each encounter is a special moment in eternity when time is not and space is consumed." —El Morya

The Pearls of Wisdom prepare you to attend 12-week, 2-week, or weekend Summit University seminars at the Royal Teton Ranch, the 33,000-acre retreat of the Great White Brotherhood in southwestern Montana—and they prepare you for life, its full savoring, morsel by morsel, every day of your loving in God.

Weekly Pearls of Wisdom $40 (1 year), $20 (6 months), $10 (3 months). Introductory 12-week series $5. Make checks payable to and mail to The Summit Lighthouse, Dept. 402, Box A, Livingston, MT 59047-1390 (406) 222-8300.